Other Chinas

RALPH A. LITZINGER

Other Chinas

The Yao and the Politics

of National Belonging

DUKE UNIVERSITY PRESS

Durham and London

2000

© 2000 Duke University Press
All rights reserved
Printed in the United States
of America on acid-free paper ∞
Typeset in Quadraat by Tseng
Information Systems, Inc.
Library of Congress Cataloging-
in-Publication Data appear on the
last printed page of this book.

For my parents

contents

preface

Pick up any book published in China in the 1980s and 1990s on minority nationality populations and you will invariably come across a chapter discussing the Yao people, one of China's fifty-five officially recognized minority nationalities. The book will have a section at the beginning with a series of black-and-white or color photographs depicting minorities engaged in an assortment of cultural activities. If you find an image of a Yao subject, she will be dressed in the traditional costume of her people and the caption will give the Han name of her subgroup—the "Tea-mountain Yao," or the "Red-trouser Yao," or the "Yao who cross mountains." If the image is of a man, it is no doubt of a Taoist priest in trance grasping in his hand a hand-copied Taoist text or some other accoutrement of his trade. There may also be an image of young Yao boys and girls, trekking across a mountain path on their way to middle school with books in hand. These Yao will not be in traditional clothing. The caption will tell you that, since the reforms initiated by Deng Xiaoping in the late 1970s, more and more schools have been opened for the Yao, that the socialist modernization of the Yao minority is underway, and advancing swiftly.

These subjects will appear in mountainous settings, probably in an "autonomous" Yao county somewhere in the south or southwest of China. For most readers in China the name of the place will be unfamiliar, but this is in part the point: to inform the reader about life on the ethnic margins of the nation. In the chapter on the Yao you will discover that, according to the 1982 census, there were some 1.4 million Yao in China in the early 1980s. Books published a decade later, in the mid-1990s, report an increase in the population to over 2 million.[1] These demographic figures are usually followed by the observation that the Yao are a migratory people scattered throughout the mountains of south and southwest China. In some accounts, you will learn that in the mid–nineteenth century this inclination to roam took them into the hills of mainland Southeast Asia, into northern Vietnam, Laos, and Thailand. You may also learn that the Yao people now have many "brothers and sisters" living abroad, in Europe, Canada, and the United States. You will learn that these brothers and sisters are refugees, but there will be very little discussion of the politics that produced the Yao refugee diaspora.[2]

This book addresses questions concerning China's reforms, the demise of Maoist ideology and the critique of the Cultural Revolution, and the role of ethnic minorities in new imaginings of the Chinese nation and state.[3] In China, the Yao are known as an isolated and relatively "underdeveloped" ethnic minority who practice an esoteric form of Taoism. They are an upland people, what anthropologists used to call a hill tribe, distributed throughout the mountains of Guangxi (860,000), Hunan (290,000), Yunnan (147,000), Guangdong (96,000), Guizhou (20,000), and Jiangxi (over 500).[4] In the 1920s and 1930s, when American, European, Soviet, and Chinese ethnologists began to visit these regions, they imagined they were entering a kind of living museum, where one could observe, study, and record the ancient peoples and cultures of China. The bureaucrats of Republican China tended to view these upland regions as danger zones, where non-Han peoples consorted with beasts, ghosts, and goblins, ate strange and exotic foods, and refused to join the modern world. The Christian missionaries who attempted to penetrate them and spread the word of God found the mountain residents to be a suspicious people, even though they recognized them as a strong, sturdy, and independent people who maintained a kind of empire of their own. China's communist revolutionaries saw these regions otherwise. The ethnic borderlands were approached as zones of peasant struggle, where various forms of feudal exploitation had crafted in the minority other an authentic revolutionary sensibility. In the reform period, China's socialist modernizers have brought a new range of discourses to bear on these regions and their inhabitants. As with other upland groups, the Yao have once again been marked as objects of ethnological fascination. Some see them as a resilient minority, a people that have retained, under the worst of political and economic conditions, the best of their cultural traditions. Others see them as a socially and culturally backward minority, a stubbornly primitive people standing in the way of the nation's development, progress, and march to socialist modernity.

In writing this book I have had to confront the question of what drove me to study the Yao. What was I after in wanting to work, study, and live in these remote regions? What did I think China's ethnic periphery would tell me about the history of socialism, the twists and turns of the "nationalities problem," and Deng Xiaoping's promise that China had entered a new age of development and progress? How could I write about the Yao without reproducing the hierarchies and discursive orderings of Chinese nationalism? What was my "investment" in the politics of cultural struggle for a people defined by popular, official, and academic discourses as ethnic, culturally backward, economically disadvantaged, socially stagnant, and stubbornly uncivilized? How could I write the ethnic subject into China's quest for a socialist modern identity? From what position of power and privilege was I writing? To what end?

To begin to answer these questions, I want to briefly describe how I first became involved with the Yao. Since the late 1970s, over one million Vietnamese, Khmer, and Laotians have fled their countries. Among these peoples were the upland Hmong and the Yao (also known as the Iu-Mien), who were known as fierce fighters in the CIA's "secret war" in Laos. The origins of this project can thus be traced to a time when the U.S. campaign to defeat "the communist threat" in mainland Southeast Asia was coming to a close.[5] In 1983, as an undergraduate looking for international work, I took a job for a year teaching English in Thailand. I worked for a consortium of international relief agencies: Save the Children Fund, a group called World Education, and a smaller agency out of Vermont called Experiment in International Living. These groups were involved with the State Department's efforts to prepare the Vietnamese, Khmer, Laotians, Hmong, and Yao for their new lives in the United States. Perhaps because I had dabbled in anthropology, they thought I could also help organize an in-camp "cultural orientation" training program. I was assigned to a camp in the province of Chonburi, not far from the sprawling metropolis of Bangkok. More like a prison than a transit facility, as it was euphemistically called, this makeshift camp was enclosed by imposing barbed wire fences, guarded by the Thai military, and staffed by a plethora of international refugee relief organizations. Whereas some of the relief workers and medical staff lived on the grounds, the language teachers (many were educated Thai) were daily transported in Jeeps and buses. Most of the American relief workers and administrators I knew saw these refugees as victims of an Indo-Chinese communism gone awry, and they were deeply committed to the principles of international humanitarian aid. Many of them were also working their way into the ranks of the U.S. State Department or searching for subsequent employment in other government and international agencies.

I had something else in mind. In the late 1970s and early 1980s, my intellectual interests had gravitated toward the Vietnam War, the history of colonialism in mainland Southeast Asia, and the politics of Third World nationalisms. Part of this interest no doubt came from a certain romance of the antiwar movement, which I caught glimpses of growing up not far from the campus of Ohio State University. Part of it also came from the world of television images and print media, which I consumed daily, wanting to know more about the lands and peoples of what was then called Indochina, an area that both fascinated and terrified the American political imagination. When I arrived in Thailand in 1983, I realized I knew very little about Laos and the people that now sat across from me in the classroom, who were known in China as Yao. I began to search libraries and bookstores in Bangkok and soon discovered an ethnological literature that spoke of the "hill tribes" as "slash-and-burn horticulturists" and "practitioners of animistic beliefs." I read articles that taught me about the intricately embroidered clothing of the Yao, and was from there introduced to the rules for Yao courtship; to thick descriptions of the expensive Yao wedding; and, as Jane Hanks once wrote, to "the dramatic quality of Yao rituals." I began to learn about the historical and contemporary relationship the Southeast Asian Yao had with the Han and non-Han groups that lived in the south of China.

These accounts took me into imagined "hill tribe" worlds where one learned of indigenous modes of economic self-sufficiency, charismatic village leaders, and esoteric ritual practices. Many of them were based on years of anthropological field research in the upland regions of mainland Southeast Asia. They provided detailed and meticulous accounts of everyday social and ritual life, even though they were strongly informed by the structural-functionalist paradigms that dominated anthropology in the 1950s and 1960s. Others bordered on the spectacular and the phantasmagoric, in large part because they were meant for popular consumption. I recall coming across one such publication, aptly called *People of the Hills*, in a bookstore in the university district in Bangkok.[6] A photographic documentary on Thailand's upland "tribes," this book promised to take the viewer into another place and time, a world where history stood still and people lived close to the natural world. It presented the mountain-dwelling tribes as peaceful and contented farming peoples, whose everyday simplicity provided relief from the social tensions and complexities of modern living. The following passage, culled from the introduction, reveals how the hills were imagined as spaces of exotic primitivism protected from the lure of Western materialism: "Happiness is a state of mind, something that is beyond price—and these hill people, poor though they may be in material things, live a life that can honestly be called 'happy.' They have, as you will see, no desires for the dubious 'delights' of the West . . . *it is felt that you will be delighted and fascinated by reading of ways of life so different from the norm*" (emphasis added).[7]

As many scholars of European modernity have pointed out, a discourse of primitivism first emerges in Europe in the latter half of the nineteenth century, when exotic others were sought out to reinforce an embattled Victorian society.[8] The book *People of the Hills* comes to us at a different historical moment. It appears when America's imperialist adventures in Southeast Asia were coming to a disconcerting close and when the need for a distant other to critique the modern world—seen as irrevocably contaminated by money, material desire, and the ravages of war—was perhaps stronger than ever. Though the norm referenced in this passage is the taken-for-granted culture of the West, what is left unspecified (at least in the introduction and captions) is how the reader's delight is enabled by the visual objectification of indigenous peoples living in remote social spaces. The cultures of the remote are made accessible by taking the reader on a tour of the customs and social practices of seven different groups, the Yao, Miao, Akha, Lahu, Lawa, Lisu, and Karen. A sparse yet authoritative English-language text is interspersed with black-and-white photographs of men and women engaged in an assortment of everyday activities, from hunting, farming, and cooking to the mending of tattered clothes. Not unlike books published on minorities in China in the 1980s, these images are meant to be pedagogical. Scenes of everyday labor are coupled with dramatic details from everyday life: pregnancy and birth, courtship and marriage, religious belief and ritual observance, sickness and death. Although the book purports to provide a window into the shared humanity of all peoples of the world, this humanity is defined entirely by the missionaries and travel guides searching for cultures believed to be far from the tortured realities of modern living. The celebration of humanity in all its splendid diversity actually refuses alterity by denying the other, as Johannes Fabian once so famously put it, a shared sense of radical contemporaneity. The primitive, the non-literate, the underdeveloped, the mountain peasant are denied copresence; they become objects of history and never its subjects.[9]

I worked in a camp drastically removed from the self-contained and socially functional indigenous worlds detailed in the anthropological studies and photographic compendia I was eagerly devouring. I was thus concerned about what was happening to the "culture" of my students and refugee friends, who told me stories about social life in the mountains of Laos before the war. I heard from them tales of forced migrations and rebellions in the distant past against the Han Chinese "outsiders," who for centuries, they argued, had attempted to tax the Yao and force them into corvée labor arrangements. The more articulate of my students boasted of literacy in classical Chinese, the written language of the imperial scholar-gentry before the popularization of vernacular Chinese in the early twentieth century. The religious specialists who performed marriages and funerals and attended to the everyday affairs of the spirit realm claimed expertise in the ways of Taoism, the only religion indigenous to China. To be sure, many of them knew much about things "traditional," if this is how we are to label ritual practice, oral histories of migrations, descriptions of households and social landscapes. Yet they also possessed a modern consciousness of history, of how the lives they once lived had been destroyed, first by French colonial administrators, then by the communist revolutionaries, and finally by the CIA. I recall as well that many of the older men and women were critical of Asian, European, and North American art collectors hunting the camps looking to buy the elaborately painted Taoist scrolls used in ritual practice. Yet there was little they could do to stop their sale, for most if not all of the refugees had very little money and the Yao were quickly becoming the new ethnic darlings in the global market of the Asian art world.[10]

By the early 1980s, then, the Yao had gone global by way of an international refugee crisis and the commodification of their ritual practices in international art markets. In thinking back on my encounters with the anthropological literature on the Yao, I remember being struck by the lack of any analysis of the modern state, the history of French colonialism in Laos and Vietnam, and "hill tribe" participation in the global opium trade. China sometimes appeared as a cultural space whence upland traditions, beliefs, and identifications were derived. History crept in by way of references to imperial regimes and charters to avoid tax and corvée labor, and to the migrations of the Yao across the vast expanse of what is today the politically charged border zone of Burma, China, Laos, and Vietnam. Contemporary governments appeared rarely in this literature, though Thailand was sometimes noted as a modernizing force involved in the reform of farming techniques and the introduction of new crops. The anthropological study of the Yao and other upland groups in China and mainland Southeast Asia in the 1970s marked a kind of turning point. Anthropologists, sensitive to changes that were going on in other area disciplines (in African studies especially), moved to disrupt dominant notions of tribal primitivity and isolation by introducing the more fluid notion of ethnicity. They turned to the Chinese historical record and to Taoist practices and beliefs to understand something about the historical nature of the Yao. They wanted to understand what constituted the taken-for-granted notions of a Yao sense of collective identity. And yet, despite this turn toward questions of history and the dynamics of cultural borrowing and exchange, Yao ethnicity was still seen to have everything to do with the reproduction of a social group through ritual activity. Who the Yao were seemed to have little to do with national programs of modernization and global conflicts such as the cold war. The modern nation-state, histories of anticommunism and socialist mobilization, and the effects of decades of war largely remained hidden in many of these studies. Not so unlike the phantasmagoric imaginings contained in the *People of the Hills*, the modern was written out of these upland regions.

When I returned from Thailand to the United States in 1984, I found that some members of the Yao refugee diaspora had begun to organize with federal, state, and private funds their own community centers and research associations. They were conducting studies into such topics as the history of the Yao in China, the beliefs and practices of ritual specialists, and the various dialects of the Yao language. They also had begun to write letters and establish contacts with Yao in China. In the early 1980s, as Jeffery MacDonald has described it in his study of the transnational aspects of Iu-Mien identity, many American Yao (who call themselves the Iu-Mien or Yao-Mien) were interested in developing a new romanized script for the Yao language.[11] The Iu-Mien Association of Oregon sponsored a conference in 1982 attended by Mien delegates from Oregon, Washington, and California and the internationally known linguist Herbert Purnell, who presented several possible orthographies. After much discussion, a "secular" script was adopted, one that could please both those who had converted to Christianity and those who argued that the diaspora Yao should retain their Taoist beliefs. Meanwhile, the Chinese Yao, led by the linguist Pan Chengqian, were involved in their own efforts to construct a pinyin-based romanized script for the Yao language. Cassette tapes were exchanged and then, in Ruyuan County, Guangdong, in May 1984, an orthography conference was held at which delegates from China and the United States agreed to incorporate elements of both the U.S. Iu-Mien system and the Chinese pinyin system. These conferences and academic exchanges allowed for the development of a unified script that could be used to communicate in the transnational space of Iu-Mien communities in China, France, Canada, Thailand, and the United States.[12]

Before long, Yao community leaders in the San Francisco Bay Area, Portland, and Seattle organized a series of international symposia exploring questions of Yao culture and history. I attended the first of these in 1987, which was held in a community center in Richmond, California.[13] Leaders of the Yao community in the United States, several American scholars, a provincial Communist Party leader from Guangdong, a young scholar from the Nationalities Institute in Nanning, Guangxi, and two prominent Yao scholars from the Central Nationalities Institute in Beijing were all in attendance. A range of topics was discussed. The conference attendees reexamined the unified script because it did not include the different Yao languages in China. They debated whether a single ethnic name should be developed for the Yao, with most of the refugee leaders calling for the use of the term Iu-Mien, and the Chinese delegates insisting on the use of the term Yao. The delegates also delved into more esoteric ethnological matters, discussing the differences between Yao and Chinese Taoism and whether different Yao groups, in the far reaches of Chinese history, had once believed in different totems. It was at this time that the refugee Yao also began to learn of the Chinese Yao myth of Qianjiadong, or the Thousand Family Grotto, the lost homeland of the Yao people in China. The legend of Qianjiadong has been the source of heated ethnological debate in China and has more recently begun to be incorporated by the American Iu-Mien into their own origin myths and narratives of identity.

The Yao leaders from the United States and China whom I met at the Richmond conference spoke of Yao culture as a complex realm of practices, languages, beliefs, and sentiments that had been reproduced for centuries. Theirs was a story of cultural resilience in the face of powerful empires, regimes, and modern nation-states. They recognized that Yao culture, however it was to be defined and delineated, had been subjected to the policies, developmental programs, and political campaigns of modern nation-states and transformed in the process. These were not a people lost in the modern world, ravaged by the geopolitics of the cold war, without histories to tell.[14] Rather, they were acutely and sometimes passionately concerned with questions of loss, displacement, and cultural survival. Perhaps more than anyone, they knew that Yao culture was an object to be struggled over and controlled. They were recreating their histories and they were doing it, somewhat ironically, by crossing the very ideological antinomies that once defined the cold war.

After much letter writing and some clever administrative arrangements, I was invited to study Yao culture and history at the Central Nationalities Institute in Beijing, the premier training ground for minority scholars and cadres in China. I was to work under the tutelage of Su Defu and Pan Cheng-qian, both of whom had attended the Richmond conference. A Yao from the Jinxiu Yao Autonomous County in Guangxi who has written extensively on the history of Jinxiu, Su also worked for the Central Nationalities Publishing House on the campus of the Central Nationalities Institute. Pan, also a Yao, is a leading linguist in China and abroad. He was instrumental in setting up the first American and Chinese Yao exchange delegations in the early 1980s. I set out for Beijing in the fall of 1988 and quickly settled into a daily routine of class instruction, one-on-one interviews, and library research. I returned to Seattle in December 1988 with a backpack full of research notes, publications on minority affairs, and the support of government officials in Beijing to conduct a study in the Jinxiu Yao Autonomous County in Guangxi.

I was unable to return to China until the autumn of 1990. As with many of my colleagues in the China field, my research was halted by the events that took place in Beijing during the spring of 1989. As with most of the world outside of China, the student occupation of Tiananmen Square came to me via National Public Radio and the nightly news. I remember watching the televised broadcasts in both amazement and horror with my colleagues at the University of Washington, a group that included not a few students and professors from Taiwan and the mainland, as the Chinese government turned on its people. I attended large rallies in the university and international districts of Seattle, where leaders from the Chinese community in Seattle gave speeches calling for democracy and the immediate dismissal of Li Peng. The more brave mainland students—brave because many of them feared there were Party moles in their midst—read aloud poems and laments for those who were perhaps dying on the Square. Many onlookers were ambivalent about what was happening in China, and I remember one elderly Chinese man tell me that he feared that the rectification campaigns would once again return to China, a reference to the Party's periodic crushing of its intellectuals. Others of us bemoaned the sensationalized press coverage; yet others used facsimile machines to bombard China with information about what was happening in Beijing. Despite these different modes of identification with the student movement, none of us could deny that the term June Fourth (*liusi*) was now etched into our memories. Months of youthful optimism and protest in China had come to an end.

The crushing of the student movement shocked many people around the world, especially those who had been optimistic about the course of Deng Xiaoping's reforms.[15] Other events soon stole the global media limelight, however. By the year's end, on 9 November, the Berlin Wall was opened, providing a symbolic end to several years of popular upheaval in East Germany. Several months later, Romania's dictator, Nicolae Ceausescu, was executed. Within two years the Soviet Union was gone, as its various nationality republics, long guaranteed the right to secede from the union if the Party ever failed them, were catapulted into the very uncertain terrain of the so-called New World Order. As one critic put it, the year 1989 is now "enshrined as a symbol of historic ruptures" felt across the globe.[16] Scholars, government officials, and journalists tell us that the period 1988–1992 will be remembered as one that swept away regimes, obliterated long-standing political and economic structures, and brought an end to the cold war. The passing of state socialism has, of course, led to all kinds of fanciful pronouncements, symbolized most forcefully in Francis Fukuyama's claim that we were now witnessing the "end of history" and the emergence of Western liberalism as the final form of human governance. Others have been less sanguine in their assessments, arguing that the passing of state socialism demands not less Marxism but more, or at least a more critical appreciation of the intricacies and contradictions of global capitalism. Still others tell us we have entered an entirely new era, one that requires new notions of politics and new understandings of culture, place, and identity in a changing global order. We read almost daily—in the popular press and in the most rigorous of humanities and social science journals—that the local, the national, and the global are now irrevocably enmeshed and entwined, and that the nation-state itself is a fading figment of the modern imagination.

Like many of my colleagues in anthropology and in the field of Chinese studies, I find much of value in all of the new and exciting work on globalization and the politics of transnationalism. The end of the cold war has most certainly altered the global landscape. And scholars in the social sciences and humanities are now looking for new conceptions of culture, history, and identity, both to move beyond the ideological assumptions that shaped cold war research agendas and to account for the emergence of new social and political formations.[17] Since I entered the field of anthropology in the late 1980s, social theorists have increasingly turned to the fragmentary, the local, and the subjugated to unmask the will to power at the heart of all modernist discourse. As I worked in China among Yao elite, the recovery of the fragmentary and the local—what I call the politics of ethnic marginality—led me into the very center of modernist discourse in China. I contend that the struggle against ethnic marginalization had everything to do with a widespread perception that the cultures and societies of various Yao communities had been tragically misrepresented during the Maoist era. This process began in the late 1950s and carried on into the Great Proletarian Cultural Revolution, when all forms of ethnic, local, and national identity were subjected to ruthless and sometimes violent criticism. Seeking new interpretive frames to represent the history and identity of their people, Yao elite turned their attention to something called "traditional culture." They began to write accounts of Yao history that treated this cultural domain less as a remnant of past "feudal" social orders that retarded the making of a modern socialist nation than as an object to be embraced and protected. They enthusiastically promoted popular ritual and other folk customs at national and international conferences, and they publicly defended Deng Xiaoping's socialist modernization agenda. And, as with many Han intellectuals who turned to minority cultures to restore what they saw as a sick and depleted national body, they presented minorities as the carriers of some of China's most ancient traditions. These images of a timeless culture appeared across the contemporary landscape, in remote autonomous regions, in slick photographic albums, in television documentaries and home videos, in theme parks in Beijing, and even in fashion boutiques in Hong Kong.

This book thus seeks to trace the various ways the Yao have been represented in China. But more than this, I have sought to draw the reader into how various members of the Yao community have represented their cultures, histories, and identities to a diverse range of interlocutors. I show

how elite members of the Yao nationality have been active agents in the making of a modern socialist and, more recently, postsocialist Yao identity. Yao scholars, intellectuals, government workers, Communist Party officials, Taoist specialists, and others who claimed expertise on matters of history and culture have all played a determining role, albeit in different ways, in how the Yao have been studied, represented, and displayed. By focusing on the role of various members of the minority elite in forging new understandings of minority realities, I hope to advance a more nuanced understanding of the history of the People's Republic and the place of minority elite in the politics of socialist and postsocialist nation building. Additionally, in attending to zones of overlap among official discourse, state policy, and practices of minority empowerment, I aim to move away from depictions of minorities as romantic subalterns outside of the sphere of critical debate in post-Mao China. Marginality emerges as a key term in this study. I use it to point to how minorities have interpreted the politics of socialism, the political predicaments and cultural struggles of present-day Chinese nationalism, and the place of the People's Republic in the changing global order of the late twentieth century.

What follows, then, is a critical ethnographic account of the politics of minority discourse in the late 1980s and early 1990s. This was a time when Chinese Marxism was being hotly debated, Maoist socialism was a troubling reminder of years of violence and ideological struggle, and global capitalism was very much in the making, when minorities were clamoring for voice and recognition and critically participating in the making of the postsocialist nation-state of the People's Republic of China.

acknowledgments

In researching and writing this book I have enjoyed support and friendship from friends, teachers, research associates, and institutions in several countries. The funding for my first visit to China in 1988 was provided by a Foreign Language Area Studies grant from the Jackson School of International Studies at the University of Washington, Seattle. The National Academy of Science's Committee on Scholarly Exchange with the People's Republic of China (CSCPRC) and a Fulbright-Hays grant provided funding for field research from 1990 to 1992. I want to thank both of these organizations for sponsoring a proposal on the role of Yao intellectuals in post-Mao Chinese nationalism. My work in China at times required complex administrative and budgetary negotiations, especially when I sought to provide assistance for several scholars at the Central Nationalities Institute in Beijing who were to accompany me into the Yao mountains of Guangxi. I want to thank Pam Pierce, who headed the CSCPRC office in Washington, D.C., and John Olsen, the Beijing director of this organization from 1991 to 1992, for their invaluable assistance in these and other matters.

I first met Assistant Professors Pan Chengqian and Su Defu, both then affiliated with the Central Nationalities Institute in Beijing, at a Yao studies symposium in Richmond, California, in 1987. I also met at this time a young, energetic Yao from Nanning, Huang Fangping. Mr. Huang graciously took me into his home in August 1988 and introduced me to his father, the well-known Yao scholar Huang Yu. I continue to learn much about Yao history, culture, and society from their many publications and books. Pan took time out in the fall of 1988 to travel with me to Yao regions in Guangxi and Hunan, a most memorable trip from which I learned much. My research during the period 1990 to 1992 owes much to Su, who arranged for me to live and work in Jinxiu County in Guangxi. His family in the village of Xidi warmly opened their home to me, providing much support and affection. Liu Yulian spent over a year with me, sharing her memories and reflections on the political history of Jinxiu County and teaching me much about the institutional structure of minority nationality studies in China. My research in Jinxiu is also indebted to Huang Zhihui, Su Fengling, and the many "Yaobao" who taught me to walk in the hills, drink the local wine, and do the waltz at the local dance hall.

I owe much to the friendship and camaraderie of Su He and Wang Hongman, whom I came to know at the Central Nationalities Institute in Beijing. These extraordinary people were two of my very best friends in China and they remain so to this day. They both magnanimously tolerated my many queries and tirades, teaching me patience and understanding, even while they remained astonished at the childlike pace at which I learned the ropes of Chinese political culture. I also express my thanks to Shi Naijun for many hours of conversation.

The reader will find many instances in this book in which I do not name the source of a particular point of view or reflection. Many of the people I worked with in both Beijing and Jinxiu asked me not to reveal their identities or link their names to certain reflections on the Communist Party and its promises for order and development. This was especially the case in the years immediately following the so-called Tiananmen incident, when many of my friends and research consultants were required to attend daily meetings on the "correct interpretation" of the so-labeled counterrevolutionary movement. As I write now in the late 1990s, it may well be that the concerns they once had are no longer relevant to a regime that, for the moment at least, seems more interested in managing an emerging consumer culture than in the politics of historical and ideological interpretation. No matter one's reading of the current directions of the reforms in the mid-1990s, I have felt it important to continue to maintain the anonymity of certain individuals. I have therefore used the real names only of people who themselves wished to be identified or whose names have appeared in the media and publications in China.

At the University of Washington, Stevan Harrell has been at once my biggest supporter and most thorough critic, encouraging my interests in cultural studies and always keeping me attentive to the ground of politics and culture in China. Charles Keyes, one of the world's foremost experts on ethnicity, always urged me to compare the Yao case in China to other places and times. Elizabeth Perry, now with Harvard University, was the first to encourage me to anthropologize the state. Ann Anagnost has been a constant teacher, friend, and intellectual companion. My thinking on the politics of culture in China owes much to her critical vision, to her readings of a wide range of scholarship, and to our many deliberations on how the business of anthropology is to be done in the late twentieth century. Purnima Manke-kar has been a close friend and intellectual inspiration since we met on the first day of our doctoral training at the University of Washington. Lousia Schein and Susan Brownell invited me to present my first paper on the Yao research at the American Anthropology Association meetings in San Fran-cisco in 1992. I thank them for that opportunity and for their continued support, friendship, and generosity. I have also benefited enormously from Jeff MacDonald's work on Yao refugee culture and politics and his writings on the transnational affiliations between Yao in China and in the United States. Jacques Lemoine's *Yao Ceremonial Paintings* is a classic in the field of Yao ethnography; his writings and lifelong interest in the Yao in mainland Southeast Asia and in China have been a major source of inspiration.

I want to thank the following individuals, some connected with the University of Washington, some residents of Seattle, some in and around the Duke campus in Durham, some spread out across the globe: Wurliq Bao, Carter Bentley, Adam Bund, Nahum Chandler, Chen Yongling, Siu-woo Cheung, Cathy Davidson, Kevin Ergil, Dru Gladney, Hugh Guster-son, John Herman, Marilyn Ivy, Almaz Khan, Chas McKhann, Tom Moran, Sarah Nelson, Tim Oakes, William O'Barr, John Pemberton, Peng Wenbing, Naomi Quinn, Rob Sikorski, Irene Silverblatt, Ren Hai, Marianne "Pie" Ryan, Anne Scheeran, Michael Strauch, Theresa Truax, Trevina Wang, Janet Upton, Mayfair Yang, and Zhuang Kongshao. Peter Moran, observing my obsessions with work, has always reminded me of the importance of friend-ship and quiet moments. I have also benefited enormously from many con-versations with my colleagues at the University of North Carolina in Chapel Hill, especially Judy Farquhar, Jim Hevia, and Yue Gang. Susan Brownell, Bruce Grant, Akhil Gupta, Hugh Gusterson, Purnima Mankekar, George Marcus, Lousia Schein, Dan Segal, and Ted Swedenburg have each read por-tions of this work over the past several years. My editor at Duke University Press, Ken Wissoker, has been behind this project from the beginning. All of these individuals have provided invaluable feedback, though I alone am responsible for the interpretations that have given shape to the chapters that follow.

Since joining the cultural anthropology faculty at Duke in 1994, I have benefited from a supportive and intellectually rich environment. The staff at Duke's Asian/Pacific Studies Institute have worked tirelessly to support its many faculty. I have learned much from my graduate students, and wish to thank especially Ya-chung Chuang, Jennifer Hasty, Marro Inoue, Ayse Karayazgan, Rebecca Karl, Jeni Prough, Ajantha Subramanian, Clare Talwalker, Nilgun Uygun, Margot Weiss, and Kim Wright. Zhou Yongming helped with translation work in the final stages of this project. Special thanks to Danny Hoffman for his meticulous reading of the page proofs. I would also like to thank my students in the 1998 Duke-Study-in-China program, which I directed as I was putting the final touches on the manuscript. I have learned much from Arif Dirlik, and Michael Hardt, and Walter Mignolo with whom I have worked in several faculty seminars and reading groups; my own thinking has been enriched by their writings on a wide range of topics and places. Leo Ching has been a best friend and writing companion since 1994, helping to make Durham home when both of us, torn from our imaginary homes on the West Coast, felt at times terribly displaced. Finally, Anne Allison, Charlie Piot, Orin Starn, Ken Surin, and Jing Wang have been constant intellectual companions. I cannot express enough what their friendship has meant to me over the past several years.

Cynthia Rivera—friend, lover, wife, dog-training companion, and so much more—has been by my side throughout the writing of this book. She has sustained me through moments of self-doubt, insisted that I remain true to my intuitions, and encouraged me to persevere. As this manuscript was going to press, she brought into this world our beautiful Zachary Evan, the new joy and love of our lives. Finally, this project would not have come to fruition without the stubborn support of my family, and especially my mother and father. Skeptics of my career choice for all the right reasons, they have nonetheless remained my greatest fans, my most enduring support network, my true sustenance. Can I ever repay them for everything they have done for me? As a small step in that direction, I dedicate this book to them.

Writing the Margins: An Introduction

The urge to have it all here and now and bring everything within
the compass of order and system is very much the ideology of
empire. —WAI-YEE LI, *Enchantment and Disenchantment: Love and Illusion in*
Chinese Literature

*A*s with many foreign scholars interested in minority politics in
China in the late 1980s and early 1990s, I began my research at the
Central Nationalities Institute in Beijing.[1] Known around Beijing
as the Minyuan, this institute was officially opened on 11 June 1951, with the
blessing of Zhou Enlai and other top officials in the Chinese Communist
Party (CCP) who felt that the study of nationalities should be concentrated
in one place.[2] I was housed on the Minyuan campus in Building 4 (*sihao lou,*
as it was called), a nondescript two-story brick structure. The building was
populated mainly by Korean and Japanese students studying the standard
northern pronunciation of Chinese (known as *putonghua* in China and as
Mandarin Chinese in much of the West), though it also served as a short-
term guest house for visiting scholars from around the world. The Minyuan
was meant to be an international place, though the administration did not
allow Chinese students and scholars to enter the building beyond the lobby.
I therefore daily made my way to the faculty apartments that towered behind the west end of the campus, just adjacent to the small urban village of
Weigongcun, where Hui Muslims and Uyghurs from Xinjiang ran the most
popular restaurants in the neighborhood.

In cramped apartments that housed from three to six family members,
I worked daily with a small coterie of scholars, all of whom were Yao.
These scholars shared similar personal histories. Their journeys began in

the 1950s, when they were recruited in their home villages in the south of China by Communist Party cadres and then brought to Beijing to be trained as ethnologists, historians, and linguists. As had other young students during this period, some of them came from relatively wealthy landowning families, and they all exhibited, almost from the start, complex identifications with the CCP and with the figure of Chairman Mao. They nonetheless told me how, in their youth, they had embraced Marxism-Leninism to understand the history and place of the minority subject in the Chinese Revolution. They devoted their attention to the solving of what the writings of Stalin and Lenin termed the "nationalities problem," or *minzu wenti*. Although some of them were able to do research on the Yao and other minorities in the 1950s, much of their work ground to a halt in the 1960s, when the study of ethnic cultures and histories was labeled a capitalist bourgeois enterprise during the Cultural Revolution. Like social scientists throughout the country, many of these young Yao intellectuals were sent to the countryside, to learn from the peasants, to rectify their thinking, and to sharpen their proletarian sensibilities.

After the death of Mao in 1976 and the rehabilitation of Deng Xiaoping as China's paramount leader, these Yao scholars, now approaching middle age, returned to their positions as teachers and researchers at the Minyuan. In the midst of Deng's frenetic "socialist modernization" drive, they were encouraged to devote their energies to the study of "local cultures and histories." This was to be the postideological era and the end of class struggle, though the CCP still ruled the country and still attempted to set the agenda for how modernization, development, and progress were to be defined and pursued. Intellectuals throughout the country were asked to now "seek truth from facts." For the minority scholars with whom I was working, this required reexamining the history of ethnic classification in remote Yao autonomous regions and counties in the south and southwest of China. My work with these scholars taught me that minority ethnologists and social historians were deeply invested in rethinking how their people had been studied, classified, and represented in China. They were especially interested in revisiting the social history investigations carried out under the leadership of the CCP in the 1950s, when Yao culture and society were marked as objects of both ethnological knowledge and ideological struggle.

For many of the people I came to know, the signifier "traditional culture" pointed to distinctive ways of life, to worlds of sentiment, belief, and feel-

The front cover of a Christmas greeting sent to the author from the Foreign Affairs Office at the Central Nationalities Institute in 1992. The image shows representatives of various minorities at the front gate of the institute.

ing ingrained deep within the Yao subject and deep within the history of the Chinese nation. Many believed that fragments of this cultural domain had somehow survived the onslaught of modern history, especially the political campaigns associated with the "ultraleftists," now held responsible for the disasters of the Cultural Revolution. Those with whom I worked most closely argued that intellectuals now had a responsibility to study this culture, to write about and represent it to other Yao communities as well as to wider national and international audiences. Yet, what exactly were they finding in the imagined worlds of custom, social practice, belief, and sentiment? What does the desire to know and recover the traditional tell us about minority agency in the People's Republic? What does it tell us about the reform regime's search for new modes of governmentality? How were different actors using tradition to speak against what they saw as histories of marginalization? With these questions in mind, the chapters that follow explore histories of ethnic classification, the role of ethnology in the study of the Yao, the politics of place and locality, and theories of marginality. I want to briefly describe each of these interests to tease out some of the issues to be addressed in subsequent chapters.

Ethnic Classification and Its Discontents

Whether I was in Beijing, a provincial capital in the south, or the mountains of Guangxi, I encountered Yao who argued that the CCP had done much to liberate minorities from the classificatory schemes of Imperial and

Republican China. References to non-Han peoples living in the upland regions of the south and southwest have appeared in histories of China for over two thousand years. It is common knowledge in China and beyond that these peoples were subjected to denigrating stereotypes and dehumanizing modes of discrimination and prejudice. For centuries, they were viewed as incomplete and imperfect human forms with strange tongues, customs, and social practices. Seen for the most part to inhabit the dangerous worlds of beasts and goblins, these peoples were at once marginal figures in the Chinese imperial imagination and yet at the same time central to it. They provided a cultural and political other against which the center of power in Imperial China defined its identity.

With the expansion of the empire further into the south after the Song dynasty, more and more knowledge on the location and distribution of the non-Han other was needed. The Yao came to be classified under the broad category of "southern barbarians" (nan man), a term that pointed to the nomadic lifestyle of swidden cultivators as well as to their propensity to raid imperial outposts and rebel against the authority of the emperor. By the time of the Ming dynasty, one begins to find an amazing amount of recorded information on the cultures, customs, and habits of these upland peoples. This knowledge was deemed necessary if these peoples were to be brought under administrative control and integrated into the tax and corvée labor schemes of the imperial system. Much of this knowledge was collated and systematized by the editors of local gazetteers (fang zhi) and nationwide gazetteers (yi tong zhi). In these accounts one finds long lists of mountain ranges, the names of villages inhabited by different kinds of peoples (often named with descriptors of clothing, headdresses, or other bodily markers), and an occasional reference to the social life and behavior of the people. These gazetteers were quasi-ethnographic accounts meant for the eyes of high-ranking officials who sought knowledge about social life on the margins of the empire. The modern notion of a world composed of socially and culturally distinct peoples sharing a common sense of identity was nowhere to be found in these official reports and gazetteers, however.[3] Non-Han others had yet to become anthropological subjects in the modern sense of the term: peoples with their own cultures, histories, identities, and desires.

Much of this began to change in the early decades of the twentieth century. After the fall of the Qing dynasty in 1911 and in the context of China's repeated defeats and humiliations at the hands of American, European, and

Japanese imperialist ventures, a range of images and discourses about the modern began to enter China. During the May Fourth period (a reference to the events that began on 4 May 1919, when students in Beijing protested the terms of the Versailles Treaty), a newly defined intellectual class—the *zhi-shifenzi*—emerged to speak against the Confucian order and European and Japanese colonialism.[4] Composed in large part of students who had studied in Japan, France, and the United States, these intellectuals began to entertain modern notions of cultural diversity, local cultures, anarchy, nationhood, the emancipation of women, and citizenship. As the conscience of the new nation, these intellectuals constituted themselves as a privileged class. Through modern education and enlightenment, they promised to liberate the nation from the past and save it from the Western imperial powers that threatened its borders.

The making of a new unified national polity required locating and defining the nature of society (*shehui*). Society came to be viewed as a space outside the state and government interests where a multiplicity of social interests, ethnic peoples, and regional cultures came into contact and, at times, conflict. Modern ethnology (*minzuxue*) was born at this time, when Cai Yuanpei and other May Fourth intellectuals promoted it as the discipline best suited to study the non-Han other. From its very inception, then, ethnology has been linked to intellectual debates about Chinese modernity and the question of how best to build a strong and prosperous Chinese nation, and it was forged in the space of Japanese and Euro-American colonialism and imperialism. Many of its ideas about ethnic difference, historical progression, and cultural survival were derived from the Japanese and from the ethnological writings of Henry Lewis Morgan, Herbert Spencer, and Marx and Engels. As ethnologists and other intellectuals attempted to write non-Han others into the nation, a range of questions was debated: What was the place of non-Han peoples in the Chinese nation? Did they constitute the most primitive or indigenous of China's people? How were observable differences in cultural traits and physical characteristics among different nationalities to be explained? Were these people in fact at one time Chinese? How did their cultures relate to the culture of the Chinese? What, in fact, was a Chinese? The anthropological writings of Marx and Lenin were appealing at this time not so much because of their calls for a proletarian revolution, but because their descriptions of primitive social forms that evolved through time provided a new, seemingly anti-Confucian interpretation of history. Morgan's work, especially his laborious *Ancient Society*, was a favorite and often-cited text, for it seemed to exhibit sensitivity to the linguistic and cultural particularities of Native American Indians and other "tribal" peoples.[5]

These questions of cultural borders and boundaries eventually gave way to the more pressing political question of how best to govern the non-Han populations. Issues of political administration and cultural policy dominated ethnological writings in the 1940s, especially when ethnologists began to study and debate how to implement the nationality theories and strategies of Lenin and Stalin. How were minorities, who were seen as socially and culturally different from the more advanced Han, to be approached? What were the costs of forced assimilation? Should their cultures be respected and perhaps even protected from the ravages of war and revolution? Given their history of resistance to China's imperial regimes, was it not the case that minority populations were potentially better revolutionaries than Han peasants and workers? How were cadres to learn more about these peoples so that they could convince them to join the socialist nation and its revolution? How to win the support of a people who for so long had been brutally mistreated by the scholars, gentry, and officials of the Ming and Qing dynasties? How to counter the Guomindang nationalists, who were approaching minorities with their own promises of liberation and their own narratives of progress and national development?

Scholars of the Chinese Revolution have pointed to the emergence of a number of cultural forms that define how the CCP approached the work of building a new nation and mobilizing the support of the people. The CCP put into place a hierarchical Leninist organizational structure, with a strong emphasis on mass political campaigns, ideological indoctrination and conformity, public struggle sessions, and self-confessions, but it also promoted the spread of literacy and strove to put an end to prostitution. Especially after the communist victory in 1949, the Party went to work to control the print and electronic media; it built monuments, museums, and other public memorials to honor its image, its revolutionary history, its leaders and martyrs. The making of a modern socialist nation also demanded a new relationship with the non-Han other, which was dictated in large part by Marxist-Leninist theory.[6] The Party had built relations with many minority communities during the civil war with the Guomindang (the Nationalist Party headed by Chiang Kai-shek) and during the Long March of 1934 and 1935. After 1949, the CCP adopted a host of new policies to continue to harness the support of minority populations. One of its first orders of business was to put an end to long-standing modes of Han chauvinism, called *da Han zhuyi*, and to local forms of intraethnic exploitation. In the constitution of 1954, for example, minorities were guaranteed rights of self-government in newly instituted autonomous regions, but not the right of secession as existed in the Soviet Union. The CCP initially promoted minority language use among Party cadres, encouraged sensitivity toward indigenous cultural practices and modes of livelihood, and lent institutional and sometimes financial support for the development of so-called traditional forms of art, music, and literature.

The new revolutionary regime also asked minorities to step forward and register the names by which they wished to be identified. By 1955, more than four hundred different ethnic groups had taken up the call.[7] This was a startling and perplexing development and the Party immediately moved to clarify the situation. Two questions were put on the table: Were these groups actually a subgroup of the Han? If they were not part of the Han, then did they belong to a larger, non-Han group? Intensive field investigations began to be carried out in the early 1950s, with the Central Branch of the CCP sending visiting research teams composed of historians, ethnologists, and linguists into minority regions around the country.[8] Proper identification was important to settle claims for state recognition, but also because official recognition would mean that a given group would be granted a number of deputy seats in the National People's Congress. The deputies could then lobby on behalf of their constituencies and even push to have a locality classified as an autonomous region, thereby ensuring access to state funds for development projects such as the building of highways, schools, and supply networks.

The revolutionary state also placed a high priority on recruitment. Promising youth and others who had strong records of revolutionary activity were moved from their homes, enrolled in newly established minority nationality institutes, and thereby introduced to the fields of ethnology, social history, political theory, and administration. The Party also recruited from landlord and rich peasant households, as well as from the families of Guomindang collaborators, all in hopes of winning converts to the revolutionary cause. These youth were introduced to a new theoretical language and a new way of seeing themselves in the world. They were enjoined to turn a critical gaze on their communities, which often were seen as socially backward and hindered from advancement by uneducated peasants who believed more in the magical realm of ghosts, gods, and ancestors than in historical materialism. They were introduced to anticolonial and national struggles in other regions of the world and were asked to consider if, when, and how class struggle should be brought to minority communities. They were asked to think about the theoretical status of their new identities as elite minority nationalities and to participate in the recording and writing of social histories of their people. These youth were to be the new minority elite. After several years of training, many of them returned to the countryside. Equipped with new theoretical tools and a strong grounding in Marxist-Leninist theory, they took charge of everyday political administration in autonomous regions and ensured that the Party had popular support for its campaigns to bring socialism to the masses.[9]

By the late 1950s, fifty-four nationalities, or minzu as they are popularly called, were recognized by the state; the Yao were one of them. Stalin's definition of a nation was employed to solve these conundrums of ethnic identification and state recognition. According to Stalin, a nation was a stable community of people that had evolved over time. The people of this nation were to have a common language, live in a common territory, and have a common economic life. They were also to have a common "psychological makeup," a kind of shared mentality that was supposed to correspond to their level of social development.[10] Although the Han were officially considered a nationality, they were rarely called a minzu. In everyday speech, this term began to refer only to minorities. Despite the CCP's declarations that the battle against "big Han chauvinism" would be waged on all fronts, the fact is that the Han were considered by many to be the most socially advanced of all of China's peoples, the most educated, and the most worthy of Party membership. In any case, by the 1980s, fifty-five groups enjoyed minority status, with several more clamoring for recognition.[11] It is now commonly acknowledged in China that these criteria were very difficult to put into practice.[12] Immense linguistic and cultural diversity existed within these groups, to say nothing of their territorial dispersal throughout China and, as with the Yao, for example, beyond the borders of the Chinese nation-state. Additionally, pre-Liberation Chinese folk categories strongly informed the identification process, which has pushed many minority researchers retrospectively to question the scientific truth claims of Stalin's identification scheme.[13]

Ethnology and Yao Studies

This process of groping and theoretical uncertainty was evident during the Yao identification process as well. In China, as I have indicated, the Yao are known as a mountain-dwelling people dispersed throughout a number of regions in south and southwest China. Many of these places were extremely difficult to reach in the early 1950s, often requiring several days' journey on foot. When minority researchers finally did reach these areas and began to collect social histories, they were overwhelmed by the cultural and linguistic diversity that existed in these remote mountain enclaves. When the Yao were eventually entered into the official minority nationality system, the category contained three mutually unintelligible languages, each with its own dialects (see map on p. 99).[14] Yao living in different parts of the country possessed over thirty names for themselves (*zicheng*), and over three hundred different terms for the Yao existed in the Chinese language (usually descriptive of clothing or styles of ornamentation). These various groups—ethnologists recognized them as subgroups or *minzu zhixi* of the larger Yao *minzu*—worshiped deities, celebrated religious festivities, and proclaimed mythological origins that, at least before 1949, were not known to some of the other subgroups to be distinctly Yao.[15] It thus was not at all clear initially just what constituted a Yao identity or how this identity had been formed throughout the long stretch of Chinese history. And all minorities were required to have a history![16]

Eventually, after the collection of extensive local histories and much deliberation, Party cadres and minority researchers argued that territorial location was the determining factor in the constitution of a shared Yao identity. The Yao were those minorities who lived at the top of the remote mountain ranges in Guangdong, Guangxi, Hunan, and southern Yunnan, where Han settlers in search of new arable land had long ago forced them to live. In these distant lands, where few dared to travel or live, they took to swidden cultivation, roamed the southern highlands, and practiced an esoteric form of Taoism. The widespread Yao adherence to Taoist practice differentiated them from other upland peoples such as the Tujia and the Miao, and it suggested a long history of cultural exchange and borrowing with the Han Chinese. Yet other evidence was at hand, evidence that would prove essential to the making of the first modern socialist mythology of the Yao. Minority researchers began to find that many Yao subgroups possessed and in cases fervently guarded copies of an old imperial document written in the classical language; it would eventually be dated to the Tang dynasty. A kind of imperial license (*quandie*), this document guaranteed its holder the right to roam the mountains of south China free of tax and corvée labor obligations, in perpetuity.[17] Party researchers thus realized early on that the historic definitions of the Yao were derived from Chinese imperial political designations. This explained in large part why different groups with strikingly different languages and cultural practices sometimes identified themselves as Yao. Historically, the term Yao pointed to a contingent and transitory collectivity of disparate groups who occasionally mobilized themselves to resist the encroachments of bandits, tax collectors, and imperial officials spreading the glories of Chinese culture. Yao identity was seen to be grounded in the experience of territorial remoteness, but also, and more important for many cadres, in the act of resistance. In short, the Party had at its disposal a perfected subaltern subject: a remote minority who repeatedly rose up against the injustices of the "feudal" imperial order. In time, historians and minority researchers would make much of these images of territorial isolation, marginal subsistence, nomadic wanderings, and repeated resistance. In official histories of the group and of particular regions and counties, the Yao were championed for their tough mountain spirit, their ancient revolutionary drive against feudal modes of exploitation, and their participation in the final battles against the Guomindang, which in some Yao regions lasted into 1952.

It bears mentioning that not all Yao recruited to be minority leaders in the 1950s became scholars and intellectuals. The majority, in fact, became government officials and high-ranking Party cadres. Some became Red Guards during the Cultural Revolution, though few were willing to revisit their involvement in this history. We need to remember that Mao Zedong's revolutionary rhetoric and practices of class struggle did not dictate every moment of this historical period, and his visions of development were often challenged at all levels of Chinese society. It is thus difficult and perhaps even misleading to speak of a unified and politically homogeneous Maoist regime. What we can say for sure is that intellectuals especially occupied an ambivalent position in the making of a socialist political culture, in part because the Party inherited the *zhishifenzi* category and its elitist pretensions from a previous era of Chinese nationalist fervor. Mao attempted to rip open the notion of the intellectual as both educator and savior of the nation and sever it from its roots in the Confucian and May Fourth traditions. As Mao saw it, one problem was that the May Fourth imaginary allowed intellectuals to imagine their class as being above the people they claimed to represent and speak for. They were too easily seduced by the language of pure aestheticism, by the comfort of moral disinterestedness, or by the search for philosophical absolutes, all of which, in Mao's view, had very little to do with China's immediate problems as a poor and war-ravaged nation.

As Sheldon Hsiao-peng Lu has summed it up, Mao's approach to the "problem" of intellectuals was both institutional and discursive. Artists, writers, professors, and scientists were assigned work in newly administrative units. These intellectuals now became the cadres and staff of a workplace (danwei), entirely dependent on a salary from the revolutionary state. Moreover, at the discursive level, intellectuals were required to do constant "ideological work" on their thinking. They were asked to voice their criticisms and then, in the next moment, found themselves the objects of ideological struggle or the subjects of reeducation. Intellectual work (art, literature, and even some scientific research) was often treated, at least in official discourse, as secondary to the advanced consciousness of peasants, workers, and soldiers: the very classes that made the revolution or in whose name the revolution was fought and won. During these campaigns intellectuals were often singled out, isolated from other intellectuals, and incarcerated in special camps. Subjected to the disciplinary practices of the Party-state apparatus, they would be asked to remold their consciousness, defeat class-based elitism, and identify with the masses they were said to disdain. Throughout much of the 1960s and 1970s, intellectuals were denied any meaningful constituency. They were denied the right to speak for anyone, except perhaps for the discursively constructed and abstract category of "the people."

In theory at least, Deng Xiaoping's reforms were designed to change all of this. As Qui Pu wrote in the early 1980s, the reforms enabled ethnology to find new life in a new era.[18] Under the leadership of a remade Communist Party, ethnology was no longer labeled a bourgeois practice contaminated by an idealist fascination with outdated cultural remnants and esoteric local practices. It was now called on to serve the larger national effort of bringing socialist modernization to the ethnic margins. The term "tradition" emerged as a key signifier in this remade historical moment. Many intellectuals, government officials, and commoners believed that Yao culture was rooted in the ancient history of the Chinese nation; many felt this culture had been radically misrepresented throughout much of the socialist period. Under the reforms, it was to be liberated, in theory at least, from its previous designation as a mere form awaiting socialist content. Ideologically loaded terms such as "feudal superstition" were jettisoned, no longer seen as sufficient to capture the complexities and richness of Yao social and cultural life. Yet many government officials and some ethnologists still felt that the Yao people, isolated in the remote mountains of south and southwest China, needed to lift themselves up, raise the quality of their people, and join the socialist modernization efforts that were sweeping through the rest of the country. It was in the context of these competing discourses on the minority subject that Yao ethnologists struggled to make sense of the history of Chinese socialism and find a place for their people in the making of a new China.

The Politics of Place and Locality

My third interest concerns the study of ethnic regions in the far south of China, what I term the moral geography of place. When I returned to China after the political fallout over the Tiananmen protests subsided in the autumn of 1990, I discovered that the scholars with whom I was working were eager to get out of the nation's capital. With the crumbling of the Soviet Union and developments in Eastern Europe, the "nationalities problem" had once again become a concern of the Party; many minority scholars and students at the Minyuan were required to attend long study sessions on the correct interpretation of the Soviet Union's historic failure. A new ideological retrenchment was in process. I began to discuss with my advisors and negotiate with administrative authorities at the Minyuan the conditions under which I might conduct a field study in the Jinxiu Yao Autonomous County in Guangxi Province. This was a sensitive topic, for no foreign scholar had ever lived in this region for an extended period of time for as long as anyone could remember. And, to top it off, I was proposing to live not in the Communist Party guest house or *zhaodaisuo* where tourists were typically required to stay, but in the house of a local Communist Party member!

Jinxiu is commonly referred to as the Dayaoshan, or the Great Yao Mountains. It is known for its stunning topography and its long history of ethnological research. Three of the scholars I was working with in Beijing were members of a small Yao subgroup from these mountains, the Chashan, or "tea-growing" Yao. They had been born and raised in these mountains before moving to the Minyuan in the 1950s; another had spent extensive time here in the early 1960s and then again in the early 1980s; another's family had been linked to the Guomindang leadership in Guangxi in the 1930s and 1940s. I traveled to Jinxiu with one of these scholars (another joined us some months later) and a Japanese graduate student studying Yao linguistics. My aim was to join and observe their ongoing ethnological research projects into the culture and social history of the Jinxiu Yao. The history of Jinxiu before 1949 was a central focus of our investigations. Before Liberation, the Chashan Yao, along with two other Yao subgroups, the Hualan and Ao Yao, controlled a local system of political and economic organization known as the "stone tablet system" or *shipai zhidu*. The primary function of this system was to establish and enforce the regulations for land ownership and tenancy. Its leaders were also called on to enforce social order, as they would issue fines and other forms of punishment for a range of transgressions, from petty thievery to adultery and murder. Communist Party cadres in the 1950s argued that this system was contaminated by feudal ideas of ethnic differentiation and hierarchy, and they began to remove and reeducate its headmen; much of the authority and local prestige of the Chashan Yao group was eroded over the subsequent decades. These scholars were particularly interested in how, in the 1950s, Party cadres and researchers had struggled against the *shipai* leaders and represented the Chashan Yao as an aristocratic people who oppressed and exploited other Yao groups in the mountains. They were invested in crafting an alternative history of the Chashan Yao, one that would return some respect to what they saw as a once proud and prosperous people.

In late November 1990, we left Beijing and boarded a hard sleeper train bound for Guilin, loaded down with luggage, books, and boxes of gifts. Once in Guilin, we caught local transportation south to the backpacker retreat of Yangshuo, a small town on the Li River where one could find cheap hotels, Western rock music, and banana pancakes. We spent a night in Yangshuo and then worked our way by bus toward the southwest and into the Dayaoshan. I eventually settled in the household of the son of Su Defu and Liu Yulian, the scholars with whom I worked in Beijing. They lived in the Chashan Yao village of Xidi, a short walk from the town of Jinxiu, the administrative seat of the county.

Before 1940, the year the Guomindang set up the first garrison command post here and called it Yongning (the town of "everlasting tranquillity"), Jinxiu had no paved roads, the nearest market was some forty kilometers away, and the majority of the trading was done with overland itinerant peddlers. Well into the reforms, many of the Yao groups living in the more distant villages of the county continued to struggle daily with basic needs. Jinxiu was of additional interest to me, then, because issues of remoteness, uneven development, and intraethnic politics were central to how minority leaders were dealing with everyday social problems and struggling with how best to represent the history and culture of the region to larger national and international audiences. Finally, popular ritual was making a comeback in a country eager to move beyond the politics of class struggle. As my advisors argued again and again, to know the Yao it was necessary to know something about the complicated and richly detailed world of Yao Taoist rites, beliefs, and history. This world of ritual, they insisted, could be found only in the remote mountains in which most Yao lived, in places such as Jinxiu.

Jinxiu was attractive as a research site for yet other reasons. Some of the other Yao scholars and officials I had met in Beijing were familiar with the social history of the region. For example, a Han ethnologist named Hu Qiwang had recently completed a book on the Pan Yao of Jinxiu, a Yao subgroup who had practiced swidden cultivation in the area until it was outlawed in the early 1950s.[19] By this time I had also met Huang Yu, who headed the Guangxi Nationalities Research Center in Nanning and was the father of a close friend. He was also the leader of one of the first Party research teams to visit the area in the 1950s.[20] I was drawn to Jinxiu additionally because it was here that the eminent Chinese anthropologist Fei Xiaotong carried out his first fieldwork project in the mid-1930s.[21] The mountains of Jinxiu are thus one of the originary sites of modern ethnological research in China, and I early possessed a certain romantic if not troubled attachment to this place. In 1935 the education department of the Guangxi provincial government, then loosely tied to the Guomindang government, had hired the young Fei to enter these remote mountains and measure the height, breadth, circumference, color, and shape of various body parts of individual Yao. Influenced strongly by the Russian anthropologist and Manchu expert Sergei Mikhailovich Shirokogoroff, with whom he studied at Qinghua University in the early 1930s, Fei seemed to have believed that taking physical measurements of people would prove helpful in developing minority education programs. He was traveling with his newly wed wife, Wang Tonghui, a rising star in Chinese sociology who was studying the relationship between landowning and nonlandowning Yao groups. For months, these two Han Chinese students from the north wandered the Yao hills, until late one afternoon Fei was crushed by rocks and other debris when he stepped into a tiger trap. With Fei unable to walk, Wang went for help, only to lose her way in the dark and fall to her death.

As a student of Chinese anthropology, I have long been fascinated by Fei's early interests in the now discredited field of anthropometrics and haunted by the tragedy of Wang's untimely death. In the course of my own travels through the Dayaoshan I would discover that hers and other stories haunted these hills. These tales concerned not only the history of Han Chinese research in the "primitive" outback, but also the history of Communist Party attempts to bring order, progress, and modernity to a people said to be desperately in need of economic development, socialist culture, and modern forms of education. The reforms and especially the widespread repudiation of Maoist socialism was forcing people in a range of social positions to ask themselves what had happened in these hills in the past, what was happening in the present, and just what a socialist modern future might look like. The reforms were leading people to ask just how modern Jinxiu actually was, and just who had the right to speak for its history and its contemporary problems.

I lived in Jinxiu on and off from 1990 to 1992. During this period, I frequently traveled to other Yao regions and provincial minority nationality institutes in the south of China, and I returned to the Minyuan in Beijing on several occasions. I attended large community Taoist rituals throughout Jinxiu County, presented papers at academic workshops, and observed large state-sponsored celebrations of the Yao in a number of different locations. I interviewed and worked with Yao ethnologists and historians, Communist Party members, research and tour guides, amateur and professional photographers, and others who had been assigned by authorities in Beijing and Guangxi to teach me about Yao culture and history. To work in and out of Jinxiu was to try to make sense of how the reforms had unleashed an intellectual fascination with "traditional culture" and memories of past social orders. It was also to understand how this fascination, however imbued in nostalgic renderings of a lost cultural past, articulated with reform-era Party concerns over how best to govern its people. Many of these issues over Party rule, social morality, and popular consciousness were played out in the proliferation of writings on and visual representations of Yao culture and society that began to appear in China in the mid-1980s. I spent a good deal of my time in Jinxiu poring over the writings of some of China's leading Yao scholars and examining Jinxiu local Party histories and other documents

The anthropologist pictured at a dinner with county officials in Jinxiu. The linguist Pan Chengqian is second from left.

produced in the 1980s on the local cultural scene. I was able to seek out and talk at length with many of the authors of some of these articles and the editors of Party and non-Party publications on Jinxiu culture and history.

At the same time, many of these new images of the Yao social and cultural order were traveling across China and the Pacific Rim at an alarming rate. I was also able to observe, for example, how foreign scholars from Japan, Thailand, and Taiwan conducted research among Yao scholars and county officials in Jinxiu. The presence of these eager and gift-bearing scholars, myself included, impressed on me how the remaking of Jinxiu into an object of reform-era research was not just a question of finding a place for "traditional culture" in Deng's socialist modernization campaign. It was also tied to the movement of dollars, gifts, and commodities such as gold, cameras, and televisions into this "remote" space. It was about turning Jinxiu into a global site for ethnological desire.

The Rectification of Names

In Euro-American contexts, intellectuals have long occupied a dominant position in the social division of labor. As Carl Boggs has put it, intellectuals are seen to stand at the summit of great political formations and events, the prime movers of local struggles, parties, revolutions, and states: "As critical repositories of world views, from traditional religions to Enlightenment rationality to liberalism and Marxism, intellectual groupings have commonly provided a linkage between power and knowledge, governance and legitimacy, moments and ideologies." [22] Recent studies on the role of intellectuals in the politics of social change have emphasized the need to situate intellectual production in concrete historical and discursive processes. There is a strong sense in much of the current literature that intellectuals can no longer be seen to stand apart and above the worlds on which they comment and act. In debates about identity politics and multiculturalism in the United States, for example, intellectuals have been linked in complex ways to institutional structures and discourses of power and knowledge. They are seen to be "in power" in two senses: they are constituted as elite subjects by dominant regimes and are constantly asked to comment on these regimes. In the introduction to the edited volume *Intellectuals: Aesthetics, Politics, Academics*, Bruce Robbins has employed the metaphor of "grounding" to capture the contradictory critical practices of "intellectuals in power." [23] The intellectual relationship to power is seen to be morally and politically ambiguous, which has made it even more important, Robbins argues, to map the specific social sites, situations, and structures that both enable and restrict critical discourse.

With the end of the cold war and the failure of Marxism to account for the emergence of "free market" ideologies in much of the world, some have argued that Gramsci's call for a "moral-intellectual" is now more relevant than ever.[24] At issue in these reappraisals of Gramsci is the question of how intellectuals are now implicated in the new hegemonic structures associated with post-Fordism. The question of "class"—as both an analytical category and a condition of lived reality—haunts this literature. For Gramsci, ideological hegemony refers to the capacity of dominant classes with their affiliated elite to get the general population to internalize the values and ideas of the ruling class. The masses would then become the very agents for the reproduction of a social system. A ruling elite draws on the state, its laws and procedures, as well as the educational systems and the mass media to mold both participation and consent. This process, as Gramsci was always quick to argue, is never complete, and it is the incompleteness of hegemonic rule that pushes the system onward. Debates might be waged around questions of freedom, democracy, prosperity, and the common good (especially in the media), but these serve less as a means to mobilize people who experience deprivation and marginalization than as a means to block collective political action. This is the space in which Gramsci's organic intellectual struggles. A counterhegemonic politics is one where the critical intellectual forges identifications with subaltern groups, broadens the spheres and spaces for public debate and social action, and seeks a "voice" for collective empowerment. Forging is the key metaphor here, for any effective counterhegemonic movement ultimately does away with the idea of the intellectual as an elite or professional class. The organic intellectual thus displaces the "traditional intellectual," who speaks only for transcendental truth, stands above and apart from the people, and reproduces the ideological doctrines of the ruling classes.

Some commentators have contrasted Gramsci's notion of the organic intellectual with Foucault's critique of the intellectual.[25] As R. Radhakrishnan has put it, for Foucault, nothing was more ignominious than being spoken for. Any attempt at representation — either to hold oneself as a representative of a collectivity or to represent the interests of others — is "disciplinary, panoptic, and coercively theoretical."[26] Radhakrishnan continues, "The best an intellectual can do is thematize her marginality and not presume to speak for others."[27] If, following Foucault and other poststructural theorists, struggles are now understood as singular, regional, and nomadic, then it is somewhat unclear how a theorist of power, knowledge, and domination could speak on behalf of a collectivity or constituency. Radhakrishnan takes up these issues in the context of the politics of ethnic representation in U.S. multiculturalism, but not in the sense of what previous theorists of ethnicity would have called the markers or diacritics of an identity (a primordial origin myth, for example, or a complex of cultural practices). He seeks rather to think representation in terms of the politics of how one defines a constituency, how one speaks on behalf of a given collectivity, what it means to do theoretical work on behalf of an ethnic collectivity. What happens when the interests of the ethnic theorist do not coincide with the collectivity? Do the academic, professional, and institutional affiliations of the theorist always already dispose him or her to a transethnic network? Discarding the view of ethnic collectivities as homogeneous social and cultural orders, the crucial question becomes how to theorize the relationship between a self-conscious intellectual project of empowerment and collec-

tivities that are split by a diverse set of experiences, interests, identifications, and desires.

This leads me to recent writings on the politics of culture and identity among marginalized social groups. Anthropologists and other scholars
critical of the discipline's ties to colonial regimes have shown how anthropology constructed its objects of knowledge through temporal and spatial
imaginaries that drew rigid boundaries around peoples and their cultural
identities.[28] More recently, in attempting to move beyond colonial modes of
cultural and ethnic classification, anthropologists and other social scientists have begun to utilize metaphors of border crossing, cultural hybridiza-
tion, and syncretism.[29] The postcolonial nation-state has emerged as the
favored object of deconstruction, as it is seen by many as the political and
cultural form of the late twentieth century that most clearly bears the traces
of the Eurocentric notions of historical progress that drove the colonial
enterprise. The concept of the "margins" has similarly appeared in the past
decade as a key term in writings on the politics of nationalism, postcolonialism, and modern forms of disciplinary power. It is of some interest, I
think, that the 1989 edition of *The Oxford English Dictionary* defines margins
singularly as the white space on the limits of a page, whereas in the 1990s
it comes to refer to the periphery, the cultural fringe, or the opposite of
the center.[30] The margins are frequently used to refer to the excluded, the
silenced, the subjugated, and the forgotten, especially in textual approaches
to power that focus on the discursive construction of cultural, social, and
political subjects. They are also increasingly seen as noisy zones of contact
and interaction, spaces of agency where hybrid cultural practices come into
existence, subvert the imaginaries of the dominant culture, and allow for
the emergence of new identities, histories, and alternative modernities.[31]

The question of how to rethink the interplay between domination and
resistance is at the heart of many of these approaches to the margins. It
is thus not surprising that the margins are often equated with minorities
and that minorities are often romanticized as subaltern agents who know
nothing but resistance. I think there are some dangers in how minorities
are generally attached to romantic images of the margins as spaces of resistance, especially in terms of how different regimes, leftist, liberal, and
conservative, construct "exemplary individuals" out of the culturally marginalized.[32] My concerns, however, mostly derive from a consideration of
the Yao case and the scholarship on reform-era Chinese nationalism. His-

torians and anthropologists of modern China have long employed models
of centers and peripheries to describe and analyze the realities of unequal
institutional and economic power in different regions of China.[33] China's
ethnic minorities are often equated with the margins of the nation, and
spatial metaphors of centers and peripheries have figured strongly in writings on the Chinese nation and the politics of minority representation.[34]
This is no doubt because they are so strongly outnumbered (constituting
a little more than 6 percent of the total population in the early 1990s), are
typically (but certainly not always) found in strategically sensitive border
provinces, and live in remote agricultural mountain environs where subsistence is a daily struggle. Yet, what happens when minorities are no longer
seen as simply reacting to or always already resisting the Chinese state,
but rather as central agents in the cultural politics of the post-Mao nation?
What might the anthropology of post-Mao nationalism look like if it refuses to find in the ethnic subject the perfected example of authenticity or
resistance?

In addressing these questions, I do not present a singular Yao view on
questions of culture, socialist history, and the meanings of Deng Xiaoping's
reform agenda. I have sought rather to highlight the partial, fragmentary,
and ideologically positioned nature of Yao knowledge production. In doing
so, I have opted to employ the term elite to capture the shared if not contradictory subject positions of my various research consultants. The term elite
has long been a slippery concept in the social sciences. There is a certain
ambiguity built into the term, in the sense that it is not always clear whether
an elite is, as George Marcus once put it, an empirically self-reproducing
fixture of social organization.[35] It is also not at all clear how an elite group
overlaps with a given socioeconomic class or with members of the state.
And, to be sure, it is certainly the case that just what constitutes a minority
elite has shifted through the years, as the CCP's approach to the nationalities problem has evolved. Katherine Verdery's work on identity and cultural politics in Ceausescu's Romania is instructive.[36] Verdery sought to
understand "how images of Romanian identity entered into battle with one
another in the politicized world of Romanian culture and, in so doing, per-
petuated a Romanian national ideology within an order claiming to be socialist."[37] Intellectuals in Romania were a broadly defined and diverse social
group who produced discourses of culture, and who, in writing and talking
about the nation, constructed it as an emotionally and politically charged
field of discourse. By focusing on these diverse cultural producers, she dem-

onstrated how intellectual activity was intricately and sometimes unpredictably related to the making of coherent ideologies about the nation, its past, present, and future. She did not seek to write from below, that is, to give voice to a subaltern intellectual class that had been silenced by socialist power. On the contrary, she showed how various groups, variously situated in Romanian society, produced images of their nation while competing with one another to be acknowledged as the nation's legitimate cultural representatives.

I use the term elite to refer to minority intellectuals, scholars, government officials, Communist Party cadres, and local tour guides, all of whom claimed to be in a position to know and speak for the Yao. These individuals came from a range of social and class backgrounds and occupied differential positions of authority and influence in minority studies. To write and speak about the Yao subject was not simply or only the prerogative of intellectuals—the zhishifenzi that have received so much attention in the scholarship on modern China. Intellectuals worked and competed with scholars (xuezhe), government cadres (ganbu), Party members (dangyuan), and Taoist specialists, the daogong and shigong who attended to the affairs of the spirit realm. My use of the term minority elite is intended to show how these various subject positions sometimes overlapped and intersected and how, in some instances, they delimited distinct modes of cultural and political discourse. For example, it was not uncommon for me to meet a Taoist specialist who was also a retired Party member. Individuals such as these provided unique perspectives on the history of the state and its attempts to suppress and sometimes promote popular ritual. These same retired cadres turned Taoist specialists also wrote reports for internal (neibu) Party publications and assisted in the research efforts of Yao ethnologists and social historians. These various actors were all involved in one way or another in the business of minority representation, and they each had a stake in how the Yao were governed. They were active in debates about culture and development in minority autonomous regions and they all claimed the right to speak about these places. The term elite, therefore, allows us to avoid a totalizing or homogenizing view of minority consciousness, as though all Yao think and behave in the same way. It allows us to ask how different social actors have critically engaged, negotiated, and even authorized the various discourses of historical progress, modernity, tradition, and political emancipation that have been at the center of Chinese socialist and postsocialist national imaginings.

My aim, then, is to show that Yao elite possessed quite contradictory ideas about the role of socialism in bringing progress and development to their people and about the promises of Deng Xiaoping's socialist modernization agenda. Although some deplored the Party's treatment of popular ritual, others admitted that they once fervently believed that the widespread belief in religion and magic was antithetical to the making of a revolutionary nation. Some of the scholars I knew in Beijing told me that during the Cultural Revolution they burned their embroidered clothing (one of the more salient markers of one's ethnic identity at the time) in large public rituals. They spoke of how they handed over headdresses and bangles made of handcrafted silver to Party activists, never really knowing where they ended up, fearful that these once-celebrated bodily markers of ethnic identity would be interpreted as evidence of a hidden capitalist tendency. They saw the reforms in the 1980s as an opportunity to remake this troubled history. This was a period in which it was once again relatively politically safe to speak proudly of one's ethnic background, and, as I have indicated, many Yao ethnologists began to return to their native villages to study the Taoist classics and interview elders about pre-1949 social practices. One man I knew, a scholar and Communist Party member who had risen to the top of his research institute in the southwest, returned to the village of his birth to become ordained in the Taoist priesthood. As he put it, he did this not because he wanted to make money from believing peasants who would pay him to perform marriages, oversee funerals, and deal with everyday sicknesses and misfortunes. He did it because this is what it meant to be Yao. He laughed and said, "All Yao are Taoists, but we also believe in the guiding wisdom of the Communist Party."

Marginality and the Question of Power

These various perspectives on Yao culture and its place in the Chinese nation are grounded in different personal experiences and collective histories. Scholars writing about the politics of marginality have increasingly turned to Foucault's notion of genealogy, essentially the idea that participants in social life can never have the final say about the significance of the practices they engage in. In using this term, Foucault sought to get beyond the shared, unproblematic meanings of social life, and he warned against methodologies that favor the hermeneutic retrieval of meaning. For those interested in theorizing marginalization, Foucault's methodological position has resulted in various approaches to the question of individual perspectives on and explanations of social life. In *The Ethics of Marginality*, for instance, John Champagne argues that it is impossible to free subjects from their marginality. Waged on the border zones between academic theorizing and progressive social action, the battle, in Champagne's view, should be one of creating, defining, and defending cultural sites that might liberate the subject from subjectivity altogether.

Others have proffered critical injunctions against the use of the term "experience." In writing about how "the experience of the other" has been a central focus of ethnographic accounts of domination and resistance and a popular methodology for historians interested in questions of difference, Joan Scott has framed the problem as follows:

> It is precisely this kind of appeal to experience as uncontestable evidence and as an originary point of explanation—as a foundation upon which analysis is based—that weakens the critical thrust of histories of difference. By remaining within the epistemological frame of orthodox history, these studies lose the possibility of examining those assumptions and practices that excluded considerations of difference in the first place. They take as self-evident the identities of those whose experience is being documented and thus naturalize their difference. They locate resistance outside its discursive construction, and reify agency as an inherent attribute of individuals, thus decontextualizing it. When experience is taken as the origin of knowledge, the vision of the individual subject (the person who had the experience or the historian who recounts it) becomes the bedrock of evidence upon which explanation is built. Questions about the constructed nature of experience, about how subjects are constituted as different in the first place, and about how one's vision is structured—about language (or discourse) or history—are left aside.[38]

Scott refuses any explanatory reference to individual beliefs, intentions, experiences, or actions except as a means to explain the operations of power. Just as Foucault's arguments against Marxism were aimed to disrupt a tradition in which "the economic is always taken as the last instance,"[39] arguments such as Scott's aim to show how the subject is always an effect of historical and social processes. Philosophical traditions such as phenomenology—in fact, the entire scope of the human sciences—that took the thinking and acting subject as the locus of explanation and promised to return autonomy to the individual and expiate that which blocked self-realization were merely technologies of discipline and mastery.

My approach to minority politics in China has been shaped by my reading of Foucault's relentless tracking of the techniques, modalities, and technologies that have taken human populations as the primary object of both scientific analysis and transformation. My argument in this book, however, is that to write a critical ethnography of the subjectivities, discourses, and social practices that have hovered around the body, culture, and history of the ethnic subject, it is necessary to recast Foucault's view that the human subject is a mere node through which power is dispersed. Many attempts to utilize Foucault's insights have ignored ambivalences in his writings about the nature of disciplinary power. This is in part because so much of the attention has been focused on the brilliantly deconstructed image of the panopticon in *Discipline and Punish*, which has led to exciting work on how subjects are differentially positioned and disciplined in institutional spaces of control and regulation. In this book, Foucault showed how institutions such as the army, the monastery, and the prison made possible the meticulous control of the body in space, "which assured the constant subjection" of the body's forces and "imposed upon them a relation of docility-utility."[40] A subject can never truly be emancipated from the entanglements of power, knowledge, and discipline; subjects are only produced and reproduced anew depending on the interconnected systems of discourses, practices, and institutions that structure any given regime.

Foucault argued that the growth of bureaucratic control over populations after the eighteenth century required new and more systematic forms of knowledge. These knowledges emerged largely in the domain of criminology, penology, psychiatry, and medicine, but also in economics and anthropology. Power is linked to the growth of scientific knowledge, which in turn is linked to the identification of deviant and marginal groups against which rational orders are both constituted and naturalized. Discourse creates difference through its seemingly objective classificatory schemes, tables, charts, and comparisons; it does not merely discover it. The study of ethnicity and nationalism has drawn extensively on Foucault, Lacan, and Derrida to highlight processes of classification and narrative figuration and to bring a more critical perspective to bear on the question of identity as a site of resistance.[41] In this theoretical frame, ethnic and national identities (as with gender, race, and sexual identities) are viewed not only as products of history but also as effects of dominant systems of power and knowledge.[42] These identities are no longer viewed as embodiments of local, premodern, or traditional social forms. Rather, they are intimately caught up in, if not reflective of, the ideologies, social practices, and developmental discourses of the modern era and of the modern nation-state, where history is seen as a process of increased rationalization, social ordering, and cultural homogenization.[43]

To be sure, there have been numerous studies since the mid-1980s critical of Foucault's omissions and oversights, especially his failure to see that much of what he described for France and other European countries was first tried out in the colonies.[44] Others have pointed to how his attack on the liberal notion that knowledge leads to greater individual freedom seemed to dispense with an interest in human agency. For Foucault—and this is especially the case in his earlier, "structuralist" writings—the exercise of power over the marginal or the deviant or the subordinated could never be reduced to a question of attitudes, motives, and intentions on the part of individuals. As Bryan Turner has put it, "Valid comparisons between deviants and normal individuals, between the sane and the insane, between the sick and the healthy, cannot be achieved by simply reforming attitudes and motives, since these distinctions themselves presuppose a discourse in which conceptual differences are expressions of power relations."[45] Foucault's ontology of the social is one "that treats exclusion, subjugation, and homogenization as inescapable presuppositions and consequences of any social practice."[46] In this way, Foucault seemed to suggest that all dispersions of power were the same. More perplexing and troubling for some is that in departing from "older" Marxist questions, such as who possesses power, with what rights, who profits and suffers from the exercise of power, and so on, Foucault seemed to have little to say about how one could turn power back against itself.[47]

It is my sense, however, that Foucault's late writings on power as a productive process (and not just a disciplinary one) open up a space for tracing the incomplete, nuanced, or ambiguous practices that accompany any process of subject formation.[48] Beginning especially with the publication of The History of Sexuality, Foucault begins to explore what he called "technologies of the self," drawing a distinction between technologies geared toward normalization and those geared toward crafting an aesthetics of existence. For instance, in an interview conducted by Hubert Dreyfus and Paul Rabinow in April 1983, Foucault characterizes a third axis of genealogical-archaeological analysis that explores the kinds of relationships that people ought to have with themselves.[49] He calls this a shift to the problem of ethics, one that moves away from coercive practices to those that seek to transform the self and attain a certain mode of being within the structures and discourses provided in any given regime. This new axis of genealogical practice constitutes a major shift from his earlier emphasis on fields of power in which individuals could be conceived only as nodal points—where individuals are "constituted in the first place," as Scott put it. Although individual action is still situated in cultural and institutional systems that organize the commonsensical way things are done, individuals are granted more agency: they can critically and reflectively detach themselves from these systems and sometimes modify them. They make creative use of new modes of subject formation. This shift to the question of technologies of the self continues to situate power at the center of forms of resistance and transgression, yet it also affords a consideration of how different actors employ dominant languages and practices to sometimes unpredictable ends. It opens up a space to approach ethnic politics in China as a process of "perpetual incitement and struggle," what Foucault once called the politics of "permanent provocation."[50]

The individuals whose writings, reflections, and ruminations fill the chapters that follow fascinated me because their personal stories of the revolution, and their active participation in it, flew in the face of the standard Western image of the totalitarian Communist Party breathing down the necks of the authentic ethnic primitive. This elite was the revolution, and I suppose in many ways they continue to be the revolution, if this is how we are to name what has occurred since the death of Mao. But these individuals were never simply agents of the state. They were members of an officially constituted minority nationality, but repeatedly asked, as members of an elite cadre of scholars and officials, to turn a critical gaze on their own people. They taught me in various ways that Chinese socialism had done much to recognize the Yao contribution to the revolution and the Chinese national order. At the same time, many of them argued strongly that the Yao had too often been treated as a reactionary force retarding China's grand march in history. The image of the Yao in the history of Chinese socialism is thus a complicated one, as different individuals brought quite different interpretations to the question of just where the Yao fit into the making of a modern socialist China. They made me realize that categories such as scholar, intellectual, Party official, cultural worker, tour guide, and even minority nationality could not fully capture the complexity of their identities, subjectivities, needs, and desires. They forced me to think about how one might begin to identify and write about forms of political practice not explicitly directed toward seizing state power. They made me question my own initial assumption that images of a traditional ethnic subject merely flatten history and render the past an inert object of nostalgic contemplation. They led me to ask how we might begin to locate forms of cultural struggle that occur not in the opposed realms of state and society but at the more diffused levels of force and consent, authority and hegemony, and agitation and propaganda.

Overview of the Study

The conception of power as a site of both incitement and struggle will allow us to think about the cultural politics of the Yao elite without replicating a totalitarian view that would mechanically pit a dominant state apparatus against a docile ethnic other. It will also help us avoid buying wholesale the view of power as a purely disciplinary apparatus. The following chapters are thus devoted to writing the ethnic margins not as a space of authentic resistance, but as a social practice where different ideas about identity, power, the state, culture, and modernity are inscribed, resisted, embraced, and denied. In chapter 1, I explore practices of ethnic history writing in the 1980s. I show how minority scholars sought out, defined, and wrote the culture and modernity of the ethnic subject into the history of the Chinese nation. Many of these scholars were interested in the Euro-American ethnohistory of the Yao, which argued that the south of China was an "ethnic mosaic" characterized by centuries of interethnic strife. I show how Yao scholars in China picked up on this theme and wrote a subaltern historical subject into the history of the People's Republic. Ironically, however, this subject is denied agency once the revolution is complete.

The subsequent chapters turn to the practice of ethnology and various debates in the study of Jinxiu County. I argue that the revitalization of ethnology spoke against the class politics of the Maoist period but also entailed the somewhat imaginative if not nostalgic reinhabitation of pre-Liberation social and political orders. In chapter 2, for example, I focus on early debates on how to classify Jinxiu and its various Yao populations, and I provide a sympathetic yet critical reading of Fei Xiaotong's vision of Jinxiu scholarship and its relationship to reform-era minority research. Chapter 3 brings the question of memory and modernity to the forefront of the analysis. I examine various narratives of socialism's arrival in Jinxiu to highlight the shifting ways Jinxiu has been represented as an ethnic place both within and outside of the space of Chinese modernity. Chapter 4 focuses on the ethnological study of Yao "traditional" social morality, the elite fascination with popular ritual, the Civilized Village Campaign in Jinxiu, and localized critiques of certain forms of state power. I show how the study of ritual and other popular cultural practices were never too far removed from debates over social order, morality, and the question of how best to govern ethnic populations. I look as well at the ways one of my research consultants, an older woman who remembered fondly the aristocratic days of her once landowning Yao family, taught me to think differently about the politics of socialist modernity in Jinxiu.

Chapter 5 inquires into the politics of what I call postsocialist belonging. I begin by showing how the reforms produced a widespread national and indeed global fascination with minority cultures. Throughout the 1980s, Han intellectuals and other cultural producers turned to the ethnic margins to fashion critiques of the Cultural Revolution, the CCP, and the strict gender and sexual mores of the Han nationality. Minority elite, as the following chapters will reveal, were also fascinated with the image of a traditional subject, and they worked to produce representational spaces—in their writings but also in visual depictions of ethnic difference—for the indigenous culture, ritual, and social morality of their people. What does the gaze turned on the traditional subject tell us about the reform-era repudiation of Maoist socialism and China's opening to global capitalism? How do we understand differences in minority and Han desires when both turn their attention to the figure of tradition? Can we speak of a space of minority difference? Is it even possible to write an account of ethnic struggle that does not engage in what some might see as the imperialist project of giving voice to those who have been denied representation?

This book is about ethnicity, but only if we recognize, as Marcus Banks has suggestively put it, that to write about ethnicity at the close of the twentieth century is to bring it into being and therefore open it up for debate and contestation.[51] Banks's point is that every account of some so-called ethnic phenomenon or problem must negotiate how ethnicity has escaped the world of Euro-American academic theorizing and entered complex fields of social and cultural struggle. Claims to identity throughout the world are often made by recourse to anthropological and other social and cultural theories, just as many ethnic and indigenous movements critique anthropo-logical writings. Anthropological research increasingly occurs in contexts where people speak back and across histories of ethnic classification, writ-ing, and representation. If we are to take seriously the work of intellectual production in discourses of culture, history, and nation, then we cannot ap-proach those who produce these discourses as unproblematically speaking for a clearly defined constituency. In China at least, ethnic minority intel-lectuals are complexly located vis-à-vis multiple work sites, interlocutors, personal and collective histories, and political ideologies.[52] In the context of these movements and shifting identifications, I was often asked to ar-ticulate the nature of my own political commitments, to work as an advo-cate, and to assist, through my writing, in the undoing of dominant and often denigrating modes of representation. I was implored by one of my research consultants, for example, to never write that the Yao are a "back-ward" or luohuo people. My job was to write an "honest" (laoshi) account of the Yao, which meant in part to write a book about how Yao culture had survived the worst years of Maoist rule. I was also repeatedly asked to par-ticipate in the mass reproduction of images of Yao "traditional" culture, to take an active role in journalistic, television, and photographic docu-mentary projects. Across these diverse representational spaces, and in the midst of these repeated entreaties, Yao ethnicity appeared to me a tenuous and fleeting object, despite (or perhaps because of!) the ways in which it was constantly marked as an object of both ethnological and ideological struggle. Its meanings and referents seemed to be constantly up for grabs: for one person a reminder of years of struggle and pain, for another a source of pleasure and wonderment.

Finally, I want to emphasize that this account focuses on a particular historical moment: the late 1980s and early 1990s. This was a period that witnessed the collapse of socialism in much of the world and the triumph of liberal market relations on a global scale. I argue that no account of eth-nicity during the late 1980s and early 1990s can afford to ignore the history of Chinese socialism, with its mobilizations and rectification campaigns, its promises and catastrophes, its narratives and counternarratives, its am-bivalences and contradictions. In the epilogue, I argue that if we are to write critically about this global capitalist order, then we have to continue to ask who occupies the center of this order and who is excluded. I argue that the desire for indigenous knowledge and the representations of tradition among Yao elite cannot simply be reduced to a problem in the recent history of Chinese nationalism; it must also be thought of as a global process. How we think about these processes has important implications for how we theorize the nature of power and subjection, domination and resistance when all the old formulations for political action seem to be lost in the rubble of the cold war.

I am not the first to draw attention to debates about how to define the nature of the political in the post–cold war period. For example, Don Robotham has pointed out that many Third World postcolonial intellectuals who once embraced socialism as an alternative to the capitalist modernity of the West are now in search of a new definition of political agency: "Now all of this seems to have been shattered by the collapse of communism, and postcolonial intellectuals who have not embraced capitalism are either overwhelmed by feelings of powerlessness and despair or, what is perhaps another form of the same thing, have reverted into an acute relativism bordering on nihilism." [53] Alex Callinicos has similarly argued that the failure of state socialism has been an "ideological event of the first magnitude," which has led many people—including many leftists—to believe that the "death agony of Stalinism amounts to the bankruptcy of the revolutionary socialist tradition founded by Marx." [54] Ernesto Laclau has also argued that the terms that once defined the conceptual terrain of leftist oppositional discourse—revolution, socialism, proletarian democracy, and imperialism—are no longer capable of capturing the uncertainties, aspirations, and transformative energies of our time. He asserts that it is increasingly difficult to define the nature of the political in the post–cold war period. [55] Alessandro Russo has proffered yet another view; he pushes the crisis in leftist discourse further back in time. For Russo, the disappointments of the Chinese Cultural Revolution, coupled with other worldwide crises in the 1960s and 1970s, have worked to bring an end to some of the basic categories of modern knowledge concerned with the investigation of politics. Since the late 1960s, Russo asserts, there has been a growing uncertainty about the political value and cultural substance of categories such as class, class struggle, mode of production, the state, equality, and so on. [56] Not only is the nation in crisis; so is the theorization of the political.

These are all compelling arguments, though I am not convinced that they are the full story. It is increasingly clear, for example, that the demise of state socialism, the fluidity of global market economies, and the reorganization of the international state system have all given rise to ethnic violence, economic decline, the intensification of state and military surveillance, and new forms of gender inequality.[57] It is also the case that minority groups around the world are increasingly speaking back to histories of marginalization and cultural misrepresentation. What, we might ask, is the nature of the political in these processes of empowerment? Are they riddled by the same "cognitive uncertainty" that characterizes Laclau's post-Marxist angst? We know that binary divisions between states and societies, centers and margins, liberation and repression, and domination and resistance are not politically neutral or natural distinctions and descriptions of the world. These binaries have been central technologies in how modern regimes of power and knowledge have mapped and naturalized the world for subjects everywhere. I argue that it is not enough to trace how different discursive configurations have turned these binaries into commonsense understandings of how social and political worlds are organized. If anthropology is to move beyond the task of simply showing the constructed nature of all political and social ideologies and the binaries on which they are based, then we must also trace how these binaries are sometimes used by social actors struggling to empower themselves in different situations.

My point in raising these questions is not to suggest that critics such as Laclau, Russo, and others who have drawn attention to difficulties in locating "discernible political objects" and defining the nature of the political in the late twentieth century have nothing to offer to this project. It is rather to point to the broader contexts of intellectual debate, in both China and beyond, in which this ethnography is produced, as well as to the global transformations of the past decade. It is to emphasize that this study, and the issues of representation, history, scholarship, and minority empowerment it addresses, is written in the midst of enormous changes in the global system. Many people are struggling to define and name this system, and others are working to negate it; there are still others struggling to find a place in it. How we write the "margins" of China's reforms, and the global system in which these reforms are situated, is thus of crucial concern, both for anthropology and for the people whose lives it claims to engage and represent.

chapter one

Inciting the Past

We now know that narratives are made of silences, not all of which are deliberate or even perceptible as such within the time of their production. We also know that the present is itself no clearer than the past. — MICHEL-ROLPH TROUILLOT, *Silencing the Past: Power and the Production of History*

This chapter explores how Yao ethnologists and social historians were writing histories of their people in the post-Mao period. What is remembered in narratives that locate the Yao subject in the history of the Chinese nation? What is forgotten? Who is empowered in the retelling of the past? Barbara Kruger and Phil Mariani have observed that history is a text of the dead dictated to the living, through a voice that cannot speak for itself. The historian is the keeper of the text, the worker, as they put it, of mute mouths.[1] Yet, what happens when history is not perceived as the instructor of origin, power, and mastery? What happens when it is seen as a crowded space, where complex reckonings of the past refuse to be encapsulated in any dominant narrative?[2] Is it possible to write against the singular universality assumed in histories of the nation that speak for the local, the plural, and a range of incommensurable knowledges?[3] Is it possible to displace the formal structures of a singular history into a space of dispersal, where different stories vie for voice? What is gained in this displacement? What is lost? Can we interpret the writing of histories of the Yao as anything but the search for origin and mastery?

Chinese Marxist historiography has long emphasized the "movement" and "development" of social groups, classes, and nations through history. History was imagined as a theoretical practice serving broader revolution-

ary goals. By focusing on urban commercial development, popular literature, and minority nationality resistance to dynastic regimes, Marxist historiography attempted to promulgate a new history, a history of and for
the masses.[4] To be sure, the writing of a Marxist-informed history has been
marked by numerous moments of struggle, debate, and controversy.[5] Yet,
certain fundamental premises have remained constant since the 1940s. One
is that the writing of history, like any intellectual pursuit, must "serve the
people." A second premise is that popular history is to be written about and
for the masses and that these histories are more valuable than are histories about feudal emperors, scholar-officials, and imperial intrigue. A third
premise is that history is alive. The past is not viewed as a document of lifeless events and facts but as a temporal frame to which one can turn for an
explanation for the conditions of the present and a vehicle for action and
change in the world. And finally, Chinese Marxist historiography has long
maintained that statements and representations of history invariably have
social and political roots and consequences.[6]

My fieldwork in Beijing at the Central Nationalities Institute, and then
later in the Jinxiu Yao Autonomous County, often revolved around long and
complex discussions with Yao scholars, government officials, and Taoist
specialists about the twists and turns of Chinese revolutionary history. My
job as a fieldworker interested in questions of Yao culture, history, and
identity required that I not only read the texts that many of these scholars
and officials produced; I also had to inhabit their language and try to make
sense of the categories and analytical perspectives they brought to their
work. In examining how they were writing the Yao subject back into the
history of the Chinese nation, I hope to show that the relationship among
culture, history, and the Chinese nation was an uncertain and often contested one. Minority histories were not marginal to the debates about the
Chinese nation that raged on in China throughout the 1980s. Rather, they
were at the very center of how the nation was being imagined, debated, and
discursively reconstructed.

I argue that the nation—understood here as both a contested category
and an object of devotion and protection—cannot be written out of our accounts of minority politics in the late 1980s and early 1990s. Yao scholars
were attempting to find a discursive place for the Yao subject in a highly
contentious and uncertain national setting. Throughout this period, intellectuals were critical of the analytical usefulness of almost all forms of class
discourse. Many were assessing the first three decades of the People's Re-

public and struggling to make sense of the calamities and disasters associated with the Cultural Revolution. In constructing historical narratives of their people, Yao scholars also sought a place for a subject that retained the cultural traditions of the Yao. They were also reading, translating, and arguing with discourses of the Yao that appeared in European and American ethnological works from the 1930s to the late 1970s. I begin in the next section by asking what Edward Said's work on orientalism tells us about these readings across borders in which different discourses of knowledge on the Yao subject were being read and translated. I then turn to the ways this subject was approached and constituted in some of the ethnohistorical literature. The literature on the ethnohistory of the Yao in particular fascinated many of these scholars, in part because they had been academically socialized in an environment in which prerevolutionary scholarship was marked as a bourgeois practice. In official denunciations of ethnology in the 1950s, for example, this scholarship was said to reinforce attachments to the ruling classes and devalue the revolutionary potential of the subaltern subject. In the next chapter, we will see that many scholars feel Maoism has left ethnology in ruins and that the remaking of the discipline requires a critical reassessment of how to go about the business of investigating the "histories and societies" of particular ethnic regions.

I conclude the chapter by turning to the writing of a standard history of the Yao in the 1980s, focusing in particular on the publication of the *Yaozu jianshi* (concise history of the Yao). Chinese and Euro-American scholars who have looked at these reform-era texts have emphasized the imaginative if not specious and contradictory constructions of these histories. They have argued persuasively that they are clearly indebted to the social evolutionary theories of such nineteenth-century figures as Lewis Henry Morgan.[7] Few have asked, however, what these history projects tell us about elite struggles to speak for and empower their people. I argue that the writing of reform-era histories was not simply about minority scholars fulfilling the responsibility that came to them with the rehabilitation of the social sciences and Deng Xiaoping's call to "seek truth from facts" and not be led by the blind dictates of ideology. These minority ethnologists and historians were involved in a more critical enterprise, one that called attention to the relationship between subaltern agency and the representation of the minority subject. Distinctions between the oppressor and the oppressed, the revolutionary subject and the feudal reactionary, modern consciousness and traditional sensibilities inform and shape the writing of these histories.

As with other nationalist histories that emphasize the nation's movement toward a higher order of progress and advancement, the historical Yao subject, with its revolutionary spirit and its refusal to submit to the tyranny of China's feudal rulers, finds its voice in the founding of the People's Republic.

For some, however, the question of the Yao subject in the history of the Chinese nation was far from settled. For this was a subject, granted revolutionary agency in histories of the Chinese nation, that looked back not only to the ancient past of the nation to find its power and voice, but also to the past of the People's Republic, a subject that told stories that haunted and troubled the official history of the Yao, in which the founding of the People's Republic marked the end of years of struggle. These narratives point to alternative ways in which a subaltern subject was being imagined, a subject now no longer brought to presence and visibility through the master narrative of class struggle. But neither was this to be a subject fully contained in the reform-era imaginary of a multiethnic nation-state finally at peace with itself, a nation that would now live in harmony with its own troubled past and its own sites of internal ethnic difference.

Traveling Anthropology

In late August 1988, I called on a friend at the Guangxi Nationalities Institute in the city of Nanning, Guangxi. A young man in his early twenties, Huang Fangping had graduated from this institute several years earlier with a specialization in ethnology and history and had only recently taken a position as a researcher and part-time teacher. I met Xiao Huang, as I called him, the previous year in the San Francisco Bay Area when he was the youngest member of a four-person contingent of Yao scholars and Communist Party officials to tour Yao communities in Portland, Seattle, and the Bay Area. I was just beginning my research in China and was on my way to Beijing. I entered China through Hong Kong and Guangzhou (Canton) and then worked my way up the West River by boat to the provincial capital of Guangxi, Nanning. I was also in Nanning to meet Xiao Huang's father, Huang Yu, a high-ranking administrator at the Guangxi Nationalities Institute and a representative to a number of provincial government and Party organizations. Huang Yu was recognized as one of the leading Yao intellectuals in all of China, in large part for his extensive writings on the social history of Jinxiu. From Nanning, I planned to travel north by train to Liu-

The mountain peaks of the Jinxiu Yao Autonomous County.

zhou and from there by bus into the Dayaoshan, also known as the Jinxiu
Yao Autonomous County. I had spent the better part of the previous summer plodding my way through Wang Tonghui's posthumously published
book, *The Social Organization of the Hualan Yao*, one of the Yao subgroups found
in the Dayaoshan. Wang had tragically died in these mountains in the 1930s
while doing research with her recently wed husband, Fei Xiaotong. Jinxiu
was thus very much on my mind.

The history of Jinxiu dominated my conversations with Huang Fangping, his father, and several other scholars I met in the course of this initial visit to the Guangxi Nationalities Institute. These scholars and officials
were interested in a number of historical questions, such as how the Guomindang had successfully penetrated the Jinxiu regions in the 1940s. They
talked about the history of Yao relations with the Han and other minorities such as the Zhuang, and they were very much concerned with how the
class struggle campaigns of the 1960s and 1970s continued to inform social relations among the Yao "subgroups" in the hills. Jinxiu history was
presented to me as an assemblage of facts, dates, and events, of heroes and
martyrs, but also as a site of long-standing ideological battles over how to
interpret the nature of local social realities. I was beginning to learn how
the Party had classified the region, battled the Guomindang reactionaries,
defeated the remaining enemies of the people, and worked with the moun-

The administrative town of Jinxiu.

tain peasants to bring this "remote" and "backward" place into the fold
of the energies enveloping the rest of the nation. I took these narratives of
Jinxiu's past to be lessons in the history of both the Yao and the Chinese
nation; they also gave me insight into how minority scholars understood
the exercise of power.

In the 1980s, Yao intellectuals increasingly turned to the ethnohistory of
the Yao written by Chinese and Euro-American scholars in the prerevolutionary period. International scholars and experts on Yao Taoism, many of
whom had done extensive field research in mainland Southeast Asia in the
1970s, began to organize conferences and workshops exploring the relationship between socialist modernization and traditional culture. In their
own way, these scholars were enjoining and critically participating in debates that were ongoing in China about how to study ethnic culture after
its near obliteration at the hands of the ultraleftists. Xiao Huang was also
interested in how Euro-American scholarship had represented the culture
and history of his people. As we talked about my proposed research to work
on the history of the "nationalities problem" in Jinxiu, he asked me if I had
ever read the work of the anthropologist Peter Kandre. He took me into his
study and showed me how he had been busy in recent months translating
Kandre's work into Chinese. I asked why the interest. He replied that by
focusing on the relationship between economy and culture in Yao society,

Kandre had explored many important issues about Yao culture, especially Yao religion and supernaturalism, that ethnologists in China had failed to fully consider.

I was skeptical. I knew that anthropologists who worked among the Yao in the late 1960s and early 1970s challenged the view that the Yao were an isolated and primitive people. They showed that they had long histories of cultural interaction and exchange with the Han Chinese and other groups. Kandre was one of the first anthropologists to entertain the proposition that Yao ritual was intricately bound up with the reproduction of the ethnic group itself. Yet, despite the emphasis on cultural interaction with other groups, this approach tended to see upland Yao communities as enclosed and functionally self-sustaining social spaces. Ritual practice was only rarely analyzed historically (Lemoine's work constitutes an exception); there was little sense of how it changed through time and how it related to larger social and political environments such as the modern nation-state. In effect, ritual was turned back on village life and explained in terms of what it did for the reproduction of the group and for the maintenance of the extant social order. I tried to explain all of this, though my Chinese kept failing me (I had yet to learn the Chinese for "structural functionalism," for example!). None of this seemed to matter. Kandre, he insisted, had much to teach China about the relationship between "traditional culture" and "socialist modernization."

What, I wondered, might be the political repercussions of my friend's interest in how Euro-American scholarship had studied and written about the traditional culture of the Yao? Was he not involved, I asked myself, in an ideologically dangerous enterprise, one that might invite criticism from his superiors? I already knew that Communist Party mobilization efforts in the 1950s attacked religious leaders and that the popular attachment to Taoism was seen as a form of "feudal superstition." The "traditional" culture of the Yao had become the object of intense hatred during the Cultural Revolution, as some Yao leaders as well as many peasants moved against it to reveal their "Redness" and love of Mao. Many Yao in villages across China criticized and sometimes violently attacked those who attached themselves to these living remnants (canji) of the feudal past, which came to be seen as contaminated by class interests and hidden desires for wealth and prestige. It occurred to me some time later that this young scholar's fascination with descriptions of Yao ritual life in other places and times had much to do with the fact that he himself had never lived in the countryside, never really seen Yao rituals in practice. His parents had been intellectuals and Party officials in China since the 1950s. He was born into and socialized in an environment in which minority intellectuals had to mind how they related to and spoke about the popular culture and religious practices of mountain peasants. It seemed that a certain exotic wonder informed my friend's interest in this world of popular rural ritual, a world that had been denied to him in his own upbringing. But his interest in Euro-American scholarship on the Yao was also part of a development in the 1980s in which ethnologists and other social scientists were questioning previously dominant modes of interpreting and classifying ethnic minority social realities. This meant, in part, turning to sources outside the Chinese ethnological and Marxist-Leninist tradition in which they had been trained.

I want to consider for a moment what these practices of readings and borrowings across national borders tell us about the politics of representing ethnic difference in post-Mao China. These minority scholars identified with the Yao minority nationality community. They saw themselves as being in positions of authority and influence to bring new perspectives to the study of particular places, regions where many of them continued to maintain close kinship, social, and political networks. And yet, as members of a reform minority elite, they were also acting in the interests of the reform regime, which was committed to bringing development and progress to regions seen by many scholars and officials as socially stagnant and lagging behind the rest of the country. Did they not also constitute the ethnic other as an object of knowledge, an object to be transformed into a new subject, one that could more effectively contribute to the nation's growth?

Questions of this sort were taken up some time ago in Edward Said's monumental study *Orientalism*. Published in the late 1970s, Said's study constituted an important shift in the analysis of how academic scholarship and other forms of representation produce and make visible the cultural worlds of others. Said's methodical readings of authors as different as Gibb, Bernard Lewis, Massignon, and others revealed how the "Orient" was made, at once, into an object of knowledge and a powerful imaginative figure through the disciplines of orientalist learning. Discourses on the Orient claimed to make visible the essential and enduring cultural traits of "traditional" peoples. The idea of the authentic culture located in the space of the untouched premodern generated and reinforced a series of colonial stereotypes. These stereotypes—the Oriental as backward, lazy, stubborn, promiscuous, dirty, and so forth—established the other as a culturally deficient subject in constant need of the projects of the colonizer, who defined himself as civilized, mature, rational, and modern. Said sought to map the various ways in which hierarchical dualisms between the "West" and the "East" (especially European writings on the Middle East and the so-called Islamic world) were established through the disciplines of orientalist learning. His project was to explore in all of their various manifestations the intricate linkages between discourses of culture and colonial and imperialist modes of global domination. What, Said asked, was the nature of "the alliance" among cultural work, political tendencies, the state, and the realities of domination?[8]

As is now well-known, Said's book has been controversial because his deconstructive method questioned the possibility of a positive knowledge of the other.[9] He challenged the objectivist claim that orientalist scholarship represents a real world not only distinct from the West but beyond the "irrational" flights of fantasy said to characterize premodern epistemologies. As Paul Bové has explained, the hostility directed toward Said resulted not just from his argument that orientalists have been complicit with practices of domination; his project delegitimated entire disciplines of intellectual practice on the power of which intellectuals have built their careers, identities, position, and influence.[10] Said also has been criticized for his reliance on Foucault's genealogical method and in particular his understanding of how the confluence of power and knowledge constitutes its object. Homi Bhabha, to take one example, has attempted to construct a more nuanced picture of orientalist practice by revisiting the psychoanalytic dimensions in Frantz Fanon's writings. Bhabha draws attention to what he calls the "dual economy" of colonial discourse. This refers, in the simplest of terms, to the constitution of the other as an object of both desire and derision; the other is the site of knowledge, but also of dreams, images, obsessions, and fantasies.[11] Bhabha has made productive use of this insight into the dual presence of desire and derision by pointing to the ambivalence and anxiety at the center of all forms of colonial representations.[12] This other site of conflicted desire in the colonizing subject has forced a reevaluation of Said's somewhat instrumentalist reading of the relation between power and knowledge.[13] Colonial power is not possessed solely by the colonizer, nor is it as monolithic as Said imagined; rather, it is diffused throughout the "colonial field" and is ultimately predicated less on control and more on instability, anxiety, ambivalence, and fear.[14]

Said, of course, is aware of the many critiques that have been launched against his work, both from sympathetic readers such as Bhabha and from those who have argued that he failed to advance a new epistemological approach for thinking seriously about the representation of cultural difference. What interests me here is how Said has often drawn on certain modes of anthropological inquiry to anticipate and engage his critics. We might recall, for example, passages at the end of *Orientalism* where he begins to ask about "alternatives" to orientalist knowledge.[15] He reiterates that the imagining of an "oriental other" sociologically and incommensurably different from the societies of the civilized "West" worked in tandem with other forms of colonial oppression. Yet he wants to exempt certain practices of cultural study from his critique. He is particularly supportive of Clifford Geertz's interpretive anthropology, in that it seems to offer a way to do "cross-cultural" studies without reproducing stereotypical accounts of other people's lives. Following Geertz's lead (and that of others such as Anwar Abdel Malek and Roger Owen), Said implores scholars to be animated by the specific societies and problems they study and not by the rituals, preconceptions, and doctrines that produce orientalist knowledge.[16] These scholars are exemplary because they work outside and beyond the narrow confines of an area studies approach (a modern version of orientalism, according to Said) by reading across and creatively borrowing from a range of academic disciplines. He nonetheless states, "But there is no avoiding the fact that even if we disregard the Orientalist distinctions between 'them' and 'us,' a powerful series of political and ultimately ideological realities inform scholarship today. No one can escape dealing with, if not the East/West division, then the North/South one, the have/have not one, the imperialist/anti-imperialist one, and the white/colored one. We can not get around them by pretending they do not exist; on the contrary, contemporary Orientalism teaches us a great deal about dissembling on that score, the result of which is to intensify the divisions and make them both vicious and permanent."[17]

Despite the misgivings of many scholars in the postorientalism literature about just how pervasive and all-consuming imaginings of the other were, few scholars have contested the claim that modernity was denied to this other and that representations of an other without civilization worked to justify colonial intervention. What Said leaves conspicuously undertheorized in his study is the question of how so-called orientalist practices have been interpreted and put to use at the site of their deployment through complex practices of borrowing and appropriation.[18] To be sure, Said is inter-

ested in how, for example, Arabs consume a vast range of material and ideological products from the United States, and he points out that the United
States in turn is the consumer of very few products from the Arabs "except
for oil and cheap manpower." [19] Said goes on to state that "there is a vast
standardization of taste in the [Arab] region, symbolized not only by tran-
sistors, blue jeans, and Coca Cola but also by cultural images of the Orient
supplied by American mass media and consumed unthinkingly by the mass
television audience." [20] The obvious example of this is how the Arab regards
himself as an Arab through the images provided by Hollywood. Yet, Said
also emphasizes that this process of uneven cultural exchange has resulted
in the production of a class of educated elite "whose intellectual formation
is directed to satisfying market needs." The intelligentsia is "auxiliary to
what it considers to be the main trends stamped out in the West." [21]

I have long thought about this passage in relation to the above described
experience of encountering my friend in his study in Nanning poring over
the anthropological texts of Western anthropologists writing about the Yao
in the 1960s and 1970s. Is the turn to these texts rooted in the same unequal relationship Said is describing at the end of his book, so that we think
of the reform-era ethnologist only as "auxiliary" to anthropological trends
"stamped out in the West"? How might Said interpret this scene of reading
and translation, where a young Yao intellectual reads outside the doctrines
of traditional ethnological scholarship in China to see how the Yao have
"appeared" in another space and time? Do we have, in this scene of reading and translating, the internalization of a "modernizing" discourse that
has been laid out in the West, the place where ideas about modernization,
culture, and progress are supposed to have originated? We can ask the question even more forcefully: Has this young scholar simply transported the
practices of orientalism (which are seen by Said to have originated in the
West) into a Chinese reform-era ethnological imaginary?

There are, of course, no easy answers to these questions. Nonetheless, I
want to suggest that these processes of reading and translation, appropriation and transfiguration were central to debates that were occurring among
Han and minority scholars about the place of ethnology in a socialist modernizing China. As I argued in the introduction, debates about the place
of ethnology in reform China often have addressed how the cultures, histories, and societies of particular places were represented under previous
regimes. Yet this was a sensitive issue, in part because it caused concern

among Party officials that critiques of the past could easily be turned against the reform regime. Several county officials I knew in Jinxiu, for example, were concerned with how the ethnological interest in popular ritual was reviving memories of pre-Liberation social and political orders. Some of these officials would go so far as to institute their own local memory research projects to teach the masses how to remember the past. Debates about ethnology also focused on how to interpret certain "traditional" cultural practices. The problem was that these practices were not always readily available for inspection and study. They had to be sought out and made visible. Scholars and officials sought out signs of traditional culture (in people's memories, in staged rituals, in their texts) as if the culture of the Yao was a ghost that refused to acknowledge its identity, a wayward spirit that was present in everyone's midst yet never fully discernable. Once the objects of tradition were identified—in ritual, in birthing practices, in agricultural techniques, in pre-Liberation social and political orders—Yao ethnologists, who often worked in conjunction with local officials, tour guides, and visiting foreign travelers and scholars, could then discuss and debate the place of the traditional in a modernizing China. Local practices of ethnological research, I am suggesting, were often about creating spaces for the representation of "traditional social worlds," worlds that were seen as rooted in the past and yet somehow persisted into the present.

As Caren Kaplan has written, "When the past is displaced, often to another location, the modern subject must travel to it. . . . History becomes something to be established and managed through tours, exhibitions, and representational practices in cinema, literature, and other forms of cultural production."[22] Reform-era ethnological research and history writing provides one such form of cultural production, in that the search for knowledge of ethnic cultures required practices of travel that often ended up rendering these social worlds mere specimens of exotic wonder. Here we find the structure of orientalism at work. As Bryan Turner has put it, "Orientalism is a discourse that represents the exotic, erotic, strange Orient [the ethnic remote] as a comprehensible, intelligible phenomenon within a network of categories, tables, and concepts by which the Orient is simultaneously defined and controlled." To know something is to make it visible for inspection and study: "To know is to subordinate."[23] It is to the politics of knowing the Yao as a historical subject that I now turn.

From Primitivity to Social Reproduction

European and American anthropologists first began to work on the Yao in the 1930s. This work was motivated by an ethnological agenda that sought to document the social organization and cultural beliefs of China's "primitive tribes." This discourse of the primitive was supplanted after World War II, when anthropologists began to work in mainland Southeast Asia and employ the then increasingly popular analytical trope of ethnicity. This scholarship also turned to the Chinese imperial record, and there had to contend with the images and ethnocentric prejudices that informed the traditional Chinese typology of non-Han groups. The ethnohistorian Richard Cushman brought some sense to the study of the Yao and the question of the relationship between a theory of ethnicity and the Chinese imperial record in his study *Rebel Haunts and Lotus Huts.* Cushman argued that much of the ethnohistorical work on the southern periphery of China had failed to develop a precise understanding of the relevant criteria of ethnic identity for the minorities of the borderlands. He and many other ethnohistorians viewed the southern ethnic borderlands as zones of sustained internecine strife between the Chinese empire and the dispersed "tribes" of the south. They wrestled with just how to understand the nature of minority agency in the face of an expanding Chinese empire. In contrast, anthropological writings on the Yao in mainland Southeast Asia in the 1960s and 1970s were much less interested in finding the Yao in history. This work was more preoccupied with how the Yao reproduced their culture and society at any particular moment and how they maintained group integrity. A strong primordialism informs the anthropology of the Yao in the 1960s and 1970s, for many of these anthropologists saw stasis and cultural coherence as the defining feature of the group and they implicitly assumed that a stable core of Yao ethnicity persisted through time. Cushman, on the other hand, sought to emphasize the role of conflicts between peripheral others and the Chinese imperium in the making of a modern Yao identity.

These paradigms are not that far apart, however, in that they were both informed by a shared assumption, namely, that political, economic, and social environments affect the character of the group and that these environments mold identity rather than completely alter it.[24] The problem of Yao ethnicity was one of figuring out how a core identity could be maintained in the face of migrations, border crossings, and Chinese imperial projects of bringing culture and civilization to the barbarian other. A liberal humanist discourse informed much of this work, for the agenda was to free understandings of the Yao and other upland peoples from Chinese practices of seeing and naming the periphery as a zone of both exotic fascination and fear. It wasn't always exactly clear just what ethnicity referred to, nor was it clear to Yao scholars in China when they began to turn to this literature in the 1980s just how Western notions of ethnicity differed from the theory of nationalities provided by Stalin. Nonetheless, as we will see, Euro-American theories of ethnicity, especially those that focused on indigenous understandings and interpretations of cultural worlds, were mobilized by some Yao scholars in China to write against the crude materialism and sometimes functionalist reductionism that informed the representation of minority realities throughout much of the 1950s, 1960s, and 1970s.

When Euro-American anthropologists began to do research in China in the 1930s, they saw the upland peoples they encountered as historically isolated peoples who were bound together by shared languages, beliefs, and cultural practices. In the late 1930s, for example, the British anthropologist Reo Fortune, then affiliated with the Department of Sociology of Lingnan University in Canton (Guangzhou), led a group of Chinese students into the far reaches of northern Guangdong to study an "isolated group of primitives," the Yao. Fortune saw the Yao as a primitive people hidden from history, by which he meant the history of modernity as defined and experienced in the West.[25] Fortune is an important figure in the history of Yao scholarship because it is in this period that a narrative of sustained internecine strife between the Han center and the marginal ethnic begins to be naturalized. He argued that all we know of the long and tragic history of these primitive peoples is that in the twelfth and thirteenth centuries they were driven south from the fertile valleys of Hunan Province by the invading armies of the Song dynasty. These "highlanders," as he often called them, had lived through centuries of violent confrontation with the southward-expanding Han Chinese. Faced with the superior technology of these armies, the Yao gave ground, but little else. Defying the cultural conventions of the Han, they refused to recognize the imperial court, to submit to official demands for taxes and corvée labor, or to receive education or medicine. Fortune portrays the Yao as a people turned in upon themselves and suspicious of the outside world, living out a miserably primitive existence in the marginal reaches of China's southern borderlands.

Scholars working on the Yao in the 1930s were aware of the existence of other Yao groups living in Tonkin (northern Vietnam) and regions south of the Chinese border.[26] These groups, related by language, ritual, dress, and other features of material and symbolic culture, provided further proof of the dispersion of the Yao. As long as they were not forced to assimilate to the more powerful, "civilized" groups below them, the Yao in these various localities were said to be a basically peaceful people. Wherever the Yao were found they were portrayed as a tribal people who maintained frequent contacts with other minority groups, colonial officials, and lowland Chinese, but a people who nevertheless possessed a distinct culture and society. In his writings, Fortune claimed the Yao had no writing system of their own and thus no written records that might shed light on their early origins, migration routes, and so forth. He and his colleagues were aware that Yao ritual specialists possessed documents written in Chinese, that the Yao had "procedures" that "corresponded" to Chinese ancestor worship and popular Taoism. Nevertheless, all of these seemingly Chinese features of the Yao were treated as anomalies, sitting on the fringes of a more pristine, more "primitive" Yao culture and society. In effect, the Yao are accused of being poor imitators of the Chinese tradition they attempted to copy. The literary elements of their culture were not seen as Yao; rather, they represented a kind of "literary pretension." As we will see below, these "pretensions" of aristocracy have long been noted, with great disdain, by Chinese imperial officials writing on the Yao, who tended to classify them as just one more group within the larger category of "southern barbarian" (nan man). Fortune undertakes an arguably more sophisticated yet still largely ethnocentric analysis: the Yao, as a primitive tribe, have a culture congruent with a bounded primitive society. For him, all of the borrowing from the more civilized Chinese merely represents the Yao's attempt to be something more than they could ever really be. Fortune shares a perspective with China's imperial officials, which allows him to state with confidence, "The Yao cannot have been characterized as barbarians by the Chinese for no reason."[27]

Fortune's depiction of the Yao as poor imitators of Chinese culture was eventually supplanted by a different ethnological and theoretical enterprise, one committed to understanding how the boundaries of an "ethnic group" are maintained in the face of outside cultural influences. Ethnicity emerges in the 1960s as a new way to name the Yao. They continued to be viewed as a hill tribe with a bounded culture and society, yet the awareness of various cultural connections to "Chinese civilization" suggested that the Yao differed from other hill tribe groups, such as their mountain neighbors the Hmong (or Miao, as they are commonly known in China). It became evident, for example, that the religious complex of the Yao had been totally "borrowed" at some point in their history, that this complex had great historical depth, and that the Yao saw themselves as carriers of a religious tradition that was indisputably "Chinese" in origin. These findings challenged the conception of the Yao as an isolated, primitive tribe possessing a distinct and unique tribal culture that set them off from other hill tribes and from the Han Chinese in the fertile valleys below.

The scholars who introduced the notion of ethnic identity to the study of the Yao and other upland peoples were thus wrestling with the question of just how to theorize the relationship among culture, society, and subjective processes of identity formation.[28] Did the Yao, as a tribe, have an identity originating in an unknowable past that was prior to their adoption of certain features of Chinese culture, as many Chinese, European, and American ethnologists had for so long assumed? Could this pristine identity be recovered amid the Taoist incantations, recitations, and exorcisms, the ancestor worship, and the use of the Chinese lunar calendar? This problem of conceptualizing the relationship between a remote society and Chinese culture is especially evident in Shiratori Yoshiro's *Yao Documents*. This book is a collection of materials written in Chinese that Shiratori and his colleagues collected in northern Thailand in the late 1960s. As Michel Strickmann has observed, Shiratori assumed, against all evidence to the contrary, that these documents were productions of an isolated, indigenous Yao culture. In an essay that has become a classic in the field of Yao studies, Strickmann analyzed Shiratori's collected texts and situated them within a Taoist ritual tradition popular during the Southern Song, known as the "True Rights of the Heart of Heaven" (*tianxin zhengfa*).[29] Strickmann tells us how the priests who worked this ritual complex were ambulant missionaries who brought the exorcisms and therapeutic techniques of the practice directly into the homes of common people. These priests also received official dynastic support.

Strickmann set forth the following hypothesis. In the twelfth century, a new, simplified, and accessible form of Taoist ritual spread throughout the south of China, with official participation and support. The Yao, one of the major ethnic groups of the region, were brought more effectively under Chinese control. By the thirteenth century, a process was underway that saw the successful Sinification of the Yao through conversion to Taoism. Strickmann summarizes the situation: "Taoist liturgical patterns were adapted to native mythology and sacred topography; Taoist social organization was integrated within native communal structure. Written memorials and the use of talismans [have] always been prominent [features] of Taoist ritual. In Taoist priests, the Yao would have had competent guides to Chinese literacy, well able to introduce them to the involved paperwork that effective communication with the heavens required." [30] He also pointed out that it was not until the Qing dynasty that Taoism, as a ritual practice and philosophy of life, began to be marginalized by Chinese imperial officials and scholars. The Qing court was obsessed with Confucian ethics and eradicated Taoism from the official repertoire of Chinese culture. In contrast, members of all classes during the Song, Yuan, and Ming thought Taoism contained everything that was most intrinsically Chinese. Strickmann's deliberations thus led in two directions. On the one hand, he forced scholars working on the Chinese imperial expansion into south China in the post-Song period to seriously consider the role of government-sponsored Taoist priests in opening up the borderlands of an ever-expanding empire. On the other, he forced scholars to pay more attention to the Taoist content of Yao cultural and religious life.

Strickmann's arguments find support in research carried out in the 1960s and 1970s on the Iu-Mien (typically known as the Pan Yao in China) of northern Thailand. In this ethnography, the Iu-Mien people are seen to have a distinct ethnic identity, though the boundaries of their culture were actually quite porous. Peter Kandre was perhaps the first to entertain the proposition that the Yao ritual complex was intricately bound up with the reproduction of the ethnic group itself.[31] One notable feature of Yao Taoism was its obvious difference from the practice of Taoism in Taiwan, Southeast Asia, and Han regions in Fujian Province. In these areas, the Taoist priesthood was hereditary and the Taoist masters formed a closed guildlike community and served a public largely ignorant of the subtleties of the Taoist rites. These Chinese Taoists were priests of intervention, specialists called on and employed by the public to perform community rituals, service funerals, and so forth. Other distinctions existed as well. As Lemoine has observed, the well-known Han *jiao* ritual, officiated by Taoist priests, is intended to renew the alliance between a village community and the supernatural structure of the Tao.[32] The Yao rituals, in contrast, were ordination ceremonies. This observation led anthropologists to argue that Yao ethnicity was grounded in and reproduced through an individual's (a male's) ritual incorporation into a patrilineal unit of a larger clan. A shared sense of Yao identity was based additionally on the tracing of descent to a singular mythological ruler (the dog king Pan Hu), as well as on the ritual introduction to and subsequent mastery of the intricacies of the Yao interpretation of Taoism. The ideal Yao community was a community of priests, where every male adult is initiated into the religious structure and therefore entitled to a place in the Taoist supernatural order.

The ethnography of the Yao thus argued that ritual incorporation into the Taoist cosmological realm was inseparable from the question of how these people reproduced their communities in the remote mountain regions of south China and mainland Southeast Asia. Ritual incorporation was a male-centered process. The Yao male is typically introduced to the Taoist pantheon at the age of seventeen. At this point, the word *fa* (glossed as law or model) replaces the second character in the young man's name, signifying his new status as an initiate. This initiation enables him to perform certain basic rituals; it confers the first of three degrees in the clerical system; and he gains knowledge of secret ritual accoutrements, which allows him to engage in certain feats of magic. After attaining the second grade, the Yao priest is entitled to conduct major ceremonies such as funerals and initiation rites. Most Yao do not make a trade of their priesthood, however. What is important is each individual's introduction to the Taoist supernatural realm. Wives are marginal figures in the process, introduced to the spirit realm through their husbands, who become, in effect, the earthly representatives of the Taoist pantheon, with its assortment of guardian and auxiliary spirits to protect the individual, family, and community. Young men who move beyond the second grade take up intensive study with a master, learning how to write memorials in classical Chinese to be sent to the gods; they are also instructed in how to perform more sophisticated and esoteric ritual practices. Yet the ethnography insists that the gap between these higher-order priests and the initiates is not wide, nor is it absolute. Young initiates are part of a larger community of practitioners who are bound by the authority and power structure of both their ancestors and the Taoist supernatural realm.

Kandre especially championed the idea of the intricate links between ritual activity and the reproduction of the group. He argued against the once dominant view that language performance was the basis for ethnic identity, noting that his informants did not view competence in the Mien dialect as central to one's recognition as Iu-Mien. Yao ethnic ascription is not grounded in linguistic competence, Kandre argued, but rather in the acquisition of a "combination of name and rank, to which graded doses of

Yao Taoist specialists in Jinxiu consult a Taoist text.

supernatural power, blessing, and purity are attached."[33] Ethnic identity is initially ascribed for the newborn infant, who is introduced to the ancestors. One becomes Iu-Mien, therefore, through the ritual incorporation into a patrilineal subunit of a clan that assumes descent from the mythological ruler Pan Hu. The assimilation into the ethnic group is a passive process, and here it is possible to get a sense of how ethnicity is grounded in the primordial facts of birth, as Charles Keyes once argued.[34] The Iu-Mien Yao readily admit that there are good Mien and bad Mien. This determination is based entirely on performance, both in terms of the fulfillment of one's obligations to one's ancestors, parents, and other community members and on the basis of one's subordination to the power of the Taoist supernatural order.

These sorts of arguments drove the ethnography of the Yao in mainland Southeast Asia throughout the 1960s and 1970s. Anthropologists argued that although the identity of a Yao was grounded in the facts of his or her birth, it was also practiced and performed throughout life. Practice and performance were viewed as ritual matters, but ritual was at the center of all social life: the community itself is reproduced through the everyday acknowledgment of one's obligations to family and social authorities and through one's submission to a realm of supernatural power. The anthropologists of the Yao in the 1960s and 1970s admired the proud, aristocratic attitudes of the Yao people. The Yao presented themselves as a literate people, the masters of a long tradition. The Taoist religion, ancestor worship, and the expensive and elaborate ritual ceremonies were seen to constitute the core of Yao society. These anthropologists, working in colonial contexts in which officials were daily trying to bring European civilization to the primitive outback, also noted how Yao stubbornly resisted the Christian missionary penetration of their communities. Lemoine, for example, writes of attending meetings of Yao in Thailand and Laos in which there were long discussions of whether they should abandon the "legacy of their ancestors" and embrace a new faith.[35] They impressed him with their comprehension of their cultural traditions and how they consciously linked tradition to their everyday lives. As he put it, "In the face of difficult conditions—repression, migration, segmentation, and scattering—Yao society has proven to be remarkably resilient. Furthermore, the continuation of their culture demands a state of permanent struggle, a struggle to maintain identity, literacy, and religious liturgy."[36]

The Search for a History

The region that comprises present-day Guangdong, Guangxi, and northernmost Vietnam has long been characterized by Chinese regimes as a land of barbarian peoples, languages, and cultures. This region is noted for its intensive and sometimes "tribal" conflicts, which usually occurred over the control of land and other resources.[37] The twentieth century has seen a thoroughgoing attempt to reconstruct the history of this region, largely by making sense of the images and cultural orderings set forth in the official documents of Chinese empire. There are many studies from the post–World War II period from which to draw on, and one of the most influential has been Wiens's *China's March to the Tropics*.[38] A lesser known but more theoretically nuanced argument, which focuses mostly on the Yao, is found, as I indicated earlier, in Cushman's *Rebel Haunts and Lotus Huts*. Both of these studies reveal how the search for a subaltern ethnic group was informed by the image of a Hobbesian nightmare of sustained conflict, in which the powerful Han are pitted against a recalcitrant tribal other. They both persuasively argue that as the Han Chinese slowly moved southward and opened up new areas for lowland rice cultivation, the indigenous peoples of the region were driven into the mountains, forced to carve out an exis-

tence on marginal land. It is difficult not to come away from these books
with a sense that the Yao and other groups must by nature be opposed to
the ruthless, selfish, and invading Han Chinese race. Through centuries of
struggle over unfair tax and corvée labor arrangements, the Yao were forced
into a life of migrations in which even their religious practices, indigenous
to China itself, were ironically held by Chinese officials to be crude and bar-
baric. To know the Yao historically is to know something about a history
of injustice, of how the Chinese empire inflicted prejudice and violence on
nomadic "tribal" minorities.

The archaeological record plays a central role in many of these ethnohistorical studies. Archaeological research has suggested that ancient peoples
occupied different ecological niches in the south of China. These peoples
later intermingled with oceangoing Malayo-Polynesians from the mainland
of Asia and Oceania. This record also suggests that the farmers of the Neolithic Age wandered from the north into this subtropical setting, bringing with them a ceramics industry and the art of polishing stones; these
peoples, in turn, interacted with Mesolithic hunters and fishers, who used
tools of chipped pebbles. This early "prehistory," then, marked the beginnings of cultural interaction and exchange and the emergence of what many
ethnohistorians called a complicated "ethnolinguistic mosaic."

Contemporary archaeological reconstructions of the south assert the
existence of three chief culture areas that emerged after the Neolithic revolution. One of these was in the lake areas of the Yangtze River basin; this
region later became the historic state of Chu. Scholars of the Yao have argued that some of the animistic practices and even folklore among contemporary Yao groups derive from this period. The Chu culture (6th–4th
century B.C.) produced a repertoire of songs and writings that tell of an
enchanted world in which deity and human sit in quasi-erotic tension and
attraction, a world of flying shamans and earthly illusions.[39] This tradition
of poems and songs is still present in the religious texts and popular ritual
practices of contemporary Yao groups.[40] A second area, stretching from
the Huai River region southward to present-day Guangdong (Canton), contained a coastal, seagoing culture. The tools of this region, characterized
by the stepped adze, differed markedly from the lake-bound culture. This
area had established contacts with cultures further north, as evidenced in
the findings of long-shan or "black pottery." This is also the region that had
the most contact with Malayo-Polynesian languages and peoples.

The third culture area has been described crudely as a jungle culture, stretching from the limestone hills of East Guangxi to the mountains of Sichuan and Yunnan. The chief tool was the shouldered adze, used for turning over jungle land torched by roaming mountain dwellers who practiced shifting cultivation. The Chinese, historically referred to as Hua or Xia, arrived much later to this region, migrating from the lands south of the Yellow River drainage basin as they escaped the "marauding nomads" of the northern steppes. Probably due to their intensive cultivation of the land, they found the subtropical south a land of fertility and plenty. In contrast to the northern frontier, characterized by its nomadic and stockbreeding culture, the south was a land of established settlements and rice-growing valleys, a dynamic, fluid, and heterogeneous borderland. This fluid and highly interactive culture area was also a political frontier. Exiled and posted Chinese officials were supported by armed troops demanding control of the rich valleys of the south, and they quickly killed off those who resisted Chinese imperial demands. They indoctrinated the survivors in the classics from the "Age of Zhou," rewarding aboriginal collaborators with official positions, the prestige of official seals and documents, and the luxuries of a settled, courtly life. The south was a wild, vibrant, and ghostly land. Yet it eventually came to be tamed by the "civilizing" practices of the Hua people.

The knowledge of the cultural and linguistic diversity of this region, of the history of settlements and migrations, of cooperation and internecine strife, is mostly derived from the Chinese historical record. All attempts at historical reconstruction must wade through the thicket of Chinese terms for those labeled the noncivilized and the noncultured, that is, those not converted to Chinese modes of speaking, dressing, dwelling, and thinking. One of the more prominent and all-encompassing terms was *man*, a term that, like its counterpart *yi*, means "barbarian." These terms were used extensively by the chroniclers of Chinese expansion, and they were often merely subdivisions of larger categories. For example, during the Tang dynasty, the peoples of Yunnan, who spoke languages related to the Tibetans, were referred to as Ts'uan.[41] They were divided into two major subgroups, the Eastern Black *man* and the Western White *man*. These epithets are meant to describe the costumes of the women of the two groups: the former wore black gowns that swept to the ground, and the latter wore knee-length white smocks. It is noteworthy that the terms *man* and *yi* fell into disrepute with the Communist Party's expressed project of cultural respect for the "special characteristics" (*tedian*) of the minority nationality. Yet the practice of classifying subgroups of *minzu* based on the costumes and bodily accessories of women continues to this day. Thus, in present-day Guangxi, there are Yao groups that are officially and popularly classified by the clothing of the women. One finds references to the "red trouser" Yao, the "flat turban" Yao, the "red turban" Yao, and the "flowery" Yao (referring to the colorful, flowery patterns embroidered on the dresses of women). I will have more to say about these modes of naming in later chapters, when I draw attention to how ethnic subjectivity is differently inscribed, and contested, at the site of the gendered body. Here I want only to note that the practice of naming and categorizing the ethnic other has persisted for centuries. The twentieth century has seen the refinement of these terms, what we might think of as a rounding up of the many signifiers once affixed to a landscape noted for its twisted tongues and bizarre cultural ways.[42]

At the beginning of the seventh century, the Chinese historical record tells of a "shoeless people" called the mo yao (sometimes referred to as the mak yao)[43] scattered throughout Hunan. As Edward Schafer describes it, white linen trousers distinguished the men, and the women wore blue linen shirts and multicolored skirts.[44] The women also wore huge, cumbersome "flatirons" (a wide board with red cloth dangling over the side) on their heads at the time of marriage. In late Tang times, these peoples wandered into the mountainous area known as Lingnan, where Chinese officials tried to expel them, finding them grotesque and animal-like. Liu Yuxi's "Song of the Mak" is instructive. It suggests that the Yao have already taken on Chinese names, but have yet to be fully integrated into the Chinese imperial bureaucracy ("lacking tallies and registers"). It also contains images of the horrific, of a mythological world of legendary reptiles ("sand mouthers") and forest goblins ("tree visitors"). Finally, we see glimpses of an "ethnographic" sensibility, of references to divination practices and agricultural methods. The peripheral other comes into existence through an imaginative economy of wonder and fear:

> The mak yao once born and grown,
> take names and epithets, but lack tallies and registers.
> In market and trade they mingle with shark-dragon men,
> in weddings and marriage, they intermingle with tree visitors.
> By the sites of stars they divine the eyes of springs,
> by sowing in fire they open up the spines of mountains.
> At night they cross gorges of a thousand fathoms,
> the sand mouthers have no power to spurt at them.[45]

Poems like this, written by Chinese gentry-scholars and officials, are found throughout the Chinese historical record. Though one might be hard-pressed to find contemporary poetry that builds equivalencies between the creatures of mythology and ethnic peoples, modes of cultural labeling based on negative stereotypes persist. I was once told by a young man in Guangdong, as I waited in the train station for a connection to Guilin, that Yao women would seduce (*gouyin*) me if I wasn't cautious, for they were known, he insisted, to wear no underwear beneath their skirts. A colleague in the United States who had lived in Guangzhou later relayed this "fact" to me, thus revealing how these stereotypes of libidinal otherness have moved across national boundaries. My point here is that the contemporary fascination with China's ethnic peoples is not unrelated to the history of Chinese folklore and scholarship, a domain of knowledge that many Euro-American anthropologists have employed in their own work. These various ways of categorizing the social world have been instrumental in the formation of images of noncultured and ethnic others. As the bearers of difference, the cultural other is desired for its curious customs, yet is also known as an elusive object that has yet to be contained by the Chinese empire.

The official records of the Chinese empire, coupled with contemporary observations of ethnic stereotypes and other modes of marking ethnic distance, reveal much about Chinese perceptions of the "barbarian" other. The imagining of a noncultured other has been central to the constitution of Chinese culture, what is vaguely captured in the phrase "Chinese civilization." This culture was never really firmly intact, a fixed, knowable entity that Chinese officials carried with them as they set out to civilize the south (that is, it was always something more than the Confucian classics and the cultural productions of the literati). As Stevan Harrell argues in a volume devoted to unpacking China's "civilizing missions," the "center" was highly influenced, even remade, in its interactions and confrontations with the "periphery."[46] The center spoke and operated from a position of cultural arrogance, in one moment paternal, in the next, patronizing. The civilizing center assumed that its cultural traditions were enough to transform the barbarian, but it also exhibited an acute awareness of the frailty of its own position:

Though as mean as foxes and rats,
not deserving a display of our might,

yet even tiny things like wasps and tarantulas
can bring destruction on living creatures.[47]

As this poem reveals, the borderlands of the Chinese empire were often
seen as zones of both fascination and fear. Chinese imperial officials and
administrators believed that the mountains of the south contained swarms
of tribes, who, if not properly controlled, would inflict great damage on
those peoples who were already within the realm of the empire's control.
Many ethnohistorians were rightfully put off by these depictions of people
as animals and ruthless barbarians who could at any moment turn against
the rule of empire, and they were correct to point out that there was little
imperial interest in the "culture" of these peoples. Thus, as they turned their
attention to the historical record and to imperial practices of naming and
classification, they did not find the south to be a zone of silence. There was
too much noise, too many uprisings, and too many competing claims for
who spoke for the people of the periphery.

Space and Subjects of Resistance

The pre-1949 ethnohistorical research on the Yao is therefore structured
by two major themes. The first is the question of the origins and social evolution of a Yao ethnic people; in fact, the turn to ethnicity as a marker of
identity and culture was meant to displace previous derogatory and stereotypical representations of barbarian primitivity. The second theme concerns the representation of the Yao as possessing a tradition of sustained
resistance to the imperial regimes ruling China until the fall of the Qing
dynasty. The Yao as an agent of resistance is derived from the historical representation of them as mountain recluses and worshipers of a mottled dog
king, as the Yao are shown to have persistently resisted incorporation into
the administrative structures of successive dynastic regimes. Both of these
themes are taken up in the post-1949 socialist historiography of the Yao,
though they are interpreted and utilized quite differently. For now, I want
to focus on the Euro-American ethnohistory.

As I indicated above, Cushman's study of Yao ethnohistory is to this day
the most comprehensive examination of Western, Japanese, and pre- and
post-1949 publications (up until early 1966) on the Yao.[48] In this expansive
and ambitious study, Cushman explicated the dominant theoretical problems in Yao ethnohistory and charted the changing Chinese perceptions of

the Yao through successive dynastic regimes. Many of the concerns in this early anthropological and linguistic literature have remained central to the contemporary field of Yao studies. Scholars in Europe, the United States, and China continue to struggle with how to account for the extraordinary linguistic diversity of the Yao; how to explain the wide geographic dispersal of the Yao; and how the Yao, given these two conditions, have resisted absorption by neighboring peoples and maintained group integrity. Cushman showed how scholars of the Yao, confounded by the seemingly inexplicable diversity of the group, retreated to the historical record, seeking to trace the origins of the Yao by reference to the earliest citations in the Chinese imperial record.

The Yao have been traced back to around 220 A.D. as one of the ethnolinguistic groups subsumed under the category *nan man* or "southern barbarian." The origins of this term are found in the first of the official histories of China, the *Shi Ji*, in a chapter entitled "The Aborigines of the Southwest" (Xinan yi). This chapter is devoted solely to describing the events and peoples of the south. Utilizing the classification system set forth in the *Shi Ji*, subsequent dynastic scholars divided the peoples of the south into two broad categories. The first was the *xinan yi*, which referred to the indigenous populations of present-day Yunnan, southern Sichuan, and western Guizhou. The second was the *nan man*, referring to the indigenous populations of present-day Guangxi, Guangdong, Fujian, Zhejiang, Jiangxi, Hunan, and eastern Guizhou. From Han to Tang times, these broad categories were refined into smaller units, usually by designating a group of people by their geographical location. The term *man* was not discarded, but was attached as a suffix to a place name. The end of the Southern Song (1127–1279) witnessed the recording of new and more detailed information about the southern peoples. This deluge of information was made possible by the transfer of the capital to Hangzhou and by the policies initiated by the first emperor of the Song, Zhao Kuangyin (known posthumously as Song Taizu). This period marks the subjugation and incorporation of the independent kingdoms south of the Yangtze (excluding the state of Nanzhao in the far southwest) into the Song's administrative system. Most of the terms in modern usage were in widespread use among imperial scholars by the late Southern Song.[49]

However, most Euro-American, Han, and Yao scholars now trace the emergence of a modern Yao ethnic group to the Tang dynasty (A.D. 618–906), when the term *mo yao* appears in the *Liang Shu* (History of the Liang dynasty) and the *Sui Shu* (History of the Sui dynasty). Meaning "not subject to corvée labor," *mo yao* points to a Chinese imperial strategy of statecraft in which upland peoples were given a document (*quandie*) allowing them to roam the hills in search of arable land free from obligations to the Chinese empire.[50] Tang Cui, an observer of events in the south during the Qing, was one of the first Chinese imperial officials to note this crucial linkage between the *mo yao* political category and a distinct non-Han people: "The aborigines who have diffused throughout Hunan, Kwangsi and Kwangtung are called *Yao* [written with the so-called bug radical]. In earlier times those who had merit were released from their corvée duties (*Yao*, written with the chi or 'step' radical) and were called *mo yao* ['not subject to corvée']. Later the name was changed to *Yao* [a similar character written with the insect radical]."[51]

Anthropologists working among the Yao in Thailand in the 1960s and 1970s found a crucial piece of evidence to support Tang Cui's description. Working among the Iu-Mien (known in China as the Pan Yao), they found a document variously entitled *King Ping's Charter* (*Ping huang quandie*) or the *Register for Crossing the Mountains* (*Guo shan bang*).[52] A long document written in classical Chinese (*wenyan*), the edict begins by recounting the myth that the Yao descended from the dog king Pan Hu. The story goes something like this. In the deepest reaches of Chinese history, there was once an emperor by the name of Gao Xin (2435–2365 B.C.), a benevolent ruler who was relentlessly badgered by one General Wu. A mottled dog lived on Gao Xin's estate. Hearing of his master's troubles with the notorious General Wu, the dog challenged Wu to battle and, in victory, was awarded one of Gao Xin's daughters in marriage. Embarrassed by her betrothal to an animal, she escaped to the mountains with the dog and there gave birth to twelve children. After some time, these offspring established a home in a magical place called Qianjiadong. Marauding Chinese soldiers eventually attacked the kingdom of Qianjiadong and the Yao became wandering nomads on the mountain peaks of south China. In short, the finding of this imperial charter in the hands of living Yao was seen as an important ethnological discovery. It allowed anthropologists and historians to trace present-day Yao groups to the so-called cult of Pan Hu and to the history of Chinese imperial expansion.

Sometime over the next few centuries — no one knows precisely when — the signifier *mo* is dropped. The term Yao itself comes to be associated less with a political category exempting certain groups from corvée labor and more with a group of upland peoples who traced their origins to Pan Hu. Unlike many ethnologists writing about the Yao in China in the 1980s, Cushman dismissed the entire enterprise of linking the present-day Yao to the category *mo yao*. He argued that there are only six uses of the term *mo yao* in five sources, the earliest occurring in the *Liang Shu* (early sixth century). In none of these sources is there any indication that the term refers to a particular ethnic group; in fact, there is evidence to suggest that it referred to both *man* and Han Chinese, the criteria being avoidance of tax and corvée obligations.[53] In other words, identity was not being constructed in these texts on the basis of observable differences in culture and language (as Cushman would prefer) but on the basis of an amorphous political category, to which any number of different "ethnic" peoples could theoretically belong. And finally, Cushman pointed out that no one had been able to offer a reasonable explanation for shortening the term *mo yao* to Yao; neither had anyone produced documentary evidence for why such a change may have occurred. The historical reconstruction of the Yao failed to convincingly show that the peoples referred to in the Tang dynasty as enjoying the privileges of *mo yao* status are the direct ancestors of those people who, in the Southern Song, were referred to as the *man yao*. In his critique of this now infamous "*mo yao* argument," Cushman argued that it was incorrect to use philological grounds to search for the origins of an ethnic group. If modern ethnohistorians did so, they could only approximate the once extant categories of the Chinese empire, which would only leave them further removed from the objective reality of Yao ethnicity.

To summarize, Cushman argued that conceptions of Yao history and identity owe much to the definitions set forth by imperial scholars and administrative officials. The ethnohistory of the shifts and transmutations of Yao identity are severely constrained by the Sinocentric and largely ethnocentric perspective that permeates the historical record on the non-Han peoples of the south. Cushman argued for the search for certain objective criteria—language, mythology, religious practices, and customs—that might indicate the existence of a historical ethnic group. But the question of subjectivity remained an elusive problem. Reflecting on his own invocation of objective markers as the defining features of an ethnic group, Cushman saw clearly the futility of talking about Yao identity when the Yao themselves have never had a voice with which to speak. He thus stumbled on the problem of voice, which has become a central preoccupation in poststructuralist approaches to writing the history of subaltern groups. Cushman showed how the Yao, defined as a noncultured other situated on the borders of empire and civilization, existed only through the creations of the imperial imagination.

There is another recurring theme in the ethnohistory of the Yao. It concerns the question of Yao resistance to an ever-expanding imperial state. This theme also emerges from the historical materials of Imperial China. The Yao were often referred to as the descendants of the dog king Pan Hu, or as a people who seldom ventured into cities and markets and who ate the strangest of foods. They were also represented as ferocious and mountain-wise, stubborn rebels who refused to be seduced by the lure of the superior, lowland Han culture, which meant paying taxes and providing corvée labor to local imperial administrators. Take, for example, the following description written by the nineteenth-century Chinese historian Wei Yuan: "The Yao are stupid and violent by nature and they do not have any intercourse with the Chinese. The Chinese take advantage of their stupidity by wresting things from them by force, by stealing from them, and by raiding and insulting them. The officials are prompt to assist wicked people to bind them fast [in this condition]. The Yao accumulate malice and hatred and then rebel, and events [tribal rebellions] have ever followed this course."[54]

The recurrence of Yao rebellions has been an important element in the construction of a historical Yao ethnic or tribal group. Major Yao "tribal uprisings," as Wiens characterized these historic events, were first mentioned during the rule of the Song emperor Renzong (1023–1064 A.D.). One occurred in Guangdong in 1035, another in Hunan in 1043. There is also mention of a rebellion that occurred in the Guangzhou region in 1281. By the mid-Ming, the incidence of Yao uprisings had increased dramatically. And then there was the famous 1832 Yao rebellion in Hunan, in which the Yao, reacting to the theft of cattle and grain by members of the Triad Society, organized an uprising that took several months and armies from three provinces to squelch.[55] The reports on these uprisings usually pointed to the refusal to pay taxes or attempts to reclaim land confiscated by the Han. In all of these accounts, regardless of the period in which they were written, there is a persistent tension between the desire to incorporate the Yao into the administrative domain and a sense of utter hopelessness in the face of the task. It should not surprise us that many of these reports argued that the failure of assimilation had little to do with the inadequacies of the civilizing regime and everything to do with the stupidity of the Yao.

The Yao are depicted as a people who both resisted Sinification (*hanhua*) and refused incorporation into the Chinese imperial political order. As local officials in the Ming responded to increasing imperial pressure to bring the recalcitrant "barbarians" under administrative control, it may well be, as Cushman argued, that this process of interaction and conflict gave rise to a Yao ethnic identity and increased the importance of its maintenance and reproduction.[56]

Whatever the relationship between Yao rebellions (and participation in major uprisings such as the Taiping) and the emergence of a Yao sense of ethnic identity, Yao resistance to Chinese imperial control is central to the construction of a contemporary Yao identity. For those writing on the ethnohistory of the Yao in the pre-1949 period, resistance was seen as an inevitable consequence of the southward expansion of northerners, be they Mongols or Han peasants in search of new rice land. Some saw conflict and loss of life as an invariable component of expansion into the southern frontier. Others, seeking to understand what drove the Yao to rise up against their oppressors, viewed violent resistance as the only course of action available to a people who were constantly forced to defend their marginal land and meager resources.

The Making of a History

Writing history . . . forces the silent body to speak. It assumes a gap to exist between the silent opacity of the "reality" that it seeks to express and the place where it produces its own speech, protected by the distance established between itself and its object. The violence of the body reaches the written page only through absence, through the intermediary of documents that the historian has been able to see on the sands from which a presence has since been washed away, and through a murmur that lets us hear—but from afar—the unknown immensity that seduces and menaces our knowledge. —MICHEL DE CERTEAU, *The Writing of History*

In this section I focus on a text called the *Yaozu jianshi*, or the *Concise History of the Yao* (hereafter referred to as the *Jianshi*).[57] This book represents the work of over thirty scholars of the Yao in China, the majority of whom are Yao themselves.[58] No one pretends that the *Jianshi* exhausts every possible historical source or that it is in any way devoid of points of controversy. This history is an encapsulated version of how the Yao have progressed through the nation's time. It aims to chart the obstacles they have encountered in their long and arduous path to realize full social and economic potential, to become, in short, a socialist modern minority nationality. The reader is essentially taken on a tour through the long historical stretch of Chinese history, as moments in the history of the Yao are situated in different dynastic regimes and related to successive social evolutionary stages.

Concise histories on ethnic minorities first begin to appear in the public domain in the mid-1980s. They can be found in many bookstores and are sometimes used in history classes in secondary schools and colleges. Although much of the research for these histories was carried out in the 1950s during the massive minority nationality identification project (*minzu shibie*), they were not published until the 1980s, well after the Cultural Revolution had rendered the disciplines of history and ethnology dangerous bourgeois practices. Recognizing the intricate relationship between power and knowledge in socialist transformation, Party researchers in the 1950s sought out Yao elders, village leaders, and ritual specialists to gain a greater understanding of local customs, traditions, and histories. These research teams—some sent down to the countryside, some trained locally—learned of Guomindang military tactics, land ownership patterns, pre-1949 class relations, and local ethnic antagonisms. They also encountered a rich store of cultural history, local knowledges of past clan leaders, family migrations, ritual activities, historical Yao uprisings, and events as remote as the dissemination of Taoist practice in the Southern Song and local encounters with Taiping rebels in the mid–nineteenth century. In addition, the many references to the Yao in the Chinese imperial record provided access to "feudal" perceptions of the non-Han ethnic other and to the cultural assumptions informing historical modes of Chinese statecraft, which the Communist Party, as a matter of official policy, strongly opposed and hoped to eradicate. A central focus of these early research missions was to discern if the same class conditions that predominated in rural Han communities also existed in minority regions. This was a crucial issue. Many of these cadres had been trained in the evolutionary theories of Marx and Engels, which stated that "primitive" societies may not exhibit the same level of social development as more advanced societies and thus may not be subject to the same sorts of class contradictions. Yet the existence of class contradiction was a central feature of early communist mobilization and recruitment strategies, for if there were no classes, then how could the Party cadre convince oppressed and exploited classes to speak against their feudal rulers? The popularization of a discourse of class struggle into local histories was thus a central aspect of Party politics in regions such as Jinxiu, just as public rallies denouncing the enemies of the revolution were used to mobilize public support for the new regime.

The writing of ethnic minority histories in the 1980s was largely about writing against this history of class struggle and its deleterious effects on everyday social and political life. It was about purging the interpretive mistakes of the ultraleftists and restoring to the official view of the ethnic minority world some semblance of order and rationality amid the chaos of revolutionary slogans and what came to be seen as nonscientific interpretations of class difference and social rank. In ethnological writings in the 1980s, as well as in brief descriptions of Yao culture and history at minority nationality museums, the Yao are portrayed as hardy and resilient mountain dwellers who have bravely overcome the stifling conditions of the past. As we saw above, the Euro-American scholarship of the 1960s and 1970s focused on the ritual practices of Chinese Taoism and how these practices reproduced the Yao social order through time. Writing against discourses of primitivity, this scholarship approached the Yao as an ethnic group who refused to participate in tax and corvée labor arrangements, a people who seemed to remain outside the administrative reach of the Chinese empire even while they sometimes borrowed from the cultural repertoire of the Han. In the historiography on the Yao in the 1980s, however, the refusal of Chinese imperial power is interpreted as evidence of revolutionary potential. As stubborn mountain recluses who repeatedly rose up against the "feudal" armies of the expanding Chinese, the Yao are placed at the center of the social and political processes that culminated in the communist victory of 1949. They are written into the history of the People's Republic as subaltern subjects and integral members of a multiethnic nation-state.

It is important to note that although the ultraleftists have been banished from the political landscape of post-Mao China, social evolutionary interpretations of history, struggle, and progress have continued to inform the writing of histories of minority peoples. Scholars and Party officials involved in writing histories of the Yao under the reforms presented their work to me as a more "real" history, one no longer contaminated by the blind submission to ideology. This was also to be a history that would give a more accurate view of the historical development of the Yao subject. The *Jianshi*, for example, delineates the successive stages of Yao social development and specifies the social forces causing the transition from one stage to another. The Yao are represented not as a hopelessly oppressed people but as historical agents who stood up and opposed the unfair and often brutal practices of successive "feudal" dynastic regimes. China's so-called feudal past is mobilized as the very cause of Yao social and economic "backwardness" (*luohou*) and, at the same time, as the source of the revolutionary spirit of the Yao people.

The *Jianshi* begins with an analysis of the theories on the origins of the Yao. The original homeland of the Yao is situated in the valleys and mountains south of Dongting Lake in northern Hunan. In pre-Han times, the people living in this area were referred to as *jing man*. By the Han dynasty they are referred to as the *changsha man* or *wuling man*. In the histories of the Liang, Sui, and Song dynasties, these peoples are then classified as *wuxi man*, "the *man* of the five streams," a reference to the river system that flows into Dongting Lake from the south.[59] As we saw in our examination of Cushman's work on the ethnohistory of the Yao, this style of argument reconstructs present-day groups on philological grounds, that is, by tracing their historical identity through the shifting terrain of linguistic practices of naming non-Han others.[60] There are moments of ambiguity in the *Jianshi* about whether its authors believe that these terms actually describe the ancestors of the present-day Yao groups. Yet this question is pushed aside by the evolutionary framework that informs the book. For, in this interpretive scheme, one cannot even begin to talk about the progress of the group through history unless one assumes the Yao once lived in the far reaches of the Chinese past. The book reveals an implicit acceptance that these various terms and classificatory schemes at least approximate the nature of ethnic realities at various moments in the history of the nation.

We learn that when Qin Shi Huang unified China in the third century B.C. and implemented the "system of prefectures and counties" (*junxian zhidu*), the Yao in the Dongting Lake region, for perhaps the first time in their history, were brought into close contact with a centralized government. The argument of interethnic or tribal contact and borrowing is an important strategic move in this narrative, in that all advances in technology, which enable social development, are seen to come from outside the group. For example, Qin Shi Huang's policy of *zheshumin*, in which low-ranking officials were sent to remote areas to establish garrison command posts, enabled the Yao to adopt more advanced agricultural tools and engage in trade activities with other tribal peoples. It was also in the reign of Qin that the Yao were first incorporated into the tribute system. This interaction with the Qin state, although marking the beginning of feudal exploitation, is presented in a positive light, as a necessary moment in Yao social and economic advancement. It is only in the Later Han dynasty that the Yao begin what was to become a long history of revolt against "feudal" systems of tribute and tax collection. The *Hou Han shu* records uprising after uprising among the recalcitrant Yiren, the category thought to have subsumed the Yao and various other present-day upland groups such as the Miao and the Tujia.[61] Around A.D. 300, due to the increased migrations of people from the north, the Yiren begin to establish closer ties with groups from the north and to adopt surnames and other elements of Chinese culture. Some of the Yiren became "aristocrats" (*guizu*) themselves, owning large tracts of land and bringing other Yi peoples under their control. This represents the beginning of processes of assimilation to Chinese culture for some Yao peoples.[62] Yet, more important, it splinters the historical Yao community due to the emergence of intra-ethnic systems of land and labor exploitation. By the middle of the sixth century, less powerful and wealthy Yao groups begin to migrate into the region that would later come to be known as the Nanlingshan, the mountain range that forms the borders of present-day Hunan, Guangdong, and Guangxi.

The *Jianshi* also addresses the controversial *mo yao* institution (which it sees as first emerging during the Tang) that, as we saw above, has long fascinated and perplexed ethnohistorians.[63] Yet, unlike the Western and pre-1949 Chinese research that concerned itself almost solely with the origins of the Yao, the *mo yao* category gets only scant attention. This is because the origins of the Yao have already been traced back to the pre-Han period. The term is presented as just one more way that feudal rulers classified the Yao; it is in no way used to search for the origins of the Yao people. Yet *mo yao*, as a category that describes a political class of subjects, is recognized as marking an important historical development. It represents a negotiation of interests between isolated tribal peoples and an imperial state extremely wary of the "barbarian" other, which, in the official imagination, was more often equated with monkeys, wild dogs, and quick and elusive deer than with the peoples who occupied and controlled the civilized center. The granting of exemption from taxes and other obligations was a way for the Tang court to maintain cultural distance; it was also a way to induce the "southern barbarians" to open up the mountains for agricultural purposes. Through the Yao's widespread adoption of iron tools and other advanced agricultural implements, these Tang dynasty institutions thus contributed to the further development of the Yao economy.

These social developments, not unlike that which occurred in Qin-Han times, brought with them a certain cost, represented in the increasing ferocity and frequency of inter- and intra-ethnic conflict. Due to the introduction of the so-called loose reign policy (jimi zhengce) of "using barbarians to rule barbarians" (yiyi zhiyi), the Yao, especially those in the area known in the Tang as Lingnandao (comprising the eastern, Guilin section of present-day Guangxi and all of Guangdong), were increasingly pitted against each other. This system was the precursor to the Ming and Qing tusi system. It was put into place in order that tribal leaders could be induced, usually through the granting of official rank, to govern Chinese-style administrative districts. These tribal chiefs were known as qiuzhang. They were required to collect taxes and goods for tribute, such as the high-quality silken products (sizhipin) produced mainly by women.[64] Yao farmers, presumably skeptical of the practical use of symbolic titles, refused the tax system and were subsequently pushed further into the mountains. The political divisions and class contradictions (jieji maodun) that Communist Party cadres found rampant in the Yao mountains in the 1940s are said to have their social roots in the expansion of the imperial state into the south of China during the Tang and Song dynasties. Although the Yao economy saw further advances in its productive base, Yao society was increasingly divided. Tribal chiefs were increasingly incorporated into the imperial system, and farmers and peasants were driven into isolation.[65] This constitutes, the Jianshi argues, the "feudalization" (fengjianhua) of Yao society.

The Song dynasty is known for its success in incorporating large tracts of "untamed" land into its administrative domain. This was accomplished in part through the further exploitation and elaboration of the Tang loose reign policy. In the Song we begin to see the use of the term tuguan. These were local officials, usually Zhuang peoples in the areas of present-day Guangxi and Guangdong, who were given the responsibility of distributing land to the Yao and other tribal groups. To receive land, however, one had to register with the tuguan through either the jikou jitian (distribution by population) or jihu shoutian (distribution by household) system, which determined the amount of land one received.[66] In return, taxes were collected in the form of crops and other locally produced goods. Those who failed to pay their required tax or refused to offer corvée labor in its place were harassed and sometimes severely punished. The *Jianshi* argues that these Song and Yuan dynasty methods of feudal control represent a shift from the stages of primitive society (*yuanshi shehui*) and agricultural communes (*nongcun gongshe*) to that of feudal society (*fengjian shehui*). Unlike other minority nationalities in the south and southwest, the Yao bypassed the stage of slave society (*nuli shehui*).[67] The reasons provided for this are consistent with the social evolutionary paradigm that informs the text. Driven to isolated regions in the mountains, the Yao were forced to practice swidden horticulture and, having never established permanent, stable residences, were unable to support political, economic, and cultural centers that would allow the emergence of a slave society. The imperial practice of *yiyi zhiyi* ("using barbarians to rule barbarians") and the *tuguan* institution assured that different Yao groups competed against each other for limited land and resources. Although some maneuvered to open up land for wet-rice cultivation (which could be acquired only through the household registration system), most remained tied to a swidden existence in the mountains. Due to historical processes beyond their control, the Yao were forced to "eat up one mountain and move to the next" (*chi yi shan, guo yi shan*).

Although the *tusi* system came into full bloom under the Ming and Qing dynasties, the patterns of development and forced migration remained the same.[68] In both periods, the Yao continued to encounter the ever-expansionary Chinese imperial state. By the mid-Qing, it is said, the present-day Yao regions in China were all established. However, certain regions, such as the Dayaoshan, or Great Yao Mountains, and the Shiwan Yao Shan, or Mountains of One Hundred Thousand Yao, in Guangxi and areas in southern Hunan, were never brought under effective control. We thus enter the time of uprisings and rebellions. In the Song, Yuan, Ming, and Qing periods the Yao were caught up in the stormy "feudalization" of the south. While Yao encounters with Han society and with the imperial administrators facilitated the development of the Yao economy, feudal exploitation and oppression drove the Yao deeper into the mountains and thus undermined any gain in social development. As more and more Yao refused administrative incorporation, local imperial officials attempted to cut off trade among various regions, blocking the importation of salt and other foodstuffs that could be had only from markets in the lower elevations. These actions left the Yao with no alternative but to attack the garrison command posts, which in turn led to imperial retaliation. In the year 975, for example, one third of the Yao in the Mei Shan area in Hunan were murdered by imperial troops.[69] This led to a series of skirmishes, which finally culminated in a large-scale Yao uprising. The Yao of southern Hunan organized themselves and on fifteen occasions attacked the command posts at Lianshan and Lianyang in the northwest corner of present-day Guangdong. The pacification officer (anfu-shi) in the area was thus forced to resort to the extant zhaofu or zhaoan policy, whereby amnesty was offered to the rebels if they agreed to halt their attacks. Five leaders of the rebellion considered these offers, but the struggle was sustained for another five years, until it eventually died out.[70]

Circulating throughout the history of the Yao is the assumption of historical continuity: bounded by distinct and essential cultural traits and ethnic practices, the Yao have been around since the beginnings of recorded history in China. In contrast to the pre-1949 ethnohistorical work, the writing of ethnic history in the 1980s is not about the search for origins. It is about the tracking of development, about tracing the movement and progression of the subject throughout the history of the Chinese nation. History is envisioned in the Jianshi as a body of knowledge that reveals the gradual emergence of a modern Yao identity. The Jianshi details all of the important events in the history of Chinese imperial expansion into the south, the events that ethnohistorians have long pointed to, but these events are subordinated to the task of revealing the unfolding, the coming into being of self-identity and self-realization. It would be correct to point out that the Jianshi is a materialist reading of history, one that traces how the Yao struggled against past systems of oppression. We also have to recognize that the focus on technology and shifting modes of production and imperial control is discursively linked to a narrative that details the teleological unfolding of social advancement through the time of the nation. The narrative is resolutely Hegelian. Of course, as many scholars in China have pointed out to me, the historical sources are continually being debated and reinterpreted. Yet, for those who write and contemplate the history of the Yao, it is an indisputable fact that the Yao have a long history. It is also a fact that they are a people who have been exploited by successive feudal regimes, a people driven to the mountains, who have for centuries carved out a meager existence on unforgiving terrain, struggling against the elements and encroaching, arrogant feudal masters. The claim that the Yao group has evolved through clearly defined stages of social development remains unchallenged: How else, as one scholar answered my stubborn queries, could

Yao history be understood? The issue for them is not that Hegel raises his teleological head in the pages of the *Jianshi*. It is that the narrative of a great unfolding offers a consistent and rational explanation of the current "backward" economic and social state of Yao communities. It justifies and gives meaning to the struggle to liberate the country and it further motivates, if only through the observation that history has yet to complete its mission, reform-era projects of socialist modernization.

The ethnologists, historians, and others who have been instrumental in these projects know perfectly well what they are doing when they "make" these histories. I was told by one scholar, for instance, that these histories were about bringing to the written page a past that has been silenced by the previously dominant Confucian-literati tradition of historiography. They were making room for a voice that has often been ignored in top-down histories of the nation and in histories that focus exclusively on the Han contribution to the revolution. To write the history of the Yao is to make visible a past of exploitation and oppression at the hands of feudal rulers, so that a once subordinated ethnic group can now reclaim its place in history. One will not find in the *Jianshi* contending historical epistemologies, modes of being in the world or modes of telling history that undo the narrative of the nation's unfolding through time. To have this kind of history, one in which you can envision your people struggling through the ages and overcoming one obstacle after another, is to belong to the Chinese nation.[71] I mentioned earlier that one of the features differentiating the *Jianshi* from previous history projects is the focus on how the subject advances toward higher orders of social development. The *Jianshi* is also about giving a new mode of consciousness, one that will recognize how the collective self was silenced under previous regimes. This consciousness of history and its silences is also about obtaining presence and representation in that history. The problem with the *Jianshi*, however, is that these regimes are defined entirely through references to the past. These regimes, as objects of resistance, are named as the exploitative, feudal, and expansionary Han, the local Yao headman who is incorporated into the imperial regime and sells out his people, or the Guomindang-era landlord who extracts land, labor, and surplus wealth from the landless mountain peasant. The postrevolutionary Party-state apparatus, with its campaigns to bring order and development and rid the social body of class enemies, is beyond reproach, almost entirely outside of the domain of critique except for occasional elliptic comments on the mistakes of the ultraleftists. If the Yao are seen in these histories as a subaltern subject with revolutionary potential, this quality, so central to the imagining of a Yao historical subject, is denied once the revolution is complete. The image of a restless, justice-driven subject, the subject who will protect the community from the enemies of progress and social development, is brought to representation only to show how the Yao have moved through history and, by their uprisings and recalcitrance, contributed to the making of revolution. There is no space for a subaltern subject once the history of revolution has done its work.

The Search for Qianjiadong

I had many discussions with different people about what the Yao were like during the Song, Ming, and Qing dynasties. In my field journal, I recorded stories of great Yao migrations across the mountains of south China. I learned that when the Yao discovered a new and fertile territory, they communicated the finding by sending a messenger on foot across the mountains, traveling from one Yao village to the next. These narratives told of extraordinary feats of travel, in which large groups of people moved across hostile territories as they sought to settle in places where they could live free of the excessive tax and labor demands of successive Chinese imperial regimes. My fieldwork in many ways was about reliving these histories, in that I was asked by my research consultants to try to imagine what it was like for a people who constantly struggled to live free of poverty and official harassment, who were never respected, always looked down upon, considered to be no better than primitives. Of course, I could find traces of these narratives of primitivity in the official histories of the Yao I was reading, in histories such as the *Jianshi*. As I argued above, these historical narratives were stories about how the ethnic subject developed and advanced through the great sweep of the nation's history. In this sense, they were often less about the Yao than about the People's Republic, and they arguably ignored other narratives of culture, history, and power that might not easily fit into the image of a subaltern people moving toward emancipation from the oppressive conditions of the past.

If the modernist narrative of the nation's unfolding in history forces people to forget or ignore other ways of telling, seeing, and being in the world,[72] then memory is one site where power enacts its violence. Scholars writing on memory in other socialist nations have argued that Party functionaries often used official campaigns of coercive forgetting to constrain and reshape personal memory.[73] This scholarship has also pointed out that the Party was never able to fully colonize or domesticate the past, but that, due to practices of collective and self-surveillance or threats of incarceration or state violence, oppositional narratives were very difficult to voice and popularize. People lived with the constant threat of humiliation, incarceration, and physical punishment, but they also lived with identities, desires, feelings, and personal histories that had been forced underground, essentially forbidden public presence. One might argue that the popularization of official histories such as the *Jianshi* is not just about how a minority elite has marked out a space for their people in reform-era narratives of the nation's history. These histories are also about the exercise of discursive forms of violence. They point to how intellectuals and others who worked to write and propagate official histories of the minority subject were working within and perhaps even reproducing new institutional structures and new hegemonic ways of classifying ethnic culture, history, and identity. These scholars were part of a privileged intellectual class who claimed the right to speak for the totality of the Yao community. They are perhaps best seen as the very agents who have made possible the making of new reform-era regimes of power and knowledge, in which the writing of an ethnic history played a vital role.

Where, then, might one find alternative histories or alternative representations of the past? What might these alternative histories tell us about the nature of these reform-era regimes of power and knowledge? Yao scholars do not need a deconstructive sensibility to tell them that their histories contain exclusions. They know that their official narratives are filled with silences and that these silences generate discontent among scholars and others about how the history is being told and who is controlling the telling. What might some of these silences or exclusions be? As I mentioned at the outset of this chapter, one is the question of traditional culture. The *Jianshi* touches only tangentially on some of the cultural features that people point to define just what a Yao is, such as the particularities of the practice of Taoism, with its exorcisms, its magic, and its cosmological political orders of power and authority. As I will show in subsequent chapters, it was not uncommon in the 1980s to encounter in ethnological and popular photographic texts images of young men in trance as they are indoctrinated into the Taoist priesthood. Yet these images, as we shall see, are meant only to be signs of the nation's ethnic and cultural diversity; they are in no way meant to teach people how and why they should believe in magical efficacy.

Magical Taoism is promoted not as a way of life and being in the world but as a remnant of a past social time. Some Yao scholars and not a few government officials argued to me that Taoism is better suited for the museum than for a community of mountain peasants who still struggle with everyday subsistence issues. Another issue pushed to the side in these official histories is the question of the relationship between subgroup identities and a larger Yao minzu identity, or, as it might be framed in the language of the nationality problem, the problem of local forms of ethnic chauvinism. As we shall see in the chapters that follow, many people I knew in Jinxiu were quite ambivalent when they spoke to me about the historical and contemporary differences among different Yao groups. This was in large part because the excessive focus on a particular subgroup's culture or identity had once been interpreted, especially during the antirightist campaign and then again during the Cultural Revolution, as a return to a feudal or politically backward sensibility. The enunciation of these points of difference unsettled the notion of a unified Yao community that saw itself only in relation to the leadership of the CCP. They called to memory histories of past struggles not only between the Yao and the Han, but also within and among different Yao groups.

For some, these memories allowed them to imaginatively return to a different time, before the Guomindang arrived in the hills with their promises of modernization and before Communist Party cadres began to redefine the nature of local social worlds. To be sure, these memories called to mind distant times and spaces, and were often presented as presocialist eras of social tranquillity that had been lost to the history of modern warfare and other forms of state and interethnic violence. Yet they also carried with them potentially subversive readings of the place of different Yao subjects in the nation's history. In some instances, these memories recalled a Yao subject who refused to look toward the utopian future promised by the revolution and Mao's emphasis on the need for continued struggle. In other instances, they pointed to a centralized state power that was doomed to misrepresent the nature of the ethnic subject and the social worlds these subjects were said to inhabit. Many people in Jinxiu and elsewhere told me of times when their ancestors were searching for a lost home, the original home of the Yao people, lost somewhere in the remote hills that stretched across the south of China.

I therefore want to conclude this chapter by recounting some of these stories, which center on the search for a particular place called Qianjiadong, literally the "thousand-family grotto." Qianjiadong is an imaginary place, the lost homeland of the Pan Yao people, the largest of the Yao subgroups in China. The Pan Yao will tell you that Qianjiadong refers to the original dwelling place of their ancestors. The name itself thus recalls a lost moment in history but also a lost place, a paradise in which abundance was once the order of the day and a time when the Yao lived in harmony with each other and with other peoples. All of this was before the Chinese imperial government expelled them and forced them to roam the mountains of south China. The loss of Qianjiadong marks the end of a sedentary existence and the beginning of a nomadic mountain life. Some of the ethnologists I spoke with about the Qianjiadong legend told me that they see the persistence of an oral history of Qianjiadong as a commentary on the failures of socialist development, as well as a projection into the future, the hope for an ideal time. Qianjiadong is also a story about endless wandering and community-based pilgrimages. Whether seen as a nostalgic longing for a past time or an idealized projection of a utopian future yet to arrive, the fact remains that Qianjiadong has lived on in the oral histories of many Yao villages. Since the 1950s, for instance, various Yao have organized the search for this lost homeland. Some of these were spontaneous (*zifaxing*) occurrences; others were well planned and brought together communities from different counties and provinces. Various interpretations of these searches emerged in the 1980s, which tell us how memories of past Qianjiadong movements continue to be used in the politics of narrating ethnic history in the reform present.

The search for Qianjiadong seems to begin in earnest among various Yao individuals and groups in the mid–nineteenth century. For example, one of the most popular tales of a Qianjiadong movement concerns a small group of people in the mountains of southern Hunan Province in the present-day county of Jianghua. Some 150,000 Pan Yao now live in Jianghua. It is the largest concentration of Pan Yao in all of China and is situated at the intersection of Hunan, Guangdong, and Guangxi provinces, an area the Yao began to settle during the Ming dynasty. In the 1840s, a man by the name of Dong Yuanzhu began to distribute a series of letters to Yao families and villages. These letters were not authored solely by Dong; they included excerpts from letters he himself had received from previous Qianjiadong pilgrims. Foot messengers transmitted these letters, which consisted mostly of descriptions of various territories, maps of how to find them, and reports on the fertility of the land, the presence of bandits, and the demands of local officials. Known as "road guides," or *luyinxin*, they tell of past so-journers who sought out Qianjiadong and the hardships encountered along the way. Perhaps most important, they incited the interests of others and motivated individuals and families to set out on their own.

Tales of individuals such as Dong Yuanzhu were circulated in Jianghua well into the 1950s. A popular folk story in Jianghua recounted one such movement as follows:

> There was once a father who took his father and his son to search for Qianjiadong. On several occasions they roamed the mountains of Guangdong, Guangxi, and Hunan but were continually thwarted in their efforts. They nonetheless maintained their faith. As they died, they told their descendants to continue the search. Some three generations later, these descendants launched a large-scale movement to find Qianjia-dong, which eventually took them to a place called Jiucailing [the land of flowering chives]. After climbing over two thousand meters, they dis-covered a wide and verdant plain with a small river cutting across it. They returned to their village, sold their land and belongings, and moved to Jiucailing. They worked the land for a year but the harvest could support them for only a month. The primitive forest around the plain contained numerous wild animals, which caused them to live in fear. Storms hit the mountain with relentless ferocity. They eventually left Jiucailing, re-turned home, but, having previously sold everything, were now forced into a life of endless wandering. They all died of hunger in the 1940s.[74]

A less tragic tale of Qianjiadong wanderings is told among the Pan Yao of Lipu County in Guangxi. This story recounts the travails of a Yao named Chao Yulin, who led an expedition of more than fifty persons into a differ-ent region of Hunan, in the mountains that border present-day Guizhou Province:

> In the fall of 1913, Chao Yulin came across a book entitled *Origin Stories of Qianjiadong* (*Qianjiadong yuanliuji*). There is mention of a place called Dao-zhou, which is said to produce rice grains the size of peanuts and where the Yao have lived in peace for centuries. Chao decides to gather some food, clothing, and money and head out in search of this land. Traveling by foot, he passes through Pingle, Gongcheng, and other places where Yao have settled; he encounters story after story about Qianjiadong. No one knows exactly where Daozhou is located, and many people are reluc-

tant to join him for fear of bandits who roam the hills. Chao eventually encounters these bandits somewhere in the hills around the border of present-day Guangxi and Hunan; he is robbed of all of his possessions except for a few pieces of cold bread and his book of Qianjiadong stories.

In the summer of 1941, Chao, now in old age, is rewarded with the birth of a grandson, Chao Debiao. To celebrate, he gives his son, Chao Rutian, his coveted book on the origins of Qianjiadong. He implores his son to keep searching for this lost land. Chao Rutian is unsuccessful, but the grandson heeds the call and wanders the mountains repeatedly throughout the 1950s. He has no luck and eventually gives up the effort. In the early 1980s, however, a man named Xiong Fenglong and his niece Xiong Chunjiang, who had themselves been roaming the mountains for decades looking for Qianjiadong, visited him. On August 15 of the next year the three of them set out and soon arrive in the same Jiucailing region related in the story from Jianghua, Hunan. The three go their separate ways after they survey the area and decide that it is much too small to support a large community. Chao Debiao sets out on his own the next month and soon encounters two men from a distant county who have likewise been searching for the lost homeland of the Yao. These men are brothers, known as Chao Shunwang and Chao Shunde, who come from Dayuan Village in Jiangyong County in Hunan. They make their living as hunters and boast of traveling by bus and foot throughout the many remote mountains that border the provinces of Guangxi, Guangdong, and Hunan. Eventually they return to the village of Dayuan. Upon arrival, Chao Debiao is suddenly hit with the force of an uncanny recognition. He opens the book his grandfather had passed on decades earlier, the *Qianjiadong yuanliuji*, and then looks out at the fertile plain and the mountains that surround it. He proclaims in a moment of enlightenment: "My Yao brothers and I have searched for decades for Qianjiadong. Little did we realize that we had been living in Qianjiadong all along!"

There are many such tales told in villages throughout Guangxi and Hunan, and they often contain images of Yao sojourners studying letters and handwritten books and surveying the land, trying to match the stories in the texts to the landscape around them. I talked to several ethnologists in China, some Yao, some Han, who thought this a ridiculous enterprise, a clear sign of how mountain peasants continue to be idealistically tied to the mythologies of the feudal past. The specter of large groups of Yao peasants roaming the hills of south China was a concern of the CCP throughout the 1950s and 1960s. This was not only because of the persistence of superstitious beliefs in a phantasmagoric land, but also because the political administration of the peoples of the People's Republic required that everyone be locatable in a village, township, or commune.

I want to recount one last story about Qianjiadong wanderings, this one from the township (*xiang*) of Guanyin in Gongcheng County in the northeast hills of Guangxi Province:

In 1954, the CCP, in a hurried attempt to fill the state coffers, instituted a relatively high tax across the country known as *dinggou dingxiao*. At this time, the Party was giving special consideration to the minority populations, in part to win their support after the Liberation in 1949; the Yao of Gongcheng, as were other minority groups, were to be exempted from this tax policy. The county government didn't enforce the policy, however. The head of the township (the *xiangzhang*) was a Yao by the name of Zhou Shenglong. With the assistance of another Yao township leader known as He Zhaoli and several other locals, they reported the abuse to higher-ranking authorities, arguing that county authorities were ignoring the special exemption that should be granted to the Yao under the Party's nationalities policy. Nothing came of their protests, however.

Several years passed, and in 1956 Zhou Shenglong became involved in a movement to organize several Yao families to travel into the hills of southern Hunan and follow up on reports that Qianjiadong had finally been located. By this time, Zhou had been promoted to county chief (*xianzhang*) and was in a privileged position to mobilize Yao from across the county to participate in and support the expedition. In the spring of 1957, just after the Chinese New Year celebrations, a team of thirty-six adults set off on foot loaded down with comforters, kitchenware, and an assortment of food. The group walked for three days in torrential rain, crossing steep and treacherous mountain ranges, eating and sleeping outside, until they finally came to rest in a place called Kongshuling, where they were hosted by local Yao with whom they ate, played drums, danced, and sang deep into the night. The next morning they walked for another twenty or so miles until they came across a place they called Baduyuan (located in present-day Jiangyong County in Hunan). They found this to be a magnificent place, a high mountain valley surrounded by towering peaks, thousand-year-old trees, and located near a cascading waterfall of over one hundred meters. A Taoist priest, what the Yao call a *shigong*, led the people to worship in a nearby temple. They talked to Yao who lived in the vicinity and told them that they thought they had finally discovered the original Yao homeland. They wished to return, bring additional families to settle in the region, and eventually develop it as a new Yao autonomous county with the name Qianjiadong.

They set out the next morning and after eight days of walking finally arrived back in Gongcheng County. What they didn't know is that their expedition had attracted the attention of other officials in the Gongcheng County government, who had sent along two spies who took notes and recorded their activities and discussions and eventually filed a report with the Public Security Bureau. Soon after their return, the thirty-six individuals who made the trip began to tell the good news of Qianjiadong to their families and friends, and people from around the county began to gather to hear the tale. The news spread and soon several villages organized their members to approach the county government and ask for permission to relocate to Qianjiadong. More and more people began to join the movement and the government became increasingly alarmed. A large meeting was organized at which various county officials attempted to propagate the Party's nationalities policy, which at this time was based in part on getting the previously nomadic Yao in the highest reaches of the mountains to settle down and cease their endless searching for more arable terrain. With this official discouragement and with no action taken on the request for relocation, the movement began to die down. The Yao who made the trip and organized the various villages returned to their daily lives and considered their options.

The year 1957 would be an important one in the political history of the People's Republic. Within several months of their return to Gongcheng, the antirightist campaign broke out across China. This was to become a massive ideological rectification campaign in which Party officials denounced, humiliated, and punished intellectuals and others who had spoken out with critical frankness about the first years of communist rule in China. In urban centers such as Beijing and Shanghai, scholars, journalists, and some of the country's most respected professors began to question, for instance, the techniques of Party membership recruitment. Some went so far as to blast Mao Zedong for the way he carried out education and political campaigns in Yan'an, the CCP base area in the hills of Shaanxi Province, where in the

1940s Mao carried out his initial experiments in socialist reconstruction. Though Mao had initially urged intellectuals to publicly voice their criticisms of the Party and its style of rule, he soon turned against them. Over three hundred thousand intellectuals were branded "rightists" by the end of 1957, a label they carried throughout the remainder of their lives.[75]

The Gongcheng County chief Zhou Shenglong, who had initially supported the Qianjiadong expedition several months prior, faced a similar fate. Denounced as a proponent of local nationalism (*difang minzu zhuyi*) and as an antirevolutionary (*fan geming shijian*), he was sentenced to fifteen years in jail. After two years he was released on probation, but he never returned to political life. In 1971 he committed suicide.[76] It would take the death of Mao, the official denunciation of the ultraleftist line that brought humiliation and death to so many individuals, and the reemergence of Deng Xiaoping as China's paramount leader, for Zhou Shenlong's voice to be heard again. In the early 1980s, the "Qianjiadong incident" of Gongcheng County was reevaluated. No longer labeled an antirevolutionary rightist, Zhou was rehabilitated, his reputation restored as a one-time leader of the Yao people and a friend of the revolution.

Conclusion

This chapter has taken us into imaginings of the Yao past in the history of the Chinese nation. It is not uncommon in Euro-American writings on ethnicity and nationalism to encounter the claim that we now live, at the close of the twentieth century, in the midst of "the crisis of nationalism." The nation—whether conceived as a cultural form that enables a unified subjectivity, a practice of the imagination, or a mystifying ideological construct standing in the way of modernity and revolution—has been thoroughly deconstructed. The same applies to the territorial relationship long assumed to exist between the nation and the state, a relationship expressed in the hyphen that connects the term nation-state.[77] Modern states, we are now repeatedly told, can no longer claim to speak for a bounded and culturally homogeneous nation, if in fact they ever could. Claims to national identity, nationalist discourses, remembrances of the nation and its people have been radically severed from the state, with its claims to fixed territories, to principles of sovereignty, and to its everyday institutions of governmentality. The very modernity of the nation has also been questioned. Not a few scholars have pointed out that nationalism as a distinctive mode of consciousness seems to have existed long before industrialization and print capitalism, the twin motor forces of history identified in Gellner's and Anderson's respective and highly influential takes on the rise of nationalism.[78] Yet nationalism, it seems, has only grown stronger as we approach the century's end, and it often makes its appearance in extremist and violent forms of expression and struggle.

For whom has the nation been deconstructed? To what ends have scholars of transnationalism and globalization argued that the nation is losing its grip on the imagination and subjectivities of people everywhere? To whom do these claims apply? And how might these arguments smuggle in their own universalizing claims for a global subjectivity, a hegemonic "we" that is shared and experienced everywhere the same? Do all attachments to the idea of the nation, or to the idea of a territorially bounded social group, invariably lead to violence, pain, and suffering? In examining histories of Indian nationalism, Gyanendra Pandey has asked why it is that rationalist histories that situate different subjects in the long march of the nation's history are so widely accepted among so many people.[79] Why are these people not troubled by these histories, especially when it is so easy for the deconstructive gaze to unmask their multiple erasures, refusals, ambiguities, and inconsistencies? The answers may lie, Pandey argues, not only in authoritative histories that trace the nation's unfolding. They may well rest in the persistence of worldviews that do not search for consistency in the way rational scientists do; that do not see the sharp distinctions that "modernists" make between religion and culture; that do not always expect human action and history to be neatly compartmentalized—worldviews that recognize instead that ambiguity is central to the business of existence and survival, that context determines meaning, and that the same things may have very different meanings in different contexts.[80]

This image of ambiguity and context-dependent meanings enables an understanding of history—and the nation—as something more than a cultural form. As we shall see later, the nation's history is often written on the backs of women, ethnic minorities, religious practitioners, and other subjects cast as standing in its way. But the nation's history is also constantly being interpreted, represented, and fought over in large part because it is grounded in structures of feeling that are often extremely difficult to discern in texts that claim to give voice to a people. The ineffable attachment to different domains of social life, or to different kinds of communities, is what often informs and shapes how marginalized subjects struggle for voice and recognition. And these forms of cultural struggle are often focused on the meanings of the local in changing national and global settings.[81]

In the next chapter I explore these issues of history, ambiguity, interpretation, and locality in more detail. I focus in particular on debates about the unity and diversity of the Jinxiu Yao, drawing on the Yao writings of the internationally acclaimed Chinese anthropologist Fei Xiaotong. For Fei, the crucial issue is how to define the object of ethnological analysis and how to perhaps save it from the further ravages of history. In his book *Japan's Orient,* Stefan Tanaka has pointed out that one of the shortcomings of Said's *Orientalism* is that it failed to discuss how the subject who possesses the gaze comes to be "dependent" on the object.[82] Tanaka argues that dependency is heightened when the object refuses to stay the same, refuses to remain, in a sense, objectified as it was in previous discursive constructions. In this sense, orientalism works as a practice of power and knowledge not because the other becomes fully constituted and fixed permanently as an object of knowledge, but because the other is seen to constantly elude the gaze. The image of an elusive other is what drives the desire for knowledge.

In post-Mao China, research projects into the nature of local realities reveal this endless, dependent search for an object of knowledge, for new ways of making the minority subject visible for study, inspection, and perhaps, if the object relents, transformation. Young and aspiring ethnologists such as Xiao Huang were intent on turning a critical eye on the history of the CCP's practices of ethnic classification and the interpretations of minority realities that predominated in the late 1950s and 1960s. They were working to rebuild the discipline of ethnology after it had been banished from the intellectual landscape during the Cultural Revolution, then marked, as we have seen, as the quintessential "capitalist and bourgeois science." There is a tone of liberation in many of these accounts, a sense that science will no longer be subjected to the dictates of ideology. There is a sense that the "facts" will speak for themselves. I want to write against this reform-era desire for objectivity and truth. I argue that the project of ethnological revitalization and the study of local ethnic places found itself in a complex, ambivalent, and often contradictory relationship with the demands of Deng Xiaoping's socialist modernization agenda. As in previous periods, ethnology continued to be involved in complex practices of identification and naming. Minorities continued to be singled out as a "problem" people.

In the late 1980s and early 1990s, the study of regions such as Jinxiu became entangled in new practices of governmentality that were seeking to bring development to the ethnic outback and to contain and civilize the potentially unruly ethnic other. In this sense, ethnology has not simply awakened from the nightmare of the Maoist era and suddenly found itself in a new era. It has been institutionally, discursively, and materially linked to the recuperation of a rationalist vision of social science, one that was now to be applied to concrete social and theoretical problems in particular localities.

chapter two

Moral Geographies of Place

Places are fragmentary and inward-turning histories, pasts that others are not allowed to read, accumulated times that can be unfolded but like stories held in reserve, remaining in an enigmatic state, symbolizations encysted in the pain or pleasure of the body. — MICHEL DE CERTEAU, *The Practice of Everyday Life*

The study of the history of socialism in the People's Republic has often turned on the question of how to understand the changing dynamic between state and society. Anthropologists, historians, journalists, sociologists, and political scientists have all asked from their distinctive disciplinary perspectives just how successful the revolutionary state was in transforming the "local" societies it sought to study, penetrate, and transform. Others have focused on the discursive practices of the revolutionary state and have attempted to trace the meanings and contradictions inherent in the identification and imagining of new subjectivities, from worker, to woman, to peasant, to the proletariat. Scholars who have studied the history of minority policy in the 1950s have tended to focus on questions of assimilation. They have asked whether and how the CCP was able to transform China's non-Han population, which were often seen by cadres as local, backward, and politically regressive, into modern, revolutionary, and future-oriented national and socialist subjects.

Few scholars of minority politics in revolutionary China deny that the early socialist nation was committed in principle to nonexploitative forms of social and economic development. China's leaders believed that the revolutionary regime could forge new and more productive ties with non-Han populations and that histories of oppression, nationalist chauvinism, and economic exploitation could be overcome. Knowledge of these populations was crucial. The study of the histories and cultures of the non-Han people was to be based on the scientific principles of Marxism-Leninism and on the thinking of Mao Zedong, but it was also to be practical. Knowledge of internal ethnic difference was tied to the politics of classification and control of subject peoples, as well as to pedagogical projects that aimed to teach respect for the non-Han other. These pedagogical projects were eventually linked to the politics of frontier administration. Han cadres sought out young minorities, especially those who joined the underground revolutionary movement and participated in the defeat of the Guomindang, and encouraged them to take leadership roles in the newly instituted "autonomous" minorities counties and regions. They were then charged with the task of assuring minority compliance with the laws of the state. Through everyday propaganda and consciousness-raising techniques, they were to ensure that their ethnic brothers and sisters recognized the leadership of the Communist Party and embraced the task of making a prosperous socialist nation.

In the 1950s many ethnic minorities were championed for their heroic participation in the final battles of the revolutionary struggle. As we saw in the previous chapter, minorities provided a convenient figure in narratives of resistance and subaltern mobilization. The image of the minority as a subaltern subject was convincing because minorities retained oral traditions that recounted how they had opposed the injustices of Chinese imperial and nationalist rule. Party cadres recorded and popularized these narratives. Yet narratives that conjoined the modernity of the nation with tales of resistance competed with other modernist visions, especially those concerned with the question of how to bring social and economic development to what many saw as poor and backward regions. Minorities such as the Yao, who historically had lived in some of China's most remote mountainous terrain on marginal agricultural land, were said to lag behind the Han people. The Han were the unmarked category, more advanced and modern, a kind of stable center against which development and progress would be measured. Throughout the 1950s, the CCP was thus confronted with not only how to describe differences in culture and consciousness, but also how to account for divergent levels of material and social development among different populations. As we saw in the writing of the *Jianshi*, the Marxist interpretation of history told a very appealing and convincing story. It provided a materialist framework to understand how, on the long march of history, human societies passed through successive social formations. Minorities everywhere, across the expanse of China, were seen to move and advance through the stages of primitive communism, slave ownership, feudalism, capitalism, until they finally arrived, in the revolutionary present, in the space of state socialism. Many ethnic peoples were officially classified as belonging to one of these stages of history at the time of Liberation. The Yao, for their part, were stuck in that nebulous zone between feudalism and the reactionary capitalist nationalism of the Guomindang. The propagation of knowledge about the new revolutionary nation and continuous struggle against the enemies of the state would ensure the eroding of ethnic and national sentiments and differences. As these identities disappeared, the making of a communist society would become less a utopian fantasy and more a tangible social reality. This, at least, was the theory driving the revolutionary regime's early approach to the "nationalities problem," or the *minzu wenti*, as it is termed in China.

Nationalities work, or *minzu gongzuo*, depended on the acquisition of knowledge about local social and economic structures. In the 1950s one form of this work was called "the investigation of local social histories" (*difang shehui lishi diaocha*), and it became a central strategy in the CCP's attempts to know and mobilize the peoples it claimed to support, protect, and liberate from the tyrannies of "feudal" rule. The roots of this form of study can be traced back to the 1920s and 1930s, when Chinese intellectuals became interested in the ethnic margins of the nation. For example, one of Mao Zedong's earliest political tracts was written in the 1930s, when he penned a sustained sociological analysis of the social and political contradictions that existed in Xunwu County in Jiangxi Province. Mao argued that it was important to guard against mechanical applications of broad theoretical terminology (terms such as "the proletariat" and "expropriation," for instance) in understandings of local realities. He sought to detail the contours of everyday life and expose the complex social gradations that existed among different classes and social groups. Turning his attention to everything from the sale of salt, cooking oil, soybeans, meat, cigarettes, and umbrellas in local markets to the social and religious life of Taoist and Buddhist temples, he insisted that different forms and kinds of exploitation existed in these local settings. If social relations were structured and animated by class tensions, then these tensions appeared in ways that were sometimes disguised and thus difficult to discern. As far back as the 1930s,

Mao was calling for a more thorough probing of the complex workings of local social worlds.[1]

Since 1949, the Party has periodically issued the publication of local place histories.[2] Many of these studies carry on the tradition of detailed research Mao established in his Xunwu and other case analyses. Studies on Jinxiu County in the 1980s, for example, contain detailed descriptions of religious beliefs, rites, and rituals; descriptions of the cultural differences between the region's five Yao "subgroups"; accounts of the relationship between agricultural technologies and productivity levels; and descriptions of household, village, and township social organization. They explore the reasons for rebellion in local areas and trace the development of revolutionary activity in the 1930s and 1940s. They show how peasants were effectively mobilized to participate in the struggle against the Guomindang and the landed gentry classes by communist activists who were attuned to local conditions and to the specific material needs of peoples defined as subaltern classes. Appearing in the 1980s when scholars were beginning to openly criticize the history of Chinese socialism, these studies also seek to displace previous modes of representing the local. As we saw in the previous chapter, by the late 1950s and on into the 1960s local realities were viewed almost entirely through the lens of the class differentiation system. With its minute divisions and gradations among poor, middle, and rich peasants, this was the system of class differentiation that the Party had perfected and institutionalized in the Yan'an experiments in the 1940s. It was used to assist in the Land Reform Movement of the 1950s and it came back to haunt many people during the Cultural Revolution, when activist and frenzied Red Guards sought out those with "bad class backgrounds."

These studies are thus not just about the "local." They are also about the economic, social, and political disasters of the Maoist-dominated era. The failed policies of the Great Leap Forward in 1958, the widespread hunger and starvation in the countryside in the early 1960s, and the irrational onslaught of Maoist class struggle are all seen to have derailed China from its glorious progression through history. Mao's policies led to unprecedented poverty in the countryside, and radical economic imbalances emerged in different parts of the country. The so-called ultraleftists, with their overemphasis on heavy industry, had neglected to attend to basic improvements in living standards. Morale was low throughout the Chinese populace, as years of class struggle and the relentless searching for internal and hidden enemies of the state had left the body politic a tattered and tired social organism. The revolutionary march into the utopian future was effectively deferred. It had to be defined anew. "Socialist modernization" emerged as the new buzzword. The ultraleftist clique led by Jiang Qing was smashed in October 1976 and the Cultural Revolution was officially declared over. Development and modernization were reaffirmed as the primary goals of the reform regime. The Third Plenum of the 11th Central Committee of the Chinese Communist Party, held in December 1978, spelled out a new vision. It emphasized the managerial control of industry and economy and argued for guarded market incentives and agricultural reforms. The reform Party-state apparatus had to turn to the task of controlling and curtailing population growth, and, by forging new ties and educational linkages with the West, it had to turn to the task of training a new generation of experts in a number of different specialties. Development, in principle at least, was to be freed from the emphasis on ideological indoctrination and class struggle that marked the ultraleftist abuse and contamination of Mao Zedong thought.

Questions of Space and the Politics of Place

In this chapter, I turn to the ethnological study of locality under the reforms and what I call the moral geography of place. I am interested in the intellectual energies and theoretical discourses that were invested in new representations of the Jinxiu Yao Autonomous County in Guangxi. Jinxiu was one of the first Yao autonomous regions to be established in China, coming into official administrative existence in the mid-1950s. It is celebrated in Communist Party lore as an important site of political struggle, where communist insurgents, together with sympathetic Yao, waged the final battles against the Guomindang. It also has long occupied an important place in the historical memory of ethnological practice in China, owing in large part, as we shall see below, to Fei Xiaotong's and Wang Tonghui's work in the 1930s.[3]

Jinxiu reemerged as an object of study in the 1980s, when Yao and Han ethnologists turned to the question of how a people characterized by differences in language, cultural practice, and origin myth had come to identify themselves as Yao. It is known as the "home" of five different Yao subgroups—the Pan Yao, the Guoshan Yao, the Hualan Yao, the Ao Yao, and the Chashan Yao—a mode of ethnic classification standardized by the Communist Party's ethnological research teams that first began to visit the region in 1956. Many Yao scholars presented Jinxiu to me as a kind of living museum, where one could observe Taoist rituals and interview elderly men and women about their memories of the prerevolutionary past. Others saw it as a place that had been misrepresented by cadres once eager to bring class struggle to the Yao. Beginning in the late 1950s with the Great Leap Forward campaign, knowledge of the local terrain was linked almost entirely to the politics of class struggle. Many landowning Chashan Yao families were singled out in the 1950s and 1960s as agents of exploitation and oppression, a people who supported and maintained a "primitive" legal code known as the stone tablet system, or shipai zhidu.

In the reform period, knowledge of the local terrain has been linked to a very different politics. Scholars and government officials from the families of the previous landowning Chashan Yao subgroup told me they wanted to rewrite the history of how their people had been represented and struggled against. As one elderly woman said, Chashan Yao leaders felt a responsibility to bring back some dignity to this proud, highly educated, and once aristocratic people. My hosts and research consultants, most of whom were members of this once landowning group, presented the Great Leap in 1958 (when the large-scale commune system was standardized) and the Cultural Revolution as social and political disasters. These were moments when militant youth with no true knowledge of the Jinxiu past totally disregarded the traditions of the Chashan Yao. The desire to work against this history was in itself a potentially dangerous one, for it imagined a kind of unity that preceded the Guomindang presence in the 1940s and the post-Liberation establishment of the Dayaoshan as an autonomous region. The negative effects of these political campaigns on the local populace, and especially on the Chashan Yao, led these scholars to rethink the nature of Jinxiu social realities, both in the past and in the present. These Chashan Yao intellectuals, many of whom were Party members, were ardent supporters of the reforms and of Deng Xiaoping. Their local research projects aimed to document those traditions, such as community ritual, that had survived the socialist onslaught, and they moved to dissociate the meaning of ethnic culture from the ugly history of Maoist politics. They strongly supported the new official thinking that the Maoist slogan of the 1960s — "The nationalities problem is in essence a class problem" (minzu wenti shizhi shi jieji wenti) — was a mistake of the ultraleftist line (jizuo luxian). In short, they felt the reforms constituted a marked improvement over the horrors of the past. Jinxiu was thus presented to me and to many other outsider interlocutors as a place that had awakened from the nightmare of the Cultural Revolution. It was being remade as a place where the indigenous Yao cultural practices—even the once fervently denounced stone tablet system—could be studied and productively linked to the goals of socialist modernization.

How do we understand these new investments in the study of ethnic minority regions and autonomous counties? How do we theorize the desires that have swarmed around the study of "local societies and histories"? I approach the study of locality in post-Mao China as a cultural politics in which mostly elite actors attempted to redress what they argued were the interpretive mistakes of the Maoist past. One way they did this was by arguing for a more scientific ethnology, one that could accurately account for observable cultural differences among different ethnic subgroups and, at the same time, explain how these different peoples identified themselves as belonging to the same community. Though it is not my intention to explore the vast literature on the politics of place and space in recent social theory,[4] I have found de Certeau's relational notion of "space as a practiced place" to be of some import. The term space allows de Certeau to think about places as more than just figures on a map. Space is where actions occur, where things are done, and where transformations are actualized by a range of different actors who constitute themselves as subjects of will and power.[5] In his book *The Practice of Everyday Life*, de Certeau draws a distinction between place and space. Place refers to how elements are distributed in relationships of coexistence, a configuration of positions that imply some degree of stability. As David Harvey has put it in his reading of de Certeau, place is the "site of the inert body, reducible to the 'being there' of something permanent, in contrast to the instabilities of motions creating space."[6] Jinxiu, as a place, is fixed in its location to other places, just as the villages and townships within the county are known in relation to each other. Space, on the other hand, is much more fluid, in that it refers to the intersection of constantly mobile signifying elements, meanings, and social processes. For Harvey, de Certeau's relational image of space and place is theoretically suggestive because of its dialectical approach to history.[7]

When I refer to Jinxiu as a space, then, I am referring to something more than the geographical fixity of Jinxiu on a map (a problematic construct in itself), which can be located in relation to other topographical features. Rather, I am drawing attention to the multiple significations of Jinxiu as an ethnic place as different "subjects of will and power"—nation-states, government agencies, Party cadres, tourist bureaus, and ethnolo-

gists—try to fix it as an object of knowledge. To further understand these
various struggles over Jinxiu as an object of knowledge and transformation,
it is necessary to briefly trace the history of ethnology in China. This is the
topic of the next section. I then turn, in the final section of this chapter, to
the eminent anthropologist Fei Xiaotong's reading of the history of ethnic
identity formation in Jinxiu. I am interested in Fei's writings because he
shows so clearly how social scientists were working throughout the 1980s
to proffer alternative views on the history of the Jinxiu Yao. Fei is primarily
interested in how the different Yao groups in the Dayaoshan came to identify themselves as a unified ethnic group. For Fei, unification or solidarity—
a notion captured in the Chinese term *tuanjie*—was embedded deep in the
history of the Dayaoshan and was not simply an effect or result of the brilliant propaganda efforts and mobilization strategies of early Party cadres
and activists.

Fei also views the Yao as an obscure object of knowledge, in which the
established criteria of "nationalities identification" have been insufficient
to capture the Yao situation. We might read Fei's position as an acknowledgment of the limits of the socialist state's modes of ethnic classification and
identification. It could also be read as a continuation of his once expressed
belief in a utilitarian conception of knowledge in which social problems
are best approached by an impartial observer who can then work, through
rationality and realism, to instruct government officials on policy issues.
Although these are tenable positions, I propose we read it as a reform-era
discourse of power and truth, one in which ethnologists are implored to
correct the interpretive mistakes of the socialist past and pursue the study
of minority identification and difference through the scientific principles of
rationality and objectivity. Employing the scientific metaphor of "dissecting a sparrow" (*jiepo maque*), Fei urges scholars, intellectuals, and others
who study the Yao to delve more deeply into the nature of "local societies."
These realms of local culture and society are presented as spaces still in
need of further ethnological study. Yet he also sees them as economically
and socially deficient social spaces, as remote realms of backwardness and
isolation still in need of the transforming interventions of a rational modernizing state that has finally divorced the study of culture from the dictates
of ideological struggle.

Fei's ethnological imaginary allows us to see how practices of classification and interpretation worked as strategies of knowledge, surveillance,
and mobilization, and not simply as descriptions of an objective local and

ethnic reality. As historical and ideological conditions changed in the reform period, these strategies were opened up to critique. These critiques
did not simply set the record straight; rather, they entered Jinxiu into new
strategies of knowing, remembering, and representation. Some of these
strategies sought to constitute Jinxiu as a figure of the remote and the backward (*pianpi luohou difang*); others constituted it as a repository of traditional
culture; still others rendered it as a heroic site of revolutionary agency. Narratives about Jinxiu provide a window into the politics of representing the
nation's history, its progress, its failures, and, more in the context of this
chapter, its sites of internal ethnic difference. These meanings are not in-
trinsic to Jinxiu as a place. They are created and recreated through interpretive practices and strategies that are grounded in social struggles to name,
classify, see, and project Jinxiu as a particular kind of Yao place. It is in this
sense that de Certeau argues that stories about places are always spatialized
practices.[8]

A Discipline in Ruins

The founding of modern ethnology, or *minzuxue* as it is called in China,
is usually associated with the name of Cai Yuanpei. Cai was a May Fourth–
period intellectual who rose to a position of prominence when he became
the chancellor of Beijing University (Beida) in 1917. Cai's educational roots
were firmly in the late Qing, a time when many of his generation were seeking ways to respond to the series of political humiliations and military defeats China had experienced since the Opium War in the mid–nineteenth
century. He held a classical *jinshi* degree (the highest degree in the Confucian educational system) and had once served as an educational official
in his native province of Zhejiang. He traveled to and lived in Germany
in the early 1910s, where he studied philosophy, ethnology, and evolutionary theory.[9] During this period he spent considerable time in Paris, working closely with Chinese student anarchists to establish work-study programs and contributing essays to various overseas student journals.[10] Cai
was a close associate of Yan Fu, a late-Qing dynasty scholar-official who
was known widely for his translation of Thomas Huxley's 1893 book, *Evolution and Ethics*. In this book Huxley criticized the sociological and evolutionary theories of Herbert Spencer, who had attempted to apply Darwinian
theory to the development of human societies. Yan was nonetheless taken
with Spencer's ideas, and his translation of Huxley, entitled *On Evolution*,

immediately appealed to many early-twentieth-century Chinese nationalists, with its portraits of strong and weak nations struggling for survival in
a world of intense rivalry and competition.[11] Cai was very much a part of
this cosmopolitan social milieu in Beijing in the 1910s and 1920s. This was
an environment in which intellectuals were looking to Europe, to the texts
of the Chinese Confucian tradition, and, as we shall see, to the countryside
for guideposts on how to deal with the weaknesses of the Chinese nation.

Not long after he was brought in to modernize Beida's educational system, Cai Yuanpei found himself swept up in the events of May Fourth 1919.
When students in Beijing learned that the Versailles Treaty had handed
over portions of Chinese territory (previously held by Germany and other
European powers) to the Japanese, they took to the streets in an outpour-
ing of patriotic anger; they eventually occupied Tiananmen Square. When
military leaders in Beijing arrested the protesting students, Cai promptly
resigned his position as the head of Beida. A year later he was rehired,
though he never wavered in his defense of the students' calls for human
rights and open intellectual inquiry. In the midst of this turbulent period,
Cai continued to be interested in how the study of human societies could
be brought into the service of national revitalization. He became a leading intellectual in the political debates and cultural innovations associated
with the May Fourth Movement (wusi yundong).[12] He developed an increasingly radical educational philosophy at Beida, one that emphasized the need
for students to form cooperatives and independent discussion groups and
to combine mental with manual labor. Throughout this period he also remained drawn to the nineteenth-century theories of ethnology he had encountered in Germany. He believed ethnology had much to offer scholars
and students concerned with China's predicaments. Cai envisioned ethnology as a scientific pursuit as well as an applied discipline, one that could
assist the national effort to bring science, democracy, and education to all
of the nation's peoples. These themes were expounded on in his 1923 essay
"On Ethnology" ("Shuo minzuxue"), which scholars would later consider
to be the first major statement on this new field in China. Ethnology was to
encompass archaeology and history and draw on sociology and linguistics,
but it was also to include the observation of living peoples.[13] After leaving
Beida in the mid-1920s, Cai attempted to set up an ethnology institute in
Beijing but failed due to lack of funds. He was eventually successful in 1928,
when he established the Academia Sinica (Zhongyang Yanjiuyuan) in Nanjing and charged it with the study of an array of natural and social scientific

disciplines. Heavily influenced by nineteenth-century Western sociologists such as Spencer, who believed that contemporary societies contained "remnants" or "survivals" of past epochs, Cai encouraged his protégés to search for the origins of extant cultural practices among more "backward" (*luohou*) peoples, such as China's non-Han minorities.[14]

It should be noted that during the May Fourth period and well into the 1920s, many students and young scholars were drawn to the countryside. The former librarian at Beida and early Marxist Li Dazhao, for instance, urged China's youth to travel to the countryside and learn from the peasants. In one of his more impassioned essays from this period, Li wrote that urban intellectuals should "go out and develop" new forms of consciousness among the peasantry. Only in this way, Li believed, would peasants "demand liberation, speak out about their sufferings, throw off their ignorance and be people who will themselves plan their own lives."[15] The ethnologists and anthropologists that surrounded Cai in the 1920s were also captivated by this sense that the rural populace had something to offer the search for a new culture to revitalize what many saw as a sick and decaying social order. Much of the ethnological research from this period must be placed in the context of a widespread belief that the countryside, despite its astonishing poverty and "backwardness," was a source of inspiration for revolutionary ideals and a repository of information on the national condition. Cai became increasingly interested in encouraging young ethnologists to embark on studies in minorities regions. His protégés worked among the Yao in Guangxi, the Yi in Sichuan and Yunnan provinces, the aborigines in Taiwan, the Miao in western Hunan and eastern Guizhou, and the Li peoples of Hainan Island.[16] Some devoted their energies to theory; many were asked to assist in the formulation of policy in such areas as frontier politics and administration. Fei Xiaotong, Lin Yaohua, Chen Yongling, and other anthropologists who became leading fieldworkers in the People's Republic in the 1950s have all commented that scholars from this period tended to shy away from political organizing. It is not clear in any case how many ethnologists in the 1920s and 1930s believed that China's future rested in the hands of the rural masses; they were mostly interested in documenting "cultural survivals" and bringing education and cultural development to the "backward" minority.

Greg Guldin has summed up Cai's legacy as follows: "Given the uneven record on both sides of the Chinese political divide . . . and given the harassment and muzzling of Chinese scholars in both the Republic of China and the People's Republic of China, it is not surprising that many Chinese intellectuals should continue to pay homage to Cai Yuanpei." [17] The divide to which Guldin refers began after the outbreak of the Anti-Japanese War in 1937. Some of the May Fourth–period ethnologists were closely associated with the Guomindang government and moved to Chongqing after the Japanese captured Nanjing. Once in Chongqing, they retreated into the hill country of Sichuan and Yunnan and continued to dedicate themselves to the study of the ethnic cultures of the so-called border regions.[18] Fei Xiaotong, for example, returned from his educational stint in England and traveled overland from Hanoi to Kunming. By the late 1930s, Kunming was becoming a center for intellectuals fleeing the Japanese occupation of north China and Fei would there join his former teacher Wu Wenzao. Wu himself was in exile and had arrived in Kunming with Rockefeller funds to set up a sociology research center to be attached to Yunnan National University.

By this time, Mao Zedong and his rural-based Communist Party had been run out of the Jiangxi soviet; they would then embark on the Long March. As his troops moved through the mountains of south China and eventually turned northward into Sichuan, they undertook quasi-fieldwork projects, collecting ethnic folktales, songs, and local histories. They also began to recruit widely from among ethnic minorities, and Hui, Yi, and Tibetans joined the march. The most prominent of these new minority recruits was the Tibetan Sang Ji Yue Xi (also known as Tian Pao), who so impressed Party leaders that he later became the youngest person ever to be elected to the Party Central Committee.[19] Once settled in the Yan'an base area, the communists established the Yan'an Nationalities Institute and continued to recruit and train scholars to undertake minorities research and propaganda work. They also recruited heavily from among Hui and Mongols living in the Shan-Gan-Ning border region, a CCP-controlled base that comprised the present-day provinces of Shaanxi, Gansu, and Ningxia. It is unclear just how much Cai's notion of an applied ethnology informed these projects. There is little doubt, however, that "nationalities work" (or *minzu gongzuo*, as work among non-Han groups was now termed) increasingly came under the influence of Stalin's writings on the nature of socialism and its relationship to the "nationalities problem."

When I began to work with Yao and Han scholars in 1988, I found that they too recognized Cai Yuanpei as the founder of modern ethnology. The older among them possessed an awareness of China's ethnological traditions of scholarship and they had read many of the scholastic works published on minority groups in China during the 1920s and 1930s. Knowledge of this scholarship was a part of their early training. An elderly historian at a research institute in a southern province once told me that young scholars in the 1950s had an intense interest in the research that had been done among the Yao and other upland peoples in the 1920s and 1930s. As we saw in the previous chapter, much of the pre-Liberation Yao research had been carried out in northwest Guangdong, in southern Hunan, and in the mountains of Guangxi, the traditional strongholds of the Yao in the south of China. Americans, Europeans, and Russians did some of this research; their Chinese students did most of it. Yet these young students in the 1950s were constantly reminded that this research had been carried out with the help of Guomindang officials and Christian missionaries seeking ways to "open up" (kaifang) these Yao strongholds, to bring civilization to the heathen primitive. In the 1950s many of these reports were held up as examples of reactionary modes of research. Euro-American and Chinese scholars in the pre-Liberation period, indebted as they were to the local landed gentry in many of the places in which they worked, had failed to see how these "primitive" societies were structured by modes of "feudal" exploitation and class antagonisms.

In the political language of the 1950s and 1960s, pre-Liberation ethnologists were suddenly said to lack a "class viewpoint." One of the most famous of the pre-Liberation scholars at the Central Nationalities Institute in Beijing in the 1950s was a former student of Bronislaw Malinowski, Fei Xiaotong. As I've mentioned, Fei began his anthropological fieldwork career in the mid-1930s in the Yao Mountains of Guangxi, in the Dayaoshan. After the tragic event that took his wife, the promising sociology student Wang Tonghui, Fei departed for England to pursue a Ph.D. in social anthropology at the London School of Economics. He wrote a dissertation under the tutelage of Malinowski that later served as the basis for his first book, *Peasant Life in China*. He returned to China in late 1938 and, as I noted above, took up a post in Kunming at Yunnan National University, where he continued to do field research on peasant social life and to publish. In the mid-1940s, when the anticolonial war against the Japanese was coming to a close and the communist struggle against the Guomindang was reaching new levels of intensity, Fei left for the United States to visit Harvard, the University of Chicago, and the Institute of Pacific Relations in New York. He returned to China in 1947 and taught in the sociology department at the prestigious Qinghua University in the northwest suburbs of Beijing. By the early 1950s, however, Fei found himself along with other leading figures in the Chinese social sciences in the midst of intense debates with Communist Party education authorities about the future of sociology. At several conferences, Fei defended sociology by arguing that it was closer to scientific socialism than other disciplines and was useful in solving the economic and social problems of everyday peasant life.

Fei seemed to win these arguments until the political winds shifted in 1952. The sociology department at Qinghua was abruptly closed down and sociology and anthropology were repudiated as disciplines. Many of these pre-Liberation scholars suddenly found themselves transferred to such places as the Central Nationalities Institute and other minority-related government organs. They were called on to assist in the training of ethnic minority cadres who would return to their native homes and promulgate the Party's system of regional self-government. They trained researchers, recorded indigenous non-Chinese languages, and taught people about their histories and the nature of the social and economic realities under which they lived. As is now well-known, Fei became an object of serious criticism during the antirightist campaign in 1957, when the Communist Party turned on intellectuals who openly criticized the first years of Party rule.[20] Fei himself, in an essay written in the *People's Daily* in March 1957, argued that intellectuals had been "left out of the picture" and were not contributing to national affairs and debates about China's national development.[21] Sociology, anthropology, and ethnology were essential, Fei argued, if China was to become a great nation, for these disciplines were based on the concrete empirical examination of new social problems as they emerged in any given social setting.[22] Population growth, adequate housing, reeducation and employment of intellectuals, questions of work and labor relations, antagonisms and contradictions among minorities—these were the areas most in need of empirically grounded research.

In July 1957, Fei wrote a self-criticism in the *People's Daily* entitled "I Admit My Crime to the People."[23] During the Cultural Revolution, he was again forced to publicly air his crimes against the people; he eventually spent two and a half years in the countryside at a May Seventh Cadre School learning to grow cotton and rectify his thinking through labor with the masses. Some years later, in a speech given to the Second Friendship Delegation of the Committee of Concerned Asian Scholars who visited the People's Republic in April 1972, Fei had this to say, as quoted in Gene Cooper's report on Fei's remarks: "I can't even read the works I've written on the Chinese peasant in the past (he laughed). The difference is that I lacked their class viewpoint. My ideas and feelings were different from the labouring people. The problems I wanted to solve, the questions I wanted to answer were not those that the peasants wanted solved and answered. My viewpoints didn't correspond with that of the broad masses of peasants. At that time, I looked down at them as inferior, as illiterate country bumpkins. Because of this, the words I wrote did not serve the peasants but those that ruled over them. I never understood it before. Through revolution, I came to understand this, and by revolution, I meant the revolution in myself." [24]

Fei Xiaotong's struggles to reconcile his past with the ideological demands of the socialist state remind us that one of the central historical and theoretical problems of post-Mao scholarship has been the question of how to assess the Cultural Revolution. Both within China and beyond, this period is seen by many as a historical aberration, a misguided and irrational political experiment that left the country in ruins. As Arif Dirlik and Maurice Meisner have put it, the Cultural Revolution "is now held responsible for everything from retarding China's economic development to destroying public morality, making tolerable to decent and ordinary people the most intolerable acts of public and private vindictiveness." [25] Lin Yao-hua, one of the leading anthropologists at the Central Nationalities Institute in Beijing and a contemporary of Fei Xiaotong, summed up this period of attacks on ethnology in the following startling passage from an essay written in 1990:

> From Liberation up until right before the Cultural Revolution, research work in the field of ethnology, led by the Party and sustained by its concern, had moved forward uninterruptedly and achieved gladdening results. However, just as we forged ahead with confidence, Lin Biao and the "Gang of Four" and their ilk brought great calamity upon the country. As in other spheres, nationalities work and ethnological studies suffered severe damage. Lin Biao and the "Gang of Four" opposed the Party's policy toward nationalities, neglected the nationalities work, undermined their solidarity, spread discord among them, and stifled nationalities research work. For more than a decade the study of nationalities was suspended, and the entire organization became paralyzed. Much valuable research was lost and in many places the research teams were disbanded. All of this caused irreparable loss. In particular, they fabricated many absurd theories about the nationalities issue, thus creating

ideological and theoretical confusion. This severely and adversely affected ethnic research. Lin Biao and the "Gang of Four" slaughtered the Marxist-Leninist study of ethnology, which had, since Liberation, been carried out under the correct leadership of the Party, and labeled it bourgeois ethnology. They negated it in a wholesale fashion and thoroughly strangled it. As a result, the field of ethnology was entirely eliminated from the country. Many ethnologists and researchers suffered severe attacks, and some were even persecuted to death. Those who survived did not even dare to mention the word "ethnology." [26]

These critiques of the Cultural Revolution have enabled new imaginings of the role of the social sciences and, in the context of our discussion here, new conceptions of the place of ethnology in reform-era projects of development. One is immediately struck by how this passage romanticizes a golden age of socialist ethnological work before the "strangulation" and "negation" of the Gang of Four. One is also struck again by the theme of loss: of invaluable information about ethnic minorities and of careers, even lives. Lin singles out the errors of a few Chinese leaders, yet seems to retain a space for a recuperated and enlightened Communist Party system.

Not all ethnologists in China in the late 1980s could speak so openly about this period. When I moved to Jinxiu in 1990, for example, I initially discovered a great deal of ambivalence around the question of the Cultural Revolution. As we've seen, some of the scholars and Party members with whom I was working were ridiculed during this period. I also met many government officials who were once Red Guards, yet few were willing to revisit this troubling moment in China's post-1949 history. Many of the Yao and Han scholars I worked with were much younger than the elderly scholar and statesman Fei Xiaotong. Some were old enough, however, to remember these sordid political affairs and struggles against intellectuals during the 1950s and 1960s. For many of them, Fei's story was emblematic, and it was a tale I heard again and again over dinner and in private conversations. I was constantly impressed by how members of younger generations, both men and women, spoke almost tearfully about Fei's struggles to find a place for sociology and anthropology in China. They applauded how he had emerged once again as a prominent leader in the social sciences in the 1980s. Others spoke of Fei in less romantic narratives. A Party official in Jinxiu once told me that Fei was now out of touch with the problems people face in the remote hills of southern China. Another told me that Fei, during his research in the 1930s, did not have the support of the local population and that many resented having their heads and arms measured during his anthropometric surveys. It is hard to know exactly what motivates comments such as these. What is clear is how these critical yet hesitant remarks catch Fei in a kind of post–Cultural Revolution double bind. On the one hand, he has been embraced by many as an intellectual who survived the worst years of the ultraleftist reign of terror. On the other hand, his return to power at China's most prestigious universities and institutes in Beijing raises questions about how a Han intellectual from his generation can relate to and speak for the ethnic minority masses.

Nonetheless, the more advanced Yao scholars I was working with welcomed Fei's reform-era approach to the study of ethnic minorities. In a series of essays written in the early 1980s on Yao and other minority research, Fei called for a comprehensive reexamination of ethnology and its relationship to the "nationalities problem." He called for a comparative approach to understand local conditions; he supported visions of social development that were respectful of local conditions; and he championed "micrological" studies into the differences among and within minority groups. Fei seemed to implicitly understand that "nationality unity" (minzu tuanjie) had too long been nothing more than a hollow ideological slogan; it was necessary to understand what "unity" could mean in light of empirical research into the cultural practices, psychological makeup, sentiments, and living conditions of different peoples in China. Many scholars picked up on Fei's visions. They too were asking, though few could ever explicitly state this in their writings, whether Yao identity could be fully understood, fully grasped as an object of knowledge through the theories of Marxism-Leninism and the ethnological writings of Engels and Lewis Henry Morgan. I now turn to some lessons in the history of knowing places.

Modernity and the Moral Geography of Difference

Let me begin with Guangxi, a region in the south that has figured predominantly in discourses about marginality, development, culture, and civilization in modern China. Extreme poverty and persistent lawlessness have long characterized Guangxi.[27] Located in the far south of the country, the province lies in the upper basin of the West River (Xi jiang). This river connects Guangxi and Guangdong and has afforded the development of a strong regional identity between the peoples of these two provinces (at

Distribution of Yao by Language Group

present, of course, Guangxi is connected to other regions by train and air-
plane).[28] The tributaries of this river rise beyond the borders of the province
and carve deep valleys in the numerous stretches of foothills and mountain
ranges that demarcate Guangxi proper from its neighboring provinces. It
is only in the southeast of the province that a broad, flat plain connects
Guangxi to Guangdong. It was not until the Tang dynasty that this region,
which was named Lingnan after the mountains that define the present-day
Guangxi, Guangdong, Hunan, and Guizhou borders, was settled by military farm colonies.[29] Guangxi's identity as a province did not occur until
the Ming, when "tribal chiefs" were incorporated into the imperial administration through the tusi system, a process we saw detailed in the Jianshi in
chapter 1. As Han settlers moved up river valleys in search of land suitable
for wet-rice cultivation, the so-called indigenous inhabitants—the ancestors of the present-day Zhuang, Yao, and Miao—were driven further into
the hills, forced to carve out a living on the least fertile land.

This is the standard ethnohistorical narrative for how the Chinese opened and expanded into the south of China, as outlined in the previous chapter. Despite the settlement of the land by Han migrants and the historical Sinicization (*hanhua*) of the Zhuang peoples, Guangxi continues to this day to be considered one of China's poorest provinces.[30] In late 1998, for example, during the fortieth anniversary celebrations for the founding of the Guangxi Zhuang Autonomous Region, the Central Committee of the Communist Party pledged to promote ethnic unity and to help the more than three million people who still live below the poverty level. At a celebration in Nanning, Vice Premier Wu Bangguo stated that the "central authorities will pump in more capital and aid to support Guangxi's infrastructure, construction, and development . . . only by further boosting economic construction and productivity will we be able to fulfil the material demands of all ethnic groups."[31]

In addition to its privileged position in contemporary discourses of poverty, Guangxi has also long been seen as a land of mythical landscapes. As one observer has put it, "The very name of Guangxi aroused in the minds of educated Chinese the idea of a place like no other, where the fairy landscape—pine-clad mountains of fantastic shape rising abruptly from a lake-studded plain, and creaking through wreathes of mist to show glimpses of ravines and waterfalls—which for centuries haunted the imagination of poets and artists, really existed."[32]

It is, of course, the mythical character of the Guangxi landscape that has fueled the tourist industry that today thrives along the rivers and in the hills around Guilin. The limestone cliffs and contorted rock formations, the deep caves and hot springs have been presented both nationally and internationally as a kind of scenic wonderland. It was not uncommon for me to encounter Chinese in the north who spoke fondly of Guangxi as a land of abundant natural beauty, yet who also noted with some distaste the province's bizarre customs (in particular, culinary) and excruciating poverty. My initial point here is that Guangxi, as a figure of the remote in a larger moral geography of regional spaces, has always been caught within a powerfully conflicted fantasy. The natural landscape of the region constantly restores to memory the civilizing center's long romance with the pristine, untouched mountainous landscape, lands shrouded in misty clouds and populated by meditative, content farming people. Still, as with other remote regions in China, the region has never escaped its designation as a site of lack and uncivilized vulgarity. It is a land, as we saw in Wu Bangguo's statement, of economic and social malaise, of dispossessed people living in deep poverty, who have been forced to scratch out a living in some of the most infertile of China's hill country.[33]

In the 1980s, Guilin emerged as one of China's most famous tourist destinations, noted worldwide as an energetic city surrounded by ominous limestone towers and a lush paddy field landscape. It was the capital of Guangxi from the Ming dynasty until 1914 (when the capital was moved to the city of Nanning), and it witnessed the influx of millions of refugees from the countryside during the war with Japan. In the 1920s, the Guomindang set up administrative posts throughout the valleys of the region. This was part of a widespread effort to propagate ideas about the "new democratic" nation, battle the mobilization efforts of communist cadres who were organizing peasants into peasant associations and self-defense units, and extract taxes and resources to support the Guomindang regime. Today this history has disappeared in most official and popular accounts of Guilin and its surrounding environs, as it has come to be known for its fiery food, its brilliantly photogenic landscapes, and the mercenary attitude of its many entrepreneurial travel agents.

Some seventy kilometers to the south is a small town called Yangshuo, which rose to prominence in the mid-1980s as a haven for backpackers seeking to escape the rising prices and pollution that had gradually come to Guilin. For many Chinese and international tourists, Yangshuo is the terminus of a cruise on the Li River, an eighty-five-kilometer boat trip that begins in Guilin and meanders southward through some of China's most spectacular karst formations. In 1988, when I first visited this town on my way to the Yao mountains in Jinxiu some two hundred kilometers to the southwest, tourist agents were beginning to set up minority craft shops selling shoulder bags, clothing, and reproductions of religious items and figurines. The more daring among them were selling short excursions into the distant hills, where they promised one could observe Dong, Miao, Yao, and Zhuang peoples whose "culture," as one advertisement put it, "is apparent not only in their daily lives but also in traces of their prehistoric past." In those days, however, very few tourists were taking the bait. These excursions were mostly on local buses that were notorious for breaking down halfway up a mountain (in the mid-1990s, the favored mode of transportation was the newly built and imported air-conditioned Japanese buses). The word had quickly spread among the banana pancake–eating foreign tourists that the trip into the remote hills was more about seeing mountain

The town of Yangshuo.

peasants in drab clothing than encountering traces of a prehistoric ethnic past. It is perhaps for this reason that the Communist Party guest house (*zhaodaisuo*) in Jinxiu, the only place for foreign tourists to stay in the late 1980s and early 1990s, recorded a mere twelve visitors in 1988.

In the late 1980s, then, tourists and Han and Zhuang lowland dwellers felt the mountains of Jinxiu were simply too far off the beaten tourist track. I remember one German photographer telling me they were a bit "too agricultural." The political history of the region escaped many of the Han and Zhuang who lived in the lower elevations as well. I was surprised to find that many Chinese in Guilin and Yangshuo expressed little knowledge of the history of the Yao mountains in Guangxi other than the occasional reference to the Taiping revolt, which got its start in the town of Jintian on the southeastern flank of the Dayaoshan. Few people knew that the town of Jinxiu had become the administrative seat of Jinxiu County in the 1950s, or that the Dayaoshan was the name for this region before it was turned into an autonomous region (*zizhiqu*) on 28 May 1952. While living in Jinxiu, I often traveled to Yangshuo for weekends and played the role of anthropologist for the tourists and backpackers with whom I drank beer and swapped travel stories. I told them stories of how and why, for example, the Communist Party in 1955 decided the area was actually too small to be a "region" (*qu*) and then turned it into an autonomous county, a *zizhixian*. Repeating the language I had learned in the Jinxiu Tourism Bureau where I often hung out, I told them that the mountains around Jinxiu were "high and steep, surrounded by perilous rivers and covered by heavy forests." I explained that because of the area's foreboding terrain, "the feudalist rulers of past dynasties" were unable to penetrate the hills. This isolation came to an end when the Guomindang set up an outpost in the region in the 1940s, a period many people in Jinxiu refer to as the "opening of the mountains" (*kaihua*). I told them the Dayaoshan was one of the final battlegrounds in the defeat of the Guomindang. Of how Party cadres in the late 1940s, together with local Yao sympathetic to the goals of the revolution, established "bandit suppression" troops and began a series of isolated attacks on the remaining Guomindang troops. Of how victory finally came in the southwest part of the Dayaoshan, in present-day Xiuren County, when the Guomindang leader Han Mengxuan was killed and a meeting was held celebrating his death. I translated and recited what I had learned in the Party histories I was required to read by my research consultants as part of my education in

Jinxiu history and culture: "With the masses cursing between their teeth," they yelled out in angry yet jubilant defiance, "Dig out his heart!" "Skin his body!" "Cut him into pieces!"

It should not surprise us that the people who traveled to Guilin and Yangshuo, these newly emerging sites on the international and Chinese tourist scene, were little interested in the details of revolutionary history in a faraway county. Many of the tourists I met in Yangshuo and elsewhere in Guangxi and Yunnan wanted to know about traditional culture, about ethnic costumes, about weird and exotic rituals. They wanted to travel into another space and time, to see something of the ethnic and traditional life they believed existed before the socialist revolution. Although I, too, was interested in all of the trappings of the traditional, I also wanted to fight against what seemed to be an indisputable fact: the political history of the revolution was fading from national memory. Imagining myself as a kind of emerging expert on local Guangxi history, and believing that there was important knowledge to be learned behind the screen of ethnic commodification, I implored the tourists and other travelers I met to learn something of the history of these remote regions.

The problem was that the region had come alive with a different kind of activity in the late 1980s, an activity that swarmed around the signifier "modernization," or *xiandaihua*. Government officials often pointed out to me that before the revolution the Yao could not even produce a nail. Under the reforms, Yao, Zhuang, and Han Chinese traders began daily to come in over the mountains, some on foot, some by bus, all to set up shop in the local markets where they could earn off the private plots they now controlled under Deng's "responsibility system." In these narratives, Jinxiu is championed as a success story of reform-era development. The people of the county are applauded for having meticulously followed the county government's economic construction principle to "take forestry as the main production, and combine forestry and grain production together." By the end of 1986, for example, the county had over 1.9 million mu of forest, over 52 percent of the total land coverage. It seems to matter little to most people that the forest products are mainly shipped to other parts of the county, just as a large dam built in the mid-1980s provides over two billion cubic meters of water to over one million people around Guangxi. Since the late 1970s, twelve new roads were built with a total length of 212 kilometers, providing bus service between towns, townships, and villages. Though never

Another view of the town of Jinxiu, showing administrative buildings and apartments built since the late 1950s.

enunciated in quite the same terms as we saw in Wu Bangguo's candid acknowledgment of Guangxi's lack of development, poverty was an object of struggle in these new imaginings of the modern in Jinxiu. The poor life of the Yao used to be described in a short poem that went something like this: "A bamboo pipe of rice and eight ladles of water, sitting next to the fire and waiting till the sun rises." "Now," as a local tourist brochure puts it, "many families live in cement-built buildings of two or more stories, possessing television sets, radios, and washing machines."

Discourses of the modern that celebrate the arrival of dams and schools, cement buildings and television sets dominated descriptions and representations of Jinxiu throughout the late 1980s and early 1990s. These ubiquitous and typical signs of modernization, however, were not apparent in all parts of the county. The reality of uneven development raised questions for many, including myself, about how to critique contemporary social problems and just what could be gained from such critiques. But the question of the modern—and its belated arrival—was also forcing Yao in Jinxiu to rethink the history of how the Dayaoshan had been "opened" by the Guomindang and then made into an autonomous Yao county by the communists in the 1950s.

The Reimagining of Jinxiu

The present-day Jinxiu Yao Autonomous County encompasses the mountain range known as the Dayaoshan, or Great Yao Mountains. Jinxiu is located almost at the center point of Guangxi. Its mountains are the largest in the region, covering an area of over twenty-three hundred square kilometers and in many places rising to a height of over two thousand kilometers. Until the 1940s the mountains were accessible only by foot, as the area was encased in dense forests with some twenty-five different river systems. The county was created in the 1950s as an autonomous administrative entity, part of the CCP's initial nationalities policy (minzu zhengce) to bring "unity" (minzu tuanjie) to regions inhabited largely by non-Han minorities. Exactly what unity meant and how it was to be achieved in minority regions in the late 1940s and early 1950s has been the source of some debate among ethnologists in China. In Jinxiu, I found that the Communist Party's early message to the Yao, which began to be promulgated in the early 1940s through underground propaganda efforts (dixia xuanchuan gongzuo), was that autonomy (zizhi) was not a right to be granted by yet another outside force. Party cadres similarly insisted that it was not something that should rest in the hands of a few powerful Yao families or social groups. It was presented as a state of empowerment, a mode of democratic local self-rule. Part of the effort in these early days of revolutionary struggle was to eradicate the Guomindang presence in the hills and root out Yao collaborators. Party cadres presented the Guomindang's campaign to open (kaihua) the hills and assimilate (tonghua) the Yao in the 1940s as a strategy to divide and conquer the local populace, to turn one group against the other. The Guomindang were said to have turned the Han against the mountain Yao, and the landowning Yao against those who owned no land and were forced into labor and rent arrangements. Jinxiu was viewed as a fragmented social space, split by different classes and powerful landowning families and collectivities of different Yao subgroups (minzu zhixi).

Initially, Yao autonomy in Jinxiu was to be about recovering some semblance of control over the means of production for a subaltern class of subjects who lived without any access to the fertile rice-growing regions in the valleys and to the plentiful forests. Communist Party cadres came on the scene to put an end to what they called feudal (fengjian) modes of "big Han chauvinism" (da Han zhuyi). They sought to liberate landless Yao groups from their oppressive Yao and Han overlords and to bring a remote,

Guangxi Zhuang Autonomous Region

predominantly minority region into the fold of the revolutionary energies sweeping the rest of the nation. Once instituted as an administrative unit, Jinxiu County had to be remade, both politically and culturally. This required, in part, creating a local Yao subject that saw its future entwined with the revolutionary and modernizing developments occurring elsewhere. The making of a localized yet outward-looking subjectivity required that the populace overcome the ways the Guomindang had exploited local ethnic and social differences. Once this past was left behind, the Yao groups in the hills could be unified around a common project of socialist reconstruction. At stake here was the making of Jinxiu as a Yao ethnic place, where Yao could, in theory at least, participate and actively determine the course of local development. This was to be a cultural and pedagogical project as well, one that involved getting the mountain peasants to define for themselves the nature of Yao society.

I want to pause here for a moment and discuss how the term "society" (*shehui*) first came to be constituted as an object of knowledge in the May Fourth period in the 1920s. To recall the argument above on the founding of ethnology, this was a time when intellectuals were intensely debating the meaning of the Chinese nation. A number of scholars have argued that early Chinese nationalism tended to simultaneously enable and repress a plurality of voices that were clamoring for recognition within the new polity.[34] This created a tension, as Michael Tsin has put it, between the drive to create a cohesive unitary polity and the impulse to locate "society," which was largely seen to be characterized by a multiplicity of social interests.[35] As mercantile, philanthropic, native place, and a number of other associations vied to assert their interests, they increasingly did so in an environment in which they identified and conflated their interests with those of the nation, the new *guojia* that was in the process of being politically and imaginatively constituted. Echoing the work of Duara, Dirlik, Lydia Liu, Anagnost, and others who have examined early-twentieth-century nationalism, Tsin's argument is that we cannot talk about society, which was seen to comprise a plurality of voices, identities, and interests, without first tracing its career as a signifying practice in different nationalist projects.[36] For those who sought to define the nature of the social body of the nation, this multiplicity of interests and this specter of political, cultural, and social difference could not be taken for granted. These interests had to be discovered, articulated, and mobilized.

For Tsin, then, this is one way to understand the cultural struggles that existed between the Guomindang and the communists. Armed with a number of new and imported theories of the social (from Darwin to Marx to Mussolini), these parties were convinced of their own ability to identify the social interests of the nation and mobilize them accordingly. Tsin puts it this way:

> It is within the context of the remapping of social categories that such concepts as "class" (*jieji*) acquired particular significance. Indeed, the differentiation of "classes" not only facilitated the formation of the quasi-rational strategy for mobilization but also provided a new key for the articulation of the nationalist project. For despite the grounding of the nationalist discourse in the language of popular sovereignty, the question of the actual constitution of the "citizenry" (*guomin*) or the "masses" (*minzhong/qunzhong*) remained a contested issue. By representing "society" as a material body, social mapping—the demarcation of the populace into different categories as defined by "class" or "segment" (*jie*)—thus became instrumental in establishing or shifting the boundaries of the imagined national community. Selected categories could

be either incorporated or rejected. The centrality of the "social" in the political discourse, in other words, was to lead increasingly to its own reification. "Society" was to be objectified. Its body was to be dissected, its constituents classified, and their ascribed interests represented.[37]

In China in the 1950s, the administrative demarcation of ethnic minority autonomous regions was one way the Communist Party, now armed with the nationality theories of Marxism-Leninism, mapped and mobilized the interests of minorities. This required defining the social and political nature of the regions in which they lived. The imagining of a local and distinctively ethnic social body was enabled in large part by the socialist state's massive ethnic identification project, or *minzu shibie*, first put into practice in the early 1950s. An identification project was never carried out in Jinxiu, however. This was due in part to the fact that the struggle against the Guomindang "bandits" lasted until late 1951 and early 1952, which meant that the CCP did not establish a strong administrative presence in the area until late 1952. Rather, from 1950 to 1955 the Central Committee of the CCP, with the guidance and support of the Guangxi People's Government, sent various visiting research groups, known as *minzu fangwentuan*, to the Dayaoshan. These research visits were seen as an important component of "nationalities work" (*minzu gongzuo*) in the early 1950s. The top echelon of the CCP insisted that language and other overt manifestations of ethnic uniqueness were to be respected and encouraged. The Party required its cadres to approach minorities in local tongues and dressed in local attire. In theory at least, the visual demonstration of respect for ethnic forms of identity (language, costume, ritual, marriage and courting practices, etc.) would open the heart of the ethnic subject to the content of the socialist message.[38]

These teams came frequently to the Dayaoshan, though they stayed for very short periods of time, sometimes a week or two, a month at the most. One of their charges was to work with Party cadres who were attempting to mobilize different Yao peasants to join mutual aid associations, the first step in what led to the establishment of large-scale agricultural collectives during the Great Leap campaign of 1958. But mobilization depended on first determining which groups were oppressed and exploited by whom and through what kinds of political institutions and cultural practices. Subaltern groups internal to the Yao ethnic category were therefore identified, for Yao unification in Jinxiu could not be realized until the nature of intra-Yao conflict was documented and then publicly displayed, as in other re-

gions of China during this period, through struggle sessions. Local hegemonies had to be disrupted. Traditional land tenure systems were soon
nullified. Peasants without land and with no voice in local governing structures were recruited into the new government. In short, the local social
landscape, in its political and cultural dimensions, was invested with new
meanings.

In the mid-1950s, Mao Zedong called on provincial, county, and township governments to further collectivize agricultural production in the
countryside. By the end of 1955, 223 peasant cooperatives (*nongmin shengchan hezuo she*) had been established in Jinxiu County. A new wave of Party
research was soon initiated. In 1956, as part of a nationwide campaign,
the Central Branch of the Communist Party sent another research team
into the Dayaoshan to "salvage" (*qiangjiu*) social historical materials before
they were lost to these practices of socialist development. Huang Yu, along
with Professor Yang Chengzhi, led some fourteen scholars and Party officials on a research exhibition throughout the hills; they stayed in the region
from October 1956 to September 1957. They visited the newly established
cooperatives in the hills and collected an astonishing mass of historical
detail. They interviewed elders who told stories about Yao participation in
the Taiping movement in the mid–nineteenth century, about when the first
Christian missionaries arrived in the hills, and about how the different Yao
"subgroups" in the Dayaoshan had interacted and related to each other
through the years. With no photographic equipment, they drew pictures of
local agricultural implements and sketched images of plants, herbs, and
other local "special products" (*techan*). They observed popular ritual and collected narratives of local customs. They also began to discover tensions and
contradictions in the collectivization process.

What emerged from the findings of these two research teams was a picture of the local landscape split by competing class interests, though these
classes did not precisely follow the existent ethnic divisions in the Dayaoshan. The *fangwentuan* research teams that first visited the region in 1952
found that economic and social power in Jinxiu was divided between two
main social groupings. The smaller but more powerful social group comprised three small landowning Yao subgroups (the Chashan, Hualan, and
Ao Yao groups, differentiated by language use, clothing, myths of migration
into the mountains, and some religious beliefs), who were known collectively as the Changmao Yao, or "the longhaired Yao," in reference to the
Qing-style queue sported by many of the men. The second group was called

the Guoshan Yao, or "the Yao who cross mountains," who tended to live in the higher altitudes and work the least productive agricultural land. The people who belonged to this group (the Pan Yao and the Shanzi Yao) owned no land, practiced a modified form of swidden cultivation, and periodically worked as hired laborers for the landowning group. The Changmao Yao, the region's landowners, reproduced their authority and prestige through the maintenance of a local legal system, called the stone tablet system, or the *shipai zhidu*. Headmen or *touren* (a few of these positions were held by women) were elected to oversee its operation, the public dissemination of its codes, its rules of behavior, its manner of handling disputes, and the collection of taxes in the form of agricultural products or labor.

Yao who have studied and written about the *shipai* have argued that it represents two divergent yet overlapping forces at work in prerevolutionary society. On the one hand, the *shipai* comes into existence as a social and political practice (scholars admit that the precise origins of the practice are impossible to determine) in the context of the Chinese imperial policy of "using barbarians to rule barbarians" (*yizhi zhiyi*). For them, to study the *shipai* is to enter the history of Chinese imperial expansion into the frontier regions of Guizhou, Yunnan, Sichuan, and Guangxi. On the other hand, as a form of primitive self-rule, the *shipai* is believed to provide a window into the social evolution of the Yao subject. The *shipai* is thus all about the shifting dynamics of center and periphery in the history of China. As we saw in the previous chapter, Yao scholars trace the origins of the Yao subject back to the Song dynasty, when imperial armies and their bureaucrat officials moved into the mountainous regions of present-day Sichuan and Guizhou. China's imperial officials sought out local leaders, the so-called native chieftains, and rewarded them with rank, access to inheritance rights and educational opportunities, and other markers of cultural prestige. These campaigns of frontier expansion were at once materially and culturally motivated. The price of official recognition was getting one's community to participate in tax and corvée labor systems. They sought to expropriate the region's rich natural reserves, encourage the Han settlement of so-called native lands, and impose direct rule over the barbarian other by winning over local chiefs and headmen.

By the time of the Ming and Qing dynasties, this policy, known as the *jimi zhou*, was further rationalized with the implementation of the "native chiefdom system" (*tusi zhidu*). As Richard von Glanh and more recently John Herman have argued, the native chieftains who surrendered to the Song,

Ming, and Qing empires sought to strengthen their own control over the indigenous populations of the south.[39] This process created a peripheral elite
and generated new social and class divisions among indigenous populations and among the chieftain elite. By the time of the mid-Qing, intense debates emerged, for example, between the Yongzheng emperor (1723–1735)
and his retainers about whether the native chieftain system should be abolished. Yongzheng, the emerging multiethnic liberal of his day, was incensed
at how the native chieftains treated their subjects, as he daily read reports of
atrocities, "unspeakable cruelties," and internecine strife. He saw the non-
Han indigenous peoples as his innocent children. His retainers wanted to
keep the system intact, for the native chieftain system was seen as essential
for the Qing state's ability to open up frontier regions and intercede in local
affairs: "The native chieftain system, they argued, could project China's immense political-military influence and cultural prestige directly into frontier societies and transform 'savage man' into 'civilized man.' In time, respect for Chinese ways would trickle down the social hierarchy of non-Han
society. Eventually, Chinese ways would replace non-Han cultural practices
as the indigenous frontier population 'turned toward civilization' (*xiang
hua*), thereby removing the cultural barriers separating China proper and
peripheral non-Han societies."[40] When this utopian cultural oneness was
achieved, the borders and boundaries between the civilized center and the
uncivilized margin would dissolve. The native chieftains would no longer
be needed and direct bureaucratic control (*gaitu guiliu*) could be achieved
once and for all.

The Yao ethnologists and social historians who study the *shipai* have seen
a similar process of military, administrative, and cultural expansion at work
in the history of the Chinese nation. Yao scholars differ from von Glahn,
Herman, Cushman, Weins, and other historians of Chinese frontier expansion in that they want to understand these processes from below. Yao elite
have sought to write a subaltern perspective into these narratives of imperial expansion and non-Han peripheral localities to give voice to a subject
they see as long ignored, if not silenced, in the historiography of China.
They have recovered this subaltern subject by searching the many local and
regional gazetteers produced during the Ming and Qing, but also by documenting the memories and oral histories of elders. We have to be careful,
however, in how we understand and theorize the recovery of this subject.
As I argued in the previous chapter, Yao scholars and others who have written on Yao history have continued to resort to the evolutionary imaginaries

of Marx, Engels, Morgan, and others. The *shipai*, for instance, is seen to contain in its most fundamental form characteristics of the primitive commune system, a term that comes to them from Marx's take on Morgan's writing on ancient societies. Thus, although the *shipai* is understood as an important social institution in the history of the Yao people, and although it reveals much about local ethnic engagements with successive technologies of imperial rule, it is interpreted as having an ambivalent, double character (*you shuangchong de xingzhi*). On the one hand, it is a "superstructural" (*shangceng jianzhu*) reflection of the feudal social order of prerevolutionary China, and on the other, it contains certain characteristics (*tezheng*) of the primitive commune system.

For minority intellectuals trained in ethnology and the social sciences in China, feudalism marks the beginning of modern history. The primitive commune system, in contrast, is resolutely premodern, providing access to a time and space before the advent of the modern. Thus, though the Yao subject has been written into the history of the People's Republic by following this subject's movement through the time of the nation, traces of this subject are also recoverable in the premodern communal form. The image of a primitive commune has therefore allowed for the recovery of certain modes of indigenous social organization and cultural process, all of which are seen to have been instrumental in the formation of a unified Yao consciousness. As Huang Yu, Su Defu, Liu Yulian, and other Yao scholars have argued, the *shipai* represents the best of how the Yao have creatively adapted to the exigencies of imperial rule. It wears the double mask of feudalism and primitivism, yet it is nonetheless seen as a cultural and social innovation produced by marginalized subjects who were forced deep into the mountains and subjected to the ruthless and violent expansionary policies of Imperial China. In the 1950s and 1960s, Party cadres saw it as a technology of local rule contaminated by class relations and local forms of ethnic chauvinism. In the 1980s, it gained new meaning as a cultural innovation that historically allowed the different Yao groups living in the Dayaoshan to overcome their differences, unify as a people, and resist the intrusions of outsiders seeking to impose their will. Many Yao thus argue that it should be studied, respected, and perhaps even emulated.

Some ethnologists have suggested that the *shipai* system is similar in both form and practice to the village compact systems found in Han regions in pre-1949 China.[41] It seems that both systems were set up to ensure local social order, to facilitate resource and land tenancy arrangements, to regulate trade and punish those who offended established codes for correct behavior, and to organize defense units during conflicts either between competing Yao groups or between Yao and outsiders. The articles or tenets (*tiaowen*) of the *shipai*, sometimes referred to as *gongyue* or *shipai lu*, were both orally transmitted and carved on wood or stone; some were written down in booklets. In some villages, these carved tablets were publicly displayed; usually, however, they were held in the possession of the *shipai* leaders. In the 1940s, after the Guomindang entered the area and outlawed *shipai* organization, Yao leaders began to consciously record the history and organization of the *shipai*, just as they collected and stowed away the actual tablets. Most of the contemporary knowledge about the *shipai* in the Dayaoshan derives from the work of the first investigative teams referred to above.[42] As I will explore in more detail in the next chapter, the Party resurrected the *shipai*, in form, in the early 1950s in its local mobilization efforts. For example, the short-lived Dayaoshan Unification Pact (*Dayaoshan tuanjie gongyue*), signed in 1951 by representatives of the Yao and Party cadres to promote political unity among the region's five subgroups, was modeled directly on the *shipai*.

The *shipai*, then, was a mode of community surveillance organized by village leaders, the *touren*. These leaders entered into positions of authority not through rights of inheritance, but through their proven ability to mediate conflict and effectively organize production and defense. Organizationally, the most prominent *touren* were located in the Chashan Yao villages in the present-day Jinxiu County seat, and they commanded a mountainwide system made up of smaller and more diffuse regional units. The dominant Chashan Yao *touren* thus oversaw the entire system; every Yao village was subject to the *shipai* rule, requiring *touren* throughout the mountains to maintain frequent contact. The term *shipai* thus refers both to the actual tablet used in the recording of the system's legal code and to the units of "village" organization. A single *shipai* could comprise anywhere from one to ten villages, but, in some instances, *shipai* overlapped so that at any one time a village could belong, and thus be subjected to, the authority of more than one *shipai*. For example, a single village often belonged to a *shipai* that regulated production and to one that mobilized defense teams. This is one reason why ethnologists and historians of the Yao have found it difficult to determine precisely just how many *shipai* units existed. A *shipai* would form, disband, and, when the situation demanded, once again come together. I was often told that it is impossible to fix the number because of this shifting nature of formation and dissolution. Nonetheless, most official documents claim that thirty-two different stone tablet groups once existed in the Dayaoshan, a number derived from the reflections of Yao elders collected in the 1950s during the first social and history investigations.

In theory, every Yao was subjected to at least one *shipai touren*. However, it was not uncommon for a more prestigious *touren* to be requested to adjudicate conflict in another *shipai*. This was usually the case for the *shipai touren* in the Chashan Yao villages around Jinxiu, who often traveled to other parts of the hills to assist in the mediation of disputes, ferret out punishments, and organize defense units. The significance of this is that Yao across the expanse of the mountains were exposed to an assortment of different *touren*, which provided a kind of flow and movement of authority across the region's different groups. On the one hand, then, flexibility was built into the system. The system was hierarchically ranked, but a leader skillful and fair in judgment (*pingli*) worked to unite the various Yao regions and groups within the mountains around a common moral code. Moreover, *shipai* enforcement only came into effect in moments of crisis and conflict, when crimes occurred (pillaging was the most common, but rape and murder were not unheard of), when taxes were not paid to landowners, and so forth. On the other hand, the system was very rigid, for the landless Guoshan Yao group was essentially excluded from positions of rank. This practice of exclusion is evidenced in the fact that very little intermarriage occurred between the Changmao and Shanding Yao peoples. The landless Yao could never afford to marry into the landowning families and the tenets of the *shipai* largely forbade intermarriage. This allowed control of the system to remain in the hands of the large landowning families.[43]

The real power of the *shipai* system rested in the headmen's right to define the nature of local transgressions. For instance, the more influential *shipai touren* determined when it was necessary to establish a new *shipai*, a new code of tenets. They decided on the nature of the new code (*gongyue*) and only then did they convene a large meeting (*shipai hui*), at which every household was required to have a member in attendance. Because of the socially ritualized nature of these meetings (which entailed some feasting and drinking and the presence of a Taoist ritual specialist to bless the proceedings), they were major community events. A *touren* noted for oratory skills was selected and he or she chanted out (what the Yao call *liaohua*) the new tenets, proclaiming publicly why they were necessary and what they hoped to achieve. This was thus an occasion for public discussion, when village commoners were given the opportunity to voice their opinions and express their agreements and disagreements. This flavor of villagewide, public debate, in which the *shipai touren* subjected their leadership and visions for social order to public scrutiny, led early Party researchers to see the *shipai* as a form of primitive democratic socialism. In these public arenas of debate, the masses were seen to be exercising a form of local self-rule.

The early focus on the dynamics of local self-rule did not mean, of course, that Party leaders embraced the *shipai* leadership. Party documents from the immediate post-1949 period reveal a widespread belief that the *shipai* system and its leadership had to be dismantled through the gentle force of propaganda and persuasion. By the time the land reform (*tudi gaige*) campaign began in 1953, government and Party cadres were implementing the central policy of the CCP that different regions and nationalities exhibited complications (*you quzhe*) and distinctions (*you qubie*) that should be respected. Though there was a landlord problem in Jinxiu, and though the Changmao group owned and controlled the majority of the land, the problem was not deemed to be as severe as in many Han areas. Class struggle was thus carried out with an eye turned toward the particularities of local Jinxiu society. Cadres emphasized the complex relations and interactions between what they saw as the region's two economic classes, the Changmao and Guoshan Yao, and the five different Yao subgroups, which were seen more as autochthonous cultural units with their own languages, mythologies, origin myths, and cultural practices.

The economic realm was thus initially seen as separate from the cultural. The Changmao Yao–Guoshan Yao groups defined the nature of the economic landscape, with the five subgroups representing the ethnic landscape in its most fundamental primordial forms of difference. Cadres who first visited this region argued that class interests manifested themselves through a range of different forms of exploitation and oppression that sometimes replicated the economic division between landowners and the landless. But forms of exploitation also existed among families and individuals in the landless Guoshan Yao economic category. These forms were mostly evident in modes of social interaction, exchange of goods and services, and stipulations against intra-ethnic marriage and sexual intercourse. Cadres felt that they had become totally naturalized and ingrained in the social fabric of the region and that they could only be extinguished through political outreach and consciousness raising. Despite the fact that the division between two main economic groups defined most forms of social and political interaction, all five of the groups were marked as objects of education and material and cultural transformation. Only in this way could the Dayaoshan be lifted up and brought within the fold of the revolution.

Before long, the labels Changmao Yao and Guoshan Yao were officially banished from everyday use. Cadres began to argue that these social categories too easily called to mind the history of intra-ethnic forms of exploitation, a history that was now to be left behind with the defeat of the Guomindang and the Liberation of the hills. They also believed that the class antagonisms that existed before land reform would simply disappear with the reallocation of land and wealth. Yet the local landscape could not so easily be redefined, and past modes of interaction, prejudice, and social hierarchy did not disappear. This became abundantly clear with the collectivization movement begun in the mid-1950s. Collectivization required the various groups that had been forbidden to interact socially under the rules of the *shipai* to now live and work together. Yet, because these groups were now forced to live, work, and eat together, class antagonisms and associated ethnic stereotypes and modes of discrimination were resurfacing with new force and intensity. By the 1950s, the Party and county government together would call for more vigilant struggle against these "feudal" and "class-based" modes of thinking. The Yao subgroups that belonged to the former Changmao Yao economic category were increasingly seen to harbor dangerous counterrevolutionary sentiments. The subgroups that belonged to the Guoshan Yao category were increasingly marked as the true subaltern agents; they defined the space in which revolutionary sentiment could be found and harnessed. Yet, as one former county chief in retirement told me, these calls for vigilance against the remnants of the Changmao group backfired, for they only further alienated different Yao subgroups from each other and from the Party cadres working in the mountains.

Toward the end of the 1950s, then, the relationship between past forms of class exploitation and local ethnic relations—and the enduring question of what to do about their capacity to resurface in the revolutionary present—led to heated and sometimes acrimonious debates among Party cadres. How to maintain the struggle against the "remnants" of the Jinxiu landed gentry? How to remake the consciousness of the mountain Yao, regardless of their position in the social landscape? How, in short, were these cadres and government officials—many of whom increasingly were Yao, we must recall—to redefine the meaning of local society? Some argued that gains could be made through the support of local cultural customs, insisting, for instance, that Yao popular ritual and its associated ritual specialists should be respected if the Party was to continue to win support for the new regime. Others, however, saw ritual and other local cultural forms as too steeped in the past. With its local customs, religious specialists, and supernatural deities, Yao social life, they believed, followed a different spatial and temporal order than was necessary for active participation in the making of a socialist nation. In the late 1950s and throughout much of the 1960s, the winds of official policy began to blow in a different direction. Yao religious practice and its associated forms of social organization, which supported a hierarchy of ritual specialists, were soon labeled "feudal superstitions" (*fengjian mixin*). Local Party officials, sensitive to changes occurring in Beijing and other urban centers, began to see Jinxiu as a dangerous and contaminated place, where the remnants of once extant classes persisted into the present. Different Yao families, clans, and subgroups (*minzu zhixi*) were repeatedly criticized for having once engaged in forms of local exploitation to advance their own power and prestige.

The social history research team that arrived in Jinxiu in 1956 began to pick up on these shifts in the politics of ethnic and class interpretation. Though it fell somewhat out of their purview, some of the members of this team reported that rapid collectivization was having a negative effect on the local populace. With great risk to their own careers as cadres and scholars, they argued that collectivization efforts in Jinxiu were losing sight of Mao Zedong's dictum that class struggle was to be more gentle when carried out in minority regions. Mao believed, they pointed out, that only in this way could the Party win the support of the ethnic masses. When the social history research team left the Yao mountains toward the end of 1957, there was an abiding sense that improvements were needed in the way the Party was carrying out its "nationalities work" in the Dayaoshan. These reports and indeed the entirety of the social history research collected in Jinxiu in 1956 were never published, for the antirightist campaign of 1957 soon kicked into gear. Many of the scholars who participated in this social history research urged sympathetic Party leaders to protect them by not publishing what they correctly felt would be seen as capitalist or feudal interpretations of minority realities.

Their findings would not reach the printed page until 1983 and the publication of the *Guangxi Yaozu shehui lishi diaocha* (An investigation of the social history of the Guangxi Yao). The editors of the volume, including Huang Yu, attributed the suppression of these historical findings to the Red Guards and to the ultraleftist thinking (*jiyou sixiang*) of such figures as Lin Biao.[44] Now that the ultraleftists were defeated, the social history of the Dayao-shan could be revisited; the knowledge of the Jinxiu social world that had been collected in 1956 could enter the official record. This, in turn, would allow contemporary ethnologists and social historians to study the social history of the Dayaoshan to not only learn about this most important of Yao places, but also to see a successful application of Deng Xiaoping's principle of "seeking truth from facts." As we shall see when we examine Fei Xiao-tong's view of the Jinxiu situation, this search for truth meant not letting ideological considerations or the demands of a political campaign guide the nature of one's social scientific inquiries. It meant the end of ideology and the emergence of a more rational and scientific appreciation of the history of class and ethnic tension among the Jinxiu Yao.

In the early 1980s, after the third national census, there were 58,289 people living in Jinxiu County, of which 33,731 were members of the Yao *minzu*. Five Yao subgroups lived in the hills; the Pan Yao were the largest. As I indicated previously, I had come to Jinxiu at the invitation of several Cha-shan Yao scholars. The Chashan Yao constituted a little less than 27 percent of the population and mostly lived in the fertile valleys. They were addition-ally the dominant group living in the vicinity of the county administrative seat, also known as Jinxiu. Along with two other smaller groups known as the Ao Yao and the Hualan Yao, they belonged to the landowning Chang-mao Yao class before Liberation, and much of their economic and political power had been depleted over the past thirty years. Before Liberation, land-owning and nonlandowning groups rarely if at all married, and the elders (*touren*) of the Chashan Yao forbade various forms of social intercourse with any of the renters. A strict and sometimes ruthless ethnic hierarchy was maintained in the mountains. As I mentioned above, the laws and public edicts of the stone tablet system supported this social hierarchy, a system of political and social organization that many claimed was indigenous to the Dayaoshan. In the early 1950s, Party cadres saw this system as central to the maintenance of the divisions between the landowning and landless groups. They also recognized that the forms of exploitation and oppression were rampant throughout the mountains; the relationship among local forms of economic and political power, class, and ethnicity were highly complex and difficult to discern. The *shipai* was seen as fully entrenched in the local social order, based on class divisions but also on assumed notions of cultural dis-tinction and hierarchy. As conflict emerged in the collectivization process, local Party authorities began to move away from their earlier position that it was necessary to use more gentle mobilization strategies in ethnic minority regions. The landless groups were encouraged to speak out against the landowners; large public struggle sessions were organized. Many of the leaders of the Changmao group, seen as the local agents of the feudal system, were increasingly linked to the Guomindang "bandits" who still roamed the hills after 1949. By the mid-1950s, many would be imprisoned or executed.

So far, I have attempted to show how the research and propaganda efforts of Party research teams in the 1950s brought new interpretations and meanings to the question of Jinxiu's place in the making of a socialist nation. This process of instilling meaning into the local social landscape resurfaced again in the 1980s. Already a complex figure in the history of the People's Republic, Jinxiu continued its career as a contested signifier in the imagining of the Chinese nation. As we shall see, the question of socialism and the history of practices of ethnic classification and struggles against local hegemons resurfaced again and again in my interviews and, more obliquely, in some published writings. Memories of the 1950s and 1960s haunted the imagining of a harmonious and united multiethnic national order in the 1980s. Jinxiu, as a Yao place, was subjected to competing conceptions of the practice of ethnic classification and the question of which group now, after the Cultural Revolution, spoke for the "socialist modern," Deng Xiaoping's new slogan for development after Mao. Minority scholars and others turned to popular ritual and the meanings of social morality to secure a place for "traditional culture" in the modernization of Jinxiu. Cha-shan Yao intellectuals were especially invested in these research projects, as they tried to play a leading role in local debates about development and as they attempted to rethink the history of the involvement of their people in pre-Liberation modes of exploitation and oppression. They also paid close attention to Fei Xiaotong, one of the first Han to do research in the Yao mountains in the 1930s and one of the most influential anthropological and sociological researchers in all of China.

"Dissecting" the Local

In the mid 1980s, Fei penned the introduction to a book written by two of his former students at the Central Nationalities Institute in Beijing, Hu Qiwang and Fan Honggui. The book, one of the first full-length ethnographies of a minority group to appear in post-Mao China, was simply titled *Pancun Yaozu*, or *The Yao of Pan Village*. Fei was asked to introduce the book because he had previously urged them to conduct a social investigation in the Dayaoshan, the very site of his first ethnological research in the 1930s.[45] He begins by explaining that after he graduated from the Graduate School of Qinghua University and went to study abroad in 1935, he heeded the suggestion of his advisor, Professor Shi Luguo, to conduct a field investigation in a minority area. In the fall of 1935, he entered the Dayaoshan with his wife, Wang Tonghui. They divided the work. He was to conduct physical investigations on residents in the Dayaoshan, and she was to concentrate on a social investigation of the Hualan or "blue-flower" Yao living on the southern flank of the mountains. He recounts the tale of her tragic death: "On December 16, 1935, on the way from a Hualan Yao area to an Ao Yao area, I accidentally fell into a hunter's trap and my legs were wounded. My wife ran down the mountains for help and was drowned in the dark. Though I was rescued from the mountains, that investigation was never completed. During the recovery period, I sorted out the materials left by my wife and edited her work into a volume."

He then goes on to explain how the materials he himself had collected on the physical characteristics of the Yao were lost in Kunming. The loss of this material haunted Fei, and, as he explains, he long wanted to return to Jinxiu to follow up on the study. This opportunity came in 1978, when he was invited to attend the twentieth anniversary of the founding of the Guangxi Zhuang Autonomous Region; the celebration would be carried out in Nanning, the provincial capital. He travels during this time to the Dayaoshan, his first visit in over forty-five years. He meets many old friends and has long discussions about Jinxiu society. This leads him to reflect on a number of unanswered questions: In what ways were the Yao people formed throughout the long stretch of Chinese history? What are the special characteristics one finds among minorities such as the Yao who have lived so long in mountain environments? What has been the direction of their development? And finally, the methodological question: How does one begin to study these questions? (2)

On the surface, this all seems innocuous enough. But astute readers in China would quickly recognize that Fei is measuring his words carefully, that he is writing in a period, the early 1980s, when the actual direction and focus of ethnological research was still being debated by leading scholars and Party officials at nationality research institutes around China. Fei thus begins with the common observation that the Yao are a nationality with a long history. "As early as the South and North Dynasties, we find the name 'moyao' in Chinese records. This name for the Yao can be seen in the poems of the great Tang poets Du Pu and Liu Yuxi. The earliest Yao ancestors are generally referred to in the Chinese records as barbarians. From the existing written records we can discern that the Yao lived in the mountains south of the middle reaches of the Changjiang, from Hunan province to Guangdong province" (2). Fei goes on to acknowledge the extensive research on the historical origins and migration routes of the Yao since the Tang dynasty. A crucial moment then occurs in the text as he outlines the view he has long had on how the Yao have maintained a sense of unity (*tuanjie*) through the centuries. This is a sensitive topic because there are many scholars in China who would argue that the Yao were never really a unified people until after Liberation. This is crucial because, as we saw in the previous chapter, the assumption of Yao unity throughout the long stretch of Chinese history has been central to the writing of a standard history (*jianshi*) of the Yao people. Additionally, Fei seems to be questioning the basic Stalinist definition of just what constitutes a nationality group, and he is implicitly raising the question of just how a common Yao identity has been formed given the heterogeneous linguistic, cultural, and territorial nature of the group.

Fei explains that he has always believed there are some basic characteristics defining the Yao as a distinct people, and that these characteristics have been passed on from generation to generation. He points out that they are a mobile people who have lived in different areas of the country at different times. This has meant that some of the subgroups have been scattered over vast territories, whereas others, presumably not unlike the Han, have been able to live for long periods of time in compact communities. The nature of Yao society and its economy has naturally experienced many changes, and it is this growth and development that constitutes for Fei the core of Yao history. Fei explains that he has always assumed that the origins of the Yao can be derived from Chinese historical materials, that there is a fundamental line passing through Yao history regardless of the plethora of names for the group found in the historical record. This is common sense in his view, for who would question the argument that all human beings reproduce themselves from generation to generation? He has long believed that all nationalities existing today have origins that can be traced far back into the Chinese past. Fei then distances himself from this long-held belief and claims that his thinking has been too simplistic, that it just doesn't accord with the concrete process of how the Yao have formed as a people (3). His views, he acknowledges, have actually hindered his quest for a deeper understanding of the nature of Yao history.

Fei then turns to the question of the nature of ethnic diversity in the Dayaoshan. In the present historical moment, there are five different autochthonous names in use for the people who identify themselves as Yao. We are already familiar with these: Chashan Yao, Hualan Yao, Ao Yao, Pan Yao, and Shanzi Yao. Except for the Ao Yao, the Chinese names for the groups are not based on direct translations of their own pronunciations. For example, the Chashan Yao call themselves Lajia; the Hualan Yao call themselves the Jiongnai; the Pan Yao call themselves the Mian; and the Shanzi Yao refer to themselves as the Jindiemen. Despite these self-appellations, all of these groups readily admit they are Yao, yet they never add the character Yao to their own names. That is, they do not call themselves the Lajia Yao or the Jiongnai Yao. It is very possible, Fei argues—and here again he is measuring his words carefully—that the term Yao is nothing more than a name that has been placed on a diverse group of people by the Han Chinese. Yet this name is nonetheless used, he points out, by these five different subgroups to designate a common collective ethnic entity, the Yao *minzu*.

Fei is fascinated if a bit perplexed by this seemingly muddled linguistic picture, for it implicitly raises important questions about the politics of naming different ethnic groups in China. He admits that when he first entered the Dayaoshan in the 1930s, he had no training in linguistics and therefore failed to examine the relationship among these five different groups from the perspective of language use. He simply viewed them as five different branches of the Yao people who happened to live in the Dayaoshan. He argues that the use of the term "branch" (zhi) in the word for ethnic subgroup (zhixi) mistakenly implies that all of these people have emerged from a single common root (3). This again is a subtle critique of a standard ethnological perspective in China, one that dates back at least to the 1950s minority identification projects. He admits that it is only on this trip to the Dayaoshan in 1978 that he learns that the Yao in this region don't all use the same language—a startlingly honest acknowledgment. There are three languages in use in the Dayaoshan: Mian, Bunu, and Lajia. They all belong to the Han-Tibetan language family, though they do not represent different dialects of one language. The Mian language, used by the Pan Yao, belongs to the Yao branch of the Miao-Yao language; Bunu, used by the Ao Yao, belongs to the Miao branch of the Miao-Yao language, and is quite close to

A Pan Yao family.

the language used by the majority of the Miao minzu. The Lajia language belongs to the Dong-Shui branch of the Zhuang-Tong language, which is very similar to the language spoken by the Tong minzu and the Zhuang, two large minority groups residing in other parts of Guangxi.

These diverse languages suggest that the five subgroups have entirely different origins. This is a brash statement, for it raises the possibility that the various peoples of the Dayaoshan were once not of the same nationality, which, administratively speaking, would mean the Party had made a mistake classifying this region as an autonomous county. Fei states in no uncertain terms his new hypothesis: It was only after these various peoples entered the Dayaoshan that a common Yao identity was formed. A new metaphor is proposed: These peoples do not represent branches of the same root, but are rather more like a river composed of many different tributaries. When we refer to them as branches, he states, what we really mean is tributaries. Fei wants to jettison the use of the term branch, but he will not go so far as to think of these groups as constituting different minority nationalities, or minzu. Fei is again careful in this regard, for such a position would be to question the entire history of Yao identification in China. For Fei, the Yao of the Dayaoshan are most certainly a collective national entity; it is only the nature of their origins and the historical process of collective formation that is open to question.

Fei then delves into the world of ethnic legends and indicates that these five subgroups migrated into the Dayaoshan by different routes and at different times. The Chashan Yao entered the mountains from Guangdong through Wuzhou, Guangxi. They then lived for a period in Deng Xian and Pingnan before they entered the Dayaoshan. Another view has it that the Chashan Yao entered the Dayaoshan from Hunan after crossing Xingzhou, Guixian, and Xiangzhou. The Hualan Yao entered the mountains from Guizhou after crossing Liuzhou and Xiangzhou. The Pan Yao were long ago driven from Hunan, and then made their way into the mountains through the northeastern mountains of Guangxi. The Shanzi Yao came from Guangdong, entering the mountains through Pingnan. Finally, the Ao Yao moved into Guangxi from Guizhou to Guangxi, having worked far to the south through Baise. Each of these groups has a different opinion about who entered the mountains first. One view holds that the Pan Yao and the Shanzi Yao, who never possessed their own land, arrived after the other three. This view is based on the assumption, Fei explains, that the Chashan Yao, Hualan Yao, and Ao Yao had already occupied the region's arable land. The Pan

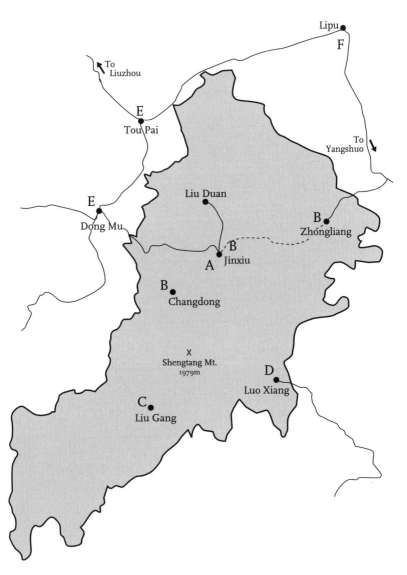

Jinxiu Yao Autonomous County

Yao, however, think they entered the mountains earlier; because they had long been nomadic, they claim they never sought to possess any land. Fei doesn't pursue this issue further. As we will see in a later chapter, this was a crucial debate among these groups when Communist Party cadres in the early 1950s began to organize the Pan Yao and the Shanzi Yao—the pre-Liberation Guoshan Yao social group—against the landowning Changmao Yao group.

For Fei, the Yao collectivity (*jituan*) is a muddled and confused (*buxiang huntong*) mess. I don't want to pursue how he supports this observation other than to point out that he focuses at some length on the fact that some subgroups share surnames and others do not. He also discusses the genealogy of some of the Yao groups, in particular the Pan Yao, to show that the analysis of surnames and genealogy suggests that the Dayaoshan is a collective cultural entity that has experienced long and complex histories of interethnic borrowings, including adoptions. For Fei, the Dayaoshan collectivity is not a static (*yicheng bubian*), pure blood group (*xueyuan jiti*), what ethnologists might call a race (*zhongzu*). The point he is driving at—the lesson for contemporary Chinese ethnology—is that the question of how an ethnic minority comes into formation must be analyzed in terms of concrete historical processes and contexts. To understand the formation of the Dayaoshan Yao, one cannot rely on language use, for the region is littered with different languages and dialects. Likewise, one cannot rely on surname comparison and reconstruction or on blood types to determine what constitutes a Yao collectivity. Fei therefore lays out a theoretical challenge for his readers. What, he asks, is the cohesive force (*ningjuli*) that gives form to a collective ethnic identity? To what degree can we think of common identity given the obvious differences that exist among the Yao in terms of language, custom, and economy? When did a Yao collective consciousness (*minzu gongtong yishi*) originate? How has it been transformed throughout the broad sweep of history? If we can assume that the Yao once lived in a common area, and that this group dispersed into different areas over time, then how did they maintain their collective consciousness? Is it possible for an ethnic group to absorb or assimilate (*xishou*) cultural and linguistic elements from other groups and still strengthen its identity? Only by considering these sorts of questions—all of which, incidentally, implicitly call into question the widespread idea that the Yao have long shared a common identity and history—will ethnology thrive in the future, Fei argues (5).

What really concerns Fei is the question of just what constitutes the Chi-

A Chashan Yao musician and daughter of the ethnologist Liu Yulian.

nese nation. He sees the Chinese nation as having a long history, yet it is a complex and ever changing entity that seems to resist generalization. He argues that the present state of knowledge of the nation's history is so sparse that it is even difficult to know much about the formation process of the Han. This even despite the fact that the Han have a long history of written records and are currently the most populous nation in the world! It is easy for ethnologists to see that the People's Republic is made up of more than fifty nationalities, yet little is known, Fei argues, about how the cohesion of the nation has been accomplished. For Fei, the study of the history of the Yao in the Dayaoshan provides a window into the study of the formation of the Chinese nation as a whole (6). Fei advocates what he calls the micro case study (*weixing yanjiu*). The analysis of local processes of identity formation will reveal little by little the general rules that apply to all nationalities. The major task for the new generation of minority nationality researchers is to seek out these rules through participant observation and the analysis of local conditions. This, in turn, will allow scholars to build theories of China's special national characteristics.

What, then, do we know about the historical processes of identity formation in the Dayaoshan? Ethnologists know from the existing source of historical materials that in the Ming dynasty the Yao lived in the Nanling Mountains, the area that comprises the borders of present-day Hunan, Guangdong, and Guangxi. The historical record reveals that Yao rebellions against the oppressive policies of China's feudal dynasties began in the Song dynasty. The center of the struggle against feudalism slowly moved with each generation from the north to the south, from low-lying valleys and hill country to more remote mountainous areas. As the Yao engaged in battle with each successive Chinese imperial regime, they (note that at this point Fei writes of the Yao as though they were a unified collectivity) were scattered into "the cold mountains," a process that would last for more than a thousand years. The last large-scale struggle would take place during the Ming in an area called Datengxia, not far from the present-day Dayaoshan. During this battle, the Ming dynasty mobilized thousands of troops and, over a period of one hundred years, conducted three large-scale massacres. Fei reports that the Yao community was devastated. After this struggle, from the late fifteenth century onward, they were continually forced to give up low-lying ground and take refuge in small, compact communities scattered over the highest mountain peaks of the south.

Fei reminds us that the Yao were not the only minority people who suf-

Three generations of Pan Yao.

fered this fate. The Miao experienced a similar history of violence and migration, as did the Dong and Shui peoples and other groups that once lived
in the Nanling Mountains. As these peoples were defeated they were effectively sent into exile, forced to migrate from one mountainous region to
the next. Mere survival was the central issue for many of them, Fei tells us.
The Yao eventually came upon the Dayaoshan, a remote place located in
the center of the Liu, Gui, and Jin Rivers, with some peaks of over nineteen
hundred meters towering above a hidden central plain. The Dayaoshan became a safe haven, for the steep grade of the surrounding peaks made them
easy to defend and difficult to penetrate. It is for these reasons, Fei tells us,
that the Yao have lived in this region for more than five hundred years with
very little interference from outsiders. It was not until the 1940s, with the
arrival of Guomindang troops, that the mountains were penetrated by yet
another oppressive force, a force not to be driven out until the arrival of the
Communist Party. This, then, is Fei's explanation for how a shared collective identity in the Dayaoshan comes into existence: histories of resistance,
migration, and retreat push disparate groups into isolated mountain country, where they come together to battle outsiders perceived as enemies. The
making of a Yao ethnic group went hand in hand with the formation of a
collective self-defense force. In Fei's view, the struggle to survive and defend common interests was the cohesive force that led disparate groups to

identify with each other and eventually accept the name Yao. Differences in language, custom, and habits (*fengsu xiguan*) are not to be interpreted as disintegrating or fragmenting factors. They merely characterize the nature of an internally diverse ethnic group that has long stood up for its rights and protected lands it claimed as its own (8).

To further explicate this point about cohesion and unity in the face of oppressive outsiders, Fei has to negotiate a politically sensitive topic in the study of the Jinxiu Yao. This topic harks back to the early Party mobilization efforts in the 1950s and the first official Party proclamations on the class situation in the Dayaoshan. Fei begins by recounting his first trip to the Dayaoshan in the 1930s. He remembers how at this time he was deeply impressed by the high moral standards of the Yao and their ability to maintain social order. He noted then that each of the various subgroups in the area kept marriage within their own clan and that this was due in part to the fact that the rules of the stone tablet system, the *shipai zhidu* mentioned earlier, forbade intermarriage between different Yao groups. As I argued above, many people in Jinxiu spoke to me of this system as a clever social innovation, one that they used to protect themselves against outside intervention. Fei himself stands in wonder at the genius of a local system of authority and law (he does not employ the term "primitive law" used by other ethnologists) that could successfully get a local populace to obey its rules and regulations. This obedience to a local rule of law brought stability to the mountains before the Guomindang arrival and helped forge solidarity among different groups. Nonetheless, he is forced to admit that the system was based on contradictions (*maodun*) and that these were of an exploitative (*boxue*) nature.

How, then, to interpret these contradictions, and how did they become manifest in everyday social relations? He answers this question by reminding us that the five current groups—the Chashan, Hualan, Ao, Pan, and Shanzi Yao—were once divided into mountain lords and tenants. As we saw earlier, the first three constituted what the Guomindang and other Han outsiders once called the Changmao Yao group. The last two, called the Guoshan Yao, paid rent, land, and labor service, the terms of which were established and enforced by the *shipai* system. Obviously, Fei notes, under such a system economic development would be unbalanced. The Changmao Yao, with their ownership of land, used the flat land in the mountain valleys to plant paddy rice. No real gap exists between them and the Han and Zhuang outside the mountains in terms of agricultural technology and development; they produced high-quality rice. The Shanzi Yao and the Pan Yao, on the other hand, with no ownership rights, were forced to rent lands on infertile mountain slopes, and they often adopted the technique of slash-and-burn cultivation. As the fertility of the land decreased, they were forced to move to other hillsides. This prevented them from settling down in one place. Many officials in Jinxiu told me that getting these groups to settle down after the founding of the People's Republic was essential for the social development of the Guoshan Yao groups, though Fei does not pursue this argument in his text. He does tell us that the output of corn and upland rice was extremely low on these mountain slopes, supporting only one or two households; many Pan and Shanzi Yao in fact never lived in villages of larger than several households. These groups were additionally subjected to a system called "returning the land with planted trees" (*zhongshu huizu*), requiring them to plant trees on the mountain slopes they rented from the mountain landlords; when the saplings matured, they could not be burned for fertilizer but rather were returned to the landlords as rent in kind. This was the system that forced the Guoshan Yao to move frequently from one slope to the next, yet their movements would only take them into another area controlled by the Changmao Yao and enforced by the *shipai*. The cycle of "rent in kind" would be repeated once again.

The argument comes full circle, and Fei asks again how it was that this exploitative relationship did not cause social disintegration. Now he provides an answer. In the 1940s, he argues, the main contradiction was between the groups in the mountains (the Yao collectivity) and those that lived outside, namely, the reactionary Guomindang forces. Certainly there were contradictions, exploitative economic relationships, and even class antagonisms between the Changmao and Guoshan Yao groups. Yet these contradictions never resulted in the Guoshan Yao rising up against the landlords because the landless group saw it in their interests to identify with the landlords in the struggle against the Guomindang penetration of the hills. As we saw in the writing of an official history of the Yao in the 1980s, class and ethnic antagonisms are resolved by overcoming systems of oppression and exploitation external to the minority itself. This narrative is propelled by the invocation of a split not within the mountains but between the isolated mountain community and the feudal empires of the past, of which the Guomindang are the most recent example. Despite the Yao ability to unify in moments of danger, and despite the fact that landless groups saw it in their best interest to support their apparent oppressors, such a system could only result in a static and backward economy and in a local culture isolated and conservative in nature. All of this, Fei tells us, comes to an end with the establishment of the new China, as he begins to speak the ritual language of national unification seen in much of the ethnological writing of the 1980s (9). Not only have the diverse Yao groups in the Dayaoshan gained equal status with other minority nationalities, but the exploitative historical relationships among different Yao groups have been abolished. The system of mountain landlords and mountain tenants is a figment of the past. These fundamental changes in the nature of local societies and in ethnic relations have allowed different minorities to achieve social and economic development, to catch up with the advanced standard of the world — to become, in short, modernized nationalities.

Fei ends his preface with an appeal to all future minority researchers: To understand situations such as the Dayaoshan, it is necessary to analyze the concrete situations that have led to the formation of collective ethnic identities. On the one hand, he says, we know that different ethnic groups share many common characteristics; yet, on the other hand, we also know that each has its own unique characteristics (*tedian*). We have to start, he argues, with the technique called *jiepo maque*, or "dissecting a sparrow." We have to discover all of the different types of minority characteristics, compare them with each other, and then discover their general character. The Yao of the Dayaoshan, for example, is only one part of the larger Yao *minzu* group (spread throughout China), which in turn is only one part of the big family of the Chinese nation. He provides some statistics. There are more than 1.2 million Yao in total (a population figure from the late 1970s) scattered in more than 130 counties in six provinces. Sixty-seven percent, or about 800,000, live in Guangxi; 30,000 of these people live in the Dayaoshan, about 2.5 percent of the total population. That 30,000 Yao would live in such a compact area is a rarity among this group. The average population of the Yao living in any county in China is less than 10,000. If there is any one Yao community worth "dissecting," it is most surely the Dayaoshan, where five different groups have a set of common characteristics as well as their own unique ones. Their languages are different, their degree of economic development is different; there are also differences in customs and everyday habits. "Dissecting a sparrow" requires working from one group to the next and building comparisons from there.

Fei imagines the Dayaoshan as a kind of laboratory for the testing of ethnological ideas about ethnic formation and ethnic change. It is a scene of past forms and practices of exploitation. These modes of exploitation sometimes occurred among people of the same group. They more often occurred between an isolated group and a feudal power such as the Ming rulers during the Datengxia suppression (discussed in the next chapter) or the Guomindang reactionaries who sought to "open" (*kaihua*) the mountains and bring to the Yao the culture of the more advanced Han. Although these mountains provide a space for the dissecting gaze of the ethnologists, they also provide moral and political lessons about historical progress. Fei is especially impressed by one of the themes developed in the book *Pancun Yaozu*: the narrative that the Yao have successfully moved from a state of isolation (*fengbi*) to one of openness (*kaifang*; 12). This process began with the abolition of feudal forms of oppression and with the Party's declaration that all minorities would now be equal under the law. I am repeating myself here, but only to capture a sense of the ritual repetition in Fei's text. In the past, there was no equality; all minorities were subjected to oppression and discrimination. Feudal rulers, unable to penetrate the remote mountains, set up systems of blockade. Daily necessities such as salt and tea were forbidden to enter these areas, as were tools for production and advanced forms of weaponry. Stalemates such as these, which kept groups in isolation, were detrimental to the social and economic development of all minority peoples.

Moral judgments and ethnic stereotypes begin to creep into the text. For the first time in his essay, Fei tells us that this historical situation led to an isolation psychology (*fengbi xinli*) among minority peoples. Their unfortunate experiences created a consciousness that led them to move further away from the forces of oppression, to find places to be safe, away from the ugliness of feudal history. They became indifferent to the outside world, suspicious of outsiders, and interested only in people like themselves. Isolation, for Fei, is not a natural condition for the human subject; it is an undesirable product that has come with a history of oppression. The CCP destroyed the blockade policy and replaced it with a policy of mutual assistance among all ethnic minorities. And what is the nature of this mutual assistance? Under the current regime, it is to call on the more advanced Han to provide both material and intellectual assistance to backward minority peoples. This requires the Han to overcome the historic practice of great Han chauvinism (*hanzu zhuyi*), and minorities to change their stubborn clinging to an ideology of isolation (*zifeng de sixiang*; 12). Social and cultural exchange among different peoples is the key to common prosperity. In the great march of the socialist construction, it has become more and more evident that minority peoples cannot prosper without the Han people, and the Han cannot do the same without minorities (13).

What is the place of scientific ethnology in all of this? For Fei, scientific research is the process of knowing the objective world. This process moves from the rough to the fine, the shallow to the deep, the partial to the comprehensive (13–14). A proper scientific disposition is one that seeks truth from facts, is persistent and not self-satisfied. For Fei, this process of knowing is never-ending: the more knowledge of reality we have, the more power we have to control the objective world. This is how human societies develop: step by step, increasing and renewing knowledge. Development is the gradual understanding and control over the objective world by the subjective human being.

Conclusion

I have undertaken this reading of Fei's work on the nature of Yao identity in the Dayaoshan to advance several arguments about the relationship between reform-era ethnology and the study of minority regions. The first is that Fei's narrative of mountain isolation, of struggle with feudal rulers and indigenous systems of exploitation is in fact quite consistent with the view expressed in evolutionary histories such as the *Jianshi*. This narrative of isolation is authored by one of China's most famous anthropologists, a scholar who claims his authority in part because he once did research in these distant hills. Fei shows us how different configurations of knowledge and different conceptions of research and science have been brought to the study of the Jinxiu Yao. In particular, he focuses his gaze on the question of how to understand the dialectic between identification and difference within the Yao group in the Dayaoshan. Second, the Yao case provides Fei with a venue to pursue his own theories about minority classification, questions of minority formation, and the more general yet nonetheless pressing and hotly contested issue about how to locate and define those points of diversity and unity within the Chinese nation. Ethnology, for Fei, remains an incomplete project. If it is to survive and thrive as a meaningful and useful disciplinary enterprise, then it must be infused with new research, new ideas, and new perspectives, all of which should be animated not by the dictates of ideology but by the realities of local social worlds. The nature of local conditions should determine the production of ethnological theory and the understanding of the nature of difference within the space of the Chinese nation. For Fei, nothing demonstrates this more than the Yao case in the Dayaoshan.

I hope it is clear that my intention has not been to take issue with Fei's interpretations in order to offer up a more accurate reading of Jinxiu. Rather, I have sought to situate his vision of the Dayaoshan in the context of post-Mao debates about what Maoist socialism did to ethnology and how it might possibly be recovered as a useful and coherent means of social inquiry. The Yao have to be an obscure object of knowledge for Fei, for it is this obscurity that propels the ethnological gaze. One should also note how his narrative skips selectively over the history of the People's Republic. We move with him from questions of pre-Liberation exploitation and local systems of rule to an image of the Communist Party as the agent of modernization and history, the agent that has freed the Yao from the yoke of the Guomindang and other rulers. Evidently, through a magical identification with the Party's vision of itself as a guiding force for change and historical progress, the Yao have found it in their interest to abandon their attachments to old and outmoded systems of authority and rule and to their psychology of isolation. Fei invites the Yao, a minority living in some of China's most remote land, to join the nation. He invites his Han compatriots to throw away their own sense of greatness and national superiority. He invites ethnologists to commit themselves to the principles of science, to discard ideological commitments and let the facts speak for themselves. He is also inviting the Yao to forget the history of pain and suffering that came with the excesses of the ultraleftists. He wants the Yao, and indeed the entire nation, to hold no grudges. He wants the people of China, and perhaps any reader who comes to his text, to see that Deng Xiaoping's nation is a very different regime of power and knowledge.

Fei's arguments touch on many issues that were being debated among Yao scholars and government officials interested in rethinking the history of Jinxiu. As I will show in the next chapter, a recurrent theme has been the question of how to interpret the historic relationship between the landlords and the landless (the Changmao–Guoshan Yao divide). Many also turned their attention to the indigenous *shipai* system and asked if it contained modes of traditional morality that, if properly harnessed and encouraged, might prove useful in the governing of Jinxiu in the post-Mao period. These research questions raise the issue of how to interpret the nature of Yao ethnic consciousness in the reform period. Did the Jinxiu Yao subject (or subjects) still retain, for example, a consciousness of its prerevolutionary modes of social morality, those modes of behavior and interaction that many believed maintained an ordered local social world before it was transformed first by the Guomindang and then by the revolutionary activists of the CCP? As we shall see, this question was informed by an assumption that fundamental distinctions could be drawn between revolutionary and traditional forms of consciousness, between modern and backward places, between the exploiters and the exploited, between the revolutionary and the reactionary.

These binaries were everywhere in my interviews, in the documents I read, in the stories I was told about the past and the making of Jinxiu into an autonomous Yao place. We might see them, in the manner of our best and most often quoted poststructuralist theories of the subject, as forms of representational violence. They are no doubt intricately tied to the will for modern power we have traced in our reading of the classificatory practices of both socialist and reform-era China. And they no doubt lead us into the thicket of all kinds of orientalist imaginings of difference within China and between China and the so-called West. Yet they also tell us something about the politics of minority intellectual work in the China of the late 1980s and early 1990s. These binaries have been central to how minority intellectuals talk about the nature of class hegemony in Jinxiu. They have enabled new interpretations of the historical reproduction of indigenous institutions of culture, authority, and political power, and new and often critical understandings of the disruption of indigenous practices by "modern" practices that attempted to "open" (kaihua) the hills and bring a "remote and underdeveloped" ethnic people within the fold of the new nation. They speak to the shifting terrain of China's moral geographies of place.

chapter three

Remembering Revolution

Political errors are political errors, and they have to be analyzed
and understood, not consigned to a waste-basket category called
"nationalism." —JAMES BLAUT, *The National Question: Decolonizing the*
Theory of Nationalism

By the spring of 1991 I had been living in Jinxiu for five months.
Because so few foreign anthropologists had lived in this region,
I was beginning to attract some attention from the residents of
the county seat. I was staying in the village of Xidi in the home of a local
Party member, the son of two of my research consultants in Beijing, Liu
Yulian and Su Defu. Many people in Xidi and the surrounding villages often
came by to visit, sometimes to just stand and stare, sometimes to be photographed with the *laowai*, the outsider, as I was sometimes called. It is late
one afternoon when I suddenly hear footsteps on the stairs that lead to my
room. A Mr. Huang is at the door. Huang is a cadre from the county's recently established tourism agency who claims to be a Yao himself, though
his father, as residents sometimes pointed out, was a Han. Lao Huang, as I
called him, has taken a liking to me, probably because he admires my ability
to drink with the village men, to play drinking games in the local Chinese
dialect, and to exchange cigarettes at the appropriate moment in the correct ritual fashion. He has told me on several occasions that he respects my
interest in things Yao, and my willingness to live in a region "as remote and
underdeveloped" as the Yao mountains. Huang fancies himself an expert on
local culture and he often boasts that he is much more knowledgeable than
the Yao scholars who visited the mountains from afar. On several occasions
already Huang has guided me into the mountains beyond the county seat

to attend weddings and observe and photograph Yao ritual activities (*yishi huodong*).

Early on in my research I sensed that Huang was different from other county officials, who tended to see the mountains beyond the bustling town of Jinxiu as dangerous terrain. Huang viewed the more distant Yao villages as areas of delight and splendor. These were places removed from the everyday tensions of bureaucratic life in the county seat, places where, he often argued, traditional culture flourished even while Yao peasants struggled daily with poverty and backwardness. On our several excursions into the mountain villages, Huang and I talked of how we felt free from these constraints, able to find time to visit and understand the common people (*laobaixing*). I too had taken to Huang. Within a very short time after my moving to Jinxiu, he became a trusted friend, an excellent informant, and a useful translator, fluent as he was in the region's three Yao languages. He was also immensely popular throughout the mountains, as many people seemed to ignore his history as an activist Red Guard during the height of the Cultural Revolution.

I greet Huang at the door and immediately sense his excitement. I'm anticipating another invitation into the hills. Yet the unexpected occurs, and I am taken out of my fantasy world in which Huang and I travel off into the hills and evade the surveillance of those officials who always sought to restrict my movements. I am being invited to participate in a television documentary depicting the "culture and history" of the Yao.

"Brother Li," Huang exclaims, "it is your day to become a famous Yao scholar. Everyone all over China will see you on the television. The Guangxi Provincial Television station is here to interview you. Come quick, please."

As we make our way down the village path and enter the main street of the town, I see that a contingent of journalists and cameramen have assembled at the bridge that spans the Jinxiu River. Many people view this bridge, named the Gongde Qiao after a Taoist ritual of community renewal, as a mixed icon of both the modern and the traditional. Recently refurbished with steel grates and thick planks of Chinese fir, it is painted in vibrant greens and blues and adorned with phoenixes and other lucky creatures from Chinese mythology. A cameraman is already busy choreographing the shoot. As I join him and several others, I overhear him instructing a young woman from the Tourism Bureau to walk across the bridge. I also learn that I am to be included in the shoot. He tells her to engage the for-

Lao Huang and friends.

eign anthropologist in conversation, and he shows her how to gesture with
her hands to the town that surrounds us and how to point to the paintings
on the rafters above our heads. Before I know it, our little drama is underway. We walk across the bridge, pleasantly taking in the sites around us.
A camera follows our every movement. She does all of the talking. I nod
my head in agreement, forcing an occasional smile, playing along with this
manufactured stroll across the Jinxiu River. When we reach the other side, a
journalist approaches us and the interview begins. The female tour guide is
now silent, her task almost complete. She is instructed to stand alongside
the anthropologist.

Without anyone's coaching me on what is about to take place, the interview begins. The journalist, a young man from Nanning, the capital city of
Guangxi, who I later learn is on his first trip to these mountains, turns to
the camera and provides some background information. "Mr. Li is a scholar
from America affiliated with the Central Nationalities Institute in Beijing.
He is a friend of the Yao and Chinese people, who has come to these splendid mountains to study the relationship between Yao traditional culture and
socialist modernization. Let us turn to Mr. Li, who speaks Chinese, and ask
him what he thinks about his stay in the Dayaoshan."

Journalist: Mr. Li, could you tell us about your impressions of the Yao people?

Anthropologist: The Yao are a very hardworking people with a long and glorious history. While they have their own languages, many Yao are literate in Chinese. They live in a very harsh environment, in which it is very difficult to make a living, but the Yao are a very hardy people making the best of their circumstances.

Journalist: So how do you pass your time here? I understand you are very busy studying Yao customs. Do you miss your home and your family?

Anthropologist: Well, of course, I sometimes feel homesick. However, the Yao have warmly welcomed me here and I feel as though I am a member of the family with whom I live. During the New Year I was very busy recording Yao rituals, marriages, and other local customs. But now I mostly interview older people, talking to them about history and the changes that have occurred in these mountains.

At this point Huang, who has been standing off to the side and conferring with a man I have never seen before, signals to me not to talk about local history. The journalist continues.

Journalist: So what are your impressions about China's socialist modernization effort here?

Anthropologist: Actually, I have many different thoughts about this problem. It is obvious that the streets are full of activity, many new shops have opened in recent years, and many people are making a lot of money. But, many new problems are arising.

Journalist (suddenly interjecting): Thank you, Mr. Li. Hope you have much success in your research. Good luck!

The interview is over as quickly as it began. Local officials gather around me, shaking my hand. Huang is boasting of my ability to climb mountains; several other men hand me their name cards, imploring me to visit if I am ever in Nanning, Liuzhou, or Guilin, the major cities in the valleys below. We are then asked to pose for photographs. From nowhere appear two young Yao women adorned in traditional Yao clothing, each representing the two dominant Yao subgroups found in the vicinity of the county, the Chashan Yao and the Pan Yao. They are first photographed alone and then together with the various members of the documentary team. They are familiar faces around the Tourism Bureau and this, I know from other similar kinds of documentary visits, is a typical part of their job. The photo session complete, I bid my farewells. The crowd that has gathered disperses.

This was not the only time I was interviewed by a provincial television station in the course of my fieldwork. Indeed, it was not rare for me to be asked to speak to larger audiences about my research interests, to share my thoughts about Yao culture and history and China's modernization effort. In most instances, I welcomed these opportunities. On this particular occasion, however, I felt a certain distance from the aims of the television crew and how they seemed to want to see the world of the mountains in which I had been living. On the one hand, I knew that this was just one more visiting "research" team here to photograph and document the peoples of Jinxiu for provincial and perhaps national consumption. On the other hand, as far as I could ascertain, these people had little interest in learning about and giving representational priority to the everyday problems Yao peasants were facing. They seemed to care little about the rising inflation in the local markets, grain shortages in the upper elevations of the hills, and problems with the Party's family planning methods. I understood clearly that it was not my place to address these issues in this particular context. Yet I nonetheless felt a desire to tell a different story, a story that would not simply be about the splendors of the Yao tradition, the colorful costumes of Yao women, or how Jinxiu was becoming daily, under the guiding wisdom of a now reformed Communist Party, a modern town in this remote region of southern China.

Several days after the television interview, I sat down with Lao Huang and attempted to explain my frustrations with these kinds of documentaries. I argued to him that we (to again reveal how I imagined that he and I somehow possessed the same complex of interests) had a responsibility to tell these journalists from outside the hills that the reforms were not all the central authorities thought they were. He laughed at me. "Who are we to think that we can tell a different history? The Yao in the hills have long been telling outside authorities what they wanted to hear. What would be gained in criticizing the reforms?" I asked him what would be the appropriate history to tell in this context. He left the room and I could hear the shuffling of papers in the distance. When he returned he handed me a photocopy of a five-page document called "Brief Introduction to the Yao Nationality in the Jinxiu Yao Nationality Autonomous County." It had been prepared, he told me, for the festival of King Pan (Panwang Jie) in November 1989, when an American delegation of Yao from Seattle and Portland had visited Jinxiu.

He pointed to one particular passage that explained the great changes that had occurred in the politics and economy of Yao society since the founding of the People's Republic of China. Here is what it said:

> In history, the Yao people had always been treated as a low-class nationality. They had suffered from the severe political repression and economic exploitation of the past feudalist ruling class. After the Yao autonomous county was founded, the Yao people became the main nationality in the county. The Yao people have the right and authority to make decisions for themselves in politics and economic construction. This change enabled the Yao people to fully exercise their talents and creativity in changing their country's backward look. Over thirty years, under the guidance of the nationality policies of the Chinese Communist Party, the Yao people's rights and authority as the master have been gradually reinforced and strengthened. Among the last nine county chiefs, eight of them were of the Yao nationality. At the end of 1987, there were a total of 3,432 cadres, among whom 2,442 were minority nationalities, making up 71.2 percent of the cadre body. Of these, 1,253 were Yao, or 51.3 percent of the minority nationality cadre.

This, Huang explained to me, was the story of how the Yao had taken control of their lives. Evidently, the Jinxiu Yao had become the masters of their destiny.

As I have argued in previous chapters, the writing of Yao history during the reforms has moved away from the strict class-based interpretations that dominated the first three decades of post-Liberation China. Throughout my work in Jinxiu, I was struck by the lack of reference to the political culture of Chinese socialism, which seemed to amount to a refusal to write the postrevolutionary subject into the history of the Yao people. The scholars involved in the research and writing of these histories told me that it was nearly impossible to detail the history of China's political campaigns and projects of socialist development in minority regions in these official histories. In my formal interviews with Party officials, Taoist priests, and government workers in Jinxiu, I was encouraged by my Yao academic friends and advisors to veer away from direct references to the events of the past twenty or thirty years. History after 1949 was off limits. Initially at least, no one wanted to talk about the Cultural Revolution, except by making vague illusions to the mistakes of the ultraleftists. Specific individuals were rarely named, in large part because many of them still lived in the villages and township in which I was working. I therefore assumed that events in the distant past would be a safer topic of inquiry. I quickly found this to be misguided, however, as even the interpretation of events in the 1920s—who brought the first Christian missionaries to the area, for example—were still being disputed and continued to inform contemporary social relations. A Taoist priest (*daogong*) in Jinxiu, Su Xianting, once told me about the eradication of Guomindang troops in the area in the early 1950s and the attempts of the then underground Communist Party cadre to win the trust of the Yao. He recounted the important actors and events in the underground movement, but also the exposure of families who harbored Guomindang sympathizers, of public executions, of Yao friends and families turned against each other. As he presented it, Yao history was tragic, filled with sadness, destruction, and betrayal. Yet he also assured me that there was much else that happened during and since the Cultural Revolution. There was eating and drinking, marriages and divorces, births and deaths—in short, a life that went on despite the many vicissitudes of any given political campaign.

Su Xianting was once an active member of the CCP in Jinxiu. A man of three marriages, a local authority on history and ritual, he became one of my best informants and also a good friend. He taught me social history (*shehui lishi*), local history (*difang lishi*), and Party history (*dang lishi*), parceling my knowledge along the same contours anyone could find in the official historiography of the People's Republic. I bought him books on the Great Leap and the Cultural Revolution during my trips to Beijing, Nanning, Guangzhou, and Hong Kong, books published in China that never made their way to the local bookstalls and the Jinxiu branch of the New China Bookstore (Xinhua Shudian). In the context of my research with him, I felt that we were reliving this history as we recorded it, wrote it down, taped it, and read articles and books on the history of Jinxiu and China. And yet, as I interviewed him and read through the documents I collected in libraries and archives, I kept searching for "other ways" of telling history. I was convinced that there must be a local historical epistemology that did not reiterate the official, Marxist-inspired history of the Party. I even attempted to uncover a Taoist conception of time in local narratives of ritual. Yet the language of progress, change, movement, and development constantly crept into the ways people reflected on the past. Even when the forward movement of history was suspended, when things were remembered as they once were (a temple along a river, a magical tree above a village, the wealth of a local

Su Xianting, center, attending to a ritual for a deceased Chashan Yao elder.

family), history was presented as a dialectical movement of destruction and construction. Because so much of the past social order had been destroyed, and because practices such as Yao Taoism were being quickly forgotten as elder practitioners passed away, it was necessary, Su argued, to organize ritual events, even if they were staged inventions for tourist consumption. In this way, images of the past worlds could be recorded in film, video, photographs, and ethnological texts; in this way, knowledge of the Yao social world could be passed on from generation to generation. It seemed to matter little that this knowledge was no longer as widespread and popular as it was at one time in Yao villages. The pressing task was to record the image, to have a mechanical reproduction of the rituals and cultural practices that once animated the local landscape.

Su had a very internationalist perspective. He reminded me that the CCP was simply one actor—though no doubt one of the more powerful—in a long history of regimes that attempted to penetrate the mountains and control the Yao. The Party, he insisted, had inherited many problems from past regimes, not the least of which was the Han Chinese attitude toward non-Chinese peoples. Party cadres working on the "nationalities problem" had to learn Stalin's theories of minority subject constitution in places such as the Central Nationalities Institute and then apply them to local conditions.

The Party would take the question of the local very seriously, especially in its emphasis on the collection of local histories and knowledge of customs and modes of social organization. Inclusion in the new revolutionary regime required disciplinary action. The minority subject was called on to know the world through a new language and lens of understanding and to go to work transforming those "feudal" modes of thought that were said to retard the Yao movement in history. Practices of mobilization and political campaigns such as land reform were not simply about the redistribution of land as a form of capital. They were also concerned with questions of social structure and the relationship of these structures to ethnic modes of consciousness. Potential class enemies had to be identified and indeed were, which only later assisted the Red Guards in deposing Party leaders, county officials, and other Yao in positions of power in the 1960s who were marked as corrupt and dangerous elements. As many older Party cadres in Jinxiu told me, at the height of the Cultural Revolution one could not even mention one's Yao subgroup affiliation without the risk of being labeled feudal and, much worse, a capitalist-roader out to undermine the ever continuing Maoist revolution.

Remembering Rebellion

There was a time worth remembering, Su Xianting would tell me, before the Cultural Revolution, a time when many people in Jinxiu were enthusiastic supporters of the Party and its socialist project. If I wanted to understand the current social and political predicaments that people in Jinxiu faced, and why some groups had become skeptical about all of the promises of progress and modernity, then I would have to know more about the history of Jinxiu. This history, he told me, was a history of heroic struggle, one that I, as a student of the Yao, should be proud of. There were many military struggles against feudal rulers in the history of Yao people in the Dayaoshan, struggles that would continue to be carried out well into the period of Guomindang penetration in the 1940s. For many people in Jinxiu, this history of struggle begins with what is known as the Datengxia uprising.

Datengxia is an old term for the mountainous region that comprises the present-day counties of Wuxuan, Xiangzhou, Guiping, Tengxian, Pingnan, Mengshan, and Lipu. When different Yao peoples began to enter these mountains in the early days of the Ming dynasty, they set up villages at the foot of the mountains and along the rivers: *yishan lizhai, yishui jiancun,* as one would find it in written accounts on this period. They also went to work reclaiming and opening up (*kaibi*) the primitive forests for agricultural purposes, turning the area into a garden of abundance.[1] According to legend, there was an old vine as thick as a *dou* (a unit of dry measure for grain) extending across the Xun River in a deep gorge in the town of Guiping. Datengxia (literally, the great vine gorge) was named after it. A series of Yao uprisings occurred in this region during the Ming, lasting from the seventh year of the Zhengtong reign (1442) to the eighteenth year of the Jiajing reign (1539), a span of nearly one hundred years. Today, in villages throughout the Dayaoshan, men and women, young and old know the leaders of this period of resistance, for the names of such heroic figures as Lan Shouer, Hou Dagou, Hou Zhengang, Wang Niuer, and Hou Gongding are an established part of local knowledge. Yet this period of sustained uprising against the feudal policies of the Ming is also a national knowledge. Yao groups across China consider it to be one of the greatest rebellions in the history of the Yao, a movement that revealed ingenious organization and military maneuverings, skills rarely seen in the revolutionary history of China's nationalities.

In the middle of the fourteenth century, the Datengxia was a Yao stronghold. As we saw in the *Jianshi* in chapter 1, during this period the Ming rulers employed the policy of "using barbarians to rule barbarians" (*yiyi zhiyi*) and appointed local headmen, known as *tuguan* or *liuguan* (a distinction of rank), to govern the local populace. This strategy of local rule was first used during the Song and Yuan dynasties and was put into place mostly to seize and reclaim fields that were said to belong to the emperor. The Ming rulers in Guangxi also attempted to control the Yao by instituting an economic blockade, prohibiting certain Yao groups from obtaining tools made of iron, or rice, salt, and certain kinds of cloth. In the sixth year of the Zhengtong reign, the office for household registration (known then as the *qianhusuo*) in a place called Fengyi was relocated to Beijiao, in present-day Pingnan County. In the hope of cornering and further isolating the mountain Yao, the *tuguan* dispatched some of his subordinates to guard the mountain passes. The encirclement of the Datengxia region lasted for well over a year. This enabled the Ming ruler to send more and more troops to the Datengxia, again with the intent of seizing the fields the Yao had already opened up for cultivation. Surrounded in their own land, the Yao began to organize. Under the leadership and inspiration of Lan Shouer, several hundred of the poorest peasants (note that it is always the poorest who

are marked as the revolutionary subjects in these narratives) began to initiate surprise attacks on the Ming soldiers. Eventually, during one of these
skirmishes, Lan was lured into a trap and captured. He would be held in
captivity until the commander of the Guangxi military force ordered his
death.

With the death of Lan, Hou Dagou stepped in to lead the uprising. With
guerrilla troops secretly moving throughout the hills, he was able to gar-
ner the support of over ten thousand people. The fighting lasted for more
than thirty years. In the spring of the tenth year of the Zhengtong reign,
Hou divided his forces into more than fifty groups, each consisting of thirty
to fifty people. Using Datengxia as a base, they attacked the neighboring
areas controlled by the Ming rulers and captured and killed many people.
The situation, now out of control, was reported to the Yingzhong emperor,
who immediately issued an edict promising one thousand tael of gold and
a rank promotion to the person who could capture Hou Dagou. Additional
troops were also ordered to advance on Datengxia. The officials sent to attack Datengxia came from around the south of China, from Guizhou to
Zhejiang. In the first year of the Chenghua reign, the Ming troops came at
the Yao from five different directions with more than sixty-eight thousand
government troops. With their knowledge of the local landscape, the insurgent Yao relied on the natural barriers of the mountains to launch counterattacks and beat back the Ming troops. However, the insurgent force was
outnumbered and eventually overwhelmed by the government troops. In
the last year of the fighting, more than seven hundred Yao were slaughtered
in the Jiucenglou mountain range along the border of the Dayaoshan. Hou
Dagou was caught and killed.

The Yao resistance entered a nadir, yet it would return with even greater
force. During the middle of the Jiajing reign several years later (1520s),
a new insurrection army led by Hu Yuaner and Huang Gongbao emerged
along the banks of the Qian River in the south of the Dayaoshan. By this
time the Yao had managed to wrestle up the support of other nationalities
in the region, especially the poorer Han and Zhuang peasants who lived in
the lower elevations. Their attacks on the Ming forces grew in intensity. The
Ming commander, Zhu Houchong, sent one of his deputies, Wang Shouren,
to Guangxi. In April of the seventh year of the Jiajing reign (1528), Wang
commanded more than six thousand government troops as they stormed
the Datengxia from two directions. The Yao insurrectionists had to retreat,

but they kept returning to harass the government troops, making use of their superior knowledge of the local mountain passes and the region's natural barriers. As reported in one of the histories of the Dayaoshan produced in the 1980s, Wang once lamented, "As our troops moved further into the hills we were constantly attacked by flying projectiles made of rock and wood."[2] After two more months of fighting, the insurrectionary force divided itself into small groups and eventually broke through the blockade set up by the government troops. Wang Shouren was one of the Ming's most famous military leaders in the south. Exhausted by the relentless guerrilla warfare of the Yao rebels, he fell ill and died en route to the Ming imperial stronghold of Nan'an.

As Su Xianting would often tell me, it was important to realize that the Yao were valiant fighters who were determined to protect their land, no matter the cost and no matter the fact that they were greatly outnumbered by the Ming soldiers. The Datengxia uprising was sustained through local forms of storytelling that brought together villages in different parts of the mountains and by a determined peasant will. The movement eventually ground to a halt. In the fifteenth year of the Jiajing reign (1536), several Ming officials trapped and killed Hou Shenghai, who had emerged as the new leader of the Yao forces, and seized large tracts of Yao land. Led by Hou Gongding, the younger brother of the now deceased leader of the insurrection, more than two thousand fighters attacked the Ming outpost. After battling through the night, the outpost was wiped out and three hundred government soldiers had fallen to their bloody deaths. Huang Gui and Wei Xiang, the commanders of the Ming force, managed to escape. The Ming court–appointed Cai Jing, a notorious general known for his exploits in pacifying the barbarians, advanced on the Datengxia area. His troops successfully bribed a relative who knew of Hou Gongding's whereabouts; within days a trap had been set for the last of the Yao rebel leaders. After three years of repeated small-scale attacks and counterattacks, the next Ming advancement came in February of the eighteenth year of the Jiajing reign. Advancing on the Yao with over fifty thousand troops, the entire rebel force was surrounded at Mount Luoyun in the southeast corner of the Dayaoshan, in the area around the present-day villages of Luoxiang and Liuxiang. The Yao forces divided into small groups and took to the steepest elevations in the mountains, forcing the government troops to trample through and climb unknown land. Though this exhausted the Ming troops, the Yao forces had become scattered and disorganized. The Yao uprising, which had lasted for almost one hundred years, had come to an end. The families of the insurrectionists were forced deeper into the forests of the Dayaoshan.

Revolutionary Struggle in the New Democracy Period

These local narratives of struggle are known throughout the hills, and, of course, different people have different versions. These were the stories of uprising and rebellion that the first Communist Party work teams heard when they began to organize among the Yao in the fight against the Guomindang in the late 1940s, the same stories that would be recorded by the visiting ethnological and social history research teams that were sent to the Dayaoshan in the 1950s. The underground Party movement in the 1940s and the research teams in the 1950s were naturally interested in the Guomindang's efforts to set up administrative posts in the Dayaoshan, in large part because by this time many Yao had been won over to the Guomindang side. The history of the Guomindang presence, which for many Yao ethnologists constitutes the beginning of the modern period in the area, begins in the 1920s, the period known in Chinese historiography as the "new democracy period," or xin minzhu zhuyi shiqi.[3] Throughout the 1930s, the Yao in the Dayaoshan would be watched closely by the Guomindang rulers Li Zongren, Bai Chongxi, and Huang Xuchu, who made their way between Guilin and Nanning. The Dayaoshan separated these two cities. For many Han in the river valleys and flat plains below, it was a dark, imposing, and densely forested region where few dared to travel. Guomindang officials saw it as an isolated ethnic enclave, but they also respected the Yao to a degree, for they knew from many local accounts that they had long resisted outside encroachments on their territory. The Guomindang leaders in Guangxi made it their mission to "civilize" the Dayaoshan, to bring modern culture to the heathen ethnic other. They also sought to bring them within the fold of the mutual security system known as the baojia zhidu, a mode of household registration, village governance, and police surveillance with roots in the Qing yet modernized by the Guomindang in the 1930s.[4]

Communist organizers also had their eyes on the mountains. In the spring of 1927, the Wuzhou District Committee of the CCP began to organize peasant associations (nongmin xiehui) in Pingnan and Guiping Counties, on the southeastern flank of the Dayaoshan. At this time, the Yao and

Han living in the small mountain towns of Luoxiang and Luoyun were under the jurisdiction of Pingnan County; these towns would be incorporated into the Jinxiu Yao Autonomous County in the 1950s. In the summer of 1927, the Jinxiu communist leaders Su Qili and Huang Qitao went to Malian and Penghua, two smaller districts (*qu*) in Pingnan to organize several peasant associations and to establish a peasant self-defense army (*nongmin ziweijun*). The Malian Party chief, Long Tiejun, often traveled to Luoxiang to conduct propaganda (*xuanchuan*), which at this time meant teaching the poorer peasants about the aspirations of the communist movement and the benefits of joining the peasant associations and self-defense armies. On April 18 of the lunar calendar, several thousand peasants attended a large public meeting organized by the Malian peasant association. A large pine gate was set up to mark the entrance of the meeting grounds, a tactic often used by Party propaganda teams to distinguish those who had joined the revolution from those who still waffled. Peasants from different villages lined up with flags in their hands and military weapons strung across their shoulders; they beat drums and gongs and chanted revolutionary slogans. By this time the peasant association around Luoxiang had some five hundred members, led by Mu Weilin and Huang Duanfu. With the peasant associations and self-defense armies established, the struggle against what Party cadres called the "local tyrants and evil gentry" (*tuhao lieshen*) was initiated. The peasant self-defense armies of Luoxiang and Luoyun, in conjunction with those of Malian and Penghua, took part in attacks against the landowner Liu Jintang of Daping Village in Guiping County; Feng Zuoqing of Changduan Village in Malian; and the landlord bureaucrat Lan Mingbo of Tongsheng Village. These landlords were all members of the Changmao Yao group, the quasi-ethnic coalition of landowners that controlled the *shipai* system. A life-and-death struggle then began against the Guomindang troops led by Huang Guidang, who were then setting up garrison posts on the outskirts of the Dayaoshan. The fight with the Guomindang initially failed; the houses of members of the peasant association were set ablaze and some members were killed in the vicinity of Mount Luoyan. When military support eventually arrived from a peasant association in Luoxian district, the Guomindang troops retreated.

Battles such as these continued through the 1930s and the Guomindang began to make headway. In 1940, the Guangxi Provincial Government (*shengfu*) decided to set up the Jinxiu Garrison Command Post (*jingbei qushu*) in the vicinity of the present-day county seat. To do this they would have to enter the mountains from the south, travel for days overland, and engage local Yao forces resisting their advance. A Han named Pan Yaowu was appointed commander; he entered the Dayaoshan with a force of three detachments with more than three hundred troops. The Yao in Jinxiu fought back ferociously, mostly with sticks, rocks, farming implements, and a few rifles, and Pan had to temporarily establish his headquarters in Xiuren County for about half a year. On July 14 of the lunar calendar, during the time of the Zhongyuan festival, Pan launched another attack on Jinxiu. Traveling overland with few supplies, his troops met fierce resistance from Yao in Tianchun, though he was able to send a telegram asking for reinforcements to the Guomindang militia headquarters in Pingle District. A massive battle ensued, as the Pingle district commander Jiang Tiemin with an army of several hundred troops fought their way into Jinxiu. Supported by nearby villagers, the people of Liuchun and Tianchun waged a brave resistance, with fighting and hand-to-hand combat breaking out in the streets. To this day, Party officials and others in Jinxiu, including Su Xianting, recall the number of casualties. Eight of the reactionary soldiers were killed and six Yao lost their lives with three severely wounded. The Guomindang troops entered the villages around Jinxiu; they confiscated all of the domestic animals they could find and most of the Yao homes were burned to the ground. Jiang began to arrest any local Yao in sight, arguing that they were all enemies of the new revolutionary government. Pan Yaowu entered Jinxiu shortly thereafter and set up his garrison command post. In March 1941, he would be dispatched elsewhere, succeeded by Liu Yannian, a Han and Guomindang official from Guilin. In September 1942, the garrison command was renamed the Jinxiu *shezhiju*, literally the "bureau for establishing control of the mountains." The transformation from a mere district post (*qushu*) to the higher administrative order of a bureau (*ju*) did not go unnoticed by the Yao who opposed the Guomindang presence. The Guomindang were here to stay, and, as Su Xianting told me, the local Yao were weary of battle.

The Yao would, of course, fight back; the Guomindang, in due time, would be driven from the hills. Su Xianting and others would tell me the story of the defeat of the Guomindang with pride. This was one of those moments in his narrative when the Party, which he joined in his youth in the 1950s, was remembered with fondness and a sense of exhilaration and joy. Listening to and recording these narratives, I was infected with his enthusiasm; it was difficult for me to maintain the position of objective anthropologist with an eye toward the truth of history. I was, after all, a long-

time student of the Vietnam War and of Third World anticolonial nationalist movements and I had spent much of the late 1970s and early 1980s as
an antinuclear activist in Colorado and California. I told Su and others of
my opposition to the U.S. involvement in Nicaragua and how the CIA supported death squads in El Salvador and other Latin American countries. I
was in a sense striving to establish my credentials as a leftist and sympathetic student of the Chinese revolution with Su and other Jinxiu Yao who
sought to teach me the history of their people and lives. These narratives of
underground revolutionary activities heightened my desire to identify with
an international socialist opposition, one in which the history of animosity
between China and America, the great imperialist power, would somehow
not figure into our relationship. This desire was arguably naïve, myopic,
and utopian; it was perhaps even colonial. Yet it gained a further sense of
urgency given that such a position and a politics were increasingly being
marginalized by the Reagan era and by Deng Xiaoping's seemingly weekly
intimations of China as a capitalist nation with socialist characteristics, or
whatever the slogan of the day happened to be.

   Additionally, as I mentioned above in the vignette about my interview
with the Guangxi television station, I wanted to find ways to speak out
against what I saw as the new inequalities and injustices that were so obviously coming to China with the economic reforms. I was having a difficult time removing my scholarly interests from my political commitments.
But this was entirely my own decision, for people such as Su and many
others in Jinxiu were teaching me, despite Deng's proclamation "to seek
truth from facts," that politics and questions of ideology could never be
removed from our research interests. This was not simply a theoretical position, but a practical one thickly and complexly grounded in how different
people defined the stakes of ethnic knowledge and classification. There is
a short passage in Ann Anagnost's book *National Past-Times* in which she
responds to a question posed by Michael Taussig about when and how anthropology might move beyond the mere deconstruction of all discursively
constructed social forms. She states, and correctly I think, that it is difficult
to imagine how the transformations in Chinese society, especially those
that have resulted from the increased presence of market forces, offer any
possibilities for a universalizing theoretical project.[5] She is especially wary
of projects that would seek to emancipate the Chinese subject from the market, yet at the same time she wants to write against the celebration of the
reforms as a progressive history that has liberated the masses from the so-

cialist stranglehold. Anagnost seeks to resist the colonizing logic inherent in modes of discourse and social practice in which a theoretically fashioned self, with knowledge or insight into the human condition, speaks for the other. Yet this was precisely the position I was finding myself in, as I was increasingly drawn (in what we might think of as an Althusserian "hailing") into these narratives of how the communist spring had come to the Dayaoshan and into contemporary struggles to rethink the history of the region. I was drawn in not only because of my commitment to understand the nature of socialist revolution in a remote part of China and my ideological refusal to see the early revolutionary struggle as a form of symbolic and material state violence enacted on a docile ethnic subject. I was also drawn in because these narratives were central to how so many people in the Dayaoshan, especially those who had lived through the history, were rethinking the past and the place of local struggles in the history of the Chinese nation.[6]

From March 1941 on into the winter of 1942, the Communist Party agitators Sima Wangsun, Song Enyi, and Yan Wei infiltrated the Guomindang *shezhiju* as underground agents. In the evenings they would make their way to different Yao villages and hang out with the commoners. Using their undercover status in the government bureau, they labored with the peasants in the fields, established primary schools, and taught evening classes in Chinese history. They began to teach the people to sing revolutionary songs; they spread the word on the anti-Japanese effort and told the Yao of the victories and defeats that were occurring in other parts of the country. They spread the revolutionary principles of Mao Zedong, and people began to hear for the first time of the land reform efforts that had been carried out in the Yan'an base area in Shaanxi. Su Xianting was a young boy in his teens at the time. He told me of how he would sit transfixed listening to these stories of a revolution sweeping an invaded and almost defeated Chinese nation. He told me that it was through one of Sima Wangsun's associates that he learned to read the underground newspapers and pamphlets of the Party. Speaking for himself, he said that he knew before long that these educational activities and secret revolutionary meetings were changing the political consciousness (*zhengzhi juewu*) of the Yao people. It was a transformation he and many others, including many Chashan Yao who were tied to landlord families, wholeheartedly welcomed.

During this time, of course, the Guomindang government was implementing its own methods of assimilation, but they were doing it mostly by

force. In large measure they were acting in accordance with the cultural requirements of the New Life Movement, which had been instituted by the
Guomindang national leader Chiang Kai-shek in the mid-1930s. Chiang
sought to create a new national consciousness and a new cultural ideology
by reviving the virtues of "etiquette, justice, integrity, and conscientious-
ness" that had long been emphasized in the Confucian tradition. Foreign
Christian missionaries also influenced him, and he had a morbid fascination with Europe's fascist dictators. In Jinxiu, this cultural movement
would be put into practice in a number of ways. For example, the Guomindang police officers would hold public rallies at which they would gather
together the younger Yao women and cut off their long braids. Anyone who
resisted would be arrested, but only after being paraded through town. They
ordered the Yao in the vicinity of Jinxiu to demolish their village temples
and to cease their religious practices, for these were thought to be antithetical to the making of national subjects; also, and perhaps more important,
they feared the rites were being used as covers for political organizing. For
both men and women, they outlawed the wearing of locally made clothing
(difang fuzhuang), the embroidered skirts, turbans, and other markers that
were used to differentiate one subgroup from the next.[7]

The troops and government staff in the shezhiju were also permitted to
openly seize crops, kill cattle, and rape women. On 26 February 1943 of
the lunar calendar the Yao launched a military attack on the government
bureau. Among the Chashan Yao, this is known as the zuoriliu, or the "uprising of the twenty-sixth." It began when the ox of a villager, Tao Sheng-
zhong, wandered into the garden of a bureau soldier and ate some vegetables. The soldiers came to his house and fined him. The Yao in the village
were outraged, for the penalty flew in the face of local custom. In the winter
months, as the weather turned cold and wet, the Yao allowed their livestock
to wander outside unattended for two- or three-day periods. There was an
understanding that every family had a responsibility to protect their own
vegetable plots and that no one would be held responsible if livestock wandered onto someone else's plot. This was seen as the most reasonable way
to exercise and feed the animals without constant monitoring in the cold-
est months of the year. Several days after this incident, the soldiers seized
several oxen; one was nearly frozen to death. The villagers grew angry and
began to organize. Tao Yuanzheng and Su Xingdao approached several shipai headmen and traveled to other villages in the vicinity to request their
assistance. Su Daoda and Lin Shengyin of nearby Xidi Village invited Quan

Jinbiao of Dishui, who was already known as a vociferous opponent of the Guomindang and their "civilizing," what the Yao would call *tonghua*, antics. A secret meeting, known among the Chashan Yao as a *juier*, was held. An attack on the bureau headquarters, the *shezhiju*, was set for 26 February.

Led by Quan and other underground Party leaders, Yao villagers from Dishui, Longhua, Changer, Luomeng, Yonghe, and Pingzhu divided into two groups. One attacked the *shezhiju*, the other the police station. They eventually occupied part of the military storage facility attached to the bureau and seized a dozen rifles. With no reinforcements, they had little choice but to retreat. Bureau Chief Liu Yannian immediately sent telegraphs to the Guangxi government in Guilin and to neighboring counties asking for reinforcements. The Goumindang militias of Pingnan, Mengshan, Xiuren, Lipu, Xiangxian, and Liujiang were quickly sent to Jinxiu. Guomindang soldiers first attacked the villages of Xidi and Liula. They went on a rampage, burning, killing, and arresting many local Yao. Six houses were burned in Xidi, and eighteen of the twenty-four houses in Xidi were set ablaze; the remaining houses were looted for their valuables. Those who could escape fled into the hills. Su Defu, one of the Chashan Yao ethnologists who grew up in these mountains and with whom I had worked for some months at the Central Nationalities Institute, was eight years old at the time. He escaped out of the back of Xidi as it was ablaze and soon met up with other "refugees" (*taonan ren*) on the top of a nearby hill. They wandered through a pitch-black night, as it was late in the month with no moon, and they feared lighting bamboo torches lest they be discovered. They spent the night in a cave and ate wild vegetables. In the morning they peered down into the valley and watched the Guomindang soldiers stab and kill their oxen with the bayonets on their rifles. Within a week the villagers returned. Su Daosheng, Tao Xiucai, Liu Shengyin, and Su Daoda had been captured. A massive execution ground had been set up where they would soon be publicly shot to death. Meanwhile, I was told, the Yao hid in the few remaining homes, burnt incense, prayed for revenge, and cursed the executioner, Liao Cheng. A month later Quan Jinbiao would enter into negotiations with the Guomindang officials to settle the situation and bring back some normalcy to the valley. He would be tricked into attending a meeting with leaders of the provincial government in Guilin. He would never return to the Dayaoshan.

I never met another Yao in Jinxiu who thought of this period as anything but a living hell. Yao in Jinxiu remember this as an indigenous uprising, one they organized and instigated without the help of Communist Party activists, who had yet to establish a presence in the hills. Yet the Party, which had already set up bases in villages in lower-lying elevations outside of the Dayaoshan proper, had heard stories of the uprising. Party organizations in neighboring counties thus began to send more and more cadres into other regions of the Dayaoshan. In 1947, Su Shengping was sent to the township of Dongbei (known as Changtong in the 1980s) as a lion dance performer. He eventually settled in Longhua Village, a predominantly Hualan Yao region, and began to organize a poor peasant association (*qiongren hui*) and a revolutionary military unit (*geming wuzhuang dui*), in which he taught young men and women how to use rifles and engage in hand-to-hand combat. Using Longhua as a base, he gradually established ties with Changtong, Dishui, Zhenchong, Pingdao, Guitian, Zhanger, and Liutuan villages through the organization of revolutionary mass organizations (*geming qunzhong zuzhi*). These organizations, comprising mostly poor peasants, orchestrated struggle sessions against the Guomindang's "three taxation system" (*sanzheng*), in which land, labor, and forest products were extracted from the peasants, often against their will. The Changmao Yao leaders connected to the indigenous *shipai* system were paraded through the village and denounced by the poorer peasants both within the Hualan Yao group as well as those from the Pan Yao and Shanzi Yao groups who lived in the more upland villages. These efforts would begin to pay off. In the early months of 1949, a *qiongrenhui* (poor peasants association) and a *renmin wuzhuang* (people's militia) were set up in the township of Dazhang. In August and September, the eighth regiment of the Guizhong guerrilla force (*youji dui*) stormed the troops of the Guomindang magistrate in Xiang County with the assistance of the Changtong and Dazhang poor peasant and military associations. By July the revolution would be taken into the heart of the mountains, as underground Party cadres from Xiuren County entered the villages around the present-day towns of Jinxiu and Sanjiao and quickly organized a military unit. On 28 November 1949 Comrade Li Shengping destroyed the Jinxiu *shezhiju*, which had recently been transferred to Changtong. He was supported by a detachment from the Eighth Regiment of the Guizhong guerrilla force and by military units sent to Changtong and other districts in the mountains. The head of the *shezhiju*, Li Chengdi, and his sixty soldiers were defeated within an hour. The revolutionary forces captured several light machine guns, more than forty rifles, four handguns, and ten telephone sets. The people's government of Changtong, or the Changtong renmin zhengfu, was established, a largely symbolic gesture in which a revolutionary star was hung over the door of a poor peasant's home and a small office and telegraph machine were set up. Within weeks other Guomindang outposts were captured, and additional revolutionary stars were hung above the doors of peasant homes. The remaining Guomindang troops scattered into the hills.

"Spring comes to the Yao Mountains!"

The end of 1949 brought liberation to the whole of Guangxi. In the Dayaoshan, however, the remaining Guomindang troops were unwilling to admit defeat and quickly began to reorganize their forces with the help of the more powerful Yao landlords. In fact, more than thirty-eight thousand Guomindang troops were roaming the Dayaoshan and its vicinity in the early 1950s, as the region became a final staging ground in the long civil war. Guomindang military leaders from around eastern Guangxi took refuge in the hills and began to set up their own guerrilla organization with different ranks of commander, different army divisions, and a host of small shock brigades. The Dayaoshan emerged as a Guomindang command center for subsequent attacks on the people's governments that had been established throughout the valleys and hills in central and northern Guangxi. They began to conduct antirevolutionary propaganda, but, as with the communist troops, they also killed their enemies and burned their homes. The Yao who supported the Guomindang were posted to guard the mountain passes, collect taxes, seize crops and farm animals, dig trenches, and construct new garrison posts. As in any region of China, official Communist Party documents in Jinxiu represent the Guomindang as barbarians and bandits who exercised little if any constraint. These reports indicate that the Guomindang committed unthinkable atrocities: they dug out human hearts and tendons, drank human blood, cut open the bellies of pregnant women, killed infants, and ate human flesh. Over 150 Yao were dead in the villages of Changtong, Jintian, Liula, Liuduan, and Changer by the autumn of 1950.

Thus began the phase of what Party historians call the "joint suppression of banditry in the Dayaoshan." In October 1950, Mao issued a directive demanding the eradication of the Guomindang bandits (tufei) in Guangxi before 1 May 1951. The People's Liberation Army (PLA) brought together over fourteen regiments and brigades from more than ten neighboring counties as well as the several dozen militia units that had been set up in the Dayaoshan over the preceding decade. Additionally, more than four thousand work team members from different prefectures and counties were called on to conduct propaganda about the Party's "bandit suppression" efforts and its newly formulated nationalities policies. These work teams, made up of many Yao from poor peasant families, worked to mobilize the masses to support the front, suppress the bandits, and establish people's governments at the district and township levels. The joint suppression was conducted in two phases. The first phase aimed to destroy the Guomindang troops on the periphery of the Dayaoshan by blocking the roads and rivers that led into the hills. Once these blockades were established, the second phase began, in which the revolutionary troops went on military excursions into the hills and hunted down the remaining Guomindang bandits and their collaborators.

The general attack against the Guomindang bases on the periphery of the Dayaoshan began on 8 January 1951. Though initially hindered by torrential rain storms, the Liberation Army, local troops, and militia units launched a series of surprise attacks and, over the course of ten days, forced the remaining Guomindang troops into the interior of the mountains. Guomindang commanders Gan Jingsheng, Lin Xiushan, and Han Mengxuan, in conjunction with the most hated of Yao landlords, Li Rongbao, held a meeting in the vicinity of the present-day county seat in an attempt to regroup their forces. The bandit suppression troops launched a surprise attack. In Jinxiu Party documents, this final assault recalls the mythology of both the Long March and the Yan'an days, in which revolutionary organizations of believing peasants and benevolent cadres reach out to and win over the masses:

Work teams were essential to the success of the campaign. They consisted of cadres trained in ideological work, nationalities work and commercial trade work. These teams accompanied the troops as they marched through the hills. They were in turn followed by tens of thousands of civil laborers [mingong], who carried large quantities of food, oil, salt, medicine, and other daily necessities. Guided by the leaders of several different nationalities and by activists in the militia units, the troops bravely crossed mountain after mountain and river after river. Propaganda was a central aspect of their mission. Every time they entered a village, they educated the people about the Party's nationality and bandit suppression policies. . . . When they encountered these bandits, they immediately launched an attack, sometimes destroying them on the spot, sometimes hunting them through the hills. The bandits would scatter.[8]

On 2 February, Jinxiu was liberated. The leaders of the Guomindang bandits were forced further into the hills and many were captured as they attempted to flee through the mountain passes, which were now controlled entirely by communist troops. Party documents claim, not unsurprisingly, that unlike the Guomindang, the bandit suppression troops adopted a policy of combining leniency toward the enemies with violent suppression when necessary. A typical story is of how the Guomindang leader Han Mengxuan was eventually captured. Isolated in the hills with little food and few supplies, on the evening of 27 February he sent his deputy He Qihuai to beg for food from a Yao family in Jinxiu village. They locked the deputy in their house and reported the capture to the PLA. During the interrogation, he revealed Hang's hiding place; he also indicated that a *shipai* headman supported him, a Chashan Yao named Tao Guojun. Troops were immediately sent to hunt them down. Under the leadership of Zhang Souxi, political director of the Third Battalion and secretary of the working committee to establish the Jinxiu Yao Nationality Autonomous District, the militia units from the surrounding Yao villages joined in the fight with rifles, knives, and wooden sticks. When the mountain peak on which they were hiding was captured, Han Mengxuan was killed on the spot. However, a Jinxiu Yao named Sun Guifang was also killed during the skirmish. A massive funeral service was held for him. As his body was paraded through town, his relatives cried out for his soul; they buried him according to the most solemn ceremony of the Yao people, a practice of mourning the Guomindang had forbidden a mere decade earlier. This young man would become one of the first martyrs in the battle against the Guomindang in the Dayaoshan. He would be remembered in Party histories as a dedicated revolutionary who gave his blood for the cause of the revolution, for the motherland, and for the future of the Yao people.

The Dayaoshan Unification Pact

The defeat of the Guomindang led to the administrative reorganization of the Dayaoshan.[9] The Party also turned its attention to the question of how to put the Yao back on the path of production and development. Party cadres found, however, that contradictions (*maodun*) existed between the landowning Changmao Yao group (also called the *shanzhu*) and the land-less Guoshan Yao group (also called the *shanding*) and that these impeded the development of the Dayaoshan's productive forces. Despite all of the mobilization efforts, perhaps even because of them, these contradictions remained a core feature of the local social and political situation. To resolve them in a timely fashion, the Guoshan Yao would have to be empowered so-cially and politically. This would entail allowing them to reclaim mountain wasteland and reap its products for their own use; to hunt in mountains and fish in rivers without paying a tax in kind; to cultivate native products on mountains without permission from the *shipai* headmen; and finally, to abolish the rule of *zhongshu huanshan* (explained below). The Changmao Yao leaders did not agree to these stipulations, however. As one of my neighbors in Xidi once explained to me, the Changmao Yao leaders, many of whom had participated in and assisted the underground revolutionary movement, felt cheated and betrayed by these Party efforts to rob them of their eco-nomic and social power. Her neighbor, an elderly woman who always had an opinion, chimed in, "The mountain landlords (*shanzhu*) were fools to ex-pect anything less. They should have known all along that the communists were out to get them." In the early years of the 1950s, arguments between these groups and Party cadres intensified, and the contradictions between the landowners and the landless became more pronounced as the landlords demanded the payment of back taxes and the honoring of labor agreements.

This is how many people explained the pre-Liberation social and pro-ductive system to me. As far back as anyone could remember, all of the wild mountains and the rivers of the Laoshan (as the Dayaoshan was often fondly called) belonged to the Changmao Yao. The Guoshan Yao, who arrived much later, had nothing. They were basically considered outsiders and had to pay rent or taxes if they sought to reclaim land or hunt and fish. The tenets and stipulations of the stone tablet system, the *shipai zhidu*, legitimated and re-inforced the exploitative relationship that existed between the *shanzhu* and *shanding* groups. The *shipai* was the law of the land (what many ethnolo-gists in China called, as we have seen, a primitive legal system); disobeying it meant fines, incarceration, and, in the most extreme cases of adultery or murder, execution. In reality, as many Chashan Yao told me, it was not at all true that all of their people were mountain landlords, though this is how the more exuberant Party activists saw them. The Chashan Yao, as were the Ao Yao and the Hualan Yao (the three groups comprising the Chang-mao group), were made up of landlords, rich peasants, middle peasants,

and poor peasants, essentially running the gambit of China's class identification system. The Party had misunderstood the relationship between the
ethnic divisions in the hills and the system of class exploitation. Mountain
landlords, the *shanzhu*, existed in all five of the subgroups and not just in the
Changmao Yao group. Moreover, the Guoshan Yao group, the *shanding*, was
not made up entirely of poor and dispossessed peasants. Even within this
group, there were landlords and rich peasants, though they did not possess
the same degree of power found among some of the more powerful Changmao Yao families. Party cadres never confiscated the property these *shanding*
landlords owned because they approached the land reallocation problem
by incorrectly treating the entire Guoshan Yao group as though it were a
landless collectivity. The Changmao Yao headmen repeatedly tried to point
this out to Party cadres charged with resolving these contradictions, and
they became increasingly angry when landlord families in the Guoshan Yao
group concealed their landed wealth by simply claiming to be among the
landless, subaltern class.

The exploitative relationship between the *shanzhu* and *shanding* groups
took many forms. For example, when rent for land was required, it could
be paid in kind, cash, or labor. The most common form of rent in kind
was called *zhongshu huanshan*, roughly translated as "returning the land with
newly planted trees." When a *shanding* family rented a piece of land, they
cleared their debt through the payment of product or cash. This system,
however, was seen to be even more perniciously exploitative in that the
renters also had to plant trees (typically, Chinese fir) and then nurture them.
When the fields were depleted of their nutrition (usually a ten- to twelve-
year cycle; in some places even shorter) and abandoned, the *shanding* would
return the mountain to the *shanzhu* covered with trees that the *shanzhu* could
then exploit for timber and other purposes. Party cadres also focused on
the exploitative nature of labor payments. These payments were required
during the busiest times of the agricultural season, the spring planting and
the autumn harvest. The *shipai* system required the tenants to work for the
shanzhu for several days without pay. But exploitation went beyond the economic. When rent contracts were negotiated, the *shanding* renters were required to invite the landowners to drink wine, to present gifts of pork and
chicken, and to offer their services for voluntary work on *shanzhu* mountain
estates. The mountain landowners were even given a voice in marriage de-
cisions, for the movement of bodies to different households and villages
was seen to be intricately tied up with questions of economic power and

productivity; a "consultation" price would be paid in the form of wine and pork. If these gifts were not made, the *shanding* households were subject to fines and other forms of punishment and humiliation. The *shanding* also had to pay rent for drinking water, for land on which they sought to build new homes, and even for land on which they buried their dead. Behavior was also monitored. The landless were subjected to fines if they inappropriately smiled or cajoled the landlords, and even if they broke wind in front of the *shanzhu*. In more extreme cases, the *shanzhu* would bring friends and members of their family into the home of a renter and demand to be fed chickens, pigs, or anything else in sight. This was euphemistically called *dayouhuo*, or "lighting up the stove." These multiple forms of exploitation were detailed and made public in struggle sessions and through propaganda efforts. The Changmao Yao group was asked to give up their special privileges. They were implored to allow those groups with little or no land to reclaim fields and harvest the fruit of their own labor, to cultivate the wild goods of the mountains freely without tax stipulations. They were asked to assist in transforming the tenancy relationship into a more rational and fair system, which meant of course giving up much of their social and economic power. These changes, they were told, would enhance and encourage solidarity among the different groups. This was a new mode of local governmentality, in which ethnic unification was deemed essential for the development of the productive base and the building of socialism in the Dayaoshan.

The new revolutionary regime's guiding principle at this time was captured in the slogan "Solidarity, mutual cooperation, and the development of production" (*Tuanjie, huzu, fazhan shengchan*). In the early months of 1951, the Central Committee of the CCP and the Guangxi People's Government sent numerous work teams to Yao villages. The CCP was in the process of defining its nationality policy in remote ethnic regions. There was an abiding consensus that if the Party was to win the support of the ethnic minority, it must thoroughly understand the nature of local conditions, a position that assumed that ethnic regions differed from Han ones. Ethnic groups and their local leaders were encouraged to come to new understandings of local forms of power and to resolve their conflicts through negotiations in which everyone had a voice. Solidarity and cooperation were the buzzwords. This principle would be put to the test first on 26 March 1951 by the Dongbei township people's government. Cadres decided to publicize the Party's policy of "solidarity, friendliness, equality, and mutual aid" through the use of the *shipai* system, in which a headman would publicly expound a set of rules and stipulations and ask for discussion. Many Chashan Yao told me that traditionally, these public *shipai* meetings were all about negotiation; the passing of new rules and regulations was a matter of spirited debate and based on consensus between the *shanzhu* and the *shanding*. A resolution was passed at Dongbei, but, as a friend once reflected, it was hardly done in the democratic spirit that once defined the *shipai* negotiations. In any case, the contents of the new resolution were as follows. (1) The Changmao Yao group was to forgo the privilege of land ownership on barren and uncultivated mountain land. The Pan Yao and Shanzi Yao (the two groups that comprised the Guoshan Yao) could reclaim this land and not be subject to rent. (2) The Pan Yao and the Shanzi Yao were now free to hunt wild animals and collect edible wild herbs without rent obligations. (3) The newly established village governments would administer the rivers, once owned and controlled by the Changmao Yao group; everyone was now free to fish the rivers. (4) Forests products were to be shared by everyone. The only exception was the mushroom (*xianggu*), which belonged to the person, family, or group that cultivated it. (5) Those who owned wet paddy fields (*shuitian*) could not take more than 30 percent of the harvested product from those who rented the fields. (6) All groups were free to reclaim fields or plant trees on barren mountains; the fields and trees belonged to the person, family, or group that cultivated them.

Party cadres saw this as a fair and equitable way to solve the contradictions that existed among different groups; through public announcements and further propaganda work (the distribution of pamphlets, for example), they championed the passage of the resolution as a milestone in the history of the Dayaoshan. Conflicts arose in the implementation of the new regulations, however. For example, toward the end of April 1951, a dispute emerged when a Pan Yao in Tuoshan Village refused to pay rent to a Han family in Tuochun Village in the adjacent county of Xiuren. The Han family in turn argued that the Pan Yao had damaged their water source when they reclaimed barren land above the Han village. The county and district governments were forced to intervene; they organized what was called a "solidarity meeting" (*tuanjie hui*) between the two villages. A government official in Jinxiu told me that Party cadres initially took a passive role in these meetings; they were there mostly to encourage the airing of grievances and the clarification of positions among the parties involved in the dispute. Only after heated debate would they then move in to sum up the nature of the conflict. They would admit that the new system needed adjustments, but also insist that conflicts could be resolved only through the adherence of the new regulations that had been passed in the Dongbei resolution. Yao in Lipu County, to the northeast of Jinxiu, also began to follow this method of calling solidarity meetings to resolve conflicts. Solidarity agreements were quickly passed between the Changmao Yao and the Guoshan Yao in Liu-duan, Liuding, and Liuqiping villages in Jinxiu County; the solidarity wave soon spread to other villages in the mountains.

On 19 June, the Yao Autonomous District of Xiuren County held a meeting that brought together representatives from all of the nationalities (including Han and Zhuang) in the area. A twelve-point resolution was passed, essentially reiterating the Dongbei resolution, now fine-tuned based on several months of experience and conflict resolution. News of the resolution spread throughout the county, as the Yao in the Dayaoshan were held up as a model minority in the process of socialist reconstruction. The *Guangxi Daily* reported that the Jinxiu solidarity agreement "shows that the Yao people know how to solve problems between different nationality groups." [10] Though their actions were in accordance with their own traditional sensibilities, they also followed "The Common Guiding Principles" set forth in the People's Consultative Conference of China. They adhered to the spirit of the directive issued by the Guangxi People's Government during the nationality work meeting held on 2 June. The Yao had emerged as an exemplary minority. These were a people who demonstrated, the editorial went on to argue, "that in minority areas it is necessary to first promote solidarity and mutual aid, which together enhance production. In these areas it is not suitable to reduce and refund rent or to engage in land reform before the establishment of ethnic solidarity. It is inappropriate to apply policies and practices carried out in Han areas to minorities."

The *Jinxiu gaikuang* tells us that after the establishment of the solidarity agreement in the Yao region of Xiuren County, news of the agreement spread throughout the Dayaoshan like a "spring breeze" (*xiang chunfeng yiyang, chuibian le zhengge dayaoshan qu*).[11] The establishment of local solidarity agreements at village and township levels had laid an ideological and administrative foundation for the establishment of a singular regionwide solidarity agreement. On 20 August 1951, the central government sent a visiting delegation to convey its greetings to the people of Dayaoshan. A massive festival was planned. Yao cadres greeted the visiting delegation; the common people dressed in the clothing of their particular subgroup and

Table 1. Distribution of Delegates to the Dayaoshan Resolution

Nationality	Number of Representatives	Percentage of Total
Pan Yao	111	45.12
Shanzi Yao	18	7.3
Hualan Yao	9	3.65
Chashan Yao	59	23.98
Ao Yao	19	7.72
Han	30	12.19

Source: Jinxin County Government, *Jinxiu Yaozu zizhixian gaikuang* (A survey of the Jinxiu Yao Autonomous County). Nanning: Guangxi Minzu Chubanshe, 1984, 69.

lined the road that had recently been constructed from Xiuren to Jinxiu. The Yao danced, played their traditional musical instruments, and entertained the delegates by reciting the legends and histories of their respective groups. The festival was entirely orchestrated and choreographed by the local cadre, and it was decided in advance that this would be the ideal opportunity to bring together representatives from all five of the subgroups and discuss how to go about the business of establishing a solidarity agreement for the entire region. Several weeks before the meeting, representatives to the meeting were determined in local elections according to population percentages. Each subgroup was able to elect one representative for every 150 people. These delegates were to be non-Party members, for one of the aims was to convey a sense that the ethnic masses were taking a leading role in determining their future. In all, 246 representatives were elected, 195 male and 51 female. The number and percentage of each nationality are shown in Table 1.

The meeting lasted for five days, from 25 to 29 August. The earlier Dongbei resolution was aimed at solving land ownership problems and intra-ethnic conflicts at the village and township levels. The aim now was to get elected delegates to sign a regionwide solidarity agreement for the Dayaoshan, to promote ethnic solidarity, and to raise the productive base of the mountains. The focus was on the region as a whole. The two deputy heads of the central government delegation, Jin Xiaochun and Chen An, gave speeches in which they discussed the specifics of the CCP's nationalities policy. They emphasized that, in the process of socialist construction, minorities would be treated differently from the Han. This meant in effect that landowners and other potential "enemies of the revolution" would not be publicly struggled against, forced to sign public confessions, or, as had occurred in many parts of the country, summarily executed. The former deputy head of Xiuren County, Lian Huaxin, reviewed the experience of forging a solidarity agreement among different Yao groups in the area where he lived and worked, emphasizing the nonviolent nature of the proceedings.

Representatives of the Chashan Yao then took the stage. For those not involved in the orchestration of the event, this was a moment of great anticipation, for many Chashan Yao headmen had been, as we saw earlier, some of the most vociferous critics of the solidarity agreements. Rumors about violent attacks on landowners were circulating throughout Yao villages. Especially among the Chashan Yao and other valley-dwelling Yao groups, many people were strategizing how to disguise their land holdings and how to protect friends and kin associated with the *shipai* leadership. The Chashan Yao who spoke alleviated everyone's fears, which was, of course, the intent. They proclaimed that past forms of exploitation were caused by the Guomindang reactionaries who had worked with corrupt Yao headmen to exploit the landless Yao. The Pan Yao representatives chimed in: "We have long said that all Changmao Yao were bad. Now we are aware that our Changmao Yao compatriots are good people except a handful of bad and corrupt headmen, who have been defeated by the Communist Party and the People's Liberation Army. Now the poor have stood up and become masters of their own destiny. It is time for us to treat each other like brothers and cease regarding each other as enemies." [12] On the question of how to promote development, representatives of the Pan and Shanzi Yao said they supported the policy of allowing anyone to reclaim uncultivated land on the principle that one should own the fruit of one's labor. The Changmao Yao representatives, standing on the opposite side of the raised platform, expressed their willingness to give up their special privileges, saying, "We have more than enough uncultivated mountain land. If the Pan and Shanzi Yao want to reclaim land, we will allow them to do it and they can harvest the crops they plant for their own use." These ritualized speeches, no matter how choreographed and ideologically predetermined, were meant to symbolize not only the willingness on the part of the various Yao groups to reorganize the control of the means of production. They were also about the ritualized making of a new local subjectivity, one in which long-standing differences among different groups would be set aside.

After much discussion, a consensus was reached. Eleven representatives

A 1992 image of the stele erected after the signing of the Dayaoshan Unification Pact in 1951.

elected from each group sat down on the afternoon of 27 August. They drafted a solidarity agreement with six points. On the morning of 28 August, the draft resolution was discussed in small groups composed of all the representatives; requests for revision were then presented. For instance, the Han representatives suggested that the phrasing "all wild mountains can be freely reclaimed by the Guoshan Yao" be changed to "all wild mountains can be freely reclaimed by all nationalities," a revision that would also allow Han and Zhuang living in the Dayaoshan to reclaim land. In the afternoon, the Dayaoshan Unification Pact ("Dayaoshan tuanjie gongyue") was passed. On the following day, a shortened version of the six-point agreement was engraved on a stele, a gesture that was meant to replicate symbolically the form of the traditional *shipai* system. The various representatives, in traditional *shipai* fashion, together drank chicken blood and wine from shared earthenware bowls to express their willingness to obey the agreement. On the day the stele was erected, people from all over the county, dressed in the colorful embroidered clothing worn only on certain religious holidays, filled the valley of the present-day county seat.

With the stele now a permanent fixture on the landscape, the longer version of the agreement was mimeographed and a copy was distributed to every household in the many villages in the region. Self-surveillance became a key aspect of enforcement. Party cadres urged members of the higher classes (*gezu shangceng*) especially to take a lead in carrying out the agreement. Those that had been most severely struggled against and humiliated for past forms of exploitation were required to become the models and activists. Tao Xuantian, a Chashan Yao headman and the village chief of Liula (one of the villages in the vicinity of the present-day county seat), volunteered his labor and worked with the Guoshan Yao to help them reclaim uncultivated land. He trekked from village to village, using himself as an example to persuade other headmen to give up their own privileges and join in labor projects with the Guoshan Yao. The Party eventually acknowledged him as a model solidarity worker (*tuanjie mofan*). He was soon elected to deputy head of his district; several years later he became the head of the entire county.

The Slow Death of Feudalism

Most people I interviewed in Jinxiu about the early 1950s remembered this period as a good one, certainly an improvement over the horrors wrought by the much-hated Guomindang. I often suspected that those who might tell me different tales were being deliberately kept from me. I recall once learning that a former Chashan Yao Guomindang collaborator had been released from prison and was now living in a nearby village. He was euphemistically said to be "in retirement," though a friend wryly told me that the Party had decided that it would be all right for him to die at home; it would save them the mess of dealing with the corpse. For weeks on end I requested an interview. Everything was being arranged, I was told; the elderly Guomindang official was a little ill, but more than willing to speak to me. It was made to sound as though it was his decision alone. I never got the interview.

Su Xianting told me he was raised with the knowledge that the Guomindang period in the Dayaoshan was a living hell. Most Yao lived in fear during the 1940s; temples were destroyed, homes raided, women raped. Many blamed the arrival of prostitution and syphilis entirely on the Guomindang. Others told me that the Chashan Yao headmen had long maintained their own prostitution ring. Where was one to discern the truth? Was it worth the search? In any case, this was a time, Su told me, when the Yao thought they were losing control of their land; indeed, the meaning of land, as with the meaning of ethnic identity and revolutionary subjectivity, would become key issues in the remaking of Jinxiu. Though he admitted that "contradictions" between the landowners and the landless had always existed, he claimed that the Guomindang, who had coerced Yao headmen into collaborating with them, only exaggerated these. This resulted in part from the fact that the Guomindang instituted a tax system based on the household and police registration system known as the *baojia zhidu* carried out in other parts of the country.[13] This was meant to displace the tax system regulated by the *shipai*, but it actually worked to reinforce the power and authority of the *shipai* leaders who collaborated with the Guomindang. The signing of the solidarity agreement was meant to weaken the feudal privileges held by the *shanzhu* and to liberate the forces of production by reorganizing who owned and worked the land, but this was also tied up with the struggle against the Guomindang bandits. The double battle against Yao indigenous forms of feudalism and the Guomindang influence would continue. For example, in the winter of 1952 the people's government of what was then called the Yao Autonomous District of the Dayaoshan declared that the establishment of the solidarity agreement was basically correct. The district government emphasized, however, that enforcement measures had to be increased, for the landlord classes had not entirely given up their feudal ideas of social and economic privilege. The transformation of local consciousness was lagging behind changes in the social and political structure of the Dayaoshan. Attention was turned to one particular case in which a Chashan Yao headman in a region not far from the district seat refused to allow the Guoshan Yao to cultivate wild products in the mountains by enlarging their grazing land. In a series of disputes, headmen haggled with Party cadres over subtle distinctions and unclear definitions in the solidarity agreement. A large meeting was organized in February 1953, in which the cadre clarified the nature of land ownership and specified once again, though now with more force, the "correct" relationship that was to be maintained between landlords and tenants. A supplement to the original agreement was passed. Party cadres then sat down with elders (Yaolao) from the Changmao Yao group to once again convince them to become the models and leaders of the new system. Though this case received most of the attention in many of the reports I read from this period, I also found that from 1952 to 1953, an astonishing 1,637 conflicts were resolved in this fashion.[14]

Revolution had come to the Dayaoshan, but the work of the revolution would have to continue, for Yao feudalism died a slow death. In the 1950s, the category feudalism (*fengjian*) not only signified outmoded systems of social organization that kept the Yao in the mountains isolated from the outside world. Nor did it refer only to modes of local consciousness that connected the Yao more to the spirit realm than to the notion that China was a new nation-state finally realizing its destiny in history. Feudalism also marked the fact that the Guomindang continued to be a force in the hills and that many Yao, from each of the five subgroups, had participated in and embraced the Guomindang presence. It is thus important to remember that in the midst of all these negotiations, ritualized meetings, solidarity pacts, and instances of conflict resolution, the Guomindang and their Yao collaborators were being hunted in the hills. Liberation had come to the rest of the country, but a military campaign was still being carried out in the Dayaoshan. Official Party accounts produced in the 1980s on this era give the impression that the masses, especially the landowners and older Yao headmen, had come to understand the nature of local realities and past forms of exploitation through the benevolent teachings of an enlightened and sensitive cadre. When these local histories describe the festivities that accompanied the solidarity meetings, in which Changmao Yao danced with

Guoshan Yao and everyone admitted their mistakes, when unity was in the very process of being performed on stage, the war is rarely mentioned. Perhaps the risks of unraveling the reform myths of solidarity are too high. For to remember the war is to remember a time when the Yao subject was a split subject, a subject at war with itself and with the turmoil of the time. This was a time when political and ideological differences ruled the day, and the notion of a unified traditional culture tying together all Yao in a collective consciousness and identity had yet to be popularized.

The reform-era myth of a shared, collective identity is present in the posters of minority unification that hang in tourism bureaus and in the images of a united, multiethnic nation displayed at museums. In these phantasmagoric realms of ethnic and cultural imagining, there is no sense that there is a subject in the crowd trying to make up her mind, or one struggling with his loyalties, or one worrying about a friend or kinsperson who has been accused of being a collaborator. In these scenes in which the various subgroups of the Yao participate in the making of a modern Dayaoshan, fear and uncertainty belong to the past. So does the possibility that many Yao protected the Guomindang as they hid in the hills and engaged in their own propaganda efforts to win over the local populace. Many of my research consultants told me that even to this day it is difficult for them to admit that many Yao in the 1950s protected the Guomindang, even given everything the Guomindang had done in their campaigns to bring modernity to the Yao and defeat their periodic uprisings. I was told that there was in fact much debate among Yao leaders and commoners about whether the communists offered a better alternative, and a widespread unease and uncertainty about the veracity of cadre promises that the era of "big Han chauvinism" had actually come to an end.

Many of the activists who came to the Yao hills, we must recall, were Han and from areas quite removed from the Dayaoshan. Despite the fact that the Yao were being championed in the Guangxi press in the early 1950s as model minorities, it is probably correct to assume that many of these activists thought they were bringing modernity, socialism, and revolution to a people living on the margins of the modern world. But even before the Guomindang arrival in the hills in the 1940s, and even before the eradication campaigns against the Guomindang and their local collaborators, the Dayaoshan had been the site of complex interactions and negotiations. It seems to me that if memories and accounts of the Datengxia teach us anything, it is that the Yao groups in the hills had long been actors in the politics of empire in the south of China. As we saw in chapter 1, ethnohistorians of the south of China have long emphasized the conflicted and often violent relationship that existed between the imperial center and what was seen as the nonassimilated periphery. Han officials who reported on their travels and military campaigns saw themselves as the bearers of culture and civilization and the barbarian other as obstacles to be overcome in the opening of new territories. These "others," then, were hardly an isolated and passive people. Party cadres knew this from the beginning, of course, which is why the Yao in the Dayaoshan were seen not only as contaminated by indigenous social institutions with feudal modes of exploitation but also as subaltern subjects with their own history of revolution and rebellion. Yet it is the Party that must teach the local Yao what their rebellion means *historically*. If history has meaning, then it is invariably found in the nation's coming into being.

This is why so many narratives of the modern in contemporary Jinxiu begin with the disastrous penetration of the Guomindang, the bravery of the underground communist insurrection, and the heroic feats of the bandit suppression troops. Yet these narratives also show us how the modern was imagined as an incomplete project; the struggle to constitute it and make it real for the local populace would require a constant struggle to identify and eradicate the dangerous others that stand in its way. Yao headmen who refused to give up their local economic power and prestige were accused of clinging to the old ways not in private, but in public struggle sessions. They were marked as agents of a feudal system rooted in local forms of power and prestige that refused to give way to a present that was geared toward the nation and its utopian future. Yet, unlike the Guomindang, these agents of the feudal past could not be eliminated. They had to be won over through education and propaganda; this would allow Party cadres to demonstrate to others that revolution was also about the remaking of consciousness. This is one reason why Party cadres sought out (and no doubt rewarded) landed gentry who would publicly "voluntarily" relinquish their local power and in turn speak out in support of the solidarity campaigns. As with the subaltern Guoshan Yao, who owned no land and were given new voices and new forms of economic and social empowerment, the reformed landed gentry would also become a sign of the new era. What makes the revolutionary struggles of the 1940s "modern" is how Party cadres discursively linked revolutionary struggle with narratives of the nation's progress with the transformation of local consciousness. This tripartite connection among struggle, national progress, and local consciousness could not be enunciated simply in pamphlets and propaganda sessions, however. It had to be performed in the ritualized staging of a confession for past bad deeds. It had to be enacted in public pronouncements of both struggle and forgiveness and in long discussion sessions in which government officials explained the rules and regulations of land ownership and use that had been determined with the signing of "solidarity pacts."

This, then, was one aspect of the technology of power implemented in the Dayaoshan in the early stages of the revolution: cadres made a space for people to reinvent themselves and their histories through acts of public contrition and through altered forms of behavior and consciousness. Revolutionary consciousness was demonstrated through the performance of one's assigned identity. What did it mean, then, to be a Jinxiu Yao in the 1950s? At that time, I submit, it actually had very little to do with cultural identity. At least, very little to do with the localization of identity in language, costume, territoriality, and religious practice that was stipulated in Stalin's ethnological definitions of what constituted an ethnic minority and that we see today in many museum exhibits. Identity was interpreted and inscribed almost entirely through the economic principle. The Changmao Yao–Guoshan Yao divide was always about the distribution of material and economic power. It was a terminology used to define the nature of local reality and local identity, or at least this is how Party cadres saw it when they sought to map the local landscape so they could then change it. One's identity was determined in large part by where one fit into this classificatory scheme. Many Yao told me that this mode of naming the local was invented as far back as the 1920s by the Han who lived in the lowland valleys and in the counties on the outskirts of the hills, that it was never an indigenous classificatory system. Of course, those Yao with economic power who made frequent journeys to other parts of Guangxi and who traveled even to such "faraway" places as Guilin and to Yao places in what is today northern Vietnam, internalized the discourse and popularized it among their own people. But this does not dismiss the fact that this image of the social landscape was basically a Han construction of how the Dayaoshan was socially organized. This image was embedded in a long history of interethnic relations in which outsiders attempted to penetrate the mountains and bring Yao into the fold of different administrative, tax, and corvée labor systems. It was as "feudal" as anything else in the Dayaoshan.

Conclusion: The Revenge of History

A revolution is not the same as inviting people to dinner, or writing an essay, or painting a picture, or doing fancy needlework . . . a revolution is an uprising, an act of violence whereby one class overthrows another. —MAO ZEDONG, "Report on the Investigation of the Peasant Movement in Hunan"

In this and the previous chapter I have examined the politics of ethnic classification and subaltern mobilization in the Dayaoshan in the late 1940s and 1950s. I showed that many Jinxiu Yao (especially among the older generations) fondly remembered certain moments of Yao rebellion (the Datengxia uprising, for example) and the early phases of communist mobilization and struggle against the Guomindang. After the Guomindang were defeated, Party cadres went about the task of investing a considerable amount of "taxonomic fury" in trying to figure out what they initially saw as a very complex and messy local situation.[15] Yet, their charge was to define the boundaries of ethnic groups and locate their associated classes, map the terrain of class antagonism, and bring to the Dayaoshan a new language of unity. Party mobilization efforts in the 1950s would thus begin to seek out a subaltern other to speak against the *shipai* leadership. This became especially important once the collectivization movement kicked into gear in the mid-1950s, as tensions began to emerge among different groups and as the Party became increasingly suspicious that the old system had yet to be overturned. They found this subaltern other in the once landless and exploited Guoshan Yao, whom they championed as the group that would now be empowered to further the revolution in the Dayaoshan. Party cadres in the 1950s, I maintained, interpreted the problem of local class hegemony through the popular Changmao Yao–Guoshan Yao social categories. I argued that these were essentially local folk categories that had nothing to do with scientific Marxism and everything to do with prerevolutionary depictions of the Dayaoshan as a marginal and isolated area controlled by local headmen who exploited their own people.

Today there is no doubt in anyone's mind that modes of land ownership and tenancy were supported by the indigenous *shipai* system and that the *shipai*, with its rules and regulations, fines and punishments, protected and reproduced a hierarchical system of economic power and social prestige. However, many Chashan Yao intellectuals would argue to me that this system of local social and economic power was not about Yao intra-ethnic oppression, in which groups such as the Chashan Yao looked down on and freely took advantage of their upland neighbors such as the Pan Yao. They felt that the *shipai* system enabled the various Yao groups dispersed throughout the hills to maintain social order and, when conditions demanded, to unite to protect themselves from the ever encroaching Han and Zhuang in the valleys below. They thus argued that a discourse and practice of unity existed in Jinxiu long before the Communist Party showed up on the scene.[16] Su Xianting argued to me that long histories of ritual exchange existed among the Yao subgroups in the hills, histories that cut across the Changmao Yao–Guoshan Yao divisions. Ritual specialists from different families and groups would travel throughout the hills, sharing their knowledge and techniques of how to deal with and communicate with the spirit realm. His point, one shared by many of those I lived with and interviewed in Jinxiu, is that the Changmao Yao–Guoshan Yao division was not the only mode of rendering, representing, and understanding social and interethnic relations in the Dayaoshan. The problem is that Party cadres were little interested in these other ways of seeing the local social landscape, if only because those ways did not seem to help the cause of revolutionary mobilization. They saw clear-cut class divisions when in fact what they should have been seeing was a highly complex and fluid ethnic, cultural, and social system. Class and economic interests were no doubt part of the mix, but, as my research associates insisted, they were hardly the only interests at play and probably not the most determining of how people lived and interacted on an everyday basis.

If the Cultural Revolution had not come to the Dayaoshan, if Guangxi were not the center of some of this period's most intense Red Guard activity, if class were not used to search for and expose the hidden capitalist and feudal enemies of the state, then perhaps this history would not require this critical reappraisal. My Chashan Yao research associates argued that the Cultural Revolution was not only about the unleashing of the bellicose energies of activist Red Guards. It was more fundamentally about the state's inability to rationally manage and care for the population. And yet they also asserted that the denunciation of the class system and its social effects could not in and of itself solve Jinxiu's problems, especially its problems of rampant poverty and low morale. Many people in fact felt that the nightmare of the Cultural Revolution should be forgotten. More pressing issues were at hand; it was now the time to move on. The resurgence of popular ritual increasingly became a focus of their energies. If scientific Marxism once relegated popular ritual practice and religious belief to the domain of the superstructure, a domain of culture and consciousness antithetical to the making of revolutionary subjects, the widespread resurgence of popular ritual was demanding a new theoretical perspective. Many Chashan Yao—and I heard this from other Yao groups in the Dayaoshan as well—felt that ritual resurgence was about the cultural resiliency of their people, of how the mountain Yao were successfully reconstituting their "traditional" cultural practices after the ravages of three decades of political campaigns. Development and progress in Jinxiu was no longer to rest only within the hands of the Party-state apparatus; the making of the socialist modern future would depend on the ability of the local people to lift themselves up, to overcome the conditions of their isolation and backwardness. For some, this required studying and mobilizing local practices and social meanings that had been repressed and perhaps almost forgotten. An alternative modernity in Jinxiu was not to be based on the mimesis of the Party's dictates or by copying the West. The future was to be found in the space of the local, the indigenous, and the repressed.

In trying to open up an ethnographic space for these other modes of reckoning the local landscape—these other moral geographies of place—I hope it is clear that I am not attempting to recuperate the "indigenous" or "ritual" as a more real representation of Dayaoshan. Nor am I presenting this as the only way to see the history of this region. Su Xianting, Liu Yulian, Lao Huang, and others who taught me local history were constantly trying to get me to see the Chashan Yao otherwise, as something other than an exploitative and hegemonic local group. Liu was especially invested in this reworking of the Chashan Yao identity. Teacher Liu, as I called her, was an older woman, an ethnologist at the Minyuan in Beijing, a widely published author and world traveler who wanted me to know and respect Marxism. She wanted me to be a good materialist, but she herself despised the reduction of all local realities to the economic principle. As with many intellectuals of her generation, she was forced on several occasions throughout the 1960s and early 1970s to publicly declare that her thinking about poor peasants was misguided because of her family's class background. She was born into a relatively wealthy Chashan Yao family in Jinxiu County; her family once owned large tracts of land and employed laborers from the landless Guoshan Yao group. She once recounted to me how, in the early 1950s, Han

The Chashan Yao ethnologist, Liu Yulian. The man behind her is a guide from the Jinxiu Tourism Bureau.

Party cadres working in the area to mobilize the landless peasants stormed into the home of a relative to criticize him for the way he treated his workers. A heated argument ensued in which the Chashan Yao in the village tried to convince the cadres that even though they hired workers from landless non–Chashan Yao groups, their relations were based on "mutual respect." The Chashan Yao villagers attempted to employ the rhetorical language of the Party—the reference to mutual respect—but their class background presupposed such a sentiment. She told me again and again of how the Chashan Yao treated the landless Yao with decency, how they never looked down on them, how they fed them after they labored in the fields, how they maintained friendly relations for many years. This issue of land exploitation would come back to haunt her during the Cultural Revolution, when she was ordered to leave her research institute and work among Han peasants in another part of Guangxi in order to rectify her thinking.

As did many Han intellectuals who were struggled against during the Cultural Revolution, Liu Yulian saw the period between the late 1950s and the late 1970s as one of tragic loss. As she saw it, her career as a scholar— and she was one of the most successful female scholars from Jinxiu, a point she always emphasized—was essentially wasted. In her youth and through much of her adult life she was never able to share with her colleagues in the field of ethnology the great store of knowledge she possessed about Jinxiu and its history. She had her own perspective on the nature of pre-Liberation social and ethnic relations in the Dayaoshan. She could recite from memory long passages from Taoist texts she had learned from watching rituals in her childhood; she knew the intricacies of female embroidery work and the nature of its symbolism. Her problem as an aspiring ethnologist—she would officially be called a "nationalities worker" after the Great Leap Forward in the late 1950s until the late 1970s—was that her kind of knowledge was rooted in the intricacies and details of her subgroup's customs, beliefs, and religious practices. She thought Jinxiu was a more complicated place than certain periods of Chinese socialist history allowed. As with so many from her generation, she was accused of neglecting studies that would emphasize the nature of local forms of exploitation. For her, this was a perpetual dilemma because it meant in large part openly criticizing her own subgroup as well as members of her extended family.

In the 1980s, Liu, as were so many other minority intellectuals in China, was actively and critically rethinking the socialist past. Though they were often speaking and writing against a certain view of local history, they were not doing so outside of new articulations of power and knowledge. As I have emphasized, their critical engagements with past modes of representing local social worlds took place in the context of the reform regime's attempt to distance itself from the legacy of Maoist class struggle. All of them had me read the *Jinxiu gaikuang*, which, in one form or another, they had all helped to produce in the 1980s. Toward the end of the tale, the following story is told.

> In the midst of the "ten years of turmoil" (*shinian dongluan*), the reactionaries Lin Biao and Jiang Qing promoted the idea that "the nationality problem is in actuality a class problem" (*minzu wenti shizi shi jieji wenti*). This became the theoretical basis on which the ultraleftist line (*jizuo luxian*) was carried out in minority areas. The ultraleftists abused theory in their attempt to seize power from the Party and the masses. In the early 1980s, the reform-era county government officially declared that in the long history of Party building and cadre training in Jinxiu, the Yao people were adversely affected by "leftist" ideas. Over the course of several successive political movements, class struggle was enlarged beyond reasonable control and carried out to radical extremes. Class struggle tore apart the social and political fabric of local society, and it harmed many good Party members, cadres, and dedicated commune members. The ultraleftists abolished the Party leadership; conducted activities aimed at anarchism and national division; recklessly broke the Party constitution and its rules; and left the reform present with many cases of injustice and false accusation, all of which have severely damaged the Party and its mass organizations throughout the county. With the crackdown on the notorious and much hated *siren bang* or Gang of Four, and especially since the Third Plenary Meeting of the Eleventh Party Congress, the current leadership has begun to set wrongs right. It has spoken out against the ultraleftist line and moved to redress the many pending cases of injustice. In strengthening discipline within the Party, the tradition and style of Party mobilization and recruitment has been restored.

The narrative thus ends with the quintessential rhetorical flare of the reform period: As the relationship between the Party and the masses has improved, a solid base has been established for the making of a more advanced material and spiritual national culture and civilization in the Dayaoshan. As a student of ethnology in China and of local culture and politics in Jinxiu, I was required to memorize this narrative of past ideological excesses and of a nation now coming into material and spiritual fulfillment. I couldn't help but know this narrative by heart, for it was so ubiquitous, found in nearly everything I read. We must understand this as a narrative of state power and its critique, but also as a kind of discursive blueprint for a new mode of governmentality. Liu Yulian, as did so many people I knew and lived with in Jinxiu, welcomed this narrative. It made sense to her. It spoke to her past and to many of her private sentiments. Like everyone in China, she knew it was Party rhetoric, a new political language for a new ideological time. Yet for her and many others it opened up a space to rethink the history of socialist modernity in China, and especially in the Dayaoshan. It enabled her and other minority elite to participate in the construction of what many understand as a new and more rational form of local governance, one in which local forms of indigenous knowledge will be respected and perhaps even encouraged to flourish in the new socialist modern China. To be sure, these visions of a new form and mode of governmentality seek to bring order to a local social body that is believed, and perhaps not incorrectly so, to be battered, disorganized, and disillusioned. Liu and others would find in the shipai not only the remnants of a system of class exploitation and feudalism, but also practices of social morality, order, and civility, the very things the new regime was so desperately seeking. For Liu, the representation of Yao "traditional" culture was very much tied up with the question of how the revolution was to be remembered. To clarify the distortions of the past, to know the local and find a space for indigenous culture, was to participate in the making of an alternative local future, one no longer marred by the violence of the past. What this future would look like was uncertain, but it was nonetheless a crucial question, both for her personally and for the people, the Chashan Yao, she sought to speak for and redeem. Socialist memory was at stake. So was the love of country.

In the next chapter, I take up the question of how one might begin to write a critical ethnography of the technologies of power and knowledge that have shaped reform-era discourse on minority culture and history. I show how research on the shipai engendered localized debates on the meaning of Yao culture, on the effects of Maoist politics, on social order, and on the specter of state power as a disruptive force in everyday life. At the center of the analysis is the reform-era elite fascination with Yao popular ritual. Ethnologists in China often state that Yao Taoist specialists do not like to have outsiders document their ritual practices.[17] In my interviews with Taoist priests in the village of Xidi and elsewhere in Jinxiu, I found that many were willing to recount the general contours of ritual knowledge. They were rarely willing to discuss, however, the use of Taoist magic to ward off supernatural forces and other entities believed to cause harm, sickness, and misfortune. This has less to do with some essential cultural suspicion or taboo against the sharing of ritual knowledge than with the fact that Taoist masters today practice their craft with memories of the Maoist suppression of Yao ritual and in the context of contemporary modes of government surveillance. My discussion therefore does not seek to describe and unpack the internal symbolic meanings and associations of Yao Taoism, from funerals to marriage practices to Taoist ordination rites, nor do I demonstrate how these rituals solve, in a functional sense, social antagonisms and conflicts in local society. This has been done elsewhere.[18] Additionally, I do not follow other observers and contend that, in the aftermath of the Maoist regime, popular ritual practice today constitutes a more enduring sense of moral community, that it has returned some semblance of symbolic structure to an otherwise chaotic and wounded social body. Finally, I do not think that the widespread interest in contemporary popular ritual was only about the recovery and staging of the traditional culture of the Yao in the making of a multiethnic national imaginary. Rather, I argue that it has more to do with anxieties about the politics of rule and about how the Communist Party has sought to mobilize the energies of the local populace. In short, it had to do with the politics of governmentality.

chapter four
The State and Its Ritual Potencies

The State puts itself forward as a form full of potencies.

—JOSÉ GIL, *The Metamorphoses of the Body*

The previous two chapters demonstrated how the ethnic landscape of Jinxiu was mapped in the 1950s. Party cadres, most of whom were Han, began insurrectionary work in the Yao mountains in the late 1940s and built strong relationships with Yao from different subgroups who joined the underground movement and fought against the Guomindang. They also aimed to determine the degree to which Yao intra-ethnic relations were structured by different modes of oppression and exploitation. Through mobilization strategies and the signing of unification pacts in the early 1950s, they popularized the view that the pre-Liberation Changmao Yao–Guoshan Yao social category was marred by class antagonisms. Individuals from the Changmao Yao category were asked to turn against the landowning elite, and the Guoshan Yao groups were championed as the region's subaltern subject. Knowledge of the local terrain was thus linked to the larger task of uprooting what Party cadres saw as a deeply entrenched "feudal" social structure, maintained and supported by the so-called stone tablet system (*shipai*).

I also argued that the *shipai* system itself occupied an ambiguous status among ethnological researchers sent to carry out the Party's social history research investigations in 1956. Throughout much of the 1950s, ethnological interpretations of the *shipai* revolved around one crucial issue: Was this form of "primitive law" a tool for class exploitation? Or was it an ingenious adaptation of the Yao people, isolated in the mountains and constantly forced to defend themselves from encroaching Han and Zhuang bandits? Was the *shipai* filled with feudalistic political concepts? Or did it express the unified will of a non-Han people who valiantly defended their territory against the rulers of past dynasties? In carrying out the nationalities strategy of respecting ethnic customs, Party cadres and government officials acknowledged and at times celebrated (as with the signing of the unification pact) the *shipai* for its ability to maintain social order, protect the mountains, and ensure a functioning, if rudimentary, productive base. When villages began to be organized into production brigades in the mid-1950s, cadres called their political gatherings *shipai* meetings. Party propaganda efforts were done in the spirit of the *shipai*, or at least this is what the official rhetoric proclaimed. This, then, was the application of the Stalinist theory of ethnic forms: Use ethnic forms to mobilize the masses, but fill the forms with socialist content.[1]

The politics of interpretation shifted in the late 1950s, however. Based on my interviews, I found that in the 1950s up until the time of the Great Leap Forward (circa 1958), the *shipai* was seen at once as a form of feudal exploitation and as a kind of ingenious ethnic adaptation to external systems of power. It survived as a local ethnic cultural form in this space of ambiguity. Many elders in Jinxiu told me that they knew the social structure of the *shipai* was changing, and they knew the old system of land ownership was on the way out. But they were impressed and supportive of how Party cadres tried to keep the *shipai* alive as an indigenous practice that could be used in the social transformation of the Dayaoshan. Party documents from the reform period present the Land Reform Campaign as the final blow to the *shipai* system, its leaders, and modes of local consciousness. Land reform in Jinxiu did not only redistribute the land, it also made obsolete previously hegemonic cultural orderings of the local social landscape. In the 1960s and on into the early 1970s, the policy of appropriating ethnic forms was attacked by Party officials and then later by Red Guard factions as a reactionary practice. The use of the *shipai* as an ethnic form, and the ethnic policy that defended it, was treated as a political mistake in that it allowed "bad class elements" (*huai fenzi*) to disguise their true intentions and cling to past forms of authority. Although there were occasions in the 1960s when Yao traditional clothing was still worn (during performances for visiting dignitaries, for example), almost all forms of ethnic customs were eventually labeled unwanted remnants of the feudal past. During the Cultural Revolution, no one dared to claim a lineage connection to a once powerful *shipai* leader. When I was doing household surveys in the Chashan Yao villages of Xidi and Liula, for instance, I kept coming across individuals who had changed their surnames. Thinking I was onto some kind of new twist in Yao kinship structure, I soon discovered that this was a common way individuals disguised their family background, especially if a family with a bad "hat" wanted to get a daughter or son into a regional school. It wasn't until the early 1980s that this kind of class background discrimination began to be replaced in schools and other official settings by systems of merit. Nonetheless, many of the people I interviewed and lived with told me that the class prejudice and new systems of inequality were an integral part of everyday life under the reforms.[2]

As was the shipai, Yao ritual life was extensively studied in the 1950s. As was the shipai, ritual too eventually came to be treated as an object of ideological struggle. As I previously indicated, many if not all of the ethnological reports on ritual from this period were published only in the 1980s. These reports suggest there was a widespread belief among the mountain Yao in a host of "natural" spirits, and they argue that this form of primitive animism had, over time, been integrated into the more fully developed ritual system based on the cosmologies of Chinese Taoism.[3] The animistic beliefs were said to be a vestige of a much more ancient and primitive religion, one that predated the popularization of Taoism in the south of China during the Southern Song (see my discussion of Strickmann's work in chapter 1). Consistent with the evolutionary narrative of the Jianshi, these ethnological reports argue that the religious beliefs of the Yao reflect the level of Yao social development. The introduction of Taoism into Yao belief systems, for example, is said to have occurred at the same time that the Yao came to be incorporated into the feudal economies of imperial China. When Party cadres began studying the beliefs of Yao peasants in the 1950s, they argued that the widespread "superstitious" beliefs of the mountain Yao reflected the underdeveloped (luohou) state of the local society and economy. If the local economy could be developed, then the superstitious consciousness of the Yao could be transformed; a modern, socialist, and forward-looking subject would then emerge and take its place alongside other more advanced nationalities.

The popularity of Taoism among the mountain Yao posed somewhat of a problem, however. Chinese ethnologists and Party officials recognized that they did not stumble upon a primitive people who lived under the illusion that all natural phenomena had souls and spirits, everything from mountain summits to rice paddies to the wooden drums and digging tools of the Yao farmer. They also found a sophisticated ritual system centering around a celestial cosmology interpreted and propitiated by Taoist masters of differing ranks who performed community exorcisms, engaged in spirit mediumship, and cured the sick. Many of these ritual specialists were well connected to the *shipai* leadership. The mountain peasants in the Dayao-shan could not easily be described as a preliterate "tribe" never touched by a civilized culture; they were a proud, yet seemingly suspicious people who maintained libraries of ritual texts hand-copied and passed down from one generation to the next.[4] There was something about the Yao mastery of Taoism that made them more culturally Chinese-like and thus, in some ineffable way, closer to the center of Chinese civilization.

Nonetheless, from these reports one gets the impression that the Jínxiu Yao all identified with a realm of supernatural authority. As a youth close to the Party underground movement in the village of Xidi in the late 1940s, Su Xianting was given the task of holding secret meetings with other Xidi villagers. Together they read Party newspapers and propaganda pamphlets brought into the area from other regions of China. He told me that although few villagers actually understood the finer points of Marxist-Leninist thought, what was important to him and many others is that the Communist Party offered a way to end the brutal local rule of the Guomindang. As we saw in the previous chapter, the Guomindang, for example, burned the entire village of Xidi to the ground in 1944 because Guomindang officials suspected the villagers to be harboring Communist Party sympathizers. After the victory against the Guomindang and the administrative establishment of the Yao autonomous region, many Taoist specialists continued to perform ritual ceremonies for weddings and funerals. By the mid-1960s, these activities were brought to a halt. Ritual specialists often complained about how their activities and knowledge were constructed as belonging to another historical moment; one elder told me I would be making a drastic mistake if I wrote that Yao ritual was a kind of "primitive culture" (*yuanshi wenhua*). He was no doubt exhibiting knowledge of previous modes of representation. In the Maoist period, for example, Yao ritual was attacked as one of the "vestiges" (*canji*) of the so-called feudal past, the very stuff that made possible exploitation. Many ritual texts were confiscated and burned; the entire cornucopia of healing and prophylactic interventions was basically outlawed; many ritual specialists were imprisoned, a few killed. When I asked if rituals were then carried out surreptitiously, the answer was yes, but they were always enacted in an atmosphere of great fear.

My initial point is that socialist pedagogy demanded a transformation of the "superstitious" worldview of the peasants. As in other regions of China, the Jinxiu Yao were encouraged to adopt a more materialist view of social realities and to give up their psychological dependence on a host of guardian spirits, local gods, and other magical characters sought out in times of sickness or personal or family crisis.[5] In Jinxiu, the Party approached the transformations of this superstitious consciousness by focusing on the Taoist specialists. Taoist masters, already occupying an authoritative position in local communities, were encouraged to become Party members, to study Marxist-Leninist thought, and to educate their common villagers. Four of the five Taoist priests I came to know in the Chashan Yao villages surrounding the county seat were retired Communist Party members, who, under the reforms, had once again begun to oversee the ritual affairs of funerals and weddings. One young man in his early thirties, who had recently graduated from a technical college in the provincial capital of Nanning, was the first Yao to go through the Taoist initiation rite, the *dujie*, in over thirty years. Su Xianting was one of the local priests who oversaw the details of this three-day ritual event. He explained to me that although few Yao youth were now interested in becoming ritual specialists, more and more villagers were once again turning to these specialists for ritual intervention in the affairs of everyday life. I asked him if current Party officials were concerned that this kind of ritual activity was propagating "feudal superstition" among the masses. His response was telling: it was the responsibility of Taoist priests such as he, those who had spent years working for the Party but were now returning to their ritual trade, to monitor the popularity of Yao ritual practice among the masses. He emphasized that one of the major concerns was controlling the financial outlay required for ritual practice; ritual specialists were not to exploit for personal gain peasant desires for ritual intervention and they were to encourage peasants not to be extravagant (*shechi*) in their demands.

In the 1980s the county government in Jinxiu was thus relying in large part on Taoist priests to monitor the return of popular ritual. Many of them, such as Su, were either once Party members or once connected in some way to local county government. Although some Party officials and Taoist specialists argued that superstition was still a fundamental problem in the mountains, there seemed to be less concern about what people actually believed and more concern for the effects of ritual activity on everyday production, household income and savings, and social order. In fact, the move

away from a close monitoring of the realm of belief is reflective of the reform regime's overall rethinking of the "problem of religion."[6] Religious
belief and practice, if properly monitored and developed in the "correct" direction, was being interpreted as potentially beneficial to post-Mao China's
modernization effort. Moreover, officials who sought to demonstrate how
the reform regime was adopting a more rational approach to the problem of
social development often pointed to the new policy on religion. The return
and increased popularity of ritual practice have thus been appropriated in
a symbolic struggle to demarcate the reform present, seen as a more rational and controlled form of governmentality, from the radical phases of the
Maoist era.

　　Few officials in Jinxiu employed the term "feudal superstition" (*fengjian
mixin*) when interacting with villagers and they would often talk about ritual
as a form of "traditional culture" (*chuantong wenhua*). Others were suspicious
of the local fascination with traditional culture, which they saw as a site of
potential disorder. One official told me that the peasants (*nongmin*) had become a little too interested in magic and other forms of superstition. The
mountain Yao, she asserted, needed to get on with the business of socialist modernity, which meant raising the quality of their people. They were
hindered by a psychology that enjoyed isolation; they were too attached to
their traditions and, what could be worse, they had a tendency to produce
only for everyday subsistence. These were the traits frequently said to keep
the Yao—a "backward" and "remote" minority living on the margins of the
new reform nation—from realizing their true destiny in history. My field
notes from this time record the following entry, based on a conversation
with a high-ranking official in the Jinxiu government. As he put it in the
unequivocal modernist language of the reforms: "To modernize Yao society
we need to break through the condition of Yao self-isolation in the mountains, and we must cast off [*baituo*] all outmoded concepts and customs. It is
necessary to heighten the cultural quality of the Yao, to develop educational
undertakings in order to cultivate a new generation of Yao people."

　　For intellectuals and officials especially, then, Yao ritual life would be
subjected to theoretical and epistemological frameworks that drew boundaries between the modern and the traditional, between the Maoist period
and the reforms, between the material and the spiritual, between culture
and politics. Yet, I was also impressed by how some of my Chashan Yao research associates were attempting to open up a space for the traditional
in the political practices of socialist modernization. They argued that the

traditional cultural practices of their people did not constitute outmoded concepts and customs that had to be thrown off. On the contrary, they were filled with ideas and practices—potencies, to return to the Gil epigraph at the beginning of this chapter—that could assist the reform regime. In this chapter I explore discourses on the social morality of different Yao sub-groups, the relationship between indigenous social practice and the Civilized Village Campaign, and the politics of how Liu Yulian remembered the birthing and reproductive practices of the Chashan Yao.

Questions of State

In attending to these various discourses of indigenous knowledge and social practice, my aim is to enjoin debates in the China field and other interdisciplinary arenas on the nature of the state. As I pointed out at the beginning of chapter 2, the study of Chinese politics has often turned on the question of how to understand the relationship between state and society. In the 1980s, for example, many China scholars began to argue that during the Maoist period the state-society relationship was more complex than initially believed and that a new and even more complex relationship was emerging under the reforms.[7] A central issue in these debates was the question of whether Maoist socialism had actually transformed the consciousness of the masses.[8] In what ways had the socialist project been successful? In what ways had it failed? How, after Maoism, were we to understand the nature of the state and its methods of social regulation, control, surveillance, and popular mobilization? Was it even possible to speak of a uniform state, one that could be generalized to different regions of the country? Did the Party and its various bureaucratic agencies operate in the same way in all places? Did it matter that in autonomous ethnic counties such as Jinxiu, minorities were mostly in charge, dealing with complex intra- and interethnic relations and histories of cultural struggle?

These questions point to both theoretical and methodological issues. Scholars have been certain that the term post-Mao China referred obviously enough to the events and developments after the death of Mao in 1975. But not everyone was sure whether the so-called post-Mao regime constituted a radical disjuncture from the Maoist period. Thus, some scholars have been interested in, for instance, how the socialist past, with its command politics, its mass campaigns, and its class differentiation system, has informed the reform present and its new experiments in governmentality and market economics. How, many have asked, do we understand the legacy of Mao's rule and egalitarian ideologies in a historical moment suspicious of class politics and hungry for rapid economic development? Especially after the Tiananmen crisis and the subsequent political crackdown on the movement's "counterrevolutionaries," scholars began to entertain questions of public space and public spheres; some began to note points of crisis, conflict, and tension that they argued existed in an emergent "civil society."[9] These various approaches to the state-society relationship often betrayed radically different conceptions of the nature of power and modernity, and they covered a range of political commitments to Deng's socialist modernization agenda. Many scholars were certain that the Cultural Revolution, for example, had tarnished the Communist Party's relationship with the masses. Some pushed the analysis even further and asserted that the CCP, especially after the Tiananmen crackdown, had become an alienated force in social life. If this was a regime that had lost touch with the very masses it had so long championed as the nation's heart and soul, then who spoke for the socialist modern future?

Outside of the China field, scholars have focused on the nation-state and its political and cultural imaginaries. Those who have written on the role of discourses of tradition in nation-state politics have drawn attention to the discursive construction of the nation-state and emphasized the politics of modernity in unequal global relations. In looking at Japan, for example, Marilyn Ivy has persuasively argued that like other colonized and near-colonized polities, "Japan as a nation-state was instaurated in response to the threat of domination by the Euroamerican powers in the mid–nineteenth century. It is arguable that there was no discursively unified notion of 'Japanese' before the eighteenth century, and the particular articulation of a unified Japanese ethos with the 'nation' to produce 'Japanese culture' is entirely a modern configuration."[10] Ivy's work has successfully traced how the idea of Japan as a distinct and unique cultural sphere, with its own national realm to protect, has relied on phantasmagoric imaginings of a tradition that is perpetually disappearing.[11] This sense of a constantly vanishing tradition propels national cultural industries, heritage foundations, tourist excursions to magical and haunted sites, and the practices of longing that many critics see as the quintessential marker of national cultural politics. One gets the sense, however, that the nation has received more critical attention than the state. Do the nation and the state long for the vanishing in the same way? How might we begin to understand national and state imaginaries as different kinds of political practice? How might these discourses of vanishing cultures and modes of longing speak to local forms and practices of governmentality? How, in short, does the desire to protect and recover the nation's tradition get entangled in governmental modes of protecting, mobilizing, and securing the support—and love—of subject populations?

Let me refer to one more ethnographic example that has addressed how modern nations seek out "traditional peoples," one that begins to raise the question of how to theorize the relationships between discourses of tradition and practices of governmentality. In writing about indigenous politics in Australia, Elizabeth Povinelli has traced the ways in which modern liberal nation-states have recognized and debated the worth of their interior ethnic peoples. Povinelli seeks to move beyond the essential multicultural question of why a settler nation (Australia) should recognize the worth of indigenous customary law. She asks more fundamental questions: "What is the state and nation recognizing and finding worthy when it embraces the 'ancient laws' of indigenous Australia? What is the thing 'tradition' which produces sensations; desires; professional, personal, and national optimisms; and anxieties? . . . What is this glimmering object the public support of which can produce, as if by magical charm, the feelings necessary for social harmony in the multicultural nation, for good trading relations with the Asian-Pacific, and for a new globally inspirational form of national cohesion? Why must Aboriginal persons identify with it to gain access to public sympathy and state resources?" [12] Povinelli aims to track the transformations of "traditional indigenous law" across various public, state, and commercial domains, and to map, as she puts it, "the political cunning and calculus of cultural recognition in a settler modernity." [13] For her, hegemonic domination in postcolonial multicultural societies works by inspiring in the indigenous subject a desire to seek out and identify with a lost object, to in fact turn oneself into the "melancholic subject of traditions."

The making of a multicultural and multiethnic postsocialist China has also revolved around the structuring of desire for objects lost to history. Yet my argument is that this is only the beginning of the story of power and its multifarious operations in a China seeking to move beyond the ideological excesses of the Maoist period and especially the Cultural Revolution. For the desire to know, mark, discuss, and present one's traditions has been inescapably linked to critical readings of the nature of the state and its power to transform social worlds. In the late 1980s and early 1990s, I assert, discourses of tradition were not only about the nation and its internal others. They were also about the capacity of ethnic subjects to overcome the traumas of the past and to participate in the forging of new modes of governmentality, modes of local rule that would require the recovery of indigenous knowledges and traditional cultural practices.

Travels in Surveillance

In February 1991, just after the Chinese New Year celebrations, I was invited to attend a Taoist ceremony with a contingent of Party and government officials in a village I will call Longpan. This village was located in the far southwest of Jinxiu County, in an area inhabited predominantly by the Pan Yao. We were to be accompanied on our journey by several guides connected with the county's recently established Tourism Bureau. At this point in my Jinxiu research I had been living for several months in the village of Xidi, just up the road from the main street that runs through the administrative seat of the county. I had recently begun to interview several officials in the government about the social history of the region. From them and others I had heard repeated rumblings about all of the ritual going on in the remote hills. What else was the anthropologist to do but follow the trail of ritual activity?

I thought that getting away from the administrative center of the county and far out into the hills was essential if I was to pursue my interest in the relationship between post-Mao practices of ethnicity and the history of the "nationalities problem" in the Dayaoshan. I was influenced in this respect by a long tradition of anthropological thinking that told me that ritual was a domain of symbolic action that, if properly decoded, would provide me with insight into the workings and meanings of the Yao social world. Trained in the academic field of Chinese studies, I had come to believe that ritual activity among the rural populace had much to teach me about the relationship among representations of power, ideology, and everyday social life. Yet I was also interested in the history of Chinese ethnological interpretations of ritual practice since the revolution in 1949. Since the early 1950s, if not before, many Party cadres, scholars, and government officials believed that religious thinking and ritual behavior kept the rural masses from realizing their destiny in history. The Party has consistently treated popular ritual among rural peasants as a domain of social activity that reveals the persis-

tence of "feudal" modes of thinking and localized forms of social organization that support local leaders whose political identifications are believed
to lie elsewhere. Suppression of ritual, then, was often about the struggle
over local forms of authority and local conceptions of power. In Jinxiu, for
example, though each of the five subgroups has its own local gods and its
own modes of domestic ritual practice, the *shipai* leadership often used large
ritual ceremonies to make public announcements or organize local defense
groups. *Shipai* leaders were often trained Taoist specialists, and *shipai* meetings often began with the burning of incense and the worship of various
Taoist gods. When ethnologists and researchers in the Tourism and Cultural Artifacts Bureau interviewed village elders about past ritual practice,
they would often recall the *shipai* leadership and its more memorable *shipai*
meetings. Especially among the Chashan Yao, the resurgence of ritual practice invoked memories of the *shipai* and its appropriation and suppression
in the 1950s.

This localized interest in ritual practice and its historical ties to the *shipai*
system must be seen in the context of a more generalized national interest in popular ritual among rural peasants. When I first arrived in Beijing
in 1988, I discovered that social scientists from Beijing and other parts
of China were venturing into minority regions to study the resurgence of
popular ritual. They often returned with photographs of large communities of young men and women being introduced to the Taoist pantheon,
of Taoist specialists clad in multicolored robes, and of close-ups of the
ritual accoutrements of the priesthood. These images would then appear in
academic publications detailing the religious beliefs and practices of minorities and in popular magazines that reported on minority affairs. These
academic and popular images of an ethnic populace engaged in esoteric
ritual no doubt contributed to the exoticization of minorities in the 1980s.
However, what these images did not show is that in the context of everyday life, ritual practice was subjected to official scrutiny and surveillance.
The Chinese government continued to maintain the elaborate bureaucratic
system that had been set up in 1954 under the leadership of the Religious
Affairs Bureau, which had operational branches at the national, provincial,
county, and township levels. Party members at these various levels monitored religious affairs and tracked the finances of various religious groups.
Numerous reports appeared in the official press in the 1980s noting both
the increase in religious activity among the masses and the gallant actions
of Party cadres who suppressed the "profiteers" who charged excessive

A Pan Yao village on the way to Longpan.

sums of money for their services and manipulated the uneducated peasant. These were not the only modes of surveillance. As I emphasized previously, articles began to appear in ethnological and religious affairs journals in the 1980s discussing how religious modes of thought and behavior might assist in the socialist modernization agenda. Party functionaries at all levels of the bureaucracy were examining popular ritual not only in terms of how it created disorder, but also how it might contribute to the maintenance of social order. This other mode of surveillance, one that would exceed the state's traditional repressive function and promote indigenous forms of ritual to assist in the reforms, would become clear to me during my trip to Longpan.

The trip to Longpan required a long bus ride on bumpy gravel roads. We spent the first night in a village along the side of the road, sleeping on wooden cots with thick down comforters in the empty rooms of the village head. In the morning we woke to a bowl of spicy noodle soup and then set out in a thin mist of rain on one of the trails that left the rear of the village. Reaching Longpan would require a full day's walk on narrow trails that passed through verdant mountain forests and several small Pan Yao villages of no more than twenty households. As I pointed out in previous chapters, in the pre-Liberation period the Pan Yao belonged to the landless Guoshan Yao group. To reiterate, they were among the first groups to be mobilized by

Communist Party cadres in the late 1940s, implored to struggle against the mountain landlords, the Changmao Yao group who controlled the *shipai*. For the most part, the Pan Yao continued to live in the county's more remote regions and, though they outnumbered the other groups, they tended to be the poorest and the most dependent on state subsidies. They were also known in the hills to be ardent practitioners of Taoism. Because a large community ritual and market fair was in the making, my traveling companions carried with them video cameras and photographic gear. We were each additionally stocked with gifts—candies, liquor, cigarettes, and meat—to present to our hosts.

When we reached Longpan we were met by the village Party secretary and several young men and women dressed in the costumes of their group, the men in indigo trousers, top shirts, and tunics, the women in embroidered headdresses and skirts. As I would find on many similar visits to other parts of the county, the appearance of these modern ethnic subjects in traditional garb was a cue for the photo session to begin, and everyone scrambled for their gear. Once the initial images were captured, we sat down for tea and almost immediately entered into a discussion about how arduous (*xinku*) our trip had been and how backward (*luohou*) and remote (*pianpi*) this area of the county remained. Our hosts apologized again and again for their poverty and lack of development; they insisted that the people in these parts were doing everything they could to lift themselves up and modernize the conditions of their existence. It wasn't entirely clear how this was being accomplished, for rice was still being imported to these villages and most of the timber in the forests was being cleared and sent to other parts of the province. The younger men and women in this and the nearby villages worked as day laborers for these timber projects, so that some families now had more disposable income to spend on goods they could not produce themselves. The conversation soon shifted to other topics, however, as one of the Party officials asked how much money was being spent on the ritual activities we would observe over the next few days. No one knew for sure, but everyone present agreed with the official that it was important not to be too extravagant (*shechi*) in celebrating these "traditional" ritual activities (*yishi huodong*). What I found most striking in moments such as these was how questions of traditional practice, especially those revolving around large ritual affairs that brought villages and networks of villages together, were interpreted through discourses of remoteness and historical lag. Most of the peasants in fact never employed the term "tradition" in talking about

Young Taoist initiates in the vicinity of Longpan.

what was to take place. And only a few of them could actually explain the details of initiation or the texts the Taoist masters (all of whom were members of the Pan Yao group, though one had traveled from another part of the county) would read from and recite.

Over the next few days in Longpan, I listened attentively to the Pan Yao villagers apologize for their lack of development and watched county officials express both fascination and contempt for the increased boisterousness (*renao*) of Yao community ritual. I also watched as the Pan Yao villagers built an elaborate series of bamboo bridges, some two or three meters off the ground. A number of Taoist priests had been called into the village to oversee the proceedings, which had the dual purpose of curing illnesses and prolonging the life of all of the villagers. Once the ceremony began, around one hundred men and women (it was impossible to get a precise count) gathered in a large opening on a hillside; many of them were dressed in elaborately embroidered robes. As the Yao Taoist practitioners recited aloud from ancient hand-copied texts, the young men and women climbed the ladders of bamboo bridges and were then led across the top and down the other side. The event took an entire day and was repeated on the second. A large community banquet was served in the evening. On the third day of our visit the sky turned gray and torrential rains hit the hills, turning everything into mud; most of the villagers disappeared. We waited out the storm for two days, passing our time drinking tea and local rice wine and talking about such topics as marriages, deaths, and grain shortages. Though I was traveling with several high-ranking officials in the Party bureaucracy and county government, I was impressed with how these officials seemed to know all of the villagers, how they were tied to these distant villages through complex social, political, and kin relations. It was clear that these officials had traveled to this remote region of Jinxiu to document with their cameras and notebooks the bodily markers of ethnic costume and the colorful and complex rituals of the Yao. Some of these images would later appear on the wall of the Tourism Bureau, inviting travelers to Jinxiu to venture even further into the hills, once, of course, a permit and guide had been secured. The resurgence of community ritual would become the topic of government and Party meetings and directives, and, of course, the material of ethnological accounts on Yao social life.

The county government's interest in tradition was related to larger national debates occurring among intellectuals and Party cadres at all levels of the state apparatus about the relationship among culture, tradition, modernity, and socialism under the reforms. Many people I interviewed about Yao ritual in Jinxiu felt that the reform-era Communist Party was correct in rethinking its policy on religious belief and practice. The new constitution, adopted in 1982, contained an article (number 36) on religious freedom that now allowed the masses to pursue their own spiritual affairs.[14] Members of the Communist Party were to maintain ideological distance from such affairs, to monitor ritual development, and to report on the social transgressions that sometimes attended large-scale community rituals. As one county official explained it to me, the Communist Party cared little what the masses did, especially around the time of the New Year celebrations. The main requirement was that community ritual should not interfere with labor and productivity, for productivity especially was essential if the Yao were ever to overcome their backwardness and become a socialist modern people. More important, this new thinking on religious practice was a tacit acknowledgment by the Party and by government policymakers that it was futile to try to control every aspect of religious belief and popular ritual. The reforms would be a period in which ritual would continue to be an object of ideological struggle and the old rules and practices of control, surveillance, and suppression were in the process of reconfiguration as the Party attempted to forge new relationships with the masses.

My discussion of the Longpan trip has drawn attention to the state's surveillance of the local populace and its ritual practices. In the remainder of this chapter, however, I want to explore how various practices of surveillance, especially those contained in the county's Civilized Village Campaign, worked to draw villagers into localized debates about who spoke for the meanings of socialist modernity. Practices of state surveillance actually worked to incite local memories of the pre-Liberation social order in the Dayaoshan. These memories of the past in turn led to critical assessments of the nature of the state and its successive campaigns to bring socialism, modernity, progress, and rationality to a local ethnic body. More specifically, I found that many Jinxiu Yao were interested in the relationship between what was called "traditional social morality" (chuantong shehui daode) and the state's project of bringing "spiritual civilization" (jingshen wenming) to the mountains. To understand the historical specificity of Yao claims to the socialist modern it is important to first trace shifts that were underway in China in the 1980s over the meaning of culture and material and spiritual civilization. In her study of the wenming or "civilization" discourse in post-Mao China, Ann Anagnost makes two distinctions that I think are apropos the Jinxiu situation: "In the early 1980s, the use of wenming was fundamental in formulating the reformers' position on the controlled use of the market to stimulate rapid economic development. It allowed more latitude to market forces without relinquishing political and ideological control. In the early [reform] period, the use of wenming effectively repudiated Mao's emphasis on ideology and culture (wenhua) as the primary arena for struggle and change. However, wenhua refused to go away, returning in the cultural debates of the mid-1980s as a hotly contested discursive field."[15]

The distinction between culture (wenhua) and civilization (wenming) becomes increasingly important in the late 1980s. Anagnost explains the shifting meanings, associations, and usages of these terms as follows:

> We see an important shift in the relative position of these two terms in political discourse. During the Cultural Revolution, wenhua defined the domain of struggle, in which a transformation of the superstructure could have a concrete material effect on human progress. Wenhua was the domain of cultural praxis. Wenming, on the contrary, appears to have been pretty much contained within a more specialized usage in the context of the stage theory of cultural evolutionism; its deployment was largely historiographical rather than central to debates about the pressing political struggles of the day. Wenhua, as it was used in the Cultural

Revolution, clearly had a class character, whereas the wenming discourse of the 1980s carefully skirts the issue of class by referring to the overall development of society rather than the different kinds of consciousness possessed by different class positions. In the post-Mao period, wenming is closely associated with the idea of modernization. *But it is used officially to convey an idea of modernity that distinctly differs from that of the liberal democracies of the West* [my emphasis].[16]

As Anagnost shows, the reform-era *wenming* discourse works to displace previous significations of culture and civilization. Development is envisioned as a kind of capitalism with Chinese characteristics, to use Deng's now infamous cliché. It would be different from the West in part because of the continued hegemonic role of the Communist Party, in part because of the way the new discourse of *wenming* would draw selectively on the repertoire of the Chinese tradition. Finally, the making of a new Chinese civilization—despite its claims to be an alternative to the modernity of the West—was to be based on a modernist faith in the rational management of social disorder. This sense of social unruliness was largely attributed to the effects of the socialist past, but it also had much to do with the new energies and desires unleashed by the reforms.

The *wenming* discourse in the 1980s also implicitly recognized that growth and development would entail uneven development; some regions, and nationalities, would surge ahead of others. In part, this would be the result of resource allocation and because different regions, the southeast coast for example, were geographically better positioned to forge ties with regional and global capital. But it was also the result of what many in the 1980s were seeing as a defeated social body with little or no vitality. Many officials in Jinxiu felt that the poor and weary peasant body would not easily take to another massive campaign promising rapid development. Others were embarrassed by Jinxiu's poverty relative to other regions and they were hungry for growth and development. For some, their models were the new special economic zones on the southeast coast and the images of towering skyscrapers, fast automobiles, and extraordinary wealth that came from Japan, Europe, America, and the rest of Asia. Yet others, however, were skeptical of this fascination with modernity elsewhere, if only because they thought it was impractical and totally removed from the realities of Jinxiu history and current predicaments. For them, the real issue was how to overcome the widespread low morale and peasant suspicion of new

Party campaigns. Despite these divergent opinions and views, officials were working closely with scholars, who were in turn studying local conditions and local knowledges, all in the hope of forging a new symbiotic relationship between the material and the spiritual. The everyday signs of tradition expressed one's ethnic identity and provided a kind of window into the domain of spiritual civilization, ethnic-style. Development, progress, and modernity were articulated as belonging to the realm of the material, and this was how one most effectively belonged to the reform nation.

In this new imaginary of development, the material could not exist without the spiritual. A cadre on the Longpan trip explained to me that socialist modernization was all about raising income levels, building new roads, getting farmers to use new chemicals and fertilizers for agricultural production, and getting youth to attend schools. He called this the work of building "material civilization" (weiwu wenming). The realm of the material was the hard data of development, the stuff that could easily be translated into economic indices of growth. Material civilization was forward-looking and based on the rational principles of science and technology. Traditional culture, on the other hand, belonged to the domain of "spiritual civilization" (jingshen wenming). It was seen to be more amorphous, not only manifested in rituals that accompanied birth, marriage, and death and ritual initiation, but also embedded in the psychology and commonsensical beliefs of the local populace. The disciplinary task of the reform leadership was to bring the material and the spiritual in line with each other. These two domains, many believed, could be molded into a productive, noncontradictory relationship.

The meanings of the material, the spiritual, the traditional, and the socialist modern attached to Yao popular ritual were not necessarily fixed in everyone's mind. Rather, they were highly charged ideological terms, where Yao in quite different positions of authority, power, and prestige entered into debates about just what constituted a modern Jinxiu. Practices marked as traditional were closely monitored by new technologies of state power, and images of a traditional and religious ethnic subject were often displayed in academic and popular venues as a sign of a multiethnic and culturally plural China. I am interested in how the discourse on the return of ritual articulated what I call the politics of cultural governmentality, where different social and political actors debated who could best know, manage, and care for the Jinxiu populace. In the late 1980s and early 1990s some government officials and Yao ethnologists were arguing that "traditional culture" contained moralities and modes of behavior consistent with the ideological demands of socialist modernization. In a simple twist of historical fate, the realm of the traditional would be appropriated to assist in the Civilized Village Campaign, the Party's creative attempt to get the local people to monitor their behavior and turn themselves into productive citizens.

Social Morality and the Civilized Village

As the above vignette shows, the popularity of Yao ritual was interpreted differently by different individuals. Some saw it as proof of the cultural resiliency of the Yao, of how peasant populations had maintained and even rebuilt their most important cultural practices even in the face of the ideological demands of the Maoist era. Others saw the fascination with ritual and the adherence to the authority of Taoist specialists as a sign of Yao isolation and continuing social stagnation; to them, Yao remained locked in the ancient past, unable to transform their backward and superstitious thinking and find a place among more modern nationalities. Despite these differing views, Party officials were closely watching the increased popularity of these rituals and were also encouraging villagers to monitor these affairs themselves. Popular ritual was making a comeback in Jinxiu in this contradictory space of fascination and surveillance. As I suggested previously, there are strong elements of nostalgia in recuperative constructions of the Yao past. These recuperative efforts are often linked to attachments to local places and they are politically conservative, as David Harvey might argue. And they sometimes play into the hands of nationalists in search of signs of internal ethnic difference, as those who have focused on the representation of minorities in theme parks and museums might assert. I want to shift the focus of these arguments, while recognizing their insights into the limitations of cultural attachments and their caveats about the political regressiveness of certain kinds of nostalgic cultural productions. I want to ask what they tell us about local practices of governmentality that hinge on the politics of social order. For example, in my conversations and interviews in Jinxiu, I found that many people stressed the importance of returning a sense of social morality to everyday village life. I found myself dismayed that practices once marginalized under Maoism were now being treated as something that could contribute to the making of a more rational and ordered local landscape. Many assumed that Yao practices of ritual had much to do with the reproduction of what was termed a Yao social morality

A Jinxiu County government official takes notes on a Pan Yao wedding ceremony.

(*Yaozu shehui daode*). I also found a convergence between the renewed interest in ritual life and the ideological content and disciplinary procedures of the Party's Civilized Village Campaign, or *wenmingcun yundong*. Constructed as a mode of ethnic consciousness and everyday decent behavior, Yao social morality was grounded in Yao ritual life and constructed as integral to both the Civilized Village Campaign and to debates on the quality of the Yao as an ethnic people. As I have indicated, many of the Chashan Yao I worked with argued for the moral fortitude of their customs, their traditional modes of social interaction and everyday habits. They strongly rejected the imputation of these practices to the category of "feudal superstition."

During the 1980s, ethnologists across China were picking up on this morality craze. In many publications on Yao culture and society, for example, one indeed finds an almost repetitious fixation on the customs of Yao social morality.[17] One of the dominant effects of the emphasis on social morality is seen in the discursive construction of a total Yao morality, a kind of cultural knowledge common to all Yao groups. Initially, I thought the ethnological focus on a shared morality collapsed important distinctions between different Yao groups, just as it seemed to displace once dominant class-based readings of human agency and social action. Yet I was surprised to find in my interviews with members of the various Yao subgroups in Jinxiu that morality was the one thing they said linked the Jinxiu Yao. Many in fact argued that a shared sense of social morality was first formed and then popularized through the guidelines for social behavior established in the pre-Liberation stone tablet system! I understand the fascination with everyday practices believed to inculcate a sense of social morality and thus presumably ensure social order to be the result not of the unearthing of a collective morality embedded in the *shipai*, as many Jinxiu Yao might have it. I see it as the result of the post-Mao leadership's rethinking of the relationship between state power and local cultural knowledge. Additionally, I assert that there is nothing particularly new about this identification of a problematic between indigenous knowledge and state power. For, in turning to the ethnic indigenous, the reform minority leadership was entering into a dialogue with its socialist history and, perhaps more important, with questions that hark back to the 1920s. The study of social morality among the "common folk" of China has a long intellectual and political history, as questions of morality have long been intricately linked to questions of national education and political indoctrination. In the 1920s, for example, during the heyday of the folklore movement led by such intellectuals as Zhou Zuoren, there was a movement to study the maxims, proverbs, and folktales of the common people. It was thought that these oral and collective practices of transmitting knowledge, however rustic and irrational, served to both cultivate the individual and bind the local community to a common national vision.[18] Folklore studies in 1920s China represented a certain ambivalent move away from strongly Confucian statist views that moral learning and political thought had to be drilled into the uncultured peasant. Mao Zedong, as well, was acutely aware of the didactic power of "folk wisdom" to both inspire moral cultivation and incite revolutionary action.

In the 1980s Yao ethnologists argued that a traditional social morality could be identified by three basic rules of conduct. Yao scholars in particular state that the maintenance of these rules is essential to the successful negotiation of power structures. The Yao traditionally recognize two main sources of power. The first is contained in the spirit world and in particular the hierarchies of the Taoist pantheon; the second is seen to reside in the hierarchical social structures needed for everyday government. Not surprisingly, post-Mao writings on Yao social morality focus on the rules for conduct in the maintenance of everyday social order. The first concerns a strong sense of abiding by the rules of tradition (*chuantong xing*), which, in this context, refers to respect for and awareness of one's place in everyday social hierarchies. The second concerns an emphasis on good relations and cooperation with neighbors, and a cultural emphasis on hospitality and openness to outsiders traveling in the mountains. This cultural attribute is evidenced in the Yao custom of adopting children from other ethnic groups, and a belief that Yao ethnicity is not inherited but practiced through correct behavior. The third and final feature concerns the importance the Yao place on praise and condemnation in everyday social disciplining. Yao social morality is said to reveal a dialectical relationship between social discipline and social reproduction. It is noteworthy that a positive discourse on Yao social morality is absent in Party work team documents and ethnological investigative reports written in the 1950s. Whenever I inquired about this discrepancy, I was told that Party officials ignored the question of Yao morality because of the emphasis then on locating Yao practices that revealed an inclination for revolutionary agency. In the immediate post-1949 period, Yao morality was interpreted with extreme ambivalence, constructed as excessively conservative, a form of feudal consciousness that retarded the building of a modern socialist nation. In the 1980s the making of a revolutionary subject had been displaced by an overriding concern for stability, order, and the establishment of peaceful relations between ethnic groups and social classes. The traditional customs and practices that inculcate a sense of social responsibility and morality were being embraced for their functional contribution to the post-Mao social and political order.

In the mid-1980s I attended an ethnology conference in China where a young Yao ethnologist from the Guangdong Nationality Institute, Li Xiaowen, presented a paper entitled "Traditional Yao Morality and the Construction of Spiritual Civilization." Morals, or *daode*, she wrote, are standards that function to regulate everyday life. Morality adjusts people's actions and relationships through moral ideas and moral regulations, making it congruent with its economic base as well as serving the formation and consolidation of the economic base. A society not only needs to be backed up by a strong economy, but also needs a good political and moral spirit to guide it and keep it moving on the right track. In a class society, morals tend to have a strong class character. Thus, different classes and nationalities will have different moral ideas that will then be reflected in different actions. The Yao society has had social morals with nationality characteristics. These customs, public opinions, and moral ideas, which have been formed and passed down in social practices for a long time, have been used as standards of people's words and deeds and to adjust relations within and between nationalities. They have preserved social order and propelled the development of society and production. Excellent social mentality has become a traditional virtue of Yao people in the long process of history. It is a historical heritage worthy of being inherited and carried on.

Li Xiaowen reminds us that the primary stage of socialism (the stage Deng claimed the reform period belonged to) requires a long historical process.[19] The character of socialism at any given moment will always be the result of many different social dimensions, all of which are in constant flux. As Marx argued, communism requires the highest moral standard, whereas a socialist state can and must tolerate different forms and practices of morality. Because socialism has yet to achieve the perfected state of social being promised under communism, the state and its citizens must still regulate and judge the nature of people's deeds. They must learn to distinguish between virtue and evil, impartiality and prejudice, honesty and hypocrisy, justice and unfairness, honor and shamelessness. In the primary stage of socialism—in the current epoch—the morals found in common life, in professional ethics, and in the domain of family and marriage become the basic standards to which all citizens should be held and by which all citizens should be judged. Li argues that the traditional morality of the Yao has two fundamental aspects: public social morals and morals of family and marriage. Public social morals are defined as follows. The Yao people are honest, kind, hospitable, trustworthy, and always ready to help each other. From the Yao point of view, it is a family disgrace to commit theft, a fact contained in the popular adage *Dao bu tou yi, fei yi wu bu qu* (don't take things that don't belong to you). This principle has long been maintained in the village regulations of the *shipai*. Li reminds us that the *shipai* was a primitive democratic political institution that functioned to protect social order, that it took the village as its primary social and political unit, and that villages often came together to constitute a larger *shipai* unit. The regulations of the *shipai* aimed to protect production and social order; they would be promulgated at village meetings and then engraved on stone or wooden boards. Everyone, without exception, was required to obey them. When the Yao go to work in the mountains or travel to market, it is their custom to stash unnecessary clothes and other items on the roadside or in trees and attach a grass knot to them, with the intention of picking them up on their way back. No matter where one travels in the Dayaoshan, she argues, if something has a grass knot attached to it, no one else will touch it. Yao store grain and firewood at different village outposts sometimes for as long as one or two months without worry of theft. If someone is caught stealing, he or she is reported to the *shipai* authorities and then scolded and punished in a large collective *shipai* meeting. This traditional form and ritual of public admonishment, the argument goes, is how the Jinxiu Yao maintained social order without a more advanced and centralized political system.

In her article, Li is also concerned with marriage and family life as a domain of social morality. She argues that by examining the moral conceptions (*daode guan*) surrounding and regulating marriage and family, we can learn much about the spiritual life (*jingshen shenghuo*) of the Yao. She begins by reminding us that in China's feudal past, parents often employed matchmakers to arrange marriages for their children. Though this practice influenced the Yao to some degree, the Yao are different from the Han in that they have long maintained distinct ideas about romantic love, namely, the right to freely choose one's lover through the practice of singing duets, or *duige*. If a young couple expresses their love for each other, they exchange engagement gifts and only then ask their parents to choose an auspicious date to hold the wedding. It was not uncommon for several or even a dozen young men to propose to a girl by singing. No matter who won the heart of the girl in the end, Li tells us, the others would never express envy or fight with each other. As in many ethnological accounts of minority marriage practices, she tells us this social practice has residual elements (canyu) of the freedom of social interaction found in all primitive societies. Yet this openness and warmheartedness is precisely the kind of spirit (jingshen) needed in a civilized society (wenming shehui).

The ethnological imaginary continues: The kindness of Yao not only preserves close bonds between friends, it also guarantees, because it is based on free love, a happy and everlasting marriage. This in part ensures that the status of male and female in Yao society is relatively equal. Male and female members share household and farming chores. Though men often bring a bride into their home, it is also common for men to marry uxorilocally and live in the home of the bride. Unlike the Han, the young groom is treated as a son and not subjected to any form of discrimination. If a couple doesn't get along with each other, either side can openly ask for a divorce and there are no restrictions on when a woman can marry again. In the ancient past, when the Yao population was very small and the infant survival rate not very high, women who gave birth to children enjoyed widespread respect and protection. If fighting broke out between two lineages, the women and the old often stepped forward to mediate and put an end to the conflict. If, as sometimes happened, a woman was attacked, the other side would seek revenge. Ethnological evolutionism creeps into the text. As Li tells it, the reason for this probably derives from the residual elements of woman worship found in matrilineal society.[20] But the more important reason is that the Yao pay the same respect to male and female ancestors, which inspires ideas of equality between men and women. Thus, throughout the history of the Yao, though its production and economic development have been slow, its social order has been relatively stable. Using these moral ideas, the Yao have been able to preserve social order and mutual respect between men and women, young and old. These social morals have been maintained into the present, and they have a practical and valuable role to play in the construction of China's socialist spiritual civilization.

Li concludes her essay by arguing that the making of a socialist spiritual civilization requires "cultural construction" (wenhua jianshe) and "ideological construction" (sixiang jianshe).[21] The construction of ideology includes popularizing Marxist theory and the communist ideal of being a master of one's history and a member of a collective. These Marxist ideas are consistent with the socialist public ownership system, and the ideas of obligation to a collective and the need for disciplinary action for transgressions are consistent with the socialist political system. They are both deeply embedded in the popular notion that one should serve the people, be a good socialist patriot, and identify with the goals of internationalism. Many of these ideas, she argues, are embedded in the traditional morality of the Yao. She insists the Yao case reveals that it is no use to move forward with social and economic development if social morality has deteriorated. The reforms have created imbalances and contradictions between economic and moral activities. People need to tend to their own individual material and economic interests, yet they must also adopt and promote an unselfish and sacrificing spirit. Under the reforms, the state has adopted the principle of distribution based on the amount of one's economic labor, yet it is important to promote the idea that one should do more for others and ask for little in return. The state now encourages individualism and competitiveness, allowing some people to get rich before others, yet these same individuals should be willing and ready to help others. The reforms are beginning to enhance people's living standards, yet we must also promote thrift and selfless hard work. Otherwise, incompatibilities will emerge and spread between the morality and the demands of socialist modernity. In the end, she concludes, though there are still old ideas suffocating people's thinking in Yao society, there are many traditional moral concepts that can propel the progress of the Yao society: "The making of a spiritual civilization is not about applying a model previously conceived. It is rather a lively, active garden with many different kinds of flowers. We should carry on the vitality of the traditional ethnic moral systems, inherit their good properties, and construct a spiritual civilization with national characteristics [*jianshe yige juyou minzu tese de jianshen wenming xin tiandi*]."[22]

Although Li does not spell out in detail the relationship between Yao social morality and Taoist ritual, many in Jinxiu explicitly made the connection in my interviews with them. Moreover, the significance of this ethnological discourse on the importance of Yao social morality in the making of good socialist modern citizens must be understood in the context of the reform regime's attempt to get villagers to monitor social order. In Jinxiu, this surveillance function was returned to the masses through the Civilized Village Campaign. This campaign is one of the fundamental ways the post-Mao regime continued, even after its so-called retreat from the everyday control of production, to engage in ideological work in everyday life.[23] The tenets or "compacts" (*xiangyue*) of the campaign stipulate a set of ideal behaviors that all villagers are required to follow. They cover everything from interactions between spouses, to public behavior (spitting, yelling, fighting are all discouraged), to payment of taxes under the household production system, to regulating births and the use of birth control methods. Adherence to the tenets is monitored through political meetings of members of the village households, an official from the county's Party office, and the village head. During these meetings, which last anywhere from several hours to several evenings, villagers enter into a discussion about the behavior of every member of the household. These meetings are sometimes very light-hearted and playful; at other times they are very serious and critical, especially if a major crime is involved. During the household meetings, comparisons are made to other villagers' behavior and how the village committees interpreted and handled them. When the discussions have ended and each household has been scrutinized for its adherence to the code of civility, a public village ceremony is held in which each household is awarded a red plaque to hang over the threshold of the house. In conjunction with a Party leadership that claims to have returned to the masses some governing power, the villagers have conferred upon themselves the status of being "civilized" (*wenming*).

The display of this plaque indicates that the household has demonstrated its love of country by its adherence to the tenets of the village compact. The object is for a majority of the households to receive public recognition so that the entire village can be conferred the status of being a "civilized village" (*wenmingcun*). Households yet to receive this public recognition are identified as having some outstanding problem yet to be resolved. In most cases, the problem concerns adherence to the family planning project. Perhaps a couple exceeded its birth ratio and hid a pregnancy, or admitted a certain difficulty in using birth control techniques. In this case, another committee, centered in the county hospital, is sent to consult with and educate the household members on the importance of family planning. Other common transgressions are strained relations between spouses, public displays of anger or fighting, or conflicts between other members of the household. Frequently there are intravillage skirmishes over assigned responsibilities in collective labor, such as reforestation work. There are also instances of drunken and disorderly behavior and the like, but these are usually handled by family members and never enter into discussion at the village meetings. Finally, references to civilized behavior are constantly made in everyday social interactions. If a couple is fighting, someone will yell out that they are not being civilized (*bu wenming*). Even young children who avoid their homework and sneak down to the town's video game parlor are scolded for not manifesting behavior that becomes someone of a civilized family. Likewise, households that don't encourage their children to attend school can be subject to the scrutiny of village committees.

The focus on social morality and the regulation of behavior therefore represents a quite conscious Communist Party effort to intervene in everyday social practice. What really surprised me in my work on these campaigns, however, is that there seemed to be a certain consensus that the campaign did not constitute a form of "ideological work" (*sixiang gongzuo*), at least not in the sense of how this political concept was defined and applied during the Maoist period. Moreover, most local officials and villagers did not see the project as a corrective intervention in a socially disordered moment of the reforms. Rather, they saw it as an educational practice that returned to everyday life a form of traditional moral discourse, in which villagers determine and settle among themselves rules for social conduct and punishments for minor transgressions. It was perceived as a form of democratic socialism that spoke both against the abuse of power under Maoism and for the usefulness of a "traditional" mode of regulating social life. The campaign was popular because, as did other ideological projects aimed at educating the masses, it sought to raise the villagers' consciousness, to prepare them for development, for the eventual influx of capital and investment that would one day come to these "isolated" hills. Civilizing the local social world, then, was to raise the cultural quality of the people, to remold them as subjects that would be able to participate more fully in the modernization of Yao society and all of China.

What does all of this tell us about the power of the post-Mao state to both create and limit the terrain for the imagining of identity and community at the local level? A Foucauldian reading would point not to the power of the state to define reality, but to how power has become diffused and disseminated in localized, everyday practices of social regulation. Surely, it is not hard to see here a gradual fusing of a discourse on civility into a local practice, which has, in effect, rendered invisible the origins of the discourse and, in turn, reconstituted the state's authority at the local level. It is in the movement between a civilizing project for the love of the country (in which every household seeks to earn its own red plaque) and the invocation of a "traditional" Yao morality once marginalized by previous ideological campaigns that interpretive spaces are opened up for critical evaluations of who speaks for the socialist and the modern. This tension is evident in Li Xiaowen's essay. Is socialist modernity something that is applied from outside of the mountains (by the state or by a "more advanced" nationality such as the Han or the Zhuang) or does it reside within the Yao subject itself? This distinction is important, not only in terms of how ethnic cultural discourse in the late 1980s and early 1990s was leading to essentialized conceptions of the indigenous and the local, but also in terms of the more politically loaded question of who speaks for the Jinxiu Yao, their traditions, and their modernity. In a sense, the local knowledge that the state has brought into view through its celebration of ethnic custom has slipped away from its discursive mooring, having entered the very real history of Jinxiu's encounter with projects of modern socialist development. Although the Civilized Village Campaign may establish a moral discourse on everyday behavior, one in which villagers monitor their behavior in relation to some desired goal of socialist development, it cannot fully control the local memory it has summoned. Put somewhat differently, the subjugated ethnic subject, retrieved from its marginalization under Maoist ideologies of de-ethnicized revolutionary purity, haunts the very power that has given it representation because of the critical spaces opened up for talk and reflection on the meanings of socialist modernity. I want to develop this point by exploring one final example.

Reproduction, Civility, and Difference

In Jinxiu, the Civilized Village Campaign was the political arena for the enforcement of the family planning policy. As in other minority regions in China, all of the Yao subgroups in Jinxiu were permitted to have two children.[24] This number was often exceeded in many parts of the county, especially in regions inhabited by the Pan Yao and the Shanzi Yao, who had long preferred, mostly for labor power reasons, larger families. The local government engaged in countywide educational outreach campaigns, teaching men how to use condoms and encouraging men and women, after they had reached their quota of children, to voluntarily participate in sterilization programs. I was able to observe a number of civilized village meetings in which reproduction workers discussed the family planning policy with

Yao in the Chashan Yao villages surrounding the county seat, as well as in several Pan Yao villages in other parts of the county. Almost all of the reproductive outreach workers were women and I never met one who was not a Yao. I never personally witnessed an abuse, though I heard some stories of forced sterilization, especially among the Pan Yao.[25] When I asked why the problems mostly concerned these groups, I was always told it was because of their lack of culture or *wenhua*. This did not simply mean that they were backward or lacking education; it was a euphemistic way of saying they simply did not feel that two-children families were justified for peasants whose livelihood depended so much on family labor. Family planning was one way the Chashan Yao differentiated themselves from the Pan Yao and the Shanzi Yao; it was one way they marked themselves as a more civilized people. In this sense, the ethnological fascination with indigenous cultural practices such as the *shipai* and Taoist ritual was not simply, as we saw in Li Xiaowen's essay, about marking out a space for a Yao social morality in the making of a socialist modern civilization. It was also about local forms of ethnic distinction and differentiation.

In the late 1980s, Liu Yulian wrote an essay that she subsequently presented at a workshop held in Jinxiu on the relationship between "traditional culture" and "socialist modernization." A number of county government officials and provincial and national scholars of the Yao attended this miniconference. She and I spent what seemed to be an inordinate amount of time discussing this essay, which explored how the Changmao Yao groups—the Chashan Yao, the Hualan Yao, and Ao Yao—had long limited the size of their families. I was interested in this essay because it was written at a time when the county government was stepping up its family planning campaign in Jinxiu during the introduction of the Civilized Village Campaign. It seemed at some level to be an intervention in these debates, at least in terms, as we shall see, of how it created an image of the Chashan Yao as exemplars of family planning and birth regulation. I also found the essay of interest because Liu, an academic with a "bad class background," engaged in a narrative style that seemed highly critical of the *shipai* and various forms of pre-Liberation indigenous culture. I also knew that this was part of what she and others called the *biaoxian* game, the minding of one's political thought in order not to draw the attention of authorities. What she was really doing was carving out a new narrative space for the Chashan Yao, a space that would allow them to participate in and mark their contribution to the socialist modernization of the Dayaoshan.

Liu titled her essay "What I Have Learned from the 'Theory of the Two Modes of Production': A Brief Account of the Problem of Reproduction among the Chashan, Hualan, and Ao Yao." The term reproduction (*shengyu*) refers to the bearing of children and, by extension, to the social reproduction of the family unit and the social group. She begins in the manner typical of many ethnological texts from this period. She lays out the population distribution of the region's five Yao subgroups and then, in the spirit of the reforms, provides us with a range of statistical information on the total output of industry and agriculture in Jinxiu County in the 1980s. She notes with some aplomb that there has been a 50 percent increase in total output since 1977. Nonetheless, she argues, again drawing on a range of statistical data concerning grain production, distribution, and state rations, Jinxiu has continued to rely on government food rations and imports from other regions in Guangxi. Her explanation for this is that the Jinxiu Yao as a whole have not been able to control their population growth; the population problem, she insists, has impeded (*fangai*) any discernible increase in the standard of living and the healthy development (*jiankang fazhan*) of the nationality. This view is entirely consistent with the reform regime's new thinking on the population problem (*renkou wenti*). As the national population expert Liu Zheng has written, "If we had followed the appropriate population control policy in the 1950s, our population would have been much smaller than it is now. Far from having interfered with the renewal of the labor force and the continuity of the national populace, it would have saved a huge sum of funds for national construction and the improvement of the life of the people." This observation is further refined: "The quantity and quality of the population are two inseparable aspects of population growth. Under any mode of social production, a population of a certain size is inevitably composed of individuals with given qualities. In China, population problems are not only manifested in the contradiction between the huge size and fast growth of the population on the one hand and the effort to realize socialist modernization on the other. The problems also involve the quality of the population which falls short of the requirements for socialist modernization." [26]

As a reform-era intellectual charged with thinking about the socialist modernization of the Dayaoshan, Liu Yulian was very much concerned with the quality (*suzhi*) of the Jinxiu Yao.[27] She believed, in fact, that the Chashan Yao had long been a quality people, with superior education standards, high morals and practical common sense, and a commitment to regulating population growth. Thus, for Liu, even before the reform regime came to its realization that population must be controlled if the nation is to grow and prosper, the Chashan Yao, through their indigenous family planning techniques, were blazing the path of the socialist modern future. Not so long ago, the Chashan Yao—the mountain landlords, the oppressors of other Yao subgroups—were the harbingers of the population policy now at the heart of the socialist modernization agenda.

After this brief statistical introduction, Liu turns to theory. She asserts that the best way to understand Chashan, Hualan, and Ao Yao family planning techniques is through the work of Marx and Engels. Engels reminds us, she writes, that from a materialist point of view, the two determining factors of history are production and reproduction. To survive and prosper, human populations must produce food, clothes, houses, and the instruments of production. They must also reproduce themselves; they must multiply or social life ceases to exist. Engels believed that the level of material production was determined entirely by the developmental stage of labor, whereas the reproduction of the population was determined by the developmental stage of the family. Turning her eye to the pre-Liberation period and drawing on her own field research, Liu admits that the Chashan, Hualan, and Ao Yao (she never employs the now dated category Changmao Yao) owned and controlled most of the arable land, rivers, and forests in the Dayaoshan. She readily admits that this system of ownership was regulated by the *shipai* system. Here she enters into a kind of confessional mode, which is meant to demonstrate her political ability to criticize the hegemonic order that once prevailed in these hills. She writes that these groups utilized the three modes of rent collection (rent in kind, labor, and cash) and that this and other kinds of exploitation such as hiring laborers to work in vegetable oil mills represented the sprouts (*mengya*) of capitalism. The idea of private ownership was deeply rooted in the consciousness of these groups, she tells us, who used the *shipai* to protect their control of the means of production, ensure social order, and contribute to their own social and economic advancement.

Because these three groups together owned the majority of the land in the region, they paid close attention to the rights of inheritance. Unlike the Pan Yao and the Shanzi Yao (of the former Guoshan Yao category), these three landowning groups passed inheritance through the oldest son or daughter. Wet-rice cultivation was maintained in the valleys (the upland groups, as we've seen, practiced a form of mobile swidden cultivation), and they also devoted much labor time to producing and harvesting spices, mushrooms, anise, bamboo, and other local forest products. These products were then sold in the periodic markets in the surrounding regions, which enabled these groups to accumulate a relatively large source of cash. The control of local wealth, then, was intricately tied to the question of both inheritance and family size. A smaller family size was determined in part because men were often absent from home as they worked to cultivate forest products, which naturally decreased the chance of pregnancy. It was determined also by the practice of keeping only one child at home into adulthood, while the other child—the Chashan Yao preferred only two— was married and sent off to live with another family.[28] Liu was often quick to point out to me that the Chahan Yao did not suffer from the fear and social stigmatization of uxorilocal marriage (known locally as *shangmen*), as was common among the Han. Young boys readily moved away from their natal family and took up residence in the home of their spouse. This is in fact one way that Liu and other Yao intellectuals differentiated themselves from the Han. In terms of gender relations, they felt they were well ahead of the Han. The Yao, they insisted, were far more egalitarian, less disrespectful of women, and never discriminated between boys and girls at birth. The problem of female infanticide is in fact largely unheard of in Yao regions.

The reproduction system of the Chashan, Hualan, and Ao Yao was manifest as well in the realm of marriage customs. Before liberation, these groups forbade intermarriage with the Pan Yao and Shanzi Yao as well as with other nationalities outside of the Dayaoshan, a practice that Liu finds distasteful yet understandable. Party cadres in the 1950s argued that this practice epitomized the feudal mentality of the Dayaoshan Yao, and throughout the 1950s and 1960s Party activists encouraged intermarriage among the different Yao groups, as well as between the Yao and the Han and Zhuang people. The taboo on interethnic marriage was set down clearly in the texts of the *shipai*. Liu recounts one text from the 1930s as stating, "Any woman who married a man from outside of the Dayaoshan would be fined 60 taels of silver." There is a common story in Jinxiu about an event that occurred in the 1920s, when a young Chashan Yao girl fell in love with a Han boy who used to come into the mountains as an itinerant trader. Once the word of this romance got out, the male family members of the girl expelled the young Han from the Dayaoshan. Marriage was forbidden with the Pan Yao and Shanzi Yao because many of the *shipai* leaders looked down on their lower economic status and found their slash-and-burn farming method to be crude and primitive. As I've indicated, Liu and other older men and women would often tell me that Party cadres in the 1950s misunderstood the nature of the Changmao Yao–Guoshan Yao social and economic relation. Yet in this essay, presented at an ethnological workshop in Jinxiu, she readily admits that the system of economic exploitation and ethnic prejudice influenced and indeed limited the social sphere of intermarriage. The Chashan Yao were much less receptive to the Han custom that allowed brothers and sisters to live in a large extended family, and many simply did not understand the Han preference for many children and large families. In his 1948 book *Miscellaneous Notes on the Yao Mountains* (*Yaoshan sanji*), the Han ethnologist Tang Zhaomin quotes a Yao *shipai* headman (*touren*): "Arable land in these mountains is hard to come by and not everyone is sufficiently fed. Yet you can see nonetheless that we Changmao Yao have not bandits nor beggars." [29] As Liu explains it, once the Chashan Yao (as with the Ao and Hualan Yao) gave birth to two children, the grandparents would remind them that it was now time to use birth control (*jieyu*). For every Chashan Yao, then, reproductive restraint (*jiezhi shengyu*) was an essential part of family education (*jiating shengyu*).

Why was family planning and reproductive restraint so important to the Chashan Yao? Liu tells us that raising a child from birth to adulthood was an expensive affair. If a family had too many children, the economic burden was considered too heavy, having a negative impact on their immediate lives and that of their relatives. A smaller family size was also linked to the demands of ritual life. Large families drained funds needed to carry out the numerous religious rituals required throughout the year. Liu recounts the yearly ritual cycle. Four or five days after the birth of a child, fish is offered as a sacrifice to the local gods, followed some two or three months later by an offering of frogs. When the child is six months old, ritual propriety required hiring a Taoist specialist (*shigong*) to build what the Chashan Yao called a *qixing* (spirit bridge) to ensure the health of the child. A stone, about a foot long, is erected across a mountain trail, with three smaller stones placed at each end. Using chickens, ducks, and glutinous rice wrapped in bamboo leaves (*zongzi*) as sacrificial offerings, the parents invite the gods who protect newborn infants to cross the bridge and dispel evil and other supernatural beings that seek to harm the vulnerable child. Similar rituals of spirit protection are carried out at the end of the first year and when the child is five, each occasion requiring the building of more elaborate spirit bridges and more expensive sacrificial offerings, such as a pig. When the child is between the ages of seven and fifteen, the two most expensive and elaborate rituals are held. The first is known as *huanhua* (literally, "to return the flower"), which is a sacrificial honoring of the female goddess *huashen po*, who the Chashan Yao believe guides the spirit of the child into the world of humans at birth. The second ritual is known as the *dujie*. Essentially an initiation rite into the Taoist priesthood, this ritual is held either for the son who has remained at home or the son-in-law who has married into the family. All Chashan Yao remember these rituals as hugely celebratory and community affairs, in which large amounts of pork, chicken, and duck are offered to the gods and later consumed by all in attendance. Ritual expense was a fact of Chashan Yao social life. Liu writes:

> There were two other large-scale sacrificial activities called *zuogongde* and *zuohongmen*. Zuogongde required building a large bridge. This was done by a single village or by several villages that worked together. We called the bridge *gongdeqiao* [the bridge for acquiring merit]. Once the bridge was erected, a grand ceremony was held. Shigong and daogong specialists recited scriptures and performed magic dances. Some villages held this ritual every eighteen years; in other regions of the county it was held every twelve years (the villages of Liuduan and Zhaibao, for example). For the ceremony, every family was required to sacrifice a pig and supply wine (*mijiu*) to entertain one's relatives and friends. Three hundred to four hundred jin of pork was often consumed. Zuohongmen was a sacrificial ritual held for a lineage. In Jinxiu and four villages around the county seat, it occurred only once every fifty years; in Changer and Changtan villages, every twenty years. On these rare occasions, shigong recited the Taoist scriptures and performed magical dances for three days and nights. All labor stopped, as relatives and friends joined every aspect of the carnival for the entire three days. Only pork was served, as the host was expected to spare no cost. Zuohongmen was thus much more expensive than zuogongde. If a family had an extensive kin network, the affair could cost them 400–500 jin of pork. Each family was required to contribute a share of the meat for each of these two sacrifice rituals. Thus, a family with two children at home was required to pay double the share. It is clear that with too many children, the family simply could not afford the expenses of ritual life.[30]

Most Yao, Liu tells us, did not know whether these sacrificial rituals had a positive effect on their lives, for they were following other villages and families in conducting what would later be called "superstitious" activities. At that time, however, these practices were actually called *youyu*, or "advantageous birthing," a term, incidentally, that is often translated into English as "eugenics." To achieve the aims of *youyu*, they had to give birth to fewer children. The importance that the Chashan Yao placed on ritual life demanded that family planning be put on their agenda. What we find over the course of the past decades, Liu reminds us, is that social progress (*shehui de jinbu*) for many Yao has meant that their religious consciousness (*xinjiao de yishi*) has slowly faded away. Yet the Chashan Yao have continued to maintain their family planning practices; voluntary family planning (*zijue jieyu*) is one of their most important customs.

The social reproduction system of the Chashan, Hualan, and Ao Yao also had a close relationship with the *shipai* system. The *shipai* protected women and children and, at the same time, severely punished those who gave birth to illegitimate children. Liu draws on a number of *shipai* texts that contain stipulations and rules for how to protect family structure, marriage institutions, women and children, all to illustrate that their indigenous family planning system had a close relation to the *shipai*. In the *shipai* of the Chashan Yao in Zhaibao, Yangliu, and Jiangjun villages as far back as 1786, it was stipulated that a couple could not seek divorce without good reason. In the *shipai* of Luoyun and its eight surrounding villages, an 1853 text explains that if a heated conflict emerges between a husband and wife, their families could not engage in kidnapping or ransom techniques. A *shipai* text dated 1891 in the villages of Dishui, Rongdong, Liuli, and Dajin stipulated fines for marrying outside one's clan or ethnic subgroup. If a person married outside the village without permission, he or she would be fined a certain amount of money; if the person was a Han, the fine would increase; if a man took on a second wife, the fine would increase even higher. I asked Liu and others why the *shipai* was so strict with its marriage laws and I would often explain that by American standards these practices seemed excessive if not oppressive. They would always respond that Americans did not understand the importance of social order. Forbidding men to take on a second wife or forbidding marriage with Han and others from outside the mountains was the best way to preserve peace and tranquillity within the family and the village. As I indicated in the previous chapter, Han cadres in the 1950s moved to end these "feudal" stipulations that forbade the Yao to marry outside of their group, and many Chashan Yao throughout the 1950s were encouraged to court (*tan lianai*) Pan Yao, Han, and Zhuang. Yao subgroup intermarriage was an essential strategy in the politics of ethnic unification (*minzu tuanjie*) in the Dayaoshan.

The *shipai* was also used to administer fines and punishments for birth out of wedlock, which also worked, Liu argues, to halt population growth. The punishment for giving birth before marriage was both unique and severe. The Chashan Yao euphemistically called it an "educational dinner party," or *jucan jiaoyuhui*. The money from the fine would be used to buy wine and various meats and other dishes; everyone was invited to participate in the dinner meeting. The headman of the village *shipai* would begin by explaining the reason the offender was being punished. The intent was not to overly chastise or embarrass the offenders, but to educate them about their mistake and instruct them on how to deal with the problem if it emerged again; in this sense, Liu argues, the *shipai* served a pedagogical purpose. After the dinner party dispersed, the older women would talk about the herbs in the mountains that could be harvested to induce abortion, for example. There are over nine hundred different kinds of medicinal herbs (*caoyao*) in the Dayaoshan, which have led some to call it a natural treasure house (*ziran baoku*). The Yao are masters at using spices and herbs for medicine, and this knowledge was often put to use in regulating births. For example, abortions were often induced at one month of pregnancy by drinking soup boiled from raw spices. The Yao also used an herb called *yajiao*. Cutting the sprout of the plant as long as the middle finger and then placing it into the vagina would cause a painless abortion within twenty-four hours. This was the most widely used herb in the mountains, as Yao claimed that it allowed women to continue to work in the fields as usual and did not affect labor production. Rather than see these as primitive techniques of birth regulation, Liu argues in the language of ethnological Marxism that these methods were the "fruits" (*jiejing*) of a laboring people's wisdom (*Yaomin laodong zhihui*).[31]

The third and final section of Liu's article reveals how the study of indigenous practices of birth regulation, with their complex and integral relationship to the *shipai* and the Yao ritual life cycle, is firmly situated within reform-era discourses on population control, development, and socialist modernity. I quote it at length:

> In the report of the Twelfth Party Congress, it is pointed out that "family planning is a fundamental state policy. Everyone should join the effort to keep the country's population under 1.2 billion by the end of

this century." The Chashan, Hualan and Ao Yao have responded favorably and enthusiastically to this appeal, for they have a long tradition of voluntary family planning. The Pan Yao and Shanzi Yao have gradually come to understand the importance of birth control. When I was doing research in an Ao Yao village in 1983, I discovered that 90% of the women in their childbearing years had adopted birth control measures. Cadres at various levels in Jinxiu have paid attention to the Central and the State Council document known as the "Directive for Pushing Forward the Work of Family Planning." They have organized pedagogical sessions to study the Directive, so that everyone can understand the importance of the work of population control.

In 1982, 1,002 surgeries of four kinds of birth control were performed in Jinxiu County, including 276 cases of intrauterine contraceptive ring insertions, 28 cases of tubular ligation surgery [*jiezha*], 525 cases of abortion and 173 cases of induced labor. Couples with certificates for one child increased from 51 in 1981 to 138 in 1982. The birth rate decreased by 21.4%, while the natural population rate decreased by 15.1%.

Couples giving birth to more than one child decreased by 29.28%, while those having only one child increased to 38.24%. The number of couples adopting birth control measures has increased by 63.8%. Couples with the certificate for one child increased by 16.27%. The work of family planning has been carried out extremely well, thus helping to realize the task of carrying out "two productions" [returning to the theory of Engels]. In 1983, the rate of natural population increase was 11.47% in Jinxiu County, well below the 14% requirement stipulated by the Guangxi government. All Yao subgroups and other nationalities in Jinxiu are now paying more attention to the work of family planning.

With their long and excellent tradition of birth control, the Chashan, Hualan and Ao Yao work to balance development by paying attention to these "two modes of production." Since the third plenary of the Eleventh Party Congress, when the responsibility system was implemented, the situation in Jinxiu has improved immensely. For example, Liula Brigade in the township of Jinxin had 340 households, a total population of 1,694, 728 able-bodied workers [*laodongli*]. The brigade had 818 mu of wet-rice land. As in the past, they continued to take advantage of the rich resources in the mountains, focusing their energies on the gathering of spices and other products in order to increase their income. The total income of the brigade was 570,768 yuan in 1982, around 313 yuan per person. There were 12 households with an average income per person of over 1,000 yuan, while there were 229 households with incomes over 1,000 yuan, about 3.4% and 83% respectively of the total households. There were 80-odd households in the Chashan Yao villages of Da Liula and Xiao Liula villages, with six households earning over 10,000 yuan from spices.

The situation in 1983 was even better. The total income of the brigade was 1,039,524 yuan, 613 yuan per person, an 82.2% jump. There were 30 households with over 1,000 yuan per person and 335 households with incomes over 1,000 yuan. There were 17 households with savings of over 10,000 yuan. In 1983, 23 households built 26 new homes of at least 1,659 square meters. Thirteen of these new homes were built with concrete and iron, costing in total 52,400 yuan. Today, the whole brigade has 71 TV sets, 60 of which were bought in 1983; 150 sewing machines, 20-odd of which were bought in 1983; over 200 bicycles, 80 of which were bought in 1983; 70 video recorders, 52 of which were bought in 1983. There was a family (who declined to tell their name) in the second production team of the brigade in which all four members were able to engage in farming. This was the richest family in the brigade, with a 40,000-yuan long-term savings deposit.

Luoyun Brigade of Luoxiang Commune provides us with another example of how the Chashan, Hualan, and Ao Yao have managed to realize the theory of "two modes of production." The brigade had 21 production teams, 272 households, and a population of 1,512. They had 813 mu of wet-rice land under cultivation; 6,782 mu of anise forest with 5,300 mu ready for harvest. In 1983, the total output of anise was 317,000 jin, an 87,000 jin increase over 1981 (1982 was a "small year" due to the cycle of growth of anise). The income from anise was 1,176,600 yuan, about 778 yuan per person. The brigade sold 225,000 jin of anise to the country (since anise was considered a "third class" product, the brigade could sell it to private merchants at a market price after filling its government quota), and it had an income of 832,500 yuan, 616 yuan per person. The four production teams in Luoyun Village (all Ao Yao) had 78 households, 315 members, of whom 116 were able-bodied laborers. They stood out by selling 104,662 jin of anise to the county for an income of 376,783 yuan, 1,195 yuan per person. There were five households who sold more than 10,000 yuan of anise, 29 households with income from 5,000 to 9,000 yuan, or about 3.1% of the total households in the village. Among them,

A slogan on the wall of a Chashan Yao house in the vicinity of the town of Jinxiu. It reads, "Only socialism can save China."

Pan Zhenhua of the fourth production team sold 4,040 jin of anise and produced an income of 15,544 yuan. His household was known as one of the richest.

To become rich through planting anise had made Luoyun Brigade somewhat unique in Jinxiu County. One sign of this is in the increase of the brigade members' savings deposits. At the end of 1983, the amount of savings for the whole brigade reached 397,360 yuan, among which 277,360 yuan was in fixed-term savings while the rest, 120,000 yuan, was placed in current deposit. Luoyun Village (Ao Yao) had the largest savings rate in the brigade, about 130,00 yuan. The second sign is in the increase in the building of new homes. From the period 1981 to 1983, 137 households had built new homes, about 49.7% of the total households. The third sign was that many villagers were into high-end consumer goods. According to preliminary statistics, there were 87 sewing machines and 190 video recorders (because this region could not yet receive national TV programs, no one was buying televisions). The fourth sign is that many villagers began to take tourist trips. When the demands of production slacked off, away they went: to Wuzhou, Liuzhou, Guilin and Guangzhou.

The above two brigades paid attention to birth control while promoting material production, and their lives have become better with each passing year. Some members in the production teams in Gonghe Brigade in the Jinxiu Commune did not pay much attention to birth control. In what can only be seen as an extraordinary case, because some of their families had too many children, even 30-odd years after liberation, their entire property (except the bamboo house) was worth only 50 yuan. Not a single village in this brigade had a brick house; all were made of bamboo, the very sign in Jinxiu of lasting primitivity. Their distance from the realities of Liula and Luoyun Brigades demands the attention of the relevant government department.

With loving care [guanhai] from the Party and the county government, the Yao people have been actively promoting family planning—the "fundamental state policy"—while developing their economy. As long as they continue to balance the "two modes of production," the future of the Dayaoshan will be very bright. The ever-industrious Yao people will make their own contribution to the material and spiritual civilization of the motherland.[32]

Conclusion: Beyond State and Society

My interviews and travels with Party members and government officials in Jinxiu taught me that the reform regime was struggling to make itself visible as something other than a destructive force in everyday social life. The agenda of many officials was to safeguard the identity of the reform regime as the central bearer of the power and sovereignty of the people of China, but they also knew they could do this only if they had the support of the local populace.[33] My research led me to approach the state and society question in Jinxiu less as a problem of penetration and retreat than as a politics of contested cultural governmentality. Different agents brought different views and conceptions to the question of how the CCP was to ensure development, social order, and stability. In many of my interviews, I found that government officials and Party cadres viewed Jinxiu as a space of lack, desperately in need of the guiding wisdom of a new and different kind of mobilization and rationality. In this mode of representing the local, the socialist modern discourse of development has moved away from the rhetoric of revolution and class struggle and toward the question of why certain nationalities still lag behind others in terms of their social and economic development. Jinxiu was often represented in "internal" (*neibu*) Party reports on local conditions (*difang tiaojian*) as remote, underdeveloped, and backward, a state of affairs captured in the ubiquitous phrase *pianpi luohou difang* (a remote and backward place). As we saw in Liu Yulian's narrative, different degrees of backwardness and remoteness existed in Jinxiu, with the Chashan Yao, because of their ability to balance the "two modes of production," at the apex of the development ladder.

It is important to realize that the Communist Party–state apparatus did not invent this imaginary. The language of the remote and the backward had long been in circulation in this region (going back at least to the Guomindang period), and it continued to be employed in Jinxiu and elsewhere by a range of social actors. As we saw in the previous chapter, people in Guilin and in the lowland tourist town of Yangshuo viewed Jinxiu as a place far removed from the modern energies sweeping through the rest of the nation. The trip to Longpan revealed to me that if Jinxiu was becoming a place in which one could revisit the revolutionary past and observe and study the ancient traditions of the Yao people, then it was also a place that reminded many people about the realities of uneven development. The language of backwardness and the sense that the Yao were lagging behind other nationalities appeared, as I showed above, when peasants engaged in rituals of apology as they entertained county officials and other visitors from afar. It was present when Yao farmers reflected on extant agricultural methods and called for technical and managerial assistance to increase productivity, and when Yao ritual specialists described popular ritual as too extravagant (*shechi*) and wasteful of valuable resources. One also encountered it when older women discussed embroidery patterns and insisted that the making of "traditional costumes" (*women Yaoren de chuantong fuzhuang*) demanded too much time and took away from the development of other needed areas of expertise for women. Finally, it appeared when peasants pointed out to visiting research teams how the culture and customs of one subgroup were qualitatively different from, and in some cases inferior to, those of another subgroup.

The language of the remote and backward was thus diffused throughout the social landscape of Jinxiu. In this imaginary of what constitutes a modern ethnic group, social development, or its lack, comes to be as much a marker of one's identity as is clothing, or ritual, or marriage practices and popular beliefs, the standard markers used to identify and represent ethnic minorities in China.[34] Development becomes a measure of worth, of what it means to be a productive ethnic minority citizen. Ethnic minorities thus seem to be caught in a kind of developmental double bind, a bind that, in my estimation, has to do with the rise and naturalization of discourses that distinguish between spiritual and material civilization. Minorities are viewed by many people in China (and elsewhere) as the most traditional of all of China's nationalities, the people closest to the nation's ancient or primitive past. To apprehend this other is to be struck by the very historical depth of the Chinese nation. In this way, the "traditional" always belongs to the past, and this past is somehow supposed to give access to the spiritual dimension of a people.

Critics of European colonialism and modernity have noted that binary distinctions between tradition and modernity tend to "reduce complex continuities and contradictions to the aesthetics of nice oppositions," as Jean and John Comaroff have put it with forceful eloquence.[35] This distinction between the modern present and the traditional past is one of the quintessential European myths, a narrative that reduces the uneven relations between Europe and its others to the simple "epic story about the passage from savagery to civilization, from the mystical to the mundane." The story of progress "tells of the inexorable if always incomplete advancement of the primitive: of his conversion to a world religion, of his gradual incorporation into civil society, of improvement in his material circumstances, of the rationalization of his beliefs and practices."[36] The tradition/modernization binary has been a central trope in nationalist discourses that see the nation as a kind of species that grows and develops through time. The national landscape is in turn seen as being haunted by the unwanted fragments of the past, ghosts that refuse to go away and die. This sense of history turns cultural practices into things to be measured and scrutinized for their impact on the goals of the state and the desired trajectories of the nation.

The myth that a nation's progress has to overcome the oppressive weight of tradition was a central rhetorical tool in the communist revolution in China. We have to historicize this myth, however. In China, it would be interpreted, articulated, and popularized against the backdrop of years of brutal warlord control of many regions in China, an awareness of the oppressive gender codes of the Confucian order, a knowledge of local forms of Han prejudice and exploitation of minority groups, and the history of Euro-American and Japanese colonialism and imperialism. As I argued in previous chapters, the binary between the traditional and the modern was regnant across the Chinese and Yao social landscape. Do Deng Xiaoping's reforms provide us with a different practice of modernity, one in which the binary between the traditional and the modern would be recast? In the literature on modernity, one increasingly finds the claim that there are other modernities and modalities of being modern than those that have characterized the so-called West. For many scholars interested in decentering Europe as the locus of the modern, for example, the issue is not whether the postmodern has displaced the modern on a global scale but how new or "alternative modernities" have emerged at the close of the twentieth century. Aihwa Ong, for example, has shown how in the 1990s different actors in China and throughout East and Southeast Asia have promoted the idea of a "capitalism with Chinese characteristics" as a distinct form of modernity.[37] This Chinese modernity is evidently distinct from Western capitalism and rationality and based on a Confucian familial ethic and a range of interpersonal networks. The Chinese do not see the West as the perfected model for development and growth but in fact argue—in what is often a highly racialized and essentialized mode of boundary making— that Chinese business success is based on the unique qualities of a distinct civilization. As Don Robotham has argued in an assessment of this and other recent writings on alternative modernities, one implication is that all nations now claim to possess their own potential for modernity. Many proponents of such non-Western forms of the modern believe that "what was past can return again," as he put it.[38] From business and government leaders to common citizens, there is an increasingly popular view that this past, if properly studied, mobilized, and ideologically valorized, can give shape to a more meaningful future, a future evidently different from the realities of the modern as practiced and experienced in the West.

Echoing Ong, Robotham, and others who have attempted to trace "alternative" discourses and practices of modernity,[39] Jing Wang has argued that after the "aborted utopianism" of the Tiananmen occupation in 1989, many intellectuals became aware that the course of history could not be changed by ideas alone.[40] If the conventional wisdom of the 1980s was that "knowledge is wealth," then in the 1990s it would be the economic rather than the ideological, political, or cultural that would delimit the Chinese social imaginary. Wang argues that any discussion of Chinese modernity in the 1990s must address how the search for an alternative socioeconomic model would take place not through the mimesis of the West, or through abstract economic paradigms alone. The future of modernization—as both a dis-

course and an everyday social practice of development and productivity—
would take place at the site of what the Han social theorist Gan Yang called
"rural China" (xiangtu Zhongguo).⁴¹ This, then, is another image of a nation,
one in which intellectuals, officials, and policymakers are looking not just
to the West. It is an image in which we see the gaze of development and
modernization turned inward, toward the local, the rural, and the indigenous.

I have argued in this chapter that the gaze was also turned toward the
ethnic other. I have focused on different social and cultural practices in
which Party and government agents attempted to mobilize the Jinxiu Yao to
care for their own communities, to monitor their own behavior, to assess
the productive potentiality—the potency—of their own "indigenous" cultural practices. Deng Xiaoping's agenda throughout the 1980s was to bring
a new rhetoric of progress to the national body, one in which development
would no longer be tied to the politics of class struggle; the nation was
now to enter a new, more rational era. Government officials in Jinxiu interpreted this as a call for new experiments in local government. They saw
the quest for socialist modernity as making space for the promotion of
local cultural practices that they marked as "traditional," in part to undo
the hegemony of previous dominant signifiers such as "feudal" and "class-
contaminated." Rather than expel the practices from everyday life, Party
cadres and others now sought to study and promote them, to render them
useful for the project of socialist modernization. Many argued that it was
now time to mobilize the local knowledges of the ethnic masses, which,
they believed, would raise morale and awaken the dormant energies of the
local populace. Some Yao would argue that cultural practices indigenous
to the mountains—ritual, social morality, the shipai, family planning practices—already contained the very modernity the state was seeking. I asserted furthermore that this process hinged on the question of who spoke
for and who best represented the modernity of the Yao, a position that many
Chashan Yao claimed to occupy, which, in turn, inadvertently led to the
emergence of new local forms of intra-ethnic othering. They insisted that a
traditional form of ethnic consciousness existed among their people, a consciousness that Maoist socialism had failed to fully transform. Many elders,
for example, still possessed knowledge of the shipai system and its associated forms of indigenous organization, decision making, conflict resolution, and mobilization. Popular ritual offered its own potentialities. Ironi-

cally, these indigenous practices, once marked for destruction for their ties to the systems of exploitation that the revolution had struggled to overthrow, were now to be championed as locally productive technologies of social order. If properly studied, harnessed, and encouraged, then they just might assist in the maintenance of social order and the building of a new community of subjects collectively committed to the modernization of the hills. The resurgence of popular ritual became a sign of a new possibility in local government, one in which the state would now commit itself to work with local peasants, as well as minority intellectuals, to return to everyday life some sense of normalcy, social order, and everyday routine.

In my tale of alternative modernities in the Dayaoshan I have aimed to shift the focus from the West/non-West (or North/South) binary to the politics of ethnicity, the state, and development in reform-era China. By attending to these debates about the meaning of the socialist modern in Jinxiu we not only decenter Europe, we also decenter the Han Chinese subject as the singular agent of new ideologies of Chinese modernity. I have also argued that these processes of seeking out, crafting, and claiming an ethnic minority form of modernity were underway in China well before Han Chinese intellectuals got screwed by the government in Tiananmen Square in 1989—perhaps even before a discourse of alternative modernities entered anthropological discourse in the mid-1990s, when the question of the failure of state socialism in the Soviet Union and Eastern Europe impelled scholars to trace new forms of cultural production and political discourse in China and other regions of the world.

"The true global story is appearing to be not the negative one about the fall of socialism, but the far more complicated one about the rise of Asia." [42] Perhaps this is the case in the late 1990s, though I would caution against a too easy dismissal of the problem of socialism—either as lived experience, embodied memory, or political ideology—in places such as Jinxiu. Jinxiu Yao were focusing their critical energies on the excesses of Maoism, and many were committed to the idea that traditional culture had a role to play in the making of a socialist modern China. The end of history had not yet arrived in Jinxiu; I doubt if it has yet to make its utopian appearance. In the end, we might be tempted to view this period as one in which the cultural sphere has been liberated from the work of ideology, or at least from the hegemony of class analysis. Yet, the widespread interest in popular ritual, in questions of social morality and social order, suggests a new and perhaps more pervasive convergence of the ideological and the social. The gaze turned on popular ritual and other indigenous practices was all about the power of the local ethnic subject to overcome the traumas of the past. Yet it was also about the search for new technologies of rule, new practices of governmentality, and new imaginaries of the socialist modern.

chapter five

Postsocialist Belonging

We need the power of modern critical theories of how meanings and bodies get made, not in order to deny meanings and bodies, but in order to live in meanings and bodies that have a chance for a future. — DONNA HARAWAY, *Simians, Cyborgs, and Women: The Reinvention of Nature*

When I lived in Beijing and traveled to cities such as Guangzhou, Guilin, Nanning, and Kunming, I often took to the streets in search of bookstalls, bookstores, and shopping districts. I remember being overwhelmed by the sheer abundance of academic writings on the cultures and histories of China's minority populations. I also remember encountering what seemed to be a popular ethnological fascination with minority cultures. In any of a number of popular magazines, for example, one could read accounts of the open sexual practices and matrilineal marriage practices of non-Han peoples in the far southwest. One of the more enticing tales of the time described the Tibetan practice of feeding the corpses of their dead to ravenous vultures in the Tibet highlands. Visual images of minorities were also beginning to appear on billboards and in other public spaces in the late 1980s and early 1990s. The most ubiquitous, I recall, was the image of a group of smiling minorities, dressed in the multicolored traditional garb of their people, joyously singing and dancing. In any of the hip fashion boutiques at the major hotels one could buy reproductions of authentic pieces of minority clothing, or batik, jewelry and other bodily accoutrements and look just like a Yao, a Bai, a Miao, or a Tibetan.

By the time I completed my formal research in mid-1992, images of a quaint, primitive, and colorful minority subject were making their way into China's cultural theme parks, where the commodification of ethnic culture and the erasure of the socialist past were seemingly occurring hand in hand. Ethnic minorities were active participants in these national and global economies of ethnic consumption, as they eagerly sold their handicrafts, costumes, and knowledges to those seeking out the country's most primitive and exotic peoples. Once banished from the social landscape as a remnant of the feudal past, the ethnic minority had become, in the midst of Deng Xiaoping's frenetic reforms, an object to be displayed, an identity to be tried on, a cultural world to be momentarily inhabited. The historical mission of socialist modernization was not to proceed without the comfort of ethnic culture.

As in previous periods, many people in China viewed minorities as objects of exotic fascination. It is not stretching it to say that many Han saw minorities such as the Yao as modern primitives, peoples tied to strange and superstitious traditions, living in the most remote and most poverty-stricken territories of the country. As China's tourism industry blossomed throughout the 1980s, many urban Han began to encounter ethnic minorities for the first time. In contrast, those who had been "sent down" to live with the non-Han during the early 1960s rustication campaigns had more complex histories of contact with minority communities. Many of China's filmmakers and most celebrated authors, for example, had lived among minorities in the 1960s and 1970s. In the 1980s they began to argue in their writings and interviews that it was necessary to spend extensive time in ethnic regions to understand China's current predicaments. Many imagined themselves to be amateur anthropologists, as they employed participant-observation techniques to gain access to the lifeways and cultural styles of non-Han peoples. Some of the beautifully crafted films of the internationally acclaimed Fifth Generation, for example, took the viewer into remote lands where minorities followed a more tranquil and almost melodic temporal lifestyle and where they lived according to social arrangements that allowed for more fluid definitions of gender and sexuality.[1] Though many of these films depicted a male Han subject in crisis, the minority was present mainly as an object of cultural excess. The minority other enjoyed freedoms that had been denied to the Han subject, who was seen to be doubly tormented by the strictures of Confucianism and the aesthetic practices of Maoist socialism.[2]

Appropriations of Ethnic Difference

I want a history of looking. — ROLAND BARTHES, *Camera Lucida*

Many perceptions of ethnic culture and history are found in the novels written by Han Chinese during this period. These fictionalized productions are presented as artistic explorations of the Chinese modern subject. As with some of the films produced in China in the 1980s, they also reveal the ways Han intellectuals were using images of the non-Han other for their own ideological purposes. The exploration of China's current problems required an emotionally challenging return to the Maoist past, to the ethnic peoples with whom they once lived, and to the disparate knowledges and modes of being they encountered along the way. For example, in 1988 the Han essayist and novelist Bai Hua published a novel based on his experiences among the Mosuo people in the southwest of China. It was called *The Remote Country of Women*. This is a tale of a faraway land, where marriage is an alien concept, free love is the norm, and children grow up not knowing their fathers. Associated with the "scar literature" (*shanghen wenxue*) (a reference to the suffering that occurred during the Cultural Revolution) that emerged in the years following the death of Mao in 1976, Bai's novel provides a fictionalized account of the suffering that occurred among the Chinese populace during the more radical phases of Mao's rule. Scar writers set their narratives in urban environments, in distant rural landscapes, and sometimes, as in the case of this novel, among minority populations. Their fictional imaginaries were popular in large part because they contained traces of the historical real, with riveting descriptions of political bureaucracy, Maoist aesthetics, and state-orchestrated struggle sessions against counterrevolutionaries and other enemies of the state. Bai's novel was eventually translated into English in 1994. Whereas one critic championed it for exposing the "warping banality of totalitarianism," Bai reflected on his contribution somewhat differently. The inside cover of the English-language edition contains the following quote: "When a stream flows into a big river, it loses its purity but gains breadth. When humanity walks toward modernization, what is gained and what is lost? Here I can only unfold to my readers the panorama of life as it is and wait to hear their judgement."

The panorama of life in *The Remote Country of Women* is a story that follows a male protagonist, Liang Rui, as he describes his experiences during the Chinese Great Proletarian Cultural Revolution. We learn of Liang's life in a labor camp and then follow his travails in prison. These chapters are interspersed with remembrances of a young woman named Sunamei, a member of the Mosuo, a subgroup of the Naxi minority nationality found predominantly in the mountains that form the border of Yunnan and Sichuan Provinces in southwest China. The Mosuo have long been a focus of ethnologists in China, in part because they are considered to be a matriarchal people. They live, Bai tells us, in a society without marriage, where women freely take male lovers and just as freely discard them when desire ceases. As I have indicated, this novel came on the scene when many Han Chinese authors and intellectuals were exploring the effects of the Cultural Revolution on the psyche of the Chinese people. It provides a fanciful though not entirely ethnographically ungrounded representation of ethnic difference (the detailed ethnographic descriptions work to draw the reader into the narrative) to forge a critique of the repressive policies of the Chinese Party-state apparatus during the high point of Maoist socialism. Sexuality is envisioned as belonging entirely to the realm of nature. The Cultural Revolution was a battle waged not only against the class enemies of the socialist state, but more profoundly, in Bai's view, against the nature of the human subject. All nationalities share this nature, though it is often hidden and rendered inaccessible to some by the forces of culture, politics, and history. To read about the Mosuo and the cultural life of Sunamei is to encounter a more natural social order, one that has escaped the practices of social engineering and the blind submission to ideological abstractions that characterized so much of China's revolutionary politics. Where better to discover this natural state than in the figure of the ethnic minority, the primitive other whose culture remains untarnished by the politics of modernity?

Liang Rui's experiences among the Mosuo provide him with a way to cope with his own predicaments as a desexualized and socially alienated male in post–Cultural Revolution China. As a figure of cultural difference, the ethnic minority provides him with an alternative to his own miserable existence. It allows him to reflect on the repressive patriarchal society into which he was born and the pain that accompanies practices of forced marriage, the use of lovers for political advancement, and the emotional distress that comes with living in a socialist society where eroticism has been banned. In one chapter, we are taken into the drab, lifeless environment of a labor camp; in the next, into the harmonious world of minority ritual where the events of the life cycle connect one with both the social world and the cosmos. At one point in the narrative, Liang feigns an illness so that he can leave the labor camp to visit a young Han woman. However, he is soon accosted by the authorities for a letter he has written to a trusted friend urging him to free his mind from the dictates of ideology. His friend, fearing for himself if the letter is found in his own hands, exposes Liang for his dangerous anti-Maoist thoughts. Finally, toward the end of the book, we learn why Liang has been tormented by his memories of the Mosuo and his lost love, Sunamei. Disillusioned with Maoist and socialist culture, years ago Liang had traveled to this most remote place in China and met the beautiful Sunamei, who was a member of a song and dance troupe. They fell in love and were soon married, for Liang wanted her to adhere to Han customs. Yet she could never lose her cultural identity. On a return home, she slept with an old lover. Liang discovered the betrayal, beat her, and she fled. The two cultures ultimately can never cross, nor can Liang free himself from his own culture. Liang is abandoned and devastated, left alone to sort out his twisted memories of a remote land of beauty and sexual freedom and of his years of incarceration in a labor camp.

Bai takes the reader on an imagined journey into the remote world of minority difference to critique the political excesses of socialism. His novel is an example of how post-Mao forms of historical critique often depended on the production of phantasmagoric images of ethnic difference. This practice, of course, is not unique to China, nor is it a mode of representation found only in the novel. It has long appeared, for example, in European and American travelogues, in ethnological and ethnographic writings, and in many journalistic accounts (recall my discussion in the preface of the book *The People of the Hills*). What we have in Bai's narrative is a story about a Chinese subject struggling to reconstitute his identity after years of mindless obedience to Party rule. But his novel also points to a more generalized form of cultural critique, in which the alien, the deviant, and the marginal are sought out and made visible by a subject who seeks not merely knowledge of difference but his or her own self-realization and advancement. The margins, imagined as a fixed space of radical alterity, serve as a backdrop for the reconstitution of a fractured self; in this case, a Han male subject denied freedom, sexuality, desire, the truth of his body. This mode of critique was rampant throughout the 1980s in China, as writers such as Bai were turning to the ethnic margins to reinvigorate a morally, socially, and sexually debilitated Han subject. The cultivation of marginality clearly points an accusing finger at the cultural and political center of the socialist empire, but the opposition between the center and the margin is never truly disrupted. Critique is enacted over the body of the minority other, but only to consolidate the identity of the cultural center.

Another 1980s production that has drawn some attention for its depiction of minority difference is Zhang Nuanxin's film *Sacrificed Youth*, or *Qingchun ji*, as it is known in China. As with Bai's novel, this film emerged in the spaces opened up by Communist Party censors for artistic work in post–Cultural Revolution China. It explores the subjective experiences of a particular individual and thus moves away from an earlier genre of revolutionary realism in which the travails and triumphs of class struggle dominated the screen. On one level, *Sacrificed Youth* is a personal narrative very similar to Bai's fictional account of Liang. In this instance, however, the story focuses on a sent-down Han woman who lives among the Dai people in the south of Yunnan Province. Her name is Li Chun, and she too experiences an identity crisis. As she moves and lives among the Dai, she encounters a cultural world of young Dai women who celebrate their femininity, flirt with men, and marvel at the shapely contours of their own bodies, adorned as they are in the tightly clad sarongs of traditional custom. As Li negotiates her entrance into the local community—in a familiar anthropological mode—she suddenly finds acceptance when she begins to wear Dai clothing and fix her hair in the manner of the other women. As the film critic Esther Yau has suggested, this is a crucial moment in the film, for it is here that Li is liberated from the homogeneity of her political upbringing, an emancipation clearly linked to an increasing awareness of her sexuality.[3] It is in this moment that the film functions as a form of political critique, questioning both the strictures of Confucian morality and the inscription of Maoist ideologies onto the female body.

On another level, however, the film is a highly romantic and idyllic portrayal of the non-Han other. In the cinematography we see the Dai countryside awash in gentle hues of green and blue. The pace of life is slow. Farmers move with fluidity through the wet-rice fields, oxen amble dreamlike in the summer heat, and Dai women admire their reflections in ponds and streams. It is against this backdrop of imagined tranquillity that Li's conflict with her own past erupts. As much as she struggles to cross the boundaries of cultural difference, as much as she awakens to new experiences of womanhood, she can never escape the fact that her youth has been wasted, the best years of her life sacrificed to the revolution. Confronted with the culture of Dai feminine sexuality, she is forced to come to grips with her own history as a sent-down youth, with its years of social turmoil and political indoctrination. As in Bai's novel, memory—the act of recalling the past and wrestling with its meanings—is a key trope. As the film proceeds, her memories of languid days with the beautiful Dai give way to the awareness of her own existential dilemma: she cannot escape the inscription of politics on her own body.

The film ends in tragedy when she discovers that the Dai village has been destroyed in a mudslide. She is separated forever from her surrogate Dai mother, and the man with whom she longs to reunite—another sent-down youth who stays behind to work as a schoolteacher in a Dai village—has disappeared. The Han woman, resurrected from a Maoist death as pained female, is left with only her memories, alone, isolated, alienated from the social order of Han society. Despite all of its melodrama and romantic imagery, it is difficult not to see *Sacrificed Youth* as a powerful political commentary on the disenfranchisement of the Han intellectual class. But the desire to forge a powerful deconstruction of the Maoist regime relies on what seems to be a familiar orientalist rendering of cultural difference: the marginal other is denied the history experienced by the center. As Esther Yau puts it, Zhang's "thematic obsession" with a cultural construct of beauty untouched by political socialization has resulted only in an objectified and imaginary depiction of a non-Han culture. In effect, her Dai subjects are discursively mobilized only to serve a narcissistic exploration of the intellectual's marginalized condition under Maoism. Zhang thus constructs an idealized other to make more visible to a Han audience the conflicts of the Han female self. Moreover, this strategy rests on the erasure of the history of Han–Dai relations, of the politics of Chinese economic exploitation of ethnic minority regions, and the effects of years of political campaigns in Dai villages. A genre of socialist realism has merely been replaced by a kind of orientalist humanism, in which the self comprehends its own being through its representational use of the other.

As were so many others like it, this film was produced in the space of a nation obsessed with modernization. Aspiring to a modernization that could be at once socialist and Chinese, the post-Mao subject encountered dilemmas that were being scrutinized through experimentation with narrative voice-over and through acts of self-reflection made by the subjective experiences of a single person. Zhang's filmic depiction of a Han woman in existential crisis rests on her appropriation of Western modes of personal narration and diegetic construction, as well as on her appropriation of the Maoist past as the reform-era's historical other. This form of cultural introspection and historical critique acquires an added force when an "internal other," to borrow Louisa Schein's phrase, is mobilized as the cultural opposite.[4] As with her fictional character Li Chun, Zhang draws attention to and struggles with issues of gender and sexuality through the use of ethnic peoples, remote and tranquil ethnic landscapes, all brought together in a brilliant tapestry of ethnic images. The socialist modern moment is experienced as rupture and loss.

This is also a tale about the inability to cross ethnic lines. At one point in the film, for example, Li checks out her Dai costume in a market mirror. She smiles at her newfound ethnic image, but, as her shy glance in front of the mirror suggests, this is an ethnicity she wears with awkwardness and discomfort. The film ends with her crying in front of the site of the mudslide that destroyed "her" Dai village. It is this scene of destruction that confronts her with the reality of an impossible completeness and an impossible return to the world for which she so desperately longs. She must live with the loss of the very terrain (the Dai language, the ethnic landscape, the women's clothing, the warmth of her adoptive Dai grandmother) that once promised her wholeness. To reiterate, then, the ethnic other comes to us through a double movement: as a symbol of youth and as a symbol of loss. This other provides a space of and for longing, but it is removed from any kind of historical materiality. It serves only as a site for an imagined liberation from the tyrannies of the Maoist past and the dictates of Confucian and socialist moralities.

Additionally, as we saw in Bai Hua's imaginary, the remote ethnic space is conflated with the traditional. As many feminist critics have so forcefully argued, women in settings all over the world are frequently inscribed as the carriers of tradition, the ground upon which the modern is made.[5] Because the traditional is assigned to the past or to peoples, regions, practices, and bodies associated with the primitive or the ancient, the viewing public often experiences it as the "return of the repressed." This return is meant to haunt the viewer with images of unleashed sexuality, of masculine peasant men spitting and cursing and celebrating the vulgar, and of tranquil ethnic worlds free of conflict.[6]

Memory and the Politics of Belonging

Materialist historiography does not choose its objects casually. It does not pluck them from the process of history, but rather blasts them out of it. —WALTER BENJAMIN, "N [Re the Theory of Knowledge, Theory of Progress]."

Dru Gladney has argued that many of these appropriations of ethnic difference were attempts on the part of Han intellectuals to recenter a masculine Han subject.[7] I think Gladney is correct in arguing that these filmic, artistic, and literary images were a central feature of post-Mao nationalist discourse, but I want to push Gladney's analysis further and ask what happens when the minority is the very agent of these phantasmagoric ethnic imaginings. How we are to understand and theorize minority elite participation in representations that see minorities as mere signs of tradition? Is it always the Han subject positioned at the center of Chinese nationalism?[8] I want to move beyond accounts of ethnic representation that deconstruct how Han intellectuals have appropriated signs of ethnic difference to invigorate a depleted national subject. What was the minority elite finding in the figure of tradition? Were they driven by the same desires as their Han intellectual counterparts? What happens to our understanding of Chinese nationalism when minorities see the places in which they live as spaces of enduring tradition? Is the representation of the local, the indigenous, the traditional, and the ethnic informed by the same postsocialist nostalgia that drives the Han intellectual appropriation of the ethnic margins?

There are two ways to approach these questions. The first addresses the place of minority subjects in the politics of nationalism; the second asks what the desire for tradition tells us about the problematic of Chinese postsocialism. In the field of anthropology and ethnicity studies, Brackette Williams was one of the first scholars to explore issues of minority ethnic representation in the context of dominant nationalist imaginings and processes of exclusion and inclusion. In an essay published in 1989, for instance, Williams implored scholars interested in ethnicity to attend to the intricate linkages between classification and subjection, power and knowledge, ethnic identity and nationalism.[9] She argued that ethnicity can no longer be theorized outside of the politics of race, nor can it be seen as simply made up of diacritical cultural markers or symbolic expressions of a people's identity, as many anthropologists had long argued. Because it has figured predominantly in the politics of race, nationalism, and modernity across the globe, ethnicity is best approached as a highly contested modern discourse. Williams thus argued that ethnicity provides a window into the politics of cultural struggle for peoples on the "margins" of dominant nationalist imaginings. Ethnicity becomes significant when politically dominant groups set the terms of belonging to the national center while subordinate groups are left to vie among themselves as to how best to mark their contribution to the national order. In nationalist contexts where voice and recognition are a resource, the label "ethnic" comes to denote those who are excluded from the nationalist vision by the ruling elite. This elite uses images of internal ethnic difference for its own struggles for position and authority; it also refuses to acknowledge its own ethnicity.

I find much of use in Williams's reworking of ethnicity theory. However, how we understand just what constitutes the dominant and the subordinate in post-Mao China remains a question for further exploration. As the previous chapters have shown, the scholars I came to know saw themselves as members of a privileged social class who had been marginalized, misused, and repeatedly misunderstood by the Party since the late 1950s. Yao ethnologists, historians, and other local (county-based) scholars and Party officials often spoke of themselves in opposition to the CCP and especially the campaigns that reduced ethnic realities to the politics of class struggle. They were also critical of how some Han intellectuals and Party cadres had represented the "nationalities problem" among the Yao, especially in the late 1950s and 1960s. These claims to marginalization have been intricately entwined with the reform regime's attempt to mobilize a new elite to play a leading role in Deng Xiaoping's socialist modernization agenda. If we are to see these as practices of empowerment, then we have to understand them in the historical context of post-Mao China, when spaces were being opened up to speak against the excesses of Maoist socialism and to rethink the relationship between minority culture and Chinese modernity.

The problem, of course, is that these elite often claimed to speak for the Yao community as a total collective entity. Because of their positions of power and authority, they saw themselves as having a responsibility to bring development to the poorest of Yao regions, to encourage Yao villagers to lift themselves up, join the reforms, and bring socialist modernity to their own communities and families. As did intellectuals and leading cadres throughout China, they saw themselves as the guardians of the nation's people and their rich and diverse cultural traditions. As we have seen, many believed that minority cultures were rooted in the ancient past of the Chinese nation. As I detailed in chapter 1 when we looked at the writing of Yao histories, they claimed that various practices, such as religious belief and ritual, changed and evolved as the ethnic subject advanced through successive historical stages of social development. "Traditional culture," or *chuantong wenhua*, became an object to be managed, as intellectuals, scholars, and Party cadres worked to define the correct relationship between "traditional culture" and "socialist modernization." Many people thought the traditional culture of the Yao had survived the worst years of Maoist rule. Others, in repeatedly recalling the political campaigns of the late 1950s, 1960s, and 1970s, felt that the world of traditional culture was in ruins. How to study a culture in ruins? Where was it to be found? How was it to be approached, harnessed, and restored as a meaningful dimension of social life? Publications, conference papers, and official documents on local realities from the late 1980s and early 1990s reveal that discerning the relationship between tradition and modernity was defined as one of the most important tasks of nationality work, or *minzu gongzuo*. It was often as if the future of the minority subject, and indeed of the entire nation, hinged on the resolution of this very question.

The question of tradition and its relationship to reform-era socialist modernization needs to be situated in the context of complex and often contradictory elite engagements with the history of Chinese socialism. Arif Dirlik has argued that the reform-era, especially in the realms of academic and cultural work, has been defined in large part by a crisis in the historical consciousness of socialism. As he has put it, this crisis stems from

> the repudiation of Mao Zedong and Maoist communism, which has created a profound uncertainty in Chinese consciousness concerning not only the future but the past of socialism in China. For the past four decades, the history of socialism in China has been thought and written about around the paradigm of Mao's personal biography—in China and abroad. The Cultural Revolution in particular was responsible for elevating Mao's biography to paradigmatic status in the conceptualization of Chinese socialism, although this process was already underway in the 1940s, even before the victory of the Communist Party in 1949. The repudiation of the Cultural Revolution following Mao's death in 1976

was rapidly to call into question Maoist historiography of the socialist revolution as well. The crisis in the historical consciousness of socialism that has ensued presents a predicament as well as novel opportunities. Predicaments because the history of socialism has been deprived of its reference in Mao's biography and needs to be relocated in time (the Communist Party does not provide a ready substitute, because in repudiating Mao it has deprived itself of the claim to historical infallibility). *Opportunity because the repudiation of Mao has burst open the ideological closure in which socialism has long been restricted, which has made possible new ways of seeing history* [my emphasis].[10]

Dirlik's image of an ideological closure suddenly burst open reminds us of Walter Benjamin's observation, quoted at the beginning of this section, that materialist historiography does not casually pluck its objects from the process of history; rather, it "blasts" them out of it.[11] What, we might ask, is the place of materialist historiography in a historical moment both fascinated with traditional culture and critical of the history of Maoism? By focusing on the historical consciousness of socialism, Dirlik allows us to think about the politics of ethnic representation not just through the eyes of a Han male subject seeking to reconstitute his masculinity on the back of the ethnic other. It allows us to understand the reforms as a contested cultural experiment in which new discourses and practices of ethnicity were waged around memories of the socialist campaigns, and especially the politics of class struggle, associated with the rule of Mao Zedong. The problematic of postsocialist memory gives us a different angle on the complex relationship between intellectual work and the politics of ethnic empowerment.

For many of the Yao I worked with, ethnicity was not just about marking one's difference from the Han or other groups. It was also about articulating how one belonged to different kinds of communities. These elite had to define themselves in relation to, for example, mountain peasants who were often the object of official scorn for their apparent inability to overcome the conditions of their own backwardness. They also had to think of themselves and their own writings and research projects in relation to the demands of a reform-minded CCP, which was, after all, attempting to reinvent and reimagine its relationship to the Han and ethnic minority masses. Yao scholars and other elite were also constantly defining and presenting their projects to foreign anthropologists, journalists, human rights activists, and professional and amateur photographers. They thus related to and moved among a number of different constituencies and they spoke for their people in a range of shifting political and social contexts.

In this sense, to return to Williams's approach to ethnicity and marginality, it is difficult for me to see these various elite actors as speaking from the margins. If their work is about empowering a new postsocialist ethnic subject, then I think we have to understand this process of empowerment as a struggle to effectively and productively belong to the Chinese nation. And how one belongs—to continue the line of argument I have been developing here—depends on how one remembers socialism. Put differently, it depends on the dialectics of remembering and forgetting, or what Dirlik calls the historical consciousness of socialism. The centrality of a politics of belonging is revealed, I think, in how Yao elite produced images of a pan-Yao traditional subject. I turn now to one such production.

Socialism under Erasure

In the summer of 1990, a large, magnificently produced book called *The Yao Nationality* began to appear in bookstores in China.[12] This book was unlike other ethnological texts I encountered over the course of my research, what with their sometimes dull descriptions of minority rituals and cultural practices and their seemingly robotic use of terminology from the ethnological lexicon of Marx and Engels and Lewis Henry Morgan. Filled with glossy photographs depicting different subjects (men and women, old and young, intellectual and peasant) engaged in a wide range of "traditional" activities, this book was a celebration of the Yao in all of their splendid diversity. As with many publications on minorities in China, no single person is credited with authorship. It ostensibly represents the view of the CCP, for the Nationalities Affairs Commission (Minzu Shiwu Weiyuanhui) of the Guangxi Zhuang Autonomous Region played a significant role in its production, at least in terms of financial support and distribution. Inside the back cover, for instance, one finds that more than twenty people, most of whom are Yao scholars and Party officials in Guangxi, worked on the book in an assortment of capacities, everything from editors in chief (zhubian) to advisors (guwen), photo editors (tupian bianji), and map designers (tuan sheji).

If, at some level, this book represents the view of the Communist Party, then we have to understand this as a reformed Party, one that was struggling to remake its image, redefine its relationship to the masses, rethink the relationship between Chinese nationalism and the representation of ethnic difference. This text turns away from the image of the hardened revolutionary worker of the Maoist era and refocuses on the image of a traditional ethnic subject. This subject is no longer considered a "problem," or marked for ideological transformation because of its class desires, its feudal superstitions, and its attachments to the forms and practices of local nationalism. It is here and now unambiguously linked to a diversity of enduring cultural practices. These practices occur in remote mountain enclaves far from China's bustling and modernizing urban centers, yet they are nonetheless seen as a constitutive feature of China's multiethnic reality. The front cover reveals this shift in vision. It is adorned with five color photographs, several of which show young men and women dressed in embroidered clothing, supposedly the costumes of their particular "subgroup." Another image on the cover shows several men and women, again dressed in the clothing of their particular group, sauntering through the rural countryside; one subject gazes back at the camera with what seems to be a welcoming smile.

Opening the book one encounters an even greater explosion of images, a visual celebration of the Yao in all of their geographic and cultural diversity. All of the major autonomous counties in which the Yao live are randomly included, providing the reader with glimpses of ethnic life in the remote mountains of Guangxi, Guangdong, Hunan, and Yunnan. The scenes are awash in brilliant colors and the subjects are repeatedly portrayed in mountain settings, with towering peaks, cascading waterfalls, brilliantly sculpted rice fields, and thick bamboo forests serving as backdrops. We are afforded a fleeting experience of what it might mean to inhabit the places in which minorities live. We encounter images of ritual practice, of religious specialists in trance, of young men being initiated into the Taoist spirit realm. We learn that the Yao, in villages across the south and southwest of China, yearly engage in mass cultural activities, what the text calls qunzhong wenhua. These activities are said to "liven up the people's monotonous life in the mountains." As do other nationalities in China, including the Han, the Yao play cards, watch films, and enjoy recreation and sports. We learn as well that the Yao have produced authors, photographers, calligraphers, folk painters, and internationally renowned scholars. In the penultimate chapter of the book we learn that there are now Yao who live overseas.

We also learn from the captions accompanying the photographs that the

The front cover of *The Yao Nationality*.

The back cover of *The Yao Nationality*.

Yao have overcome many obstacles in their quest for socialist modernity. Early in the text we encounter the following passage:

> They were usually called the "Yao of crossing mountains." It is recorded in the history that this distressful people, subject to endless bullying and humiliation, were unable to settle down on the plains and had to bury themselves in the remotest mountains. In southern China, especially in the southwest, the Yao lived on high mountains at elevations of 1,000–2,000 meters. There is a saying in Guizhou Province that "the Buyi nationality lives by the river, the Miao in the middle, the Yao on the peak." Even if migrating to Vietnam, Thailand, Laos, and Burma, they had to reside on mountains at 800–1,000 meters. The environment in which they live can be described as such: precipitous, dry, and scattered. The Yao are characterized by their resoluteness and indomitableness; they live in the mountains, opening up the fields, planting crops, striving for a way of life and development, so that they have been toughened into a well-known mountain nationality.[13]

This passage draws the reader's attention to a tumultuous past, a life of forced migrations, of constant bullying and intimidation, when the Yao were forced to live in the most precarious and infertile of China's southern mountain terrain. No single agent is named, for it is implicitly understood that the text is referring to the rulers and class enemies of "feudal" China. These remote mountain environments, coupled with long histories of struggle against systems of exploitation and oppression, have worked together to form the contemporary Yao. Let us look at another description of the Yao, this one culled from an academic paper presented to an international colloquium on Yao studies in 1986. Jacques Lemoine, one of the world's leading scholars of Yao religion, writes: "What I find remarkable in a relationship between a human group and its culture is not the way in which culture adapts to the requirements of economy or the struggle against nature, but rather to the capacity of the group to literally transcend the real conditions of their life through the luxury of their culture."[14]

Though these two images come from very different sources, it is productive to place them in dialogue with each other. They both emerged in the mid-1980s, when anthropologists, linguists, and social historians from Australia, Europe, Hong Kong, Taiwan, Thailand, and the United States were beginning to forge research affiliations with some of China's leading Yao scholars and Party officials. Both perspectives constitute the Yao as a subject of history. The first implicitly argues that Yao cultural and social development has been constrained by a particular kind of relationship to the natural environment and by past modes of rule. The revolutionary victory in 1949 brings an end to their nomadic lifestyle, isolation, and poverty. Under the guidance of the Communist Party, they have dispensed with slash-and-burn agriculture and adopted modern ways to improve production: "The remote barren lands have blossomed into rich granaries." [15] In Lemoine's view, however, the Yao have long used "culture" to defeat the exigencies of both nature and history; he sets forth a mode of interpretation that refuses to reduce culture to a given stage of social development. Culture is granted agency, seen here as a resource that can lift a people above and beyond the conditions of their everyday existence. The Yao "transcend the real conditions of their life through the luxury of their culture."

Some but not all ethnologists in contemporary China would argue that Lemoine's view is excessively idealist, in that he sees culture mainly through the lens of religious belief and practice. His view runs against the grain of the Marxist tradition in Chinese ethnology, which would never see culture as a means to "transcend the real conditions" of life but rather as inextricably embedded in and reflective of the material conditions of social life. Lemoine's is not simply an argument for culture against the state, however. It is in fact one made possible in part by the reform regime, which allowed him to participate in the debates in the mid-1980s on the status of the Chinese nation and the place of ethnic minority culture in this national space. His view is remarkably consistent with the narrative and visual focus in The Yao Nationality, in which the identity of the minority subject has everything to do with culture. Lemoine's intervention is part of a larger historical moment, one in which discourses of culture and ethnicity have moved across and within the borders and boundaries of the Chinese nation. We saw this earlier in chapter 1, when I discussed how my young scholar-friend Huang Fangping was reading and translating the scholarship written on the Yao by European, American, and Australian anthropologists. These interventions unsettle the ways the Yao have been classified in the typologies of modern China. They especially work against the view that ethnicity is nothing more than a lingering remnant of a primitive social formation or is always already contaminated by class interests that undermine the movement of history. Lemoine's project—and here I would say his interests overlap with many Yao ethnologists—is to reinvigorate the ethnic margins and to make the fragmented ethnic body once again whole.

The Yao Nationality clearly shows how the making of a multiethnic national imaginary has depended on the participation of minority scholars and officials. It also shows how the representation of a traditional cultural subject would be intricately tied up with how the campaigns associated with the Maoist era were to be remembered and forgotten. It is tempting to argue that *The Yao Nationality* is a perfect example of what we might call a post-Mao politics of retribution, in which the "rightists" struggled against during the Cultural Revolution have finally settled a score with history. In this sense, the book tells us less about the Yao than about the instrumental machinations of elite members of an ethnic group who have successfully positioned themselves to construct, manipulate, and maintain identities in the pursuit of their own interest.[16] I think the issue is more complicated, in that those I knew and worked with were ambivalent about how to tell the history of Chinese socialism in a period in which so much of the Maoist era had been discursively reduced to the disasters of the Cultural Revolution.

In fact, throughout much of the 1980s and on into the 1990s, Communist Party leaders forbade ethnologists and social historians to analyze, at least in print, post-Liberation society. To be sure, as we have seen, political campaigns such as Land Reform, the Great Leap, and the Cultural Revolution were often mentioned in the forewords and prefaces of many texts and certainly in many "internal" (*neibu*) documents, those texts meant only for the eyes of Party members. We also encounter descriptions of how minority leaders became leading Party officials and we encounter narratives of different groups and individuals leading uprisings against the reactionary Guomindang and other enemies of the state. And we see images of a socialist modern Yao subject working hard to bring development and progress to the ethnic outback. But many of the Yao I knew were ambivalent in talking about the worst years of the socialist project, unless they were deploying the sweeping generality that reduces all of history to the mistakes of the ultraleftists. They would have us believe that the Red Guards were mostly Han or Zhuang, that the Yao themselves played only a small role in the Cultural Revolution. The minority subject experienced the struggles, traumas, and tragedies associated with the Cultural Revolution, but mostly as victims of a state power run amok.

The Yao Nationality thus seems to be consistent with a wide range of post-Mao representations of minority culture that exhibit the flattening of socialist history, the appropriation of images of ethnic exoticism, and the feminization and eroticization of a gendered subject. It also reveals how an elite participated in the surveillance of its own people, places, and cultural traditions. I want to point out, however, that few of the people I spoke with about this book's images thought they were consuming the historical real.[17] I remember interviewing one scholar involved in the project. This man was in his late fifties and had spent most of his intellectual life tracing the history of the Yao back to the "ancient culture" of China. As we together paged through the book and talked about the many different places and people in the images, I asked him why so many of the images portrayed the Yao in traditional costumes, especially when so few people now actually dressed in this manner. He responded by saying that this is what the Yao would look like "if history never happened." I have long been intrigued by this comment. It seems to reference a subject with an immutable and enduring identity, and we might interpret it as a "primordialist" view of identity, but here tinged with a good dose of anxiety. As he explained it to me, the Yao have always marked themselves off from other groups through these modes of costume and bodily display; without these expressive, bodily markers of identity, it is not clear how the differences among Yao subgroups could ever be represented. "The problem is that throughout much of the past several decades," he went on, "the Yao have been forbidden to express the many ways in which they differ from each other and from other nationalities."

This comment seems to wish history away, but it also draws attention to a history of trauma and ruin, of suppression and denial, a history that is perhaps best forgotten. This is the history many people in China (and abroad) associate with the decades of Communist Party campaigns to bring revolutionary consciousness, socialist order, and modernity to the minority subject. The desire to write against this history is evident in Lemoine's comments above, for he is acutely aware of how theories of ethnic difference have been instrumental in many political campaigns in minority regions in China. The Yao Nationality, written by some of China's leading Yao scholars, chooses to reference this history by way of absence, through its deliberate refusal to situate the Yao in any historical event that occurred between 1949 and 1979. Its narrative focus on a "traditional" subject would have us believe that the history of Chinese socialism between the 1950s and the death of Mao never happened. Under the reforms, the minority subject can now freely embrace his or her traditions and take pleasure and pride in bodily markers of ethnic difference. Histories of political and ideological struggles are vanquished in a flash, as is any reference to how the Yao themselves participated in struggles to remake the social and political orders of "local" societies. *The Yao Nationality*, in fact, refuses to remember a particular kind of socialist subject: the radical leftist associated with the Cultural Revolution, the irrational element that brought pain and misery to the Chinese populace and momentarily derailed the nation's course toward progress. The minority exists in the space of reform China as a quintessentially traditional subject.

Tradition, Marginality, and the Politics of Postsocialism

I want to conclude this chapter by considering some recent writings on the politics of tradition and ask what these writings tell us about how we theorize the historical and cultural space of Chinese postsocialism. Perhaps more than that of any other contemporary social theorist, David Harvey's work on the time-space compressions of late modernity and globalism have drawn attention to the political function of discourses of tradition and their relationship to contemporary social movements.[18] In *The Condition of Postmodernity*, for example, Harvey argues that many social movements, in attaching themselves to particular localities, identities, and traditions, often appear to be oppositional in style and intent and yet are in fact part of the "very fragmentation which a mobile capitalism and flexible accumulation feed upon."[19] Harvey is consistently skeptical of what he sees as overly romantic and always potentially conservative attachments to places and particularistic identities. Pleas to the local, to the specific, or to repressed or subjugated traditions sometimes feed radical social movements, yet they just as easily can become the material for new forms of ethnocentrism, elitism, racism, and nationalism.

Part of Harvey's continuing project has been one of synthesizing postmodern realities and Marxist commitments to class-based politics to find ways for intellectuals and activists to forge critical linkages across various theoretical divisions. In his more recent book, *Justice, Nature, and the Geography of Difference*, Harvey returns to these themes. He argues once again that appeals to difference (ethnic, national, gender, racial, and sexual) can foster as well as obstruct social justice movements. As in *The Condition of Postmodernity*, he retains his attachments to social movements that critique capitalist practices of uneven development and environmental destruction, yet he cautions more strongly than ever that appeals to place-specific difference often fall back on stereotypical images and discourses of otherness.[20] These appeals, Harvey insists, are too easily open to commodification by tourists, nationalists, and business interests. From his perspective, the critical project is one of forging a "geography of difference" that recognizes the nature of political and economic power in the postmodern spaces of a globalized world order and yet understands "places as internally heterogeneous, dialectical, and dynamic configurations."[21] How does Harvey understand this space of heterogeneity? This is a space of anticapitalist and class-based movements that allow people to translate across the claims of ethnic, racial, gender, and sexual difference. In effect, however, Harvey collapses these differences into the all-encompassing category of class and contradicts his own sense that these spaces are characterized by heterogeneous and dynamic identities. Class remains the key foundational trope, the only way to make sense of diverse claims to difference, the only way to invigorate place-based and other social movements with a radical emancipatory trajectory.

Harvey is also interested in engaging debates about cultural margins, marginal others, and displaced centers and peripheries. As with his critique of place-based movements, what worries Harvey is that scholars concerned with issues of race, ethnicity, and nationalism, in arguing that there are marginalized social and cultural spaces outside of and opposed to dominant centers, ignore questions of class and capitalist exploitation. He can't entirely explain why these metaphors have had such appeal, nor does he fully grasp how they can be utilized for processes of coalition building, minority empowerment, and activism across the divides of gender, class, race, sexuality, and ethnicity. He also ignores how appeals to class have been utilized by modern socialist states in quite contradictory ways. For example, in thinking about the politics of socialist mobilization in China, there is no sense in Harvey's work of how class-based politics have been mobilized not just to liberate subjects from histories of exploitation and injustice, but also to confine subjects in new disciplinary orderings. It is difficult to imagine how Harvey would read class as a discursive effect of new arrangements of power and knowledge, arrangements that sought to remake people in the visions of a modernizing regime. As Ann Anagnost has put it in her study on "speaking bitterness" campaigns in early Chinese revolutionary mobilization strategies, the CCP sought to give "voice" to a subaltern class subject and in doing so "authenticated its leadership as representing the constituencies its own discourse had constituted."[22] For Anagnost, class is best approached as a signifying practice, one that has as much to do with defining the nature of social reality as with tracing how various subjects and their agency are historically constituted. For Harvey, class represents and reflects contradictions and modes of exploitation in existing social orders. Yet class is not only reflective of existing objective relations but is also constitutive of them, as Anagnost insists. Class, as with other subject positions, takes on a double and thus ambiguous status. As a description of real social conditions, it can be seen as an effect of systems of knowledge or what one might call, after Foucault, a dominant regime of truth and power. But these subject positions can also be seen as a kind of resource, a critical category of consciousness and meaning that people employ in different moments of political and cultural struggle.

This shift to discourse as a social practice is, I think, one reason that scholars working on the politics of postcolonialism have increasingly thought of the margins as a space of radical heterogeneity. To be sure, some critiques of class as a foundational explanatory trope—as a Eurocentric master narrative—have arguably ignored questions of capitalist domination and their own complicity in processes of globalization.[23] Many scholars, however, have approached the margins simultaneously as a space of unequal economic development and as a complex arena of struggle where ethnic, gender, sexual, and class identities vie for representation in dominant social orders. These struggles over identity, recognition, and representation work to unsettle how dominant regimes define just what constitutes the normal, the progressive, or the modern. Russell Ferguson, for example, has argued that when "historically marginalized groups insist on their own identity, the deeper, structural invisibility of the so-called center becomes harder to sustain."[24] New forms of agency and identity can be crafted by seizing these centers, and the critical force of these agencies and identities cannot simply be reduced to the politics of class. The African American critic bell hooks implores us to focus on how dominant discourses create particular ways of seeing reality. Writing about Black women growing up in a small Kentucky town who could cross the railroad tracks only to provide service (as a maid, a janitor, or a prostitute) to the dominant White race, she evokes an image of the margins at once real and metaphorical. The margin is the spatial actuality of racist exclusion, but it is also the imagined space for an alternative sensibility. "Living as we did—on the edge—we developed a particular way of seeing reality. We looked both from the outside in and from the inside out. We focused our attention on the center as well as on the margin."[25] In hooks's view, the margins are more than a silent other in discourses of exclusion and more than a passive receptacle awaiting social transformation. The margins constitute the very terrain of cultural struggle. Racist exclusion had much to do with modes of economic deprivation; but it was not the only way, in hooks's view, for subjects to understand the nature of their existence, to develop their own particular way of seeing reality.

This notion of the margins as a practice of cultural struggle has much to contribute to our understanding of the Yao case, especially when we see it through the lens of what I have called in this chapter the politics of post-socialist belonging. As I detailed in the preceding chapters, Yao ethnologists, social historians, Party members, and government workers—what I have termed the minority elite—were working against images of the Yao as a backward and isolated people. I argued that these various actors were contesting, albeit in different ways, the dominant image that the Yao lived on the margins of socialist modernity and were once again awaiting their enlightenment from more cultured and civilized nationalities. This view of the minority other on the margins of the Chinese world no longer holds, if it ever did. My advisors, friends, and research consultants taught me that the Yao were active agents in the processes and politics of Chinese imperial expansion. They lived with the awareness that their people were once labeled "southern barbarians," but they saw in their ancestors a people with culture, a people at the very center of what it meant to be Chinese in any period. They argued that the historic Yao were also political agents, that they had long protected their lands and their people from encroaching outsiders who claimed to be the possessors of a more sophisticated and enlightened culture. Many of their kin had interacted with the Guomindang throughout the 1930s and 1940s; some joined their new cultural movements, entered their schools, and learned about their gods. They were also at the center of the final communist mobilization efforts in Jinxiu in the early 1950s. Outraged at the Guomindang's techniques to "open" the hills, many young Yao, including some of my closest research associates, enthusiastically joined the "bandit suppression" campaigns, worked with Han cadres to sign the first Dayaoshan Unification Pact, and joined the new autonomous government. As did nationalities throughout the country, the Jinxiu Yao lived through the best and worst of times in the 1950s, 1960s, and 1970s. This is one lesson Su Xianting, for example, never wanted me to forget.

Few people in Jinxiu wanted to recall the extended nightmare of the Cultural Revolution. Some asked me to not write about their relatives and

former friends who got behind the Maoist effort to rid the country of its enemies and ensure that the capitalist roaders were exposed. But many wanted
to rethink some of this period's ideological positions, and this is why the
question of memory—the historical consciousness of socialism—is so important to how we understand the desires that swarmed around the signifier traditional culture. As we saw in chapters 3 and 4, my closest Chashan
Yao research associates, individuals such as Liu Yulian, did not see Jinxiu
as a local site contaminated by feudal cultural practices or dominant Yao
subgroups exploiting landless subaltern subjects. Though they readily admitted that social relations in the Dayaoshan were once structured by forms
of exploitation and oppression, they felt the question of class hegemony
was much more complex than many Party cadres (and not a few Yao leaders)
understood in the 1950s and 1960s. For many of the scholars and officials I
worked with, but by no means all of them, it was time to think ethnic culture beyond the narrow discursive configurations of reality provided in discourses of feudal superstition and class contamination. Minority scholars,
often working in close association with local government officials, turned
to the study of Taoist ritual, to prerevolutionary forms of social and political
organization, to traditional practices of social morality, and to the display
and circulation of the traditional subject in photo albums, videos, and other
representational spaces.

To be sure, the critical reinhabitation of the past and the reimagining of
the local—what I called in chapter 2 the moral geography of place—were
informed by an increasingly frenetic and anxious socialist modernization
agenda. Ethnological accounts of cultural traditions such as Taoist ritual
written by minority scholars competed with other gazes turned on the local,
especially those that viewed Jinxiu as a remote site desperately in need of
the transforming vision of a more rational, complete, and objective scientific gaze. And, as I argued in the previous chapter, the interest in ritual and
social morality was intricately tied up with the search for new forms of local
governmentality. Jinxiu was presented to me as one of the most important
of all Yao places, a complex region with five different Yao subgroups, one of
the original sites in the history of modern ethnology, a stunning and majestic place ripe for the tourist industry. The traditional culture of the Jinxiu
Yao—especially the stone tablet system—was an object of political scrutiny
and class struggle in the 1950s and 1960s. Although the *shipai* had been dismantled in form, many Yao felt that its spirit lived on; it was lurking deep
in the Jinxiu landscape or was embedded in the submerged consciousness

of the Jinxiu populace. The traditional had to be sought out, studied, and made visible as an object of knowledge, one that could contribute to the remaking of the People's Republic.

In drawing attention to the figure of tradition in the reimagining of China, some scholars have argued that Chinese projects of bringing modernity to the ethnic outback have been remarkably similar in both discourse and strategy to practices of colonial modernity in other places and times. In writing about the politics of gender and internal orientalism, for example, Louisa Schein reminds us that internal others have long been used by Chinese intellectuals to recover a self seen as weakened or depleted.[26] Schein argues that orientalist practice is not only about denigrating the other, but also about desiring it and loving it, seeing it as a force that can put to shame one's own "dull and feeble character."[27] This practice of orientalist appropriation was clearly at play in Bai Hua's phantasmagoric imagining of a remote country of minority women and in Zhang Nuanxin's story of a Han woman who comes to know her body and sexual desires differently through her encounter with the Dai people. If we accept that orientalism is informed in large part by a set standard of rituals, preconceptions, and doctrines based on hierarchical distinctions between an "us" and a "them," then it is difficult not to see "orientalist" practices at work in reform-era ethnological writings. For me, however, the crucial task is not simply one of determining whether or not Yao ethnology is a form of orientalism or how various modes of othering have articulated "trends" of thought and representation that may or may not have originated in the West. To pose the problem of orientalist practice in this way is to presuppose an originary site of power and knowledge, which is usually seen to reside in the space of the modern West or the Eurocenter.[28] Orientalism comes to be treated less as a discursive process that makes certain forms of knowledge fact and more as an object, a thing that can be measured in different historical and social contexts for its degree of verisimilitude to the original.

For this reason, I am not really interested in determining how notions of culture, place, and modernity among Yao elite compare, mimic, or internalize Western forms of orientalist practice. I think it is more productive to trace how actors attempting to empower themselves and their assumed constituencies have put these categories to critical use in contexts that they perceive as socially and personally disempowering or empowering. Said's project, we have to remember, was one of critical vigilance. He taught us how other cultures are created as objects of knowledge. He also

A Yao woman preparing to serve bowls of wine to visiting dignitaries during an international Yao studies conference in southern Hunan Province in 1988.

showed how, once the object is defined and delimited as an object of observation and study, the observer repeatedly acts as if this object has a world of its own, outside of history, outside of institutional structures, outside of desire. The Yao case is somewhat different, I think, in that the worlds created in the ethnological and historical texts written by elite members of the minzu group were never really taken for granted and never really seen to be outside of politics. These producers of Yao culture and history were trying to pry open a space for the Yao subject in the multiethnic imaginary of contemporary China. They did this by engaging a range of anthropological, ethnological, and historical knowledges, by writing new histories of their people, and by arguing with histories of class struggle and ethnic representation.

In chapter 1, for example, I argued that the writing of Yao histories in the reform era reveals epistemologies and representational forms that we might recognize as belonging in some fundamental way to the colonial imaginaries of the European center.[29] Minority intellectuals have used ethnological knowledges from the West, the Marxist tradition, and even from structural-functionalist ideas about how certain forms of ritual practice reproduced social groups through time in order to tell stories about their people in the long march of the nation's history. These practices of ethnological representation are not outside of the new configurations of power and knowledge that have structured and animated intellectual work under the reforms. They are very much in power, caught up in its instabilities, discrepancies, and contradictions. Yet, as I argued, they also tell us much about the politics of ethnic empowerment in reform China. These scholars were not the passive bearers of extant ideologies and new articulations of power, but active producers of new cultural and historical hegemonies. These hegemonies do not reveal how the reform-era Party-state apparatus—with its funding and support for minority research projects, its interest in displaying images of the ethnic subject in museums and theme parks, and its ideological investment in the popular idea of multicultural nationalism—has entered the minds of unsuspecting minority intellectuals. Rather, they show how existing configurations of knowledge, classification, and representation have been pried open for struggle, contestation, and reformulation.

This prying open of existing configurations of discourse and knowledge has occurred in the midst of what I have called the politics of postsocialist belonging. But what is this space of postsocialism? How do we understand it in relation to the socialist era dominated by Mao and his campaigns of class struggle and heroic utopian development? What is its relationship to the world of global capitalism in the late twentieth century, a world China has struggled to belong to and yet remain apart from? In writing about the category of postsocialism in the late 1980s, Arif Dirlik has framed the issue this way:

> China during the Cultural Revolution was to make an effort to shut off world capitalism in order to establish a firm foundation for uninterrupted progress to socialism. The disastrous failure of that attempt has made it more evident than ever that socialist societies must make an effort to incorporate themselves into the capitalist world system without abandoning the basic structure of socialism. This condition, in the period of what has been described by Marxist theoreticians as "late capitalism," is the ultimate justification for the use of postsocialism to describe it. . . . To call this condition "capitalism" would be fatuous because it remains to be seen what the incorporation of socialist systems in the capitalist world order will imply for capitalism itself. For socialist societies such as China, the opening to capitalism has created new

possibilities; among these may be included greater openness to economic alternatives (which may be greater than even that of capitalism, which, for all its flexibility, forecloses one important option—socialism), greater possibilities for democracy than ever before because of the relinquishing of faith in the immediate possibility of a coercive utopianism, and richer cultural possibilities that have arisen with the recognition of global cultural diversity, which was not possible as long as progress was conceived as a unilinear movement to a uniform human destiny.[30]

New economic alternatives, relinquishing faith in a coercive utopianism, and recognizing global cultural diversity: these are themes that many observers of post-Mao China have picked up on. Some have done so, however, to quite different ends than Dirlik's attempt to find a space for a socialist politics in an increasingly global capitalist world order. The notion of China as a culturally diverse nation-state has been particularly attractive. Some observers have argued that traditional cultural practices have returned to the countryside under the reforms either because socialism failed to transform these worlds or because the CCP has retreated from the control of everyday social life. When I first began to work on this project in 1988, for example, anthropologists, historians, and sociologists of China were debating the relationship among discourses of tradition, practices of religious revival, and the socialist project. In trying to make sense of the return of popular ritual, some delved into the relationship between traditional and socialist moralities and questioned the extent to which the socialist project had remade local communities and the consciousness of the Chinese populace.[31] These various studies have tended to treat traditional culture as a social fact, where the boundaries between state and society become crystal clear or where the CCP met the limit of its power to define and transform Chinese society.

My work among Yao elite has led me in another direction. I have approached the traditional as a complex discursive figure present in struggles over how to define local ethnic places and the subjects residing there.[32] The fascination with the figure of tradition speaks to nationalist histories that have attempted to bring modernity to a subject defined as backward, marginal, and without a forward-looking consciousness. One might argue that this fascination is not at all about speaking back to power, that it reveals how minorities in China have perhaps even been duped or coerced into participating in the making of the myth of socialist modernity's inescapable momentum. As James Clifford has put it, "Swept up in a destiny dominated by the capitalist West and by variously technologically advanced socialisms, these suddenly 'backward' peoples no longer invent local futures. What is different about them remains tied to traditional pasts, inherited structures that either resist or yield to the new but cannot reproduce it." [33] This denial of agency reproduces the idea that ethnicity is a marginal form of cultural practice, something done by ethnic subjects on the periphery of modern capitalist and socialist formations. If we are to critically grasp how Yao elite have worked to craft their own alternative modernities, then we have to refuse to see this interest in tradition as providing a window into a "traditional" Yao sensibility. Nor can we see it as reflective of a homogeneous collective ethnic consciousness that is now, with the reforms, rediscovering its true identity.

It is for these reasons that I have approached the writings, ruminations, reflections, and representations that have swarmed around the signifier Yao culture as a newly emergent interpretive practice, whereby different (mostly elite) actors have turned a critical gaze upon the history of modernity in China. These interpretive practices are informed at once by complex ideological commitments and longings for past social orders. The politics of postsocialist belonging bears traces of histories of ethnic classification and knowledge production, just as it opens up spaces for the imagining of alternative futures.

epilogue

State Power thus turned upon inscription, upon the absorption
of events into a prodigiously dispersed writing machine.

—NICHOLAS THOMAS, *Colonialism's Culture*

*M*any contemporary social critics have argued that the last two
decades of the twentieth century will be remembered for the
end of the cold war, the death of history, and the increasing
irrelevance of the nation-state form. In this book, I have argued that the
China of the late 1980s and the early 1990s will have to be remembered
differently. For this was a period in which debates about the nation, its relationship to the socialist past, and its place in the new global order of late
capitalism raged on almost daily, in the press, in academic journals, and in
popular films and magazines. These debates were often framed around the
problem of how to identify, represent, and make a space for "traditional
culture" in the socialist modern nation. For Yao in China, this was also a
period of cautious yet prolific ethnological writing, as many scholars turned
to the study of local societies, in places such as Jinxiu, and authored new
accounts of Yao culture and history. And yet, lurking restlessly behind these
debates was the question of just whose country this was. Who would speak
for the Chinese nation? Who would protect it in the midst of these criticisms and debates? How was the nation, with all of its competing voices,
memories, and disgruntled subjects, to have a history that would not replicate the violence and trauma that had defined so much of the Maoist reign
of power?

Shortly after the Tiananmen tragedy in 1989, the literary critic Rey Chow
published an essay in which she explored the relationship between intellectual work and the politics of culture in the People's Republic.[1] Focusing

primarily on the post-Mao period, she showed how various intellectuals (the novelist A Cheng, the dissident Wei Jingsheng, the physicist-in-exile Fang Lizhi) had used issues of culture, education, and intellectual freedom to launch critiques of the Communist Party. She correctly saw this as a paradoxical enterprise. For how was the nation's culture now to be reproduced when it had been torn apart, fragmented, and dismantled by the "traumas" and "catastrophes" of the modern era, especially those associated with the Cultural Revolution? How, especially given the widespread intellectual disappointment with the socialist project, was the modern to be defined and achieved? How were intellectuals to contain its disruptions and displacements? And how, finally, were they to differentiate it from the modernity of the West?

What struck me about this essay was how Chow pushed these questions into the domain of the ethical. She argued that these obsessions with culture have too often contributed to the cycles of violence that have accompanied China's tortured search for progress. At the end of the essay, she makes a series of recommendations for how to end this cycle of violence: "As long as 'Chinese' remains a fixed center of identity, Chinese intellectuals will be perpetuating the political centrism which lies at the heart of the violence that has surfaced time and time again in the modern period." [2] The problem, as she sees it, is one of loosening the discourse of culture both from the Party-state apparatus and from the ethnic-national signifier *Chinese*.[3]

Jing Wang has provided us with yet another possible approach to these issues. Writing about the "culture fever" movement in the 1980s, she has argued that for many Chinese intellectuals in the 1980s, a range of binary distinctions—what she calls binary epistemologies—were central to their own projects of resistance and empowerment.[4] These intellectuals often defined the center through the image of an autocratic father figure at home, the CCP, and through the ambivalent figure of the West, identified as both the tutor and the opponent of the contemporary Chinese elite. These were people, of course, who had lived through histories of political struggle in which the enemies of the Party and the state were frenetically sought out and exposed. They knew, perhaps more than anyone, how the naturalization of certain binary categories was at the heart of the violence that had marginalized so many people, had destroyed so many lives, had torn at the nation and its spirit for so long. Yet their struggles to imagine a new form of political subjectivity required not the abandonment of binary epistemologies, but rather their very deployment. The Communist Party, and the more ambivalent figure of the West, emerged as others against which they defined their intellectual work and their political aspirations.

The Yao ethnologists, social historians, and other intellectuals and officials I worked with provide us with a similar tale, yet I think with a twist. As were many Han intellectuals, they were deeply concerned with questions of violence, modernity, socialism, and the reproduction of culture. Many of their commonsense understandings of Yao identity were provided through the knowledge they acquired learning nationality theory, or *minzu lilun*. In China, the "nationalities problem" has long been pitched as a politics of national struggle and survival. The further advancement of the revolution necessitated that all ethnic subjectivities are amalgamated (*ronghe*, or melding, is the typical metaphor) into the larger community of the People's Republic. To accomplish this, the Communist Party often resorted to practices of state violence aimed at eradicating certain kinds of identification with ethnic signifiers such as Yao and especially with a number of "subgroup" (*minzu zhixi*) identifications. The Party was suspicious of these attachments because different individuals and social classes used them to further their own interests and to naturalize local forms of oppression and exploitation. This is what practices aimed at eradicating the stone tablet system and other forms of local hegemony were all about in Jinxiu in the 1950s. Party cadres encouraged the landless Yao groups, the Guoshan Yao, to speak against their oppressors, the Changmao Yao, all in the hope of forging a new Yao subjectivity, one that would embrace the socialist nation and discard the "feudal" practices of the prerevolutionary past.

In recounting these histories of socialist development and political mobilization, my research associates often spoke of the existence of multiple centers of power and knowledge in the social life of the Yao. The CCP and the history of liberating China from the Guomindang reactionaries and the oppressive feudal past was almost always placed at the center of their narratives. For so many of them, the Party embodied more than anything the meaning of modernity and the power associated with this term. In these narratives, the Party was often seen as a benevolent force, a kind of older brother that cared for the people it sought to liberate, protect, and speak for. Yao elite also represented the history of their people through narratives of migration and cultural borrowing, and they often asserted the importance to the Yao of modes of authority that were grounded in ritual life and that connected the people to realms of supernatural power and influence.

These images, however, competed with memories of Party-initiated campaigns of class struggle, in which friends, family members, and other acquaintances were subjected to violence and even death. When they spoke to me about the importance of writing histories of their people, they sometimes pointed to how violence had been enacted, through the long haul of history, by a number of different outside forces who had come to Yao regions to colonize, exploit, and abuse their people. In a very real sense, these histories needed the reification of an outside force, an other against which the Yao self could be empowered in the overall history of the People's Republic.

After the brutal suppression of students and workers on Tiananmen Square in 1989, China watchers began to ask how, if at all, the CCP could continue to shape and control the political terrain. Many scholars were quick to point to the CCP's tarnished relationship with the masses. It was recognized that the market reforms were transforming the nation, but scholars also had to acknowledge that the language of crisis — of state security and insecurity, of social order and disorder, of productive citizens and dangerous counterrevolutionaries — continued to be a central part of the rhetorical arsenal of the reform regime. In the 1990s, the People's Republic has faced an entirely different set of problems. We are now told, in the so-called post-Tiananmen era, that the heady days of Tiananmen have receded from popular memory. We encounter reports again and again that young urban Chinese have taken refuge from the dictates of Party ideology by "seeking entertainment" (zhaole) in the new discos, bars, nightclubs, underground and not so underground brothels, and fancy and expensive restaurants that have sprung up across China in the 1990s.[5] Michael Dutton tells us that the market has "ripped the social fabric of Chinese society to such a degree that the land beneath the cloth is more visible than ever before." "It is visible," he goes on, "in the shop display windows that vie for customers no less than the faces of the subaltern who walk the street in search of work."[6]

It is tempting to argue that all of the transformations of the 1990s hint at China's gradual entrance into the world of contemporary global postmodernism. Social theorists of the late twentieth century know the litany well. The postmodern world is characterized by a crisis in dominant metanarratives of historical progress, accelerated time-space compressions, the restructuring of global capitalist investments, communications systems, and information networks, and the rise of conservative nationalisms and ethnic fundamentalisms. Recent work on transnational cultural flows, new media forms, and the massive migration of peoples both within and beyond national borders has furthered a reading of the late twentieth century as a period marked by perils and possibilities in which, as Andrew Ross has put it, "everything is contestable, nothing is off limits and no outcomes are guaranteed."[7] Fernando Coronil has recently argued that the familiar map of modernity is being redrawn by global transformations in culture, politics, and production widely associated with the emergence of postmodernity.[8] In the process, the familiar geographical categories—the West and the non-West, for example, but also the North and the South, the capitalist and the communist—have been uprooted and relocated to new locales. The spaces and targets of European imperial subjection, Coronil tells us, have shifted.

Have the spaces and targets of Chinese nationalist subjection also shifted? How do we understand these discourses of the postmodern, of geographical reconfigurations and the relocation of power and capital, when we examine Yao cultural politics in the late 1980s and early 1990s? For me, the answer to these questions rests in moving beyond the mere deconstruction of ethnicity as an essentialist category of social identity. In an era in which minority subjects everywhere are contending for voice and recognition and actively working both for and against dominant social orders, it is no longer sufficient to argue simply that all ethnic identities are historically constructed. Elite discourses are often complicit with dominant forms of discourses and social and cultural representation, a point that would hardly escape the minority elite in China. Nor can we assume that minorities who define themselves as intellectuals or who maintain close relations with government and Party organizations unproblematically speak for the state, for a given regime of power, or for a homogeneous ethnic constituency. The Yao elite I worked with maintained complex relations with different centers of power both in Jinxiu and beyond. Many of them were, and still are, good Marxist theorists who believe the world to be animated by the spirits and gods provided in Taoist cosmology.

We also have to ask what our own desire to deconstruct the nation and its modernist discourses of identity means for people who have been classified and labeled by modern states as ethnic minorities. As I hope the preceding chapters have demonstrated, various discourses and practices of ethnicity in China have much to teach us about the history of knowledges and classificatory schemes that have aimed to define, describe, and transform the minority populations. Yet ethnicity is never simply or only an effect of power. It is also a social practice of empowerment. Ethnicity points not to the margins of the modern world, but, as a critical term, to how people work to mark out spaces from which to speak back to power and back to histories of cultural, ethnic, gender, and racial marginalization. It is thus one thing to argue that ethnic (or other) identities reveal complex social and political worlds that have been produced in large part through discursive practices. It is quite another to trace how these practices inform, shape, and structure practices of cultural struggle for peoples who have been denied recognition and representation. Especially since the revolutionary victory in 1949, minority elite, from scholars to intellectuals to government officials and Taoist specialists, have been active and critical participants in the naming and remaking of the subjects and social worlds of their communities. Many of them in turn have also been agents in the making of the very disciplinary society that has become, under the reforms, the object of critical appraisals, denunciations, and reimaginings. They identify with a pan-Yao minzu community as well as with an international collectivity of scholars and elite members of the refugee diaspora. It seems to me that in our studies of Chinese nationalism and the politics and discourses of culture we need to disengage the term "intellectual" from its association with Han elite in Beijing and with the May Fourth tradition. We need to begin to trace how the meanings of intellectual work in China are multiple and dispersed throughout the landscape of contemporary China. These meanings of intellectual work articulate with other histories, other subject positions, and other modes of being in the world than those provided to us by narratives of Han intellectual struggle. We need to consider what might be contained, for example, in the work of Taoist specialists who once fought against the Guomindang, were Party members, and who now search among Yao youth for new ritual specialists.

How we approach these subjectivities depends on how we understand the relationship between ethnicity and the politics of cultural struggle for people who have been dismissed in China as backward, isolated, primitive—in need of the helping hand of powerful outsiders. It also depends on how we understand local politics, even as we work to expand our definitions of just what constitutes locality and just what we mean by a "local" struggle. We need to keep in mind that consumer desire has not everywhere saturated the social landscape in the same way that we see it displayed in Beijing, Shanghai, Guangzhou, and Shenzhen. For many in Jinxiu, even into the late 1990s, consumerism (or at least the kind that has given shape to the new capitalist imaginary of China) is still something people do in other places. We also have to realize that ethnic struggles are not uniform throughout China, that the "nationalities problem" has been understood, negotiated, and contested in different places in different ways. I find it somewhat disconcerting that in recent writings about culture fevers, conflicted national subjects, and an emerging consumer society, scholars of China have tended to ignore minority struggles. Perhaps this is because the discourse and practice of the "nationalities problem" have never really spoken directly to the concerns of the China field, which has, after all, long been about Chinese civilization and its encounter with the modern world. We need to remember that minorities from the very beginning of the revolutionary struggle in China were required by the CCP leadership to think long and hard about the costs of local forms and practices of "ethnic" nationalism. Finally, as we revisit the late 1980s and the early 1990s, we need to recall that Tiananmen was largely an urban event, though most people in the world, thanks to the wonders of satellites, facsimile machines, and mobile phones, experienced it as a purely global event. For many rural residents in China, the Tiananmen protests cannot be forgotten because they were in fact never directly experienced, if only because of the marvelous potentiality of state censorship.

The reality of these regional and ethnic spaces of difference was brought home to me in the winter months of 1992, just when I was nearing the end of my stay in Jinxiu County. I was invited by a county official to attend a wedding celebration in a village some distance from the county seat. As with the Longpan and so many other excursions into the more "remote" reaches of the mountains, we were joined by a small group of photojournalists who sought, as they put it, to document "the colorful traditions" of the Yao people. Was there anything more colorful or festive than a Yao wedding, especially when it could be photographed against the backdrop of towering mountain peaks? I too brought my camera gear. I was put up in the household of the village head. As was the practice at the time, the electricity was turned off nightly around 10 P.M. Lying under my comforter writing notes with a mountaineering headlamp attached to my forehead, I suddenly noticed that the wall of the bedroom in which I was sleeping was covered with a Chinese-language newspaper. I rose to my knees and began to inspect the walls. I was astonished to find before me newsprint from Hong Kong dated just after 4 June 1989. Here were detailed accounts of the student occupation of Tiananmen Square, the violence that ripped through the city in the aftermath of the cleansing of the Square, and photographs of burning vehicles. Where, I wondered, did these newspapers come from?

In the morning I began to query my hosts. Everyone shrugged and told me they had been dropped from the sky in large balloons. I was incredulous, but everyone I asked confirmed that this was indeed the case. With increased excitement, I asked my hosts and those that gathered around if they had read them at the time. Were they interested in the contents? Was there debate among the villagers about what was going on in Beijing? I was somewhat taken aback when I was told that, in fact, few people, in this village at least, really cared. Those who did were worried that the Red Guards were once again storming the streets. People hoped that the chaos and disorder—the dreaded luan of a previous era—would stay far from the hills. No one wanted to revisit that past.

That past—the past of the Cultural Revolution—was of course being revisited almost daily in China throughout the 1980s and, in some regions, on into the 1990s. Intellectuals, Communist Party cadres, government officials, think tank functionaries, and policymakers were hotly debating the conjuncture between the Maoist-dominated era and the promise of late-twentieth-century capitalism. Yet, as I have tried to show in the preceding pages, other histories were also being debated at this time. Yao peasants and even some officials were interested in telling me histories of socialist development and their frustrations with the new history in the making, the history of Deng Xiaoping's reforms. This is one of the themes I attempted to develop in chapters 3 and 4. I was indeed often surprised to find that many of the people I interviewed fondly remembered the socialist period of the 1950s through the 1970s. Surprised because this kind of remembering ran counter to the frequent lambasting in the official press of the Gang of Four and its ideological excesses. Surprised because not everyone was convinced that somehow, beginning in the late 1950s and early 1960s, things had begun to go wrong with the practice of socialism and especially class struggle. Even some Party officials seemed to believe that the dividing line between a state power that was benevolent and caring and one that was malevolent and destructive could not always be so readily maintained, either historically or in the contemporary period.

Others were less concerned about the Cultural Revolution, when it began, when it ended, and just what it had done to the populace. Their attentions were focused on the growing economic disparities between the

coastal provinces of the east and southeast and the interior mountain regions of the country, to say nothing of the disparities that were beginning to emerge in Jinxiu County itself. In the late 1980s and early 1990s,
the Jinxiu Yao were being asked to participate in yet another grand plan to
bring modernity to the outback. This time there would be less ideological
struggle; prosperity would eventually come even to the remote corners of
the nation. By the time I completed my research in Jinxiu in 1992, it was
clear that the wealth and development that had come to China with such
ferocity were not to be shared and enjoyed across the board, even though,
as we saw in Liu Yulian's imaginary, the signs of material civilization had
increasingly become the dominant way for some to mark their contribution
to the Chinese nation. Official rumblings about the effects of uneven development on minority populations and on the everyday maintenance of social
and political stability were beginning to be voiced in Jinxiu. As Dali Yang
has put it, Chinese policymakers have become increasingly worried about
the potential for sociopolitical instability in areas inhabited by minorities.[9]

In the mid- to late 1990s, regional disparities and instabilities had become the new, hot issue. There was a widespread perception that economic
disparity between the interior mountain regions and the east and southeast
coasts had contributed to rising ethnic tension. As the 1990s state cut down
on subsidies and forced autonomous counties to raise their own funds, minority leaders in these regions became distraught, upset, or, as one survey
put it, "extremely unbalanced."[10] The state, in conjunction with the international development community, began to respond. In the late 1990s, for
example, Guangxi was marked for new state and international resource
allocations (the World Bank has become a major player in rural Guangxi),
in large part because it was identified as one of the poorest of China's regions. Minorities live in most of these spaces of "poverty" and "under-
development." County officials in Jinxiu now export much of the timber in
the mountains to places such as Guangzhou, and Jinxiu youth increasingly
work far away from home in the factories that have sprung up throughout the southeast, especially in Guangzhou. Jinxiu has been brought within
the fold of these capitalist modes of resource and labor exploitation, but
in many ways it remains peripheral to the astonishing development daily
championed in the official press from Shanghai to Shenzhen to Los Angeles
and New York City.

Perhaps the era of cultural fascination that dominated so much of Yao
ethnology and cultural discourse in the late 1980s and early 1990s is now

over. From the perspective of the late 1990s, this period indeed seems to belong to another time, especially if we take Beijing, Shanghai, and Guangzhou as the center of our ethnographic universe. As our gaze turns now upon the politics of globalization, the postmodern, and the transnational, we need to remain vigilant to the emergence of new discourses and experiences of marginality. Centers and peripheries have not faded with the passing of the cold war, with the rise of a new and more pervasive global capitalism (even one with Asian characteristics), or with the diminishing role of the nation-state. The margins have not gone away. Some of their locations have shifted; many have stayed the same. We will no doubt need new mappings of power and knowledge, domination and resistance, capital and development as we embark on a new century. And we will need new understandings of how China's minorities are theorizing, and seeking to change, the worlds they inhabit.

notes

preface

Unless otherwise noted, all translations are mine.

1 For a discussion of these population figures and dynamics, see Huang Yu and Huang Fangping, *Yaozu.* Government officials and demographers in China attribute the growth in the population of the Yao under the reforms to the fact that most Yao communities have not been subjected to the strictures of the one-child family planning policy. As with many of China's upland minorities, the Yao have been allowed to have two children per family, and as many as three in some regions.

2 China was also involved in the Vietnam War, for many years supplying funds, armaments, and technical personnel to the communist Pathet Lao forces in Laos, to the Khmer Rouge, and to the Vietcong armies in northern and southern Vietnam. When Vietnamese armies invaded Kampuchea in 1979, China supported Pol Pot and the Khmer Rouge and went to war with Vietnam. For studies of this period, see Geoffrey C. Gunn, *Rebellion in Laos: Peasants and Politics in a Colonial Backwater*, and Jane Hamilton-Merrit, *Tragic Mountains: The Hmong, the Americans, and the Secret War for Laos, 1942–1992.* The Chinese Communist Party's view in the late 1950s is contained in a Beijing Foreign Language Press publication entitled *Concerning the Situation in Laos.*

3 In recent years, a number of studies have appeared on minority nationalities in post-Mao China. My thinking has been influenced by the many excellent essays collected in the William Safran volume, *Nationalism and Ethnoregional Identities in China*; in Stevan Harrell, *Cultural Encounters on China's Ethnic Frontiers*; and in Melissa J. Brown, *Negotiating Ethnicities in China and Taiwan.* See also Thomas Heberer, *China and Its National Minorities: Autonomy or Assimilation?* and Colin Mackerras, *China's Minorities: Integration and Modernization in the Twentieth Century.*

4 These figures are provided in Liu Yaoquan and Hu Qiwang, "Survey of Yao Studies in China (1949–1984)."

5 There are scattered groups of Yao living in Vietnam (over 200,000), Laos

(20,000), and Thailand (16,000), with a few hundred said to be living in Burma. There are also some 5,000–6,000 Yao living in the United States, with smaller numbers in France and Switzerland, Canada, and New Zealand and Australia. See ibid.

6 See Preecha Chaturabhand, *People of the Hills*. I would soon find other publications from this period, such as the majestic and stunningly photographed *From the Hands of the Hills*, written by Margaret Campbell (1978) and photographed by Chusak Voraphitak. Campbell worked for the Thai Hill-Crafts Foundation retail shop in Bangkok.

7 Chaturabhand, *People of the Hills*, 2–3.

8 See, for example, the essays exploring the construct of the primitive in Elazar Barkan and Ronald Bush, *Prehistories of the Future: The Primitivist Project of Modernism*. See also George W. Stocking, *Victorian Anthropology*. For a discussion of how Western notions of modernity have been based on the search for marginal spaces as an escape from the ills of metropolitan centers, see Dean MacCannell's classic study, *The Tourist*, and the follow-up book *Empty Meeting Grounds*.

9 See Johannes Fabian, *Time and the Other*.

10 Diane L. Umemoto, "Yao Ritual Scrolls: From Icons to Antiques."

11 See Jeffery L. MacDonald, *Transnational Aspects of Iu-Mien Identity*. Throughout this book I use the spellings Iu-Mien and Mian to refer to the same Yao subgroup. One typically finds Iu-Mien employed by scholars working in mainland Southeast Asia or in France or the United States, and this term, as we will see below, is preferred by most Yao in the diaspora. In China, this group is often referred to as the Pan Yao, though these people call themselves Mian, which simply means "people." Mian is thus based on the pinyin transliteration system used in the People's Republic. For consistency, when I discuss the Yao diaspora or the anthropology of the Yao in Southeast Asia, I employ Iu-Mien. When I discuss the scholarship on the Yao in China, I use the pinyin spelling Mian or the Chinese term for this group, Pan Yao.

12 Ibid., 233–234.

13 For a more detailed discussion of this conference, see ibid., 245–276.

14 For a discussion of the refugee as a victim of the twentieth-century state, see Edward Said's much-discussed essays "Reflections on Exile" and "The Mind of Winter." For a discussion of the figure of the refugee in modern literature and literary criticism, see Caren Kaplan, *Questions of Travel*, where she argues that images of refugees as victims have rendered them "a faceless political construct outside the sphere of literature and aesthetics" (120). Unlike the exile, the spiritual figure of modernist travel literature, the refugee has been denied any critical positioning in discourses of creativity and loss. For another take on the problematic of refugees and the politics of humanitarian intervention, see Liisa Malkki, "Speechless Emissaries: Refugees, Humanitarianism, and Dehis-

toricization," and "Things to Come: Internationalism and Global Solidarities in the Late 1990s." See, finally, the essays in Smadar Lavie and Ted Swedenburg, *Displacement, Diaspora, and Geographies of Identity.*

15 For a discussion, see Elizabeth Perry, "Chinese Political Culture Revisited."

16 R. B. J. Walker, *Inside/Outside: International Relations in Political Theory,* 3.

17 For a discussion of the cold war and its influence on social science theories of East Asia, see Tani Barlow, "Colonialism's Career in Postwar China Studies," and Bruce Cumings, *Parallax Visions,* 173–204.

Writing the Margins: An Introduction

1 The name of this institute was officially changed in 1992 to the Central Nationalities University, or Zhongyang Minzu Daxue. The university has an Ethnology Research Institute, the Language and Literature College for Chinese National Minorities, and the College for Administrative Cadres. It boasts seventeen departments, among them Tibet studies, literature, economics, law, history, philosophy, physics, biology, applied mathematics, music, dance, and art.

2 The scholars who settled in at the Minyuan in the early 1950s were to become the new vanguard of ethnic minority researchers in China. Regional sections were initially established, allowing young scholars to focus their attention, for instance, on the minorities of the southwest, on the northeast and Inner Mongolia, or on Tibet. In theory at least, these scholars would periodically return to minority regions to undertake investigations into local conditions; they would advise the Communist Party on ethnic policy, and they would train the next generation of scholars and cadres. Greg Guldin's *The Saga of Anthropology in China* is the most informative account of the key intellectuals involved in the establishment of this institute.

3 Norma Diamond, "Defining the Miao."

4 See Tani Barlow's discussion of the shifting significations of this category in "*Zhishifenzi* (Chinese Intellectuals) and Power."

5 Some Chinese ethnologists have been critical of the relationship between materialist historiography and the theories of Morgan. For one of the more trenchant accounts, see Tong Enzhang, "Moergen de moshi yu makesi zhuyi" (Morgan's model and Marxism). Morgan remained a model for many ethnologists and social historians, however. In fact, I encountered very few ethnologists who knew anything about his view that American Indians could never be the equals of Europeans or that he actually once argued that the abolition of slavery would be good because it would lead to the extinction of the "Negro" race! For a brief discussion of Lewis Henry Morgan's view of primitivity and its relationship to other nineteenth-century theories of racial difference, see Robert Young, *Colonial Desire,* 118–141. Young reminds us that one of the first anthropological ac-

counts of Morgan as a relentless racist are provided in Marvin Harris's *The Rise of Anthropological Theory*.

6 See Walker Connor's monumental study, *The National Question in Marxist-Leninist Theory and Strategy*. For more recent approaches, see the essays collected in Berch Berberoglu, *The National Question: Nationalism, Ethnic Conflict, and Self-Determination in the 20th Century*, and the study by Ian Bremmer and Ray Taras, *Nation and Politics in the Soviet Successor States*. For an insightful ethnographic study on the politics and history of the nationalities question in the Soviet Union, see Bruce Grant, *In the Soviet House of Culture*.

7 Chen Yongling, "Applied Ethnology and the Implementation of Policy toward Ethnic Minorities in China." See also Guldin, *The Saga of Anthropology*, 105–108.

8 The Han anthropologist Lin Yaohua has framed the situation as follows: "This question not only affects the policy of equality and solidarity among the nationalities, but it has a very close relationship also with a whole series of questions, such as carrying out the autonomous self-government of minority regions, exercising self-governing rights among the national minorities, developing the politics, economics, and cultures of the nationalities, and so forth" ("New China's Ethnology," 143, cited in Guldin, *The Saga of Anthropology*, 106). I take these issues up in more detail in chapter 2.

9 These themes were arguably first pursued by June Dreyer in her important study, *China's Forty Millions*.

10 Joseph Stalin, "Marxism and the National Question." For an excellent discussion of the origins and historical context of this essay, see James Blaut, *The National Question*, 142–158. For a brief overview of Soviet "ethnos" theory, see the description of the writings of Yulian Bromley, the one-time director of the Institute of Ethnography of the Soviet Academy of Sciences, in Marcus Banks, *Ethnicity: Anthropological Constructions*, 17–24.

11 See Lin Yaohua, "New China's Ethnology." For a discussion on a group that has been denied official minority status, see Cheung Siu-woo, "Representation and Negotiation of Ge Identities in Southeast Guizhou."

12 See, for example, Cai Fuyou, "Analysis and Appraisal of Stalin's Definition of a 'Nation,'" and Tong, "Moergen de moshi yu makesi zhuyi." For a study of these issues in the case of the Naxi, see Charles F. McKhann, "The Naxi and the Nationalities Question." For an analysis of the Yi case, see Stevan Harrell, "The History of the History of the Yi."

13 McKhann, "The Naxi and the Nationalities Question," 47.

14 Xu Jiewu and Deng Wentong, "Cong Yaozu zhixi wenti tanqi" (Discussion arising from the question of Yao subgroups).

15 See the introduction to Huang Yu and Li Weixin, *Guangxi Yaozu shehui lishi diaocha* (Investigation of the social history of the Guangxi Yao).

16 For early discussions of these processes, see Ralph Litzinger, "Making Histories," and Harrell, "The History of the History of the Yi."

17 Huang Yu, "A Preliminary Study of King Ping's Charter."

18 See Qiu Pu, "Minzuxue de xin kaiduan" (A new beginning for ethnology). These developments are typically traced back to the Third Plenum of the Eleventh Central Committee of the CCP in December 1978. At this time, the social sciences had only recently been rehabilitated and Deng Xiaoping was calling on China's intellectual elite to "seek truth from facts" (shishi qiushi) and correct the mistakes of the Maoist past. Deng's speech at this meeting would come to be known as one of his most important. He called for a "bold devolution" (dadan xiafang) of state power to promote a "spirit of initiative and creativity" (zhudong chuangzao jingshen) among both intellectuals and the masses. He also called for market reforms and a material incentive program, and he urged the Party elite to develop "home-grown policies" (tu zhengce) grounded in the facts of everyday reality and broadly supported by the populace at all levels of Chinese society. The Third Plenum concluded by claiming that the struggle against and subsequent detainment of Lin Biao and the Gang of Four in 1976, held responsible for the Cultural Revolution, had been correct. The struggle against the "ultraleftists" was officially declared over, and it was now time to get on with the work of "socialist modernization." A more rational social and economic vision was called for, one that would allow for the development of agriculture, industry, national defense, and science and technology. The Four Modernizations, as they were termed, would carry China beyond the political excesses of the Maoist period and on into the twenty-first century. For a discussion of these historical shifts, see Mark Lupher, Power Restructuring in China and Russia, 233–266.

19 Hu Qiwang and Fan Honggui, Pancun Yaozu (The Yao of Pan Village).

20 Huang and Li, Guangxi Yaozu shehui lishi diaocha.

21 David R. Arkush, Fei Xiaotong and Sociology in Revolutionary China.

22 Carl Boggs, Intellectuals and the Crisis of Modernity, 1.

23 Bruce Robbins, "Introduction: The Grounding of Intellectuals," xii.

24 For an excellent reappraisal of Gramsci's relevance to contemporary social theory, see Marcia Landy, Film, Politics, and Gramsci and "Gramsci beyond Gramsci." For an excellent and critical use of Gramsci in a study of ethnicity and the state, see Charles R. Hale, Resistance and Contradiction.

25 See Michel Foucault, "Nietzsche, Genealogy, History" and "Intellectuals and Power."

26 R. Radhakrishnan, "Ethnic Identity and Post-Structuralist Difference," 204.

27 Ibid.

28 See the essays in Talal Asad, Anthropology and the Colonial Encounter, and in Faye Harrison's more recent edited collection, Decolonizing Anthropology.

29 On border crossings, see Renato Rosaldo's *Culture and Truth*. For a feminist appropriation of Deleuze's notion of nomadism, see Rosi Braidotti, *Nomadic Subjects*.

30 See Sylvia Soderlind, "The Contest of Marginalities," which addresses a series of articles that appeared in 1991 in the journal *Tulsa Studies in Women's Literature*. Two of the most notable are Helen M. Burke, "The Rhetoric and Politics of Marginality," and Jonathan Crewe, "Defining Marginality." Soderlind's work owes much to Gayatri Chakravorty Spivak's important essay, "Poststructuralism, Marginality, Postcoloniality and Value." See Homi Bhabha's essay, "DissemiNation: Time, Narrative, and the Margins of the Modern Nation." The concept of the margins has received only scant attention in anthropology, though Anna Lowenhaupt Tsing's work, *In the Realm of the Diamond Queen*, stands out as an exception. For early interventions in debates about center and periphery, locality and globality, see Arjun Appadurai, "Theory in Anthropology: Center and Periphery," and Stephen Nugent, "The 'Peripheral Situation.'"

31 See, for example, Mary Louise Pratt, *Imperial Eyes: Travel Writing and Transculturation*.

32 This argument is provocatively set forth in John Champagne, *The Ethics of Marginality*.

33 The classic essays are in William G. Skinner, *The City in Late Imperial China*. For a more recent approach to the problem of centers and localities, see David S. G. Goodman and Gerald Segal, *China Deconstructs*, and Dali Yang, *Beyond Beijing*.

34 The chapters that follow do not provide an overview of the enormous and provocative literature on minorities in China, though a number of themes can be briefly identified. Dru Gladney was perhaps the first to argue that the policies of the reform period had opened up cultural and economic spaces for the resurgence of ethnic identities. In the groundbreaking *Muslim Chinese*, for example, he demonstrated that a sense of Hui-ness was rooted in the historical past and that Hui modes of ethnic expression were in dialectical tension with reform-era modes of state classification. As Prasenjit Duara once put it, Gladney almost single-handedly redirected the study of Chinese nationalism "inwards from the margins." See Duara, "Review of *Muslim Chinese*," 644–645. Part of my task in this book is to bring a more critical perspective to bear on what it means to write "inward" from the margins. I am also indebted to a number of colleagues who have explored the relationship among ethnicity, gender, and Chinese nationalism. See, for example, Louisa Schein, "The Other Goes to Market" and "Gender and Internal Orientalism." Her ethnography, *Minority Rules*, is an excellent account of the problematic of gender and ethnicity. Others have emphasized how ethnic minorities have been celebrated as the progenitors of "authentic" and "ancient" traditions, traditions that have somehow survived the accelerated transformations of the twentieth century. See, for example, Timothy S.

Oakes, "Cultural Geography and Chinese Ethnic Tourism"; Emily Chao, "Hegemony, Agency, and Re-presenting the Past"; and Almaz Khan, "Who Are the Mongols?" On the problem of minority intellectuals, see Justin Rudelson, *Oasis Identities*, and Uradyn E. Bulag, *Nationalism and Hybridity in Mongolia*.

35 For one of the best anthropological studies of the category of elite in different contexts, see George Marcus's edited volume *Elites: Ethnographic Issues*. See in particular his excellent introductory overview of the term and its history in the humanities and social sciences.

36 Katherine Verdery, *Nationalist Ideology under Socialism*.

37 Ibid., 3.

38 Joan W. Scott, " 'Experience,' " 25.

39 See Foucault's essay "Truth and Power" in *Power/Knowledge*, 116.

40 Foucault, *Discipline and Punish*, 137.

41 For recent discussions, see Edwin N. Wilmsen, "Introduction: Premises of Power in Ethnic Politics," and John Comaroff, "Ethnicity, Nationalism, and the Politics of Difference in an Age of Revolution." See also Marilyn Ivy's book on discourses of culture and the nation in Japan, *Discourses of the Vanishing*, and John Pemberton's study of the history of cultural discourse in colonial and postcolonial Java, *The Subject of Java*.

42 Richard Handler was one of the first anthropologists to draw attention to questions of discourse in the cultural politics of nationalism. See *Nationalism and the Politics of Culture in Quebec*. Tani Barlow has explored the discursive nature of the construct of gender in the provocative essay "Theorizing Women: *Funu, Guojia, Jiating* (Chinese Women, Chinese State, Chinese Family)." See also Rey Chow, *Woman and Chinese Modernity*.

43 At issue here is the teleological view of history as the quintessential sign of the modern. See, for example, Nicholas Dirks's *Colonialism and Culture*. This is the general argument as well in Robert Young's much discussed and debated *White Mythologies: Writing History and the West*.

44 See, for example, Ann Stoler, *Race and the Education of Desire*.

45 Bryan Turner, *Orientalism, Postmodernism, and Globalism*, 21.

46 Thomas McCarthy, "The Critique of Impure Reason," 130.

47 Ibid.

48 Lorna Rhodes has been one of the more stimulating and successful anthropologists to work through the challenges of Foucault's work. See especially "Panoptical Intimacies."

49 See Hubert L. Dreyfus and Paul Rabinow, *Michel Foucault: Beyond Structuralism and Hermeneutics*, 229–252.

50 The idea of "permanent provocation" is taken from Foucault's essay "The Subject and Power," in ibid., 208–226. See also Ronald F. Wendt's discussion of this concept in "Answers to the Gaze." For studies in the China field that have made

critical use of Foucault's work on disciplinary power, see Lisa Rofel, "Rethinking Modernity: Space and Factory Discipline in China," and Mayfair Mei-hui Yang, "The Modernity of Power in the Chinese Socialist Order." For a trenchant critique of Foucault from the perspective of Chinese notions of ritual and ideology, see P. Steven Sangren, " 'Power' against Ideology."

51 Banks, *Ethnicity: Anthropological Constructions*, 189.

52 I owe this image to James Clifford's essay, "Spatial Practices: Fieldwork, Travel, and the Disciplining of Anthropology." See also Akhil Gupta and James Ferguson, "Discipline and Practice: 'The Field' as Site, Method, and Location in Anthropology."

53 Don Robotham, "Postcolonialities: The Challenge of New Modernities," 357.

54 Alex Callinicos, *The Revenge of History*, 1.

55 See Ernesto Laclau, *New Reflections on the Revolution of Our Time*, xi. Laclau's view is discussed in David Scott, "The Aftermaths of Sovereignty."

56 Alessandro Russo, "The Probable Defeat," 179–180.

57 This theme is taken up in Bob Stauffer, "After Socialism," and is central to the project that informs Katherine Verdery, *What Was Socialism, and What Comes Next?*

chapter one   Inciting the Past

1 See Barbara Kruger and Phil Mariani's introduction to the edited volume, *Remaking History*, ix.

2 Ibid.

3 Partha Chatterjee takes up a similar set of questions in *The Nation and Its Fragments*.

4 One of the best analyses of the origins of Marxist historiography in China is found in Arif Dirlik, *Revolution and History*.

5 One of the more recurrent struggles in the post-1949 historiography has been the debate between "historicism" (*lishi zhuyi*) and the "class viewpoint" (*jieji guandian*). The former, perhaps best represented by Liu Jie's arguments in the early 1960s that class analysis is an inappropriate analytical tool when applied to ancient historical events, has attempted to delineate those features of China's cultural legacy that should be preserved and embraced. Liu argued that the Confucian concept of *ren* (roughly, "benevolence") was devoid of class content, a position for which he was severely attacked. See Albert Feuerwerker, *History in Communist China*, for a discussion of these struggles over historiographical method in post-1949 China.

6 See Robert W. Weller, "Historians and Consciousness."

7 See, for example, Pamela Kyle Crossley, "Thinking about Ethnicity in Early Modern China"; Stevan Harrell, "The History of the History of the Yi"; Ralph Litzinger, "Making Histories: Contending Conceptions of the Yao Past"; and

Charles F. McKhann, "The Naxi and the Nationalities Question." For critiques among scholars in China, see Tong Enzhang, "Moergen de moshi yu makesi zhuyi."

8 Edward Said, *Orientalism*, 15.

9 For a sampling of some of these controversies, see James Clifford's reading of Said in his book *The Predicament of Culture* and Lata Mani and Ruth Frankenberg's excellent overview of postorientalism commentary in their article "The Challenge of *Orientalism*." Much of this work takes up Said's methodological challenges, but also confronts his depiction of orientalism as a monolithic and uncontested discourse. In recent years, Said's work has been read, debated, and challenged by a number of China scholars. See, for example, Tang Xiaobing, "Orientalism and the Question of Universality"; Arif Dirlik, "Chinese History and the Question of Orientalism"; and Louisa Schein, "Gender and Internal Orientalism."

10 Paul Bové, *Intellectuals in Power*, 216–217.

11 See Malek Alloula, *The Colonial Harem*, for a similar approach.

12 See Homi Bhabha, "Of Mimicry and Man: The Ambivalence of Colonial Discourse."

13 By the time he wrote the essay "Traveling Theory," Said began to move away from his previous endorsement of Foucault's approach to power. He argued in part that the theory of power was too abstract and rarefied, unable to respond to the complex unfolding of the social world. For Said, Foucault could never imagine a theory of resistances; he could see power only as universalizing, a dominant force in all aspects of human life. In turning on Foucault, Said was searching for ways to define the nature of intellectual practice; to understand how intellectuals become invested in certain discourses, institutions, and practices; to image how intellectual work after Foucault can oppose repression and imagine alternative societies. As I argued in the introduction, this view of Foucault tends to focus on the conception of disciplinary power as developed in *Discipline and Punish* and ignores ambivalences and refinements of this conception in his later work. For a further discussion of Said's reading of Foucault, see Bové, *Intellectuals in Power*, 220–223.

14 This argument is set forth in Robert Young, *White Mythologies*, 141–156. See Ann Stoler's article, "Making Empire Respectable," for an analysis of certain ambivalences in the making of the colonial elite. In fact, the November 1989 volume of *American Ethnologist*, in which her article appears, is devoted to a rethinking of Said's image of the Orient as penetrated, silenced, and possessed. Stoler is primarily concerned with the constitution of colonial power and of a colonial elite and finds that the process, though no less insidious, is much more problematic than Said's initial formulation suggested. For a similar approach, see also Gyan Prakash, "Science 'Gone Native.'"

15 Said, *Orientalism*, 325–328. See as well the statement about anthropology and representation in his article, "Representing the Colonized: Anthropology's Interlocutors."

16 Said, *Orientalism*, 326.

17 Ibid., 327.

18 For excellent examples that show how discourses and practices of modernity have been put to use and sometimes radically transfigured by administrators, scholars, and other elite in colonial settings, see Timothy Mitchell, *Colonizing Egypt*, and John Pemberton, *On the Subject of "Java."*

19 Said, *Orientalism*, 324.

20 Ibid., 325.

21 Ibid.

22 Caren Kaplan, *Questions of Travel*, 35.

23 Bryan Turner, *Orientalism, Postmodernism, and Globalism*, 21.

24 The question of what happens to the identity and cultural character of a group in the face of outside influence is of course a quintessential modern one, found in both evolutionary and diffusionist notions of culture and cultural change. It is instructive to consider this view as well in relation to early-twentieth-century ethnos theory in the Soviet Union, especially the writings of Yulian Bromley. Marcus Banks sees Bromley as a strong primordialist, in the sense that Bromley, as did many of his Soviet colleagues who began to develop theories of ethnicity in the 1970s and 1980s, believed that the expression of ethnicity persists through generations and through a variety of social formations. See Banks, *Ethnicity*, 17–24. As Banks also explains, Ernest Gellner and Tamara Dragadze have pointed out that the Soviets never developed a strong structural functionalist tradition with its rejection of history and its insistence on synchronic analysis. Images of cultures in stasis do not figure strongly in the Soviet tradition; a given social formation always contains elements of the past and presages the future. See Gellner's edited collection, *Soviet and Western Anthropology*, and Dragadze, "The Place of 'Ethnos' Theory in Soviet Anthropology."

25 Fortune's and his colleagues' writings were widely read by scholars of the Yao working in China, Europe, and the United States, if only for their ethnological descriptions of "primitive forms" of kinship, religion, social structure, and economy. See Fortune, "Yao Society: A Study of a Group of Primitives in China," 3–4. Another influential piece of work from this period is H. Stubel, "The Yao of the Province of Guangdong."

26 See, for example, the ethnographic surveys by the French colonial officer Auguste Bonifacy, as discussed in Georges Condominas, "The First French Publications on the Yao."

27 Fortune, "Yao Society," 351.

28 Richard Cushman, *Rebel Haunts and Lotus Huts*.

29 Michel Strickmann, "The Tao among the Yao: Taoism and the Sinification of South China," 23–30. See also Jacques Lemoine, *Yao Ceremonial Paintings* and "Yao Religion and Society."

30 Strickmann, "The Tao among the Yao," 28.

31 Peter Kandre, "Autonomy and Integration of Social Systems: The Iu Mien ('Yao' or 'Man') Mountain Population and Their Neighbors."

32 Lemoine, "Yao Religion and Society."

33 Peter Kandre and Lej Tsan Kuej, "Yao (Iu-Mien) Supernaturalism, Language and Ethnicity," 175.

34 Charles F. Keyes, "Towards a New Formulation of the Concept of Ethnic Group."

35 Lemoine, "Yao Religion and Society," 208.

36 Ibid., 209.

37 There has been some debate concerning whether the various peoples of China in the "premodern" era (in China studies, sometimes referred to as the pre–Opium War period) should be termed ethnic groups. See, for example, Morton H. Fried's article "Tribe to State or State to Tribe in Ancient China?", in which he explains the varying uses of the terms tribe and ethnic group in the historiography of the People's Republic of China. Crossley's "Thinking about Ethnicity in Early Modern China" looks at differences between the Chinese concept of *minzu* and the Western anthropological concept of ethnicity. In an analysis of the conflicted relations between Han and Manchu bannermen during the Qing, Mark Elliot has asserted that ethnic conflict structured much of the Chinese landscape in the eighteenth and nineteenth centuries. See his "Bannerman and Townsman: Ethnic Tension in Nineteenth Century Jiangnan." On a somewhat different beat, see Prasenjit Duara, "Provincial Narratives of the Nation." Duara rethinks the "culturalism to nationalism" thesis in the study of Chinese history and modernity and in the process debunks the theories of Gellner and Anderson that insist on the modernity of the nation. He argues additionally that such constructs have also been part of the Chinese political imagination and that the nation, in the Chinese context, does not constitute a radically novel form of consciousness. See also his "Bifurcating Linear History" and *Rescuing History from the Nation.*

38 In addition to Harold Wiens's classic *China's March toward the Tropics*, see Edward H. Schafer, *The Vermilion Bird: T'ang Images of the South.*

39 See, for example, David Hawkes, "The Quest for the Goddess," and Li Wai-yee, *Enchantment and Disenchantment.*

40 Zhang Youjuan discusses some of these in his book *Yaozu zongjiao lunji* (Collected essays on Yao religion).

41 Schafer, *The Vermilion Bird*, 49.

42 Xu Jiewu and Deng Wentong's "Cong Yaozu zhixi wenti tanqi" (Discussion aris-

ing from the question of Yao subgroups) provides a list of the many Han and Yao terms for different Yao subgroups. These terms are generally descriptive of clothing (*fushi*), beliefs (*xinying*), mode of livelihood (*shengchan*), and place of residence (*juzhu*).

43 *Mak* here is probably a reconstructed Tang pronunciation for the character now pronounced *mo*. I owe this observation to Stevan Harrell.

44 Schafer, *The Vermilion Bird*, 51.

45 Ibid. According to Schafer, Liu Yuxi's poem was written sometime in the early ninth century.

46 Stevan Harrell, "Introduction: Civilizing Projects and Reactions to Them."

47 Quoted in Schafer, *The Vermilion Bird*, 50.

48 Cushman's *Rebel Haunts and Lotus Huts* only tangentially addresses the ethnographic research carried out on Mien-speaking Yao in Thailand in the 1970s. As for Cushman's treatment of post-1949 work on the Yao in China, he does note that there was a marked increase in linguistic research in the late 1950s and early 1960s. By 1992, I had come across only nine sources on the Yao published in China between 1949 and 1979. In contrast, for the period 1979 to 1986, I found over 120 articles or books published on the Yao *minzu*. Research and writing on the Yao in the PRC has continued to proliferate since 1986, and indeed new writings continued to appear in the 1990s.

49 In the eleventh century, we find for the first time references to Yao *ren* (Yao people), in which the character *yao* is written with the insect radical and is not prefixed by the word *man*. For a discussion of these eleventh-century sources, see Cushman, *Rebel Haunts*, 50–53.

50 Lemoine, *Yao Ceremonial Paintings*, 11.

51 Tang Cui, as quoted in Cushman, *Rebel Haunts*, 56.

52 See Theraphan Thongkum, *Guo Shan Bang*. See also Huang Yu, "A Preliminary Study of King Ping's Charter," 89–124.

53 Cushman, *Rebel Haunts*, 55–59.

54 Wei Yuan, "Sheng Wu Ji," quoted in ibid., 36.

55 Cushman, *Rebel Haunts*, 225–231. See also Philip A. Kuhn, *Rebellion and Its Enemies in Late Imperial China*, 106–107, where he discusses an entirely different series of rebellions, the so-called Xin-ning rebellions, the first occurring in 1836. Xin-ning is in a valley just to the west of the Xiang River valley, which had become one of the major routes by which the opium trade spread to the north. The Yao in this region were involved in this trade as well as a number of secret societies, such as the Black Lotus (Qinglian Jiao) and the Cudgel Society (Bangbang Hui). Due to *yamen* extortion of local peasants, several Yao leaders with connections in these societies began to secretly organize and drew support from large segments of the local Han peasantry. By 1847, another revolt occurred in Xin-ning,

led by a Yao named Li Caihao. The Yao were brutally defeated by a locally organized militia after several months. Kuhn finds these rebellions instructive in two senses. On the one hand, they pointed to interethnic alliances that arose in the face of local imperial oppression. On the other, they revealed the importance of local militia, typically the instruments of lineage elite, in putting down such revolts even in the face of growing provincial-level distrust of powerful, and highly successful, locally organized militias.

56 Cushman, *Rebel Haunts*, 233. Many scholars of ethnicity have noted the links between competition and conflict over resources and the crystallization of ethnic identity. See, for example, Charles F. Keyes, "The Dialectics of Ethnic Change," and E. K. Francis, *Interethnic Relations*.

57 As there is no single author attributed, I cite this book as Guangxi Editorial Group, *Yaozu jianshi*.

58 Ibid., 132.

59 Ibid., 12–13.

60 Philology is not the only means of attack. Reconstructions of the historic Yao are based on the relationship between present-day Yao traditional customs and apparently similar practices mentioned for this region in such sources as the Hou-Han-Shu (History of the Latter Han dynasty). See Guangxi Editorial Group, *Yaozu jianshi*, 20.

61 Ibid., 21.

62 Ibid., 23.

63 Ibid., 24–25.

64 Ibid., 28.

65 This argument can be contrasted to one set forth in Cushman's *Rebel Haunts*, 168. He states that according to the Guangxi Tongzhi, eleven of the twelve tribal officers recognized by the Song court whose ethnic origins were recorded were Chinese from the province of Shantong. It is not certain, however, whether this reflects the ethnic distribution of hereditary tribal positions or whether local tribal officers fabricated Chinese descent to pursue political interests.

66 Guangxi Editorial Group, *Yaozu jianshi*, 31.

67 Ibid., 32–33.

68 For an important work on the *tusi* system, see She I-tse, *Zhongguo Tusi zhidu*. See also Wiens, *China's March toward the Tropics*.

69 Guangxi Editorial Group, *Yaozu jianshi*, 34–35.

70 Ibid., 36.

71 This is a point made by many scholars who have written on nationalist history-making projects. See, for example, Duara, "Bifurcating Linear History," and Nicholas Dirks, "History as a Sign of the Modern."

72 See Young, *White Mythologies*, for a discussion of the concept of history in the

modern West, the Hegelian roots of many materialis conceptions of history, and the problems involved in poststructuralist attempts to reconceptualize and politicize the writing of history.

73 See, for example, the many excellent essays collected in Ruby S. Watson's edited volume, *Memory, History, and Opposition under State Socialism*.

74 I first heard this story when I visited Jianghua County in 1990. Gong Zhebing recounts the same tale in an unpublished article entitled "Zhongguo Pan Yao de Qianjiadong yundong" (The Qianjiadong movement among China's Pan Yao).

75 This figure is quoted in Jonathan D. Spence, *The Search for Modern China*, 572.

76 See Gong, "Zhongguo Pan Yao de Qianjiadong yundong."

77 For a discussion of the problem of territorialization and the image of deterritorialization, see Appadurai, *Modernity at Large*. These issues are also taken up in Michael Shapiro, "Moral Geographies and the Ethics of Post-sovereignty" and *Violent Cartographies*. For an excellent discussion of the growing tension between the nation and the state in the context of both the global environmental movement and the problematic of postcolonialism, see Akhil Gupta, *Postcolonial Developments*, 291–329.

78 Ernest Gellner's classic statement on nationalism and industrialization is contained in *Nations and Nationalism*. For Benedict Anderson's account of the role of the imagination and the technology of print capitalism, see *Imagined Communities*. On the politics of modernity and nationalism in the context of China, see Prasenjit Duara, "De-Constructing the Chinese Nation." For a provocative discussion of these issues in the case of Mongolian nationalism, see Uradyn E. Bulag, *Nationalism and Hybridity in Mongolia*.

79 Gyanendra Pandey, "The Culture of History," 35–36.

80 Ibid., 35–36.

81 Nicholas Dirks, *In Near Ruins*, xi.

82 Stefan Tanaka, *Japan's Orient*, 22.

chapter two   Moral Geographies of Place

1 For a description of this study, see Jonathan D. Spence, *The Search for Modern China*, 373–379.

2 I will be drawing on two main published sources here. The first is the *Guangxi Yaozu shehui lishi diaocha* (An investigation of the social history of the Guangxi Yao), which I cite under the names Huang Yu and Li Weixin, who participated in the research for the Jinxiu section of this book in the 1950s and then again in the 1980s. They compiled and edited the 1980s edition and wrote the preface. I also draw on the *Jinxiu Yaozu zizhixian gaikuang* (A survey of the Jinxiu Yao Autonomous County), also published in the 1980s. I refer to it in my text as the *Jinxiu gaikuang*, and I cite its authorship as the Jinxiu County Government.

3 For an excellent overview of the history of Yao ethnological research in pre- and post-1949 China, see Liu Yaoquan and Hu Qiwang, "Survey of Yao Studies in China (1949–1984)."

4 A number of excellent case studies exploring the politics of space and place are found in Steve Pile and Michael Keith, *Geographies of Resistance*. I refer the reader especially to Donald Moore's article on place politics in the Kaerezi Resettlement Scheme in Zimbabwe's Eastern Highlands, "Remapping Resistance." As Moore has put it in a wonderful reading of the rage for spatial metaphor in current social theory, "Amidst the scramble for spatial metaphors, is it possible to appreciate how place, in the grounded livelihood struggles of Kaerezians, is always more than metaphor?" (102).

5 Michel de Certeau, *The Practice of Everyday Life*, 117.

6 David Harvey, *Justice, Nature, and the Geography of Difference*, 262.

7 In ibid., Harvey points out how modern states have often engaged in geopolitical strategies—the development of military technologies of surveillance over vast spaces, for example—that produce "space as an effect of the strategies they pursue." Yet, certain things imagined to be permanent, such as the flow of information, the movement of capital, money, and immigrants, as well as cultural habits and ideologies, constantly undermine these strategies. "The changing status of the state, the undermining of seemingly powerful permanences (such as the Soviet Union) then become much more readily understood as the inevitable outcome of a space-place dialectic that not only undermines the supposed 'rationality' of politics, economics, and science, but also pits the strategic world of places against the wayward trajectories of multiple spatialities defined by often divergent processes" (263). The point of all of this for Harvey is that it is in the space-place relational dialectic that we can begin to image certain kinds of oppositional practices and perhaps even spaces outside and beyond the instrumentalities of both state and other forms of disciplinary surveillance.

8 de Certeau, *The Practice of Everyday Life*, 115.

9 See Greg Guldin's discussion of Cai Yuanpei in *The Saga of Anthropology in China*, 30–34. See also Vera Schwarcz, *The Chinese Enlightenment*, and Chen Yongling and Wang Xiaoyi, "Ershi shiji qiandide Zhongguo minzuxue" (Chinese ethnology in the early twentieth century).

10 For a discussion of Cai's activities in France, see Arif Dirlik, *Anarchism in the Chinese Revolution*, 169–175.

11 For a brief discussion of these May Fourth intellectuals and their interest in Darwin, Spencer, and Huxley, see Spence, *The Search for Modern China*, 310–319.

12 For a comprehensive discussion of the May Fourth period, see Chow Tse-tsung, *The May Fourth Movement*.

13 Guldin, *The Saga of Anthropology in China*, 32–33.

14 Ibid., 31.

15 Quoted in Spence, *The Search for Modern China*, 308.

16 Chen Yongling, "Applied Ethnology and the Implementation of Policy toward Ethnic Minorities in China."

17 Guldin, *The Saga of Anthropology in China*, 34.

18 Chen Yongling, "Applied Ethnology."

19 See June Dreyer, "Traditional Minorities Elites," 421.

20 Guldin, *The Saga of Anthropology in China*, 147–172. Guldin reports how friends and colleagues turned on each other during this campaign, a fact symbolized most forcefully in Professor Lin Yaohua's public accusation that Fei was attempting to incite a Hungarian-style revolution in China. Guldin correctly reports that many of these scholars are today embarrassed by this period of their lives and would rather forget it. It is also true that many of them cannot write openly about these campaigns, and their effects on people's lives and careers and on local communities. I pick up this point in subsequent chapters.

21 Fei Xiaotong, "Zhishi fenzide zaochun tianqi" (An early spring for intellectuals).

22 My understanding of this period of Fei's life owes much to Gene Cooper's report of his interview with Fei during a visit to China in April 1972, "An Interview with Chinese Anthropologists." I have also drawn from A. R. Sanchez and S. L. Wong's follow-up commentary on Cooper's report, "On 'An Interview with Chinese Anthropologists.' "

23 See Fei Xiaotong, "I Admit My Crime to the People," cited in ibid., 789.

24 Cooper, "An Interview with Chinese Anthropologists," 481.

25 Arif Dirlik and Maurice Meisner, "Politics, Scholarship, and Chinese Socialism," 9.

26 Lin Yaohua, "New China's Ethnology: Research and Prospects." This passage is cited in Guldin, *The Saga of Anthropology*, 187.

27 The traditional one-character name for the province of Guangxi is Gui, meaning Cassia, the genus that includes the Chinese cinnamon tree. The southern part of Guangxi is often referred to as Guinan, and the northern half is called Guibei. The Dayaoshan sits in the nexus of these two regions. Historically, the valleys and foothills around this mountain chain have been the sites of many conflicts between local groups and imperial officials. The city of Wuzhou, located on the West River and close to the Guangdong border, is now a major tourist stopping point, as travelers disembark the overnight boats from Guangzhou (Canton) on their way northward to the scenic city of Guilin. Founded in the first century B.C. and known as Guangxin, Wuzhou has long been a garrison town for the control of local "tribal" peoples. Revolt has also been a historical feature of the region. To this day, the local Zhuang and Hakka (Kejia) are stereotyped as fierce fighters, no doubt due to their participation in the Taiping movement.

It was in the village of Jintian, at the southern flank of the Dayaoshan near the present-day town of Guiping, that the first Taiping uprising took place.

28 In his book *The Chinese Mosaic*, Leo Moser argues that the "subethnic" picture of Guangxi is highly complex (see 226–227). Guangxi is today an autonomous region for the Zhuang people, the largest of China's non-Han minority groups. Moser uses the term "subethnic" to advance his observation that the Zhuang are a strongly Sinicized people. An originally Tai-speaking people, many of the Zhuang have lost their native language and now speak only local dialects of Mandarin. They were classified as a minority nationality in the 1950s on the basis of family tradition and a few lingering cultural habits (the building of the Zhuang long house and various Zhuang dances, for example), said to set them off from their ethnic neighbors. Moser also makes the important point that Zhuang identity, despite the apparent assimilation of the group to Chinese ways, owes much to the memory of past ostracism as one of the "southern barbarians." The assertion of a Zhuang cultural tradition, historically deep and persisting into contemporary times, is one way by which the Zhuang contest this historic legacy of marginality. But their apparent assimilation to Han culture also works against them. Zhuang provincial leaders in Guangxi are known to often complain that foreigners rarely come to research them: they don't exhibit enough alterity to be considered a proper object of anthropological analysis.

29 Wiens, *China's March toward the Tropics*, and Huang and Li, *Guangxi Yaozu shehui lishi diaocha*.

30 Guangxi is also known as a final stronghold of the ultraleftists. Many of Guangxi's leaders owed their political allegiance to the Cultural Revolution, and some of them purposefully stalled the introduction of Deng's market reforms and material incentive programs until the late 1980s. For a fruitful discussion of the recent political history and economy of Guangxi, see Hans Hendrischke, "Guangxi: Towards Southwest China and Southeast Asia."

31 Quoted in the Internet version of the *South China Morning Post*, 12 December 1998. I thank Saul Thomas for pointing this article out to me. During the course of my fieldwork in the late 1980s and early 1990s, many officials were hesitant to enunciate issues of poverty, for they directly pointed to the failure of the Party to bring growth and development to the peasant masses. Though I can't explore this in more detail here, I think the change has everything to do with the presence of nongovernmental organizations in development projects in rural regions of China in the late 1990s, which have forced the government to come clean on its record of failed development. Wu Bangguo's statements come in the midst of the CCP's position in late 1998 that one of the main agendas of the government is the fight against poverty, which it had promised to eliminate by the year 2000.

32 Diana Lary, *Region and Nation*, 21.

33 Ibid., 23.

34 For a sampling, see Prasenjit Duara, *Rescuing History from the Nation*, and John Fitzgerald, *Awakening China*.

35 Michael Tsin, "Imagining 'Society' in Early Twentieth-Century China," 213.

36 See Dirlik, *Anarchism in the Chinese Revolution*; Lydia Liu, "Translingual Practice"; and Ann Anagnost, *National Past-Times*.

37 Tsin, "Imagining 'Society,' " 214.

38 See Walker Connor, *The National Question in Marxist-Leninist Theory and Strategy*.

39 See Richard von Glahn, *The Country of Streams and Grottos*, and John Herman, "Empire in the Southwest."

40 Ibid., 49.

41 Yao Shunan, "Investigating the Dayaoshan Stone Tablet System."

42 Huang and Li, *Guangxi Yaozu shehui lishi diaocha*, 31–78.

43 Hu Qiwang and Fan Honggui, *Pancun Yaozu*, 106–130.

44 Huang and Li, *Guangxi Yaozu shehui lishi diaocha*.

45 Fei explains that his remarks are based on a talk he gave at the Nationality Research Institute at the Central Nationalities Institute in December 1981. The transcript of that talk was later included in the book, *Congshi shehuixue wushinian* (Fifty years of sociological research). The same paper was then reproduced, with a few minor changes, in Fei's preface to Hu and Fan's ethnography on the Pan Yao of Jinxiu, *Pancun Yaozu*. I was required by my Yao advisors during my first stay at the Central Nationalities Institute in 1988 to translate and study this article. All citations below are from this prefatory essay; page references are in parentheses.

chapter three   Remembering Revolution

1 This image of the Dayaoshan as a garden of abundance is taken from the *Jinxiu gaikuang*. See Jinxiu County Government, 50.

2 From the *Wang Wenzheng gongquan shu* (Collected works of Wang Shouren), vol. 15, as cited in ibid., 52.

3 This is the term employed in most ethnological accounts of Yao history. See Jinxiu County Government, *Jinxiu gaikuang*, 55.

4 For a discussion of this period, see Su Defu and Liu Yulian, "Dayaoshan Yaozu renmin fandui Guomindang fandong tongzhi de gaoya zhengce—Jinxiu baodong" (The Jinxiu uprising: Opposing the high-handed policies of the Guomindang reactionaries), hereafter cited as "Jinxiu baodong."

5 Ann Anagnost, *National Past-Times*, 158–159.

6 For an excellent discussion of the politics of scholarship and political commitment in another part of the world in which ethnicity would be a hotly contested

issue, see Charles R. Hale's study of the Miskitu Indians in Nicaragua, *Resistance and Contradiction*.

7 Su and Liu, "Jinxiu baodong," 2.

8 Jinxiu County Government, *Jinxiu gaikuang*, 61.

9 After the Party drove the Guomindang from the hills and established a new administrative structure for the Dayaoshan and the surrounding counties, they counted 5,133 households in the Dayaoshan with a total of 25,885 residents. The Yao subgroup breakdown was as follows: 831 Hualan Yao, or 3.2 percent of the population; 1,215 Ao Yao, or 4.6 percent; 5,345 Chashan Yao, or 20.1 percent; 1,056 Shanzi Yao, or 4.1 percent; and finally, for the largest group, 9,380 Pan Yao, or 36.2 percent. There were 8,058 Han, or 31.1 percent of the total population. No figures are provided for the Zhuang or other nationalities at this time. See ibid., 64–65.

10 *Guangxi ribao*, 20 July 1951, quoted in ibid., 68.

11 Ibid.

12 Accounts of this meeting are narrated in many government documents in Jinxiu, and I recorded this account in many of my interviews. See, for example, ibid., 69–70.

13 The Guomindang tax and surveillance system is discussed in Su and Liu, "Jinxiu baodong."

14 Ibid., 72.

15 This term is borrowed from Bob Jessop, *State Theory*, 254.

16 This view is very similar to Fei Xiaotong's views on the formation of a collective Yao identity and consciousness in the Dayaoshan. See Fei, preface, and my discussion of Fei's writings on the Dayaoshan in chapter 2.

17 For discussions on ritual and secrecy, see Jacques Lemoine, "Yao Religion and Society," and the detailed ethnological religious studies of Zhang Youjun, especially *Yaozu zongjiao lunji* (Collected essays on Yao religion).

18 See Cao Zhipeng, *Chashan Yao de chengnian li* (A Chashan Yao rite of passage), and Liu Yulian, "Shilun Daojiao wenhua yu Chashan Yao minjian wenhua zhi guangxi" (An inquiry into the relationship between Taoist culture and the folk culture of the Chashan Yao).

chapter four The State and Its Ritual Potencies

1 See Walker Connor, *The National Question in Marxist-Leninist Theory and Strategy*.

2 See Richard Curt Krauss, *Class Conflict in Chinese Socialism*, 165–183.

3 An early study of Yao religious beliefs is found in an article written by Jiang Yingliang in 1948 entitled "Xinan bianjiang minzu luncong" (A Discussion on the minorities of the southwestern frontier). Jiang argued that Yao religious beliefs could be summarized as centering on three main points. First, the so-

called Yao belief system exhibits a process of "Taoistization" (*daojiaohua*) at the hands of the Han Chinese. Second, it shows the continued presence of a host of "primitive" beliefs and practices that predate the penetration of Taoism into the Yao belief system. Third, it suggests the infiltration of some Buddhist beliefs. This is in effect a description of what Arthur Wolf, Steve Sangren, and others have discussed as the Chinese folk religion. Zhang Youjun, on the other hand, disagrees with the argument of a strong Buddhist influence among the Yao. He argues that although Yao ritual texts contain Buddhist expressions, the Yao do not believe in Buddhism at all. They are resolutely Taoist. See his book, *Yaozu zongjiao lunji* (Collected essays on Yao religion). Rob Weller has informed me that when he visited Yao villages in the vicinity of the once Taiping stronghold of Jintian, Guangxi, in the late 1980s, the Yao he met asserted that they were Taoist. In my own research, I found that Yao point to Taoism as the source of their religious belief in large order to assert that they are a literate people, a people with culture or *wenhua*.

4 During my initial months of research in Beijing, I had the opportunity to photocopy a number of these ritual texts. Some of the titles: *He jing shu* (The book for joining the worlds); *Dao shen lu* (The way of the deities of the Yao); *Dao jie ke* (The code of the ordination rituals); *Fa zang ke* (The code for conducting a funeral). A list of other ritual texts used in the Yao Taoist practice can be found in Zhang Youjun, *Yaozu zongjiao lunji*.

5 The battle against feudal superstition can be traced back to the May Fourth period. See Prasenjit Duara, "Knowledge and Power in the Discourse of Modernity." For a discussion of state representations of ritual under the reforms, see Ann Anagnost, "The Politics of Ritual Displacement." For an analysis of ritual politics in different contexts, see Nicholas Dirks, "Ritual and Resistance: Subversion as a Social Fact," and Talal Asad, *Genealogies of Religion*.

6 Ya Hanzhang, *Minzu wenti yu zongjiao wenti* (The nationalities problem and the problem of religion).

7 See, for example, Vivian Shue, *The Reach of the State*. Helen Siu takes up these issues in *Agents and Victims in South China*. One might also consult Andrew G. Walder, *Communist Neo-Traditionalism*. It is important to realize that these various works address state and society dynamics mostly in the 1980s. I want to remind the reader that the material for this chapter was collected during the late 1980s and early 1990s. Deng Xiaoping's "southern excursion" to Guangzhou in 1992 launched a new era of economic reforms, and many scholars see this event as the impetus behind the spectacular capitalist and consumer energies of the late 1990s. Scholars have thus begun to pay attention to the changing role of governmental elite and the relationship between an emerging middle class and an entrepreneurial class with close ties to the Party-state apparatus. As David

Goodman reminds us, echoing a point made some time ago by Elizabeth Perry, these transformations remind us that research into state and society relations will be more productive if it adopts a perspective of spatial difference across China rather than assume uniformity. I would argue that the same applies to the late 1980s and early 1990s. My ethnographic material and analysis in this chapter is thus meant to highlight the local particularities of the Jinxiu situation, but also to set forth what I think are some general theoretical issues in how scholars have imagined the state and society binary. See Perry, "Trends in the Study of Chinese Politics," and Goodman, "State-Society Relations in Reform Shanxi." Many social science approaches to the state take up where Louis Althusser left off in his classic essay, "Ideology and Ideological State Apparatuses." For a sampling, see Philip Abrams, "Notes on the Difficulty of Studying the State"; Martin Carnoy, *The State and Political Theory*; Jean Cohen and Andrew Arato, *The Political Theory of Civil Society*; and Bob Jessop, *State Theory: Putting Capitalist States in Their Place.*

8 See, for example, Arif Dirlik and Maurice Meisner, "Politics, Scholarship, and Chinese Socialism," and many of the essays collected in their volume *Marxism and the Chinese Experience.*

9 Questions of civil society and the public sphere are explored in Tony Saich, "The Search for Civil Society and Democracy in China"; Craig Calhoun, "Tiananmen, Television and the Public Sphere: Internationalization of Culture and the Beijing Spring of 1989," and "Civil Society and Public Sphere." See also two essays by Elizabeth Perry, "State and Society in Contemporary China" and "Trends in the Study of Chinese Politics."

10 Marilyn Ivy, "Mourning the Japanese Thing," 93.

11 See also Ivy, *Discourses of the Vanishing.*

12 Elizabeth A. Povinelli, "Settler Modernity and the Quest for an Indigenous Tradition," 22.

13 Ibid., 23.

14 For a discussion and reprint of this article, see Donald E. MacInnis, *Religion in China Today.*

15 Ann Anagnost, *National Past-Times*, 84.

16 Ibid., 85.

17 See Song Enzhang, "The Family System and Its Ethos among the Yunnan Yao."

18 See Hung Chang-tai, *Going to the People.*

19 Li Xiaowen, "Yaozu chuantong daode yu jingshen wenming jianshe" (Traditional Yao morality and the construction of spiritual civilization), 2–3.

20 Ibid., 5.

21 Ibid., 10–12.

22 Ibid., 12.

23 For discussions, see Ann Anagnost, "Socialist Ethics and the Legal System," and Arif Dirlik, "Spiritual Solutions to Material Problems: The 'Socialist Ethics and Courtesy Month' in China."

24 I was informed that the Yao cadre families who lived in the county seat were allowed only one child (as with the Han and Zhuang who lived in Jinxiu).

25 Many sociologists and demographers of China have focused on the politics of forced sterilization, but another issue that has emerged in the literature is the question of the abandonment and infanticide of infant girls. All Yao in China claim that they are different from the Han in that they do not discriminate against women. As we saw in Li Xiaowen's discussion above, Yao claim equality of the sexes. There are many grounds on which to dispute these claims (for example, many Yao ignore the feminization of their women in popular representations of Yao culture). I would argue that we need to understand these assertions in the context of Yao attempts to differentiate themselves from the Han and other nationalities who have long claimed to be educators and liberators. When I asked questions about female infanticide in Jinxiu, I was always told that this was a disgusting (taoyan) Han practice, something the Yao could never fathom. For an excellent discussion of these issues of reproductive policy, data reporting, and feminist demography, see Susan Greenhalgh and Li Jiali, "Engendering Reproductive Policy and Practice in Peasant China."

26 Liu Zheng, "Population," 536–537.

27 The best theoretical discussion of the relationship between these discourses of population quality and family planning practice is found in Anagnost's essay, "Neo-Malthusian Fantasy and National Transcendence," in National Past-Times, 117–137.

28 In her essay, " 'Liang zhong shengchan de lilun' gei wo de qishi–luolun Chashan, Hualan, Ao Yao de shengyi wenti" (What I have learned from the "Theory of the two modes of production), Liu Yulian explains that there were two basic forms of family structure. The first was known locally as "two, two, two," in which a couple would have two children who would each support one of the parents. The second was known as "two, two, one," in which a couple would have two children who would share the support of one widowed parent. The most common family had five or six people and it was quite rare to have more than seven people in a single family. Each family kept one child at home, male or female, to inherit the property and carry on the family line, and one child would be married out. It was thus often common to find Chashan Yao families with a live-in son-in-law. Liu's research was conducted among the Chashan Yao in Jinxiu, Baisha, Liula, and Xidi, the main villages surrounding the county seat. She also conducted interviews among the Ao Yao in Luoxiang, Luoyun, and Shanggu villages, finding that they too had the custom of keeping one child at

home and marrying out the other. They called this system "a single child carries on the family line" (*yimai danchuan*).

29 See Tang Zhaomin, *Yaoshan sanji*. The quote is taken from Liu, " 'Liang zhong shengchan de lilun' gei wo de qishi."

30 Liu, " 'Liang zhong shengchan de lilun' gei wo de qishi," 7–8. For a discussion of appropriations of the *gongdeqiao* name in the building of modern pedestrian bridges in Jinxiu, see Ralph Litzinger, "Memory Work."

31 In her essay, Liu footnotes the fact that her own knowledge of these techniques came from an eighty-one-year-old woman in Jinxiu, who refused to give her name. On several occasions we interviewed older women about their knowledge of indigenous herbs and birthing practices. The point was not to recover techniques that could be used in the present. The local county hospital had entirely usurped this regulatory function, though Jinxiu Yao families sometimes clandestinely induced abortion through the use of herbs.

32 Liu, " 'Liang zhong shengchan de lilun' gei wo de qishi," 11–14.

33 These issues of state power and sovereignty are taken up in William E. Connolly, *Identity/Difference: Democratic Negotiations of Political Paradox.*

34 For an excellent ethnographic study of how development comes to be linked with the politics of identity, see Akhil Gupta, "Blurred Boundaries: The Discourse of Corruption, the Culture of Politics, and the Imagined State" and *Postcolonial Developments: Agriculture in the Making of Modern India.*

35 Jean Comaroff and John Comaroff, *Modernity and Its Malcontents*, xii.

36 Ibid.

37 See, for example, Aihwa Ong's essay, "Anthropology, China and Modernities: The Geopolitics of Cultural Knowledge."

38 Don Robotham, "Postcolonialities: The Challenge of New Modernities," 369.

39 Gupta, *Postcolonial Developments.*

40 Jing Wang, *High Culture Fever*, 97.

41 Ibid. The Gan Yang article is "Wenhua Zhongguo yu xiangtu Zhongguo" (Culture and rural China).

42 Robotham, "Postcolonialities: The Challenge of New Modernities," 358.

chapter five Postsocialist Belonging

1 As Zhang Xudong explains in his masterful analysis of the so-called New Chinese Cinema, the Fifth Generation movement came into being in 1984 with Chen Kaige's *Yellow Earth*: "As radical innovators, Fifth Generation filmmakers not only set new standards of cinematic manufacturing; they further accommodated and cultivated a new collective spectator (and implicitly an international market demanding quality images of a changed society). By inventing and jux-

taposing landscape, selfhood, and the cinematic medium in an allegorical way, the Fifth Generation put together a cinematic language disassociated from the mandarin discourse of 'socialist realism,' thus creating a space of representation for an emergent public" (*Chinese Modernism in the Era of the Reforms*, 5).

2 For discussions, see Paul Clark, "Ethnic Minorities in Chinese Films" and *Chinese Cinema: Culture and Politics since 1949*. These issues are also discussed in Esther Yau, "Is China the End of Hermeneutics?" See also Dru Gladney, "Representing Nationality in China" and "Tian Zhuangzhuang, the Fifth Generation, and Minorities Film in China."

3 Esther Yau's reading of Li Chun's entrance into Dai society raises questions about the anthropological desire to disguise one's identity through language mastery and the wearing of local dress in order to carry out successful fieldwork. Yau writes that Li's character is so appealing to the audience because of "the ability of a single Han body to take up and sustain two different cultural discourses—the taking up of a superficial Dai identity by a Han intellectual. This disguise enables the intellectual to preserve the superiority of a traveler and insures him/her a better access to the inside knowledge of the Other under scrutiny" ("Is China the End of Hermeneutics?," 127).

4 Louisa Schein, "Gender and Internal Orientalism."

5 For a discussion of this process in colonial and postcolonial India, see Lata Mani, "Contentious Traditions."

6 For a discussion in the context of China, see Wang Yuejin, "Mixing Memory and Desire." For a critical analysis of the limitations of the metaphor of the repressed and its return, see Marilyn Ivy, *Discourses of the Vanishing*.

7 Gladney, "Representing Nationality in China."

8 Louisa Schein has also raised this question through her notion of the mobile other. See "The Other Goes to Market."

9 Brackette Williams's most influential statement is found in "A Class Act: Anthropology and the Race to Nation across Ethnic Terrain."

10 Arif Dirlik, *Anarchism in the Chinese Revolution*, 5. Dirlik also explores this question in "Postsocialism? Reflections on 'Socialism with Chinese Characteristics,'" 362–384. See also Katherine Verdery, *What Was Socialism and What Comes Next?*

11 Walter Benjamin, "N [Re the Theory of Knowledge, Theory of Progress]," 66.

12 I first encountered this book in a bookstore in Guangxi. It would later be presented to me as a gift at an international Yao studies conference held in Chenzhou, Hunan, in late 1990. I cite it under the name of Lan Kexuan, one of the principal editors-in-chief. The first printing was five thousand copies, and many of these were distributed to bookstores in Guangdong, Guangxi, Guizhou, Hunan, and Yunnan, the major provinces in which the Yao live. For a preliminary discussion of this text, see Ralph Litzinger, "Memory Work."

13 Lan, *The Yao Nationality*, 8–9.

14 Lemoine's paper was later published as "Yao Culture and Some Other Related Problems," 604.

15 Lan, *The Yao Nationality*, 194–195.

16 See Arjun Appadurai, *Modernity at Large*, for a critique of these approaches. A typical example of the instrumentalist approach is found in Abner Cohen, *Urban Ethnicity*. For an elegant resolution of the primordialist and instrumentalist divide, see G. Carter Bentley, "Ethnicity and Practice." For an excellent overview of ethnicity theory in anthropology and beyond, see Marcus Banks, *Ethnicity: Anthropological Constructions*.

17 In drawing attention to these photographic images, it is not my intention to provide a visual reading, which is beyond the scope of my project in this chapter. Although the literature on photography and its relationship to historical realism is too extensive to cite in full, Roland Barthes's *Camera Lucida* has been a major influence. See also Bill Nichols, *Ideology and the Image*. For a series of critical essays on visual culture, see Trachtenberg, *Classic Essays on Photography*; Richard Bolton, *The Contest of Meaning*; and Christopher Phillips, *Photography in the Modern Era*. For an excellent discussion of Walter Benjamin's writings on photography, see Eduardo Cadava, *Words of Light*. For a critical reading of the circulation of photographic images in an ethnographic context, see Rosalind C. Morris, "Surviving Pleasure at the Periphery."

18 This is a central theme in David Harvey, *The Condition of Postmodernity*. For others who have written on these themes, see Edward W. Soja, *Postmodern Geographies*, and the various articles collected in Michael Keith and Steve Pile, *Place and the Politics of Identity*. For a concise and critical discussion of many of these themes, see Caren Kaplan, *Questions of Travel*, 143–188.

19 Harvey, *The Condition of Postmodernity*, 303.

20 David Harvey, *Justice, Nature, and the Geography of Difference*, 320.

21 Ibid., 294.

22 Ann Anagnost, *National Past-Times*, 31–32.

23 See Arif Dirlik, "The Postcolonial Aura," for a critique.

24 Russell Ferguson, "Introduction: Invisible Center," 10.

25 See bell hooks, *Yearning*, 149.

26 See Louisa Schein, "Gender and Internal Orientalism." See also Arif Dirlik, "Chinese History and the Question of Orientalism."

27 Schein, "Gender and Internal Orientalism," 73. The quote is taken from Fei Xiaotong's introductory comments to a 1982 collection of minority poetry.

28 See Dipesh Chakrabarty, "Postcoloniality and the Artifice of History," for a discussion of how the search for the origins of a discourse often ends up turning categories such as "Third World" and "West" into hyperreal abstractions.

29 For similar approaches, see Anagnost, *National Past-Times;* Tani Barlow's no-
    tion of the "localization of the sign" in "*Zhishifenzi* (Chinese Intellectuals) and
    Power"; and Lydia Liu, "Translingual Practice."

30 Arif Dirlik, "Postsocialism? Reflections on Socialism with Chinese Character-
    istics," 379–380.

31 See, for example, Vivian Shue, *The Reach of the State;* Richard Madsen, *Morality and
    Power in a Chinese Village;* and Anita Chan, Richard Madsen, and Jonathan Unger,
    Chen Village: The Recent History of a Peasant Community in Mao's China.

32 My approach here owes much to Helen Siu's important and, to my mind, under-
    appreciated study, *Agents and Victims in South China: Accomplices in Rural Revolution.*
    See also her essay, "Recycling Rituals: Politics and Popular Culture in Contem-
    porary Rural China."

33 James Clifford, *The Predicament of Culture,* 5.

epilogue

1   Rey Chow, "Pedagogy, Trust, Chinese Intellectuals in the 1990s: Fragments of
    a Post-Catastrophic Discourse."

2   Ibid., 203.

3   Chow also pursues these issues in her essay, "Violence in the Other Country."

4   Jing Wang, *High Culture Fever,* 196–198.

5   See Zha Jianying, *China Pop,* and Orville Schell, "China: The End of an Era."

6   Michael Dutton, *Streetlife China,* 273–274.

7   Andrew Ross, *Universal Abandon,* cited in Ellen E. Berry, "Introduction: Post-
    communism and the Body Politic," 1.

8   Fernando Coronil, *The Magical State,* 393.

9   Dali L. Yang, *Beyond Beijing,* 73.

10 Ibid.

bibliography

Abrams, Philip. "Notes on the Difficulty of Studying the State." *Journal of Historical Sociology* 1:1 (1988): 58–89.

Alloula, Malek. *The Colonial Harem.* Minneapolis: University of Minnesota Press, 1986.

Althusser, Louis. "Ideology and Ideological State Apparatuses (Notes toward an Investigation)." In *Lenin and Philosophy and Other Essays,* 121–173. New York: Monthly Review Press, 1977.

Anagnost, Ann. "Socialist Ethics and the Legal System." In *Popular Protest and Political Culture in Modern China: Learning from 1989,* ed. Jeffrey N. Wasserstrom and Elizabeth J. Perry, 177–205. Boulder, CO: Westview Press, 1992.

———. "The Politics of Ritual Displacement." In *Asian Visions of Authority: Religion and the Modern States of East and Southeast Asia,* ed. Charles F. Keyes, Laurel Kendall, and Helen Hardacre, 221–254. Honolulu: University of Hawaii Press, 1994.

———. *National Past-Times: Narrative, Representation, and Power in Modern China.* Durham, NC: Duke University Press, 1996.

Anderson, Benedict. *Imagined Communities.* London: Verso, 1983.

Appadurai, Arjun. "Theory in Anthropology: Center and Periphery." *Comparative Studies in Society and History* 28:2 (1986): 356–361.

———. "Putting Hierarchy in Its Place." *Cultural Anthropology* 3:1 (1988): 36–49.

———. "Disjuncture and Difference in the Global Cultural Economy." *Public Culture* 2:2 (1990): 1–24.

———. "Global Ethnoscapes: Notes and Queries for a Transnational Anthropology." In *Recapturing Anthropology,* ed. Richard Fox, 191–210. Santa Fe, NM: School of American Research, 1991.

———. *Modernity at Large.* Minneapolis: University of Minnesota Press, 1996.

Arkush, David R. *Fei Xiaotong and Sociology in Revolutionary China.* Cambridge, MA: Harvard East Asian Monographs, Harvard University Press, 1981.

Asad, Talal, ed. *Anthropology and the Colonial Encounter.* London: Ithaca Press, 1973.

———. *Genealogies of Religion: Discipline and Reasons of Power in Christianity and Islam.* Baltimore: Johns Hopkins University Press, 1993.

Banks, Marcus. *Ethnicity: Anthropological Constructions*. London: Routledge, 1996.

Barkan, Elazar, and Ronald Bush, eds. *Prehistories of the Future: The Primitivist Project of Modernism*. Stanford: Stanford University Press, 1995.

Barlow, Tani. "Zhishifenzi (Chinese Intellectuals) and Power." *Dialectical Anthropology* 16:3–4 (1991): 209–232.

———. "Theorizing Women: Funu, Guojia, Jiating (Chinese Women, Chinese State, Chinese Family)." *Genders* 10 (1991): 132–160.

———. "Colonialism's Career in Postwar China Studies." *positions: east asia cultures critique* 1:1 (1993): 224–267.

Barthes, Roland. *Camera Lucida: Reflections on Photography*. Trans. Richard Howard. New York: Farrar, Straus, and Giroux, 1981.

Beijing Foreign Language Press. *Concerning the Situation in Laos*. Beijing: Foreign Language Press, 1959.

Benjamin, Walter. "Theses on the Philosophy of History." In *Illuminations*. Trans. Harry Zohn, 253–264. New York: Schocken Books, 1969.

———. "The Work of Art in the Age of Mechanical Reproduction." In *Illuminations*, 217–251. New York: Schocken, 1969.

———. "N [Re the Theory of Knowledge, Theory of Progress]." In *Benjamin: Philosophy, History, Aesthetics*, ed. Gary Smith, 43–83. The University of Chicago Press, 1983.

Bentley, G. Carter. "Ethnicity and Practice." *Comparative Studies in Society and History* 29:1 (1987): 24–55.

Berberoglu, Berch, ed. *The National Question: Nationalism, Ethnic Conflict, and Self-Determination in the 20th Century*. Philadelphia: Temple University Press, 1995.

Berry, Chris, ed. *Perspectives on Chinese Cinema*. London: British Film Institute Publishing, 1991.

Berry, Ellen E. "Introduction: Post-communism and the Body Politic." *Genders* 22 (1995): 1–14.

Bhabha, Homi. "The Other Question: Difference, Discrimination and the Discourse of Colonialism." In *The Politics of Theory*, ed. Francis Barker, 148–172. Colchester: University of Essex, 1983.

———. "Of Mimicry and Man: The Ambivalence of Colonial Discourse." *October* 28 (1984): 125–133.

———. "DissemiNation: Time, Narrative, and the Margins of the Modern Nation." In *Nation and Narration*, ed. Homi Bhabha, 291–322. New York: Routledge, 1990.

Blaut, James. *The National Question: Decolonizing the Theory of Nationalism*. London: Zed Books, 1987.

Boggs, Carl. *Intellectuals and the Crisis of Modernity*. Albany: State University of New York Press, 1993.

Bolton, Richard, ed. *The Contest of Meaning: Critical Histories of Photography*. London: MIT Press, 1989.

Bové, Paul. *Intellectuals in Power: A Genealogy of Critical Humanism*. New York: Columbia University Press, 1986.

Braidotti, Rosi. *Nomadic Subjects: Embodiment and Sexual Difference in Contemporary Feminist Theory*. New York: Columbia University Press, 1994.

Bremmer, Ian, and Ray Taras. *Nation and Politics in the Soviet Successor States*. New York: Cambridge University Press, 1993.

Brown, Melissa J., ed. *Negotiating Ethnicities in China and Taiwan*. Berkeley: China Research Monograph, Institute of East Asian Studies, University of California, 1996.

Bulag, Uradyn E. *Nationalism and Hybridity in Mongolia*. Oxford: Clarendon Press, 1998.

Burke, Helen M. "The Rhetoric and Politics of Marginality: The Subject of Phillis Wheatley." *Tulsa Studies in Women's Literature* 10 (1991): 31–45.

Cadava, Eduardo. *Words of Light: Theses on the Photography of History*. Princeton, NJ: Princeton University Press, 1997.

Cai Fuyou. "Analysis and Appraisal of Stalin's Definition of a 'Nation.'" *Social Sciences in China* 8:1 (1987): 209–221.

Calhoun, Craig. "Tiananmen, Television and the Public Sphere: Internationalization of Culture and the Beijing Spring of 1989." *Public Culture* 2:1 (1989): 54–71.

———. "Civil Society and Public Sphere." *Public Culture* 5:2 (1993): 267–280.

Callinicos, Alex. *The Revenge of History: Marxism and the East European Revolutions*. State College: Pennsylvania State University Press, 1991.

Campbell, Margaret. *From the Hands of the Hills*. Hong Kong: Media Transasia, 1978.

Cao Zhipeng. *Chashan Yao de chengnian li* (A Chashan Yao rite of passage). Master's thesis, Anthropology Department, Taiwan National University, 1991.

Carnoy, Martin. *The State and Political Theory*. Princeton, NJ: Princeton University Press, 1984.

Chakrabarty, Dipesh. "Postcoloniality and the Artifice of History: Who Speaks for 'Indian' Pasts?" *Representations* 37 (winter 1992): 1–26.

Champagne, John. *The Ethics of Marginality: A New Approach to Gay Studies*. Minneapolis: University of Minnesota Press, 1995.

Chan, Anita, Richard Madsen, and Jonathan Unger, eds. *Chen Village: The Recent History of a Peasant Community in Mao's China*. Berkeley: University of California Press, 1984.

Chao, Emily. "Hegemony, Agency, and Re-presenting the Past: The Invention of Dongba Culture among the Naxi of Southwest China." In *Negotiating Ethnicities in China and Taiwan*, ed. Melissa Brown, 208–239. Berkeley: China Research Monograph, Institute of East Asian Studies, University of California, 1996.

Chao Wei-yang. *Evolutionary Theory and Cultural Diversity: A Study of the Ethnology of China's National Minorities*. Unpublished dissertation, Stanford University, 1986.

Chatterjee, Partha. *The Nation and Its Fragments: Colonial and Postcolonial Histories.* Princeton, NJ: Princeton University Press, 1993.

Chaturabhand, Preecha. *People of the Hills.* Bangkok: Editions Duang Kamol, 1980.

Chen, Han. "A Reflection on the Chinese Traditional Culture: A Summary of the First International Conference on Chinese Culture." *Guangming Ribao.* 17 February 1986.

Chen Yongling. "Applied Ethnology and the Implementation of Policy toward Ethnic Minorities in China." Paper presented to the Chinese Studies Program, University of Washington, Seattle, 27 April 1989.

Chen Yongling and Wang Xiaoyi. "Ershi shiji qiandide Zhongguo minzuxue" (Chinese ethnology in the early twentieth century). In *Minzuxue Yanjiu* (Ethnological research), ed. Chinese Ethnology Society, 1:261–299. Beijing: Nationalities Press, 1981.

Cheng Hirata, Lucie. "Leadership in China's Minority Nationalities Autonomous Regions: Continuity and Change." In *Intergroup Relations: Asia Scene*, ed. Tai S. Kung, 39–49. Buffalo: International Studies, State University of New York, 1979.

Cheung, Siu-woo. "Millenarianism, Christian Movements, and Ethnic Change among the Miao of Southwest China." In *Cultural Encounters on China's Ethnic Frontiers*, ed. Stevan Harrell, 217–247. Seattle: University of Washington Press, 1994.

———. "Representation and Negotiation of Ge Identities in Southeast Guizhou." In *Negotiating Ethnicities in China and Taiwan*, ed. Melissa Brown, 240–273. Berkeley: China Research Monograph, Institute of East Asian Studies, University of California, 1996.

Chow, Rey. *Woman and Chinese Modernity: The Politics of Reading between East and West.* Minneapolis: University of Minnesota Press, 1991.

———. "Pedagogy, Trust, Chinese Intellectuals in the 1990s: Fragments of a Post-Catastrophic Discourse." *Dialectical Anthropology* 16:3–4 (1991): 191–207.

———. "Violence in the Other Country: China as Crisis, Spectacle, and Woman." In *Third World Women and the Politics of Feminism*, ed. Chandre Talpade, Lourdes Torres, and Ann Russo, 81–100. Bloomington: Indiana University Press, 1991.

Chow Tse-tsung. *The May Fourth Movement: Intellectual Revolution in Modern China.* Cambridge, MA: Harvard University Press, 1960.

Clark, Paul. "Ethnic Minorities in Chinese Films: Cinema and the Exotic." *East-West Film Journal* 1:2 (1987): 15–31.

———. *Chinese Cinema: Culture and Politics since 1949.* New York: Cambridge University Press, 1987.

Clifford, James. *The Predicament of Culture: Twentieth-Century Ethnography, Literature, and Art.* Cambridge, MA: Harvard University Press, 1988.

———. "Spatial Practices: Fieldwork, Travel, and the Disciplining of Anthropology." In *Anthropological Locations: Boundaries and Grounds of a Field Science*, ed. Akhil

Gupta and James Ferguson, 185–222. Berkeley: University of California Press, 1997.

Cohen, Abner. "Introduction: The Lesson of Ethnicity." In *Urban Ethnicity*, ed. Abner Cohen, ix–xxiv. London: Tavistock Publications, 1974.

——, ed. *Urban Ethnicity*. London: Tavistock Publications, 1974.

Cohen, Jean, and Andrew Arato. *The Political Theory of Civil Society*. Cambridge, MA: MIT Press, 1992.

Cohn, Bernard, and Nicholas Dirks. "Beyond the Fringe: The Nation State, Colonialism, and the Technologies of Power." *Journal of Historical Sociology* 1:2 (1988): 224–229.

Comaroff, Jean, and John Comaroff, eds. *Ethnography and the Historical Imagination*. Boulder, CO: Westview Press, 1992.

——. *Modernity and Its Malcontents: Ritual and Power in Postcolonial Africa*. Chicago: University of Chicago Press, 1993.

Comaroff, John. "Of Totemism and Ethnicity." In *Ethnography and the Historical Imagination*, ed. Jean Comaroff and John Comaroff, 49–68. Boulder, CO: Westview Press, 1992.

——. "Ethnicity, Nationalism, and the Politics of Difference in an Age of Revolution." In *The Politics of Difference: Ethnic Premises in a World of Power*, ed. Edwin N. Wilmsen and Patrick McAllister, 162–184. Chicago: University of Chicago Press, 1996.

Condominas, Georges. "The First French Publications on the Yao." In *The Yao of South China: Recent International Studies*, ed. Jacques Lemoine and Chao Chien, 577–590. Paris: Pangu, Editions de l'AFEY, 1991.

Connolly, William E. *Politics and Ambiguity*. Madison: University of Wisconsin Press, 1987.

——. *Identity/Difference: Democratic Negotiations of Political Paradox*. Ithaca, NY: Cornell University Press, 1991.

Connor, Walker. *The National Question in Marxist-Leninist Theory and Strategy*. Princeton, NJ: Princeton University Press, 1984.

Cooper, Gene. "An Interview with Chinese Anthropologists." *Current Anthropology* 14:4 (1973): 480–482.

Coronil, Fernando. *The Magical State: Nature, Money, and Modernity in Venezuela*. Chicago: University of Chicago Press, 1997.

Crewe, Jonathan. "Defining Marginality." *Tulsa Studies in Women's Literature* 10 (1991): 121–130.

Crossley, Pamela Kyle. "Thinking about Ethnicity in Early Modern China." *Late Imperial China* 11:1 (1990): 1–34.

Cumings, Bruce. *Parallax Visions: Making Sense of American–East Asian Relations at the End of the Century*. Durham, NC: Duke University Press, 1999.

Cushman, Richard. *Rebel Haunts and Lotus Huts: Problems in the Ethnohistory of the Yao.* Ph.D. diss., Cornell University, 1970.

———. "The Wayward Peoples: Taoism, Ethnic Identity and Ethnohistory among the Yao on the South China Frontier." Paper presented at the Workshop on Southwest China, Harvard University, 14 July–22 August 1975.

de Certeau, Michel. *The Practice of Everyday Life.* Trans. Steven F. Rendall. Berkeley: University of California Press, 1984.

———. *The Writing of History.* Trans. Tom Conley. New York: Columbia University Press, 1988.

Desai, Gaurav. "The Invention of Invention." *Cultural Critique* (spring 1993): 119–142.

Diamond, Norma. "Defining the Miao: Ming, Qing, and Contemporary Views." In *Cultural Encounters on China's Ethnic Frontiers,* ed. Stevan Harrell, 92–116. Seattle: University of Washington Press, 1994.

Dirks, Nicholas. "History as a Sign of the Modern." *Public Culture* 2:2 (1990): 25–32.

———. "Ritual and Resistance: Subversion as a Social Fact." In *Contesting Power: Resistance and Everyday Social Relations in South Asia,* ed. Douglas Haynes and Gyan Prakash, 213–238. Berkeley: University of California Press, 1991.

———. *Colonialism and Culture.* Ann Arbor: University of Michigan Press, 1992.

———. *In Near Ruins: Cultural Theory at the End of the Century,* ed. Nicholas Dirks. Minneapolis: University of Minnesota Press, 1998.

Dirlik, Arif. *Revolution and History: The Origins of Marxist Historiography in China, 1919–1937.* Berkeley: University of California Press, 1978.

———. "Spiritual Solutions to Material Problems: The 'Socialist Ethics and Courtesy Month' in China." *South Atlantic Quarterly* 81:4 (1982): 359–375.

———. "Postsocialism? Reflections on 'Socialism with Chinese Characteristics.' " In *Marxism and the Chinese Experience: Issues in Contemporary Chinese Socialism,* ed. Arif Dirlik and Maurice Meisner, 362–384. New York: M.E. Sharpe, 1989.

———. *Anarchism in the Chinese Revolution.* Berkeley: University of California Press, 1991.

———. "The Postcolonial Aura: Third World Criticism in the Age of Global Capitalism." *Critical Inquiry* 20:2 (Winter 1994): 328–356.

———. *After the Revolution: Waking to Global Capitalism.* Hanover, NH: University Press of New England, 1994.

———. "Chinese History and the Question of Orientalism." *History and Theory* 35 (1996): 96–118.

Dirlik, Arif, and Maurice Meisner. "Politics, Scholarship, and Chinese Socialism." In *Marxism and the Chinese Experience,* ed. Arif Dirlik and Maurice Meisner, 3–26. New York: M.E. Sharpe, 1989.

———, eds. *Marxism and the Chinese Experience.* New York: M.E. Sharpe, 1989.

Dragadze, Tamara. "The Place of 'Ethnos' Theory in Soviet Anthropology." In *Soviet and Western Anthropology,* ed. Ernest Gellner, 161–170. London: Duckworth, 1980.

Dreyer, June. *China's Forty Millions: Minority Nationalities and National Integration in the People's Republic of China.* Cambridge, MA: Harvard University Press, 1976.

———. "Traditional Minorities Elites and the CRP Elite Engaged in Minorities Nationalities Work." In *Elites in the People's Republic of China,* ed. Robert A. Scalapino, 416–450. Seattle: University of Washington Press, 1972.

Dreyfus, Hubert L., and Paul Rabinow. *Michel Foucault: Beyond Structuralism and Hermeneutics.* Chicago: University of Chicago Press, 1983.

Duara, Prasenjit. "Knowledge and Power in the Discourse of Modernity: The Campaigns against Popular Religion in the Early Twentieth Century." *Journal of Asian Studies* 50:1 (1991): 67–83.

———. "Review of *Muslim Chinese: Ethnic Nationalism in the People's Republic* by Dru C. Gladney." *Journal of Asian Studies* 51:3 (1992): 644–645.

———. "Provincial Narratives of the Nation: Centralism and Federalism in Republican China." In *Cultural Nationalism in East Asia: Representation and Identity,* ed. Harumi Befu, 9–35. Berkeley: Institute of East Asian Studies, University of California, 1993.

———. "De-Constructing the Chinese Nation." *Australian Journal of Chinese Affairs* 30 (July 1993): 1–29.

———. "Bifurcating Linear History: Nation and Histories in China and India." *positions: east asia cultures critique* 1:3 (1993): 779–804.

———. *Rescuing History from the Nation: Questioning Narratives of Modern China.* Chicago: University of Chicago Press, 1995.

Dutton, Michael. *Streetlife China.* Cambridge: Cambridge University Press, 1998.

Elliot, Mark. "Bannerman and Townsman: Ethnic Tension in Nineteenth Century Jiangnan." *Late Imperial China* 11 (1990): 36–74.

Fabian, Johannes. *Time and the Other: How Anthropology Makes Its Object.* New York: Columbia University Press, 1983.

Fan, Honggui. "Zai Dayaoshan jinxing weixing yanjiu de tihui" (Reflections on carrying out research in the Dayaoshan). *Guangxi minzu xueyuan xuebao* (Journal of the Guanjxi Nationalities Institute) 1 (1983): 1–12.

Fei Xiaotong. *Peasant Life in China.* New York: Dutton, 1939.

———. "Zhishi fenzi de zaochun tianqi" (An early spring for intellectuals). *Renmin ribao* (People's Daily) 24 March 1957.

———. "Xiang renmin fa zui" (I admit my crimes to the people). *Renmin ribao* (People's Daily) 13 July 1957.

———. *Towards a People's Anthropology.* Beijing: New World Press, 1981.

———. "Minzu shehuixue diaoche de chengshi" (My attempts at ethnic sociological research). *Zhongyang minzu xueyuan xuebao,* no. 1 (1982): 1–10.

———. *Congshi shehuixue wushinian* (Fifty years of sociological research). Tianjin: Tianjin renmin chubanshe. 1983.

————. Preface to *Pancun Yaozu* (The Yao of Pan Village). By Hu Qiwang and Fan Honggui. Beijing: Minzu Chubanshe, 1983.

Ferguson, Russell. "Introduction: Invisible Center." In *Out There: Marginalization and Contemporary Cultures*, ed. Russell Ferguson, Martha Gever, Trinh T. Minh-ha, and Cornell West, 9–14. New York: New York Museum of Contemporary Art and MIT Press, 1990.

Feuchtwang, Stephan, and Wang Ming-ming. "The Politics of Culture or a Contest of Histories: Representations of Chinese Popular Religion." *Dialectical Anthropology* 16:3–4 (1991): 251–272.

Feuerwerker, Albert, ed. *History in Communist China*. Cambridge, MA: MIT Press, 1968.

————. "China's History in Marxian Dress." In *History in Communist China*, ed. Albert Feuerwerker. Cambridge, MA: MIT Press, 1968.

Fitzgerald, John. *Awakening China: Politics, Culture, and Class in the Nationalist Revolution*. Stanford: Stanford University Press, 1996.

Fortune, Reo. "Yao Society: A Study of a Group of Primitives in China." *Lingnan Science Journal* (Canton) 18 (1939): 3–4.

Foster, Robert J. "Making National Cultures in the Global Ecumene." *Annual Review of Anthropology* 20 (1991): 235–260.

Foucault, Michel. *The History of Sexuality*. Vol. 1: An Introduction. New York: Vintage Books, 1978.

————. *Discipline and Punish: The Birth of the Prison*. New York: Vintage Books, 1979.

————. *Power/Knowledge*. New York: Pantheon Books, 1980.

————. "Nietzsche, Genealogy, History." In *Language, Counter-memory, Practice*, ed. D. B. Bouchard, 139–164. Ithaca, NY: Cornell University Press, 1977.

————. "Intellectuals and Power: A Conversation between Michel Foucault and Gilles Deleuze." In *Language, Counter-memory, Practice*, ed. D. B. Bouchard, 205–217. Ithaca, NY: Cornell University Press, 1977.

Francis, E. K. *Interethnic Relations: An Essay in Sociological Theory*. New York: Elsevier, 1976.

Frankenberg, Ruth, and Lati Mani. "Crosscurrents, Crosstalk: Race, 'Postcoloniality' and The Politics of Location." *Cultural Studies* 7 (May 1993): 292–310.

Fried, Morton H. "Tribe to State or State to Tribe in Ancient China?" In *The Origins of Chinese Civilization*, ed. David Keightley, 467–493. Berkeley: University of California Press, 1983.

Gang Yang. "Wenhua Zhongguo yu xiangtu Zhongguo: houlengzhan shidai de Zhongguo qianjing jiqi wenhua" (Cultural China and rural China: China's prospects and culture in the post cold war era). Paper presented at the conference "Cultural China: Interpretations and Communications," Harvard University, 3 September 1992.

Gellner, Ernest. *Nations and Nationalism.* Ithaca, NY: Cornell University Press, 1983.

————, ed. *Soviet and Western Anthropology.* London: Duckworth, 1980.

Gil, José. *The Metamorphoses of the Body.* Trans. Stephen Muecke. Minneapolis: University of Minnesota Press, 1998.

Gladney, Dru. *Muslim Chinese: Ethnic Nationalism in the People's Republic.* Cambridge, MA: Harvard University Press, 1991.

————. "Representing Nationality in China: Refiguring Majority/Minority Identities." *Journal of Asian Studies* 53:1 (1994): 92–123.

————. "Tian Zhuangzhuang, the Fifth Generation, and Minorities Film in China." *Public Culture* 8:1 (1995): 161–170.

Gong Zhebing. "Zhongguo Pan Yao de Qianjiadong yundong" (The Qianjiadong movement among China's Pan Yao). Unpublished manuscript.

Goodman, David S. G. "State-Society Relations in Reform Shanxi: Elite Interdependence and Accommodation." *Provincial China: Research, News, and Analysis* 6 (April 1999): 37–65.

Goodman, David S. G., and Gerald Segal. *China Deconstructs: Politics, Trade, and Regionalism.* London: Routledge, 1994.

Grant, Bruce. *In the Soviet House of Culture: A Century of Perestroikas.* Princeton, NJ: Princeton University Press, 1995.

Greenhalgh, Susan, and Liali Li. "Engendering Reproductive Policy and Practice in Peasant China: For a Feminist Demography of Reproduction." *Signs* 20:31 (1995): 601–641.

Gregory, Derek. "Interventions in the Historical Geography of Modernity: Social Theory, Spatiality and the Politics of Representation." In *Place/Culture/Representation,* ed. James Duncan and David Ley, 272–313. New York: Routledge, 1993.

Guangxi Editorial Group. *Yaozu jianshi* (A concise history of the Yao). Nanning: Guangxi Minzu Chubanshe, 1983.

Guldin, Greg. *The Saga of Anthropology in China: From Malinowski to Moscow to Mao.* New York: M.E. Sharpe, 1994.

Gunn, Geoffrey C. *Rebellion in Laos: Peasants and Politics in a Colonial Backwater.* Boulder, CO: Westview Press, 1990.

Gupta, Akhil. "Blurred Boundaries: The Discourse of Corruption, the Culture of Politics, and the Imagined State." *American Ethnologist* 22:2 (1995): 375–402.

————. *Postcolonial Developments: Agriculture in the Making of Modern India.* Durham, NC: Duke University Press, 1998.

Gupta, Akhil, and James Ferguson. "Beyond Culture: Space, Identity, and the Politics of Difference." *Cultural Anthropology* 7:1 (1992): 6–23.

————. "Discipline and Practice: 'The Field' as Site, Method, and Location in Anthropology." In *Anthropological Locations: Boundaries and Grounds of a Field Science,* ed. Akhil Gupta and James Ferguson, 1–46. Berkeley: University of California Press, 1997.

Hale, Charles R. *Resistance and Contradiction: Miskitu Indians and the Nicaragua State, 1984–1987.* Stanford: Stanford University Press, 1994.

Hamilton-Merrit, Jane. *Tragic Mountains: The Hmong, the Americans, and the Secret War for Laos, 1942–1992.* Bloomington: Indiana University Press, 1993.

Handler, Richard. *Nationalism and the Politics of Culture in Quebec.* Madison: University of Wisconsin Press, 1988.

Haraway, Donna. *Simians, Cyborgs, and Women: The Reinvention of Nature.* New York: Routledge, 1991.

———. "The Promises of Monsters: A Regenerative Politics for Inappropriate/d Others." In *Cultural Studies,* ed. Lawrence Grossberg, Cary Nelson, and Paula Treichler, 295–337. New York: Routledge, 1992.

Harrell, Stevan. "Ethnicity, Local Interests, and the State: Yi Communities in Southwest China." *Comparative Studies in Society and History* 32:2 (1990): 515–548.

———, ed. *Cultural Encounters on China's Ethnic Frontiers.* Seattle: University of Washington Press, 1994.

———. "Introduction: Civilizing Projects and Reactions to Them." In *Cultural Encounters on China's Ethnic Frontiers,* ed. Stevan Harrell, 3–36. Seattle: University of Washington Press, 1994.

———. "The History of the History of the Yi." In *Cultural Encounters on China's Ethnic Frontiers,* ed. Stevan Harrell, 63–91. Seattle: University of Washington Press, 1994.

Harris, Marvin. *The Rise of Anthropological Theory: A History of Theories of Culture.* New York: Columbia University Press, 1968.

Harrison, Faye, ed. *Decolonizing Anthropology: Moving Further toward an Anthropology of Liberation.* Washington, DC: American Anthropological Association, 1991.

Harvey, David. *The Condition of Postmodernity.* Cambridge, MA: Basil Blackwell, 1990.

———. *Justice, Nature, and the Geography of Difference.* Cambridge, MA: Basil Blackwell, 1996.

Hawkes, David. "The Quest for the Goddess." In *Studies in Chinese Literary Genres,* ed. Cyril Birch, 42–68. Berkeley: University of California Press, 1974.

Heberer, Thomas. *China and Its National Minorities: Autonomy or Assimilation?* Armonk, NY: M.E. Sharpe, 1989.

Hendrischke, Hans. "Guangxi: Towards Southwest China and Southeast Asia." In *China's Provinces in Reform: Class, Community, and Political Culture,* ed. David S. G. Goodman, 21–52. London: Routledge, 1997.

Herman, John. "Empire in the Southwest: Early Qing Reforms to the Native Chieftain System." *Journal of Asian Studies* 56:1 (1997): 47–74.

Hershatter, Gail. "The Subaltern Talks Back: Reflections on Subaltern Theory and Chinese History." *positions: east asia cultures critique* 1:1 (1993): 103–130.

hooks, bell. *Yearning: Race, Gender, and Cultural Politics.* Boston, MA: South End Press, 1990.

Hu Decai and Su Shengxing. *Da Yao shan fengqing* (Flirtatious expressions of the Yao Mountains). Nanning: Guangxi Minzu Chubanshe, 1990.

Hu Qiwang. "Yaozu chuantong wenhua yu xiandaihua de jige wenti" (Problems in the study of Yao traditional culture and modernization). Paper presented at Yao Studies Research Conference, Chenzhou, Hunan, 1988.

Hu Qiwang and Fan Honggui. *Pancun Yaozu* (The Yao of Pan Village). Beijing: Minzu Chubanshe, 1983.

Huang Yu. "A Preliminary Study of King Ping's Charter." In *The Yao of South China: Recent International Studies*, ed. Jacques Lemoine and Chao Chien, 89–124. Paris: Pangu, Editions de l'AFEY, 1991.

Huang Yu and Huang Fangping. *Yaozu* (The Yao nationality). Nanning: Minzu Chubanshe, 1990.

Huang Yu and Li Weixin. *Guangxi Yaozu shehui lishi diaocha* (An investigation of the social history of the Guangxi Yao). Nanning: Guangxi Minzu Chubanshe, 1983.

Hunan Editorial Group. *Yaozu "guoshanbang" xuanbian* (Collected documents from the Yao nationalities' "King Ping's Charter"). Changsha: Hunan People's Publishing House, 1984.

Hung Chang-tai. *Going to the People: Chinese Intellectuals and Folk Literature, 1918–1937*. Cambridge, MA: Harvard University Press, 1985.

Ivy, Marilyn. "Critical Texts, Mass Artifacts: The Consumption of Knowledge in Postmodern Japan." In *Postmodernism and Japan*, ed. Masao Miyoshi and H. D. Harootunian, 419–444. Durham, NC: Duke University Press, 1989.

———. *Discourses of the Vanishing: Modernity, Phantasm, Japan*. Chicago: University of Chicago Press, 1995.

———. "Mourning the Japanese Thing." In *In Near Ruins: Cultural Theory at the End of the Century*, ed. Nicholas B. Dirks, 93–118. Minneapolis: University of Minnesota Press, 1998.

Jao Tsung-I. "The She Settlements in the Han River Basin, Guangdong." In *Historical Archaeological and Linguistic Studies on Southern China, South-East Asia, and the Hong Kong Region*, ed. F. S. Drake, 101–109. Hong Kong: Hong Kong University Press, 1961.

Jessop, Bob. *State Theory: Putting Capitalist States in Their Place*. State College: Pennsylvania State University Press, 1990.

Ji Hongzheng. "Wenhua 'xungen' yu dangdai wenxue" (Searching for cultural roots in contemporary literature). *Wenyi yanjiu* 2 (1989): 69–74.

Jiang Yingliang. "Xinan bianjiang minzu luncong" (A discussion on the minorities of the southwestern frontier). Guangzhou: Guangzhou Publishing House, 1948.

Jinxiu County Government. *Jinxiu Yaozu zizhixian gaikuang* (A survey of the Jinxiu Yao Autonomous County). Nanning: Guangxi Minzu Chubanshe, 1984.

Jinxiu Editorial Group. *Yaozu jianshi* (A concise history of the Yao). Nanning: Guangxi Minzu Chubanshe, 1983.

Kandre, Peter. "Aspects of Wealth Accumulation, Ancestor Worship and Household Stability among the Iu-Mien Yao." In *Felicitation Volumes of Southeast Asian Studies Presented to His Highness Prince Dhaninivat Kromamun Bidyalabh Bridhyakorn*, 129–148. Bangkok: The Siam Society, 1965.

———. "Autonomy and Integration of Social Systems: The Iu Mien ('Yao' or 'Man') Mountain Population and Their Neighbors." In *Southeast Asian Tribes, Minorities, and Nations*, ed. Peter Kunstadter, 583–638. Princeton, NJ: Princeton University Press, 1976.

Kandre, Peter, and Lej Tsan Kuej. "Yao (Iu Mien) Supernaturalism, Language and Ethnicity." In *Changing Identities in Modern Southeast Asia*, ed. David J. Banks, 173–197. The Hague: Mouton Publishers, 1976.

Kaplan, Caren. *Questions of Travel: Postmodern Discourses of Displacement*. Durham, NC: Duke University Press, 1996.

Keith, Michael, and Steve Pile, eds. *Place and the Politics of Identity*. New York: Routledge, 1993.

Keyes, Charles F. "Towards a New Formulation of the Concept of Ethnic Group." *Ethnicity* 3 (1976): 202–213.

———. "The Dialectics of Ethnic Change." In *Ethnic Change*, ed. Charles F. Keyes, 4–30. Seattle: University of Washington Press, 1981.

Khan, Almaz. "Who Are the Mongols? State, Ethnicity, and the Politics of Representation in the PRC." In *Negotiating Ethnicities in China and Taiwan*, ed. Melissa Brown, 125–159. Berkeley: China Research Monograph, Institute of East Asian Studies, University of California, 1996.

Krauss, Richard Curt. *Class Conflict in Chinese Socialism*. New York: Columbia University Press, 1981.

Kruger, Barbara, and Phil Mariani. Introduction to *Remaking History*, ed. Barbara Kruger and Phil Mariani, ix–xi. Dia Art Foundation Discussions in Contemporary Culture, no. 4. Seattle: Bay Press, 1989.

Kuhn, Philip A. *Rebellion and Its Enemies in Late Imperial China: Militarization and Social Structure 1796–1864*. 1970. Cambridge, MA: Harvard University Press, 1980.

Laclau, Ernesto. *New Reflections on the Revolution of Our Time*. New York: Verso, 1990.

Lagerwey, John. *Taoist Ritual and Chinese Society and History*. New York: Macmillan, 1987.

Lan Kexuan et al. *The Yao Nationality*. Beijing: Renmin Chubanshe, 1990.

Landy, Marcia. *Film, Politics, and Gramsci*. Minneapolis: University of Minnesota Press, 1994.

———. "Gramsci beyond Gramsci: The Writings of Toni Negri." *boundary 2* 21:2 (1994): 63–97.

Lary, Diana. *Region and Nation: The Kwangsi Clique in Chinese Politics, 1925–1937*. New York: Cambridge University Press, 1974.

Lavie, Smadar, and Ted Swedenburg. "Introduction: Displacement, Diaspora, and Geographies of Identity." In *Displacement, Diaspora, and Geographies of Identity*, ed. Smadar Lavie and Ted Swedenburg, 1–26. Durham, NC: Duke University Press, 1996.

————, eds. *Displacement, Diaspora, and Geographies of Identity*. Durham, NC: Duke University Press, 1996.

Lee, C. B. "Local History, Social Organization, and Warfare." *Lingnan Science Journal* (Canton) 18 (1939): 357–370.

Lee, K. K. "The Yao Family in Birth, Marriage, and Death." *Lingnan Science Journal* (Canton) 18 (1939): 371–382.

Lemoine, Jacques. *Yao Ceremonial Paintings*. Thailand: White Lotus Co., 1982.

————. "Yao Religion and Society." In *Highlanders of Thailand*, ed. John McKinnon and Wanat Bhruksasri, 194–211. Kuala Lumpur, Malaysia: Oxford University Press, 1983.

————. "Yao Culture and Some Other Related Problems." In *The Yao of South China: Recent International Studies*, ed. Jacques Lemoine and Chao Chien, 591–612. Paris: Pangu, Editions de l'AFEY, 1991.

Lemoine, Jacques, and Chiao Chien, eds. *The Yao of South China: Recent International Studies*. Paris: Pangu, Editions de l'AFEY, 1991.

Li Wai-yee. *Enchantment and Disenchantment: Love and Illusion in Chinese Literature*. Princeton, NJ: Princeton University Press, 1993.

Li Xiaowen. "Yaozu chuantong daode yu jingshen wenming jianshe" (Traditional Yao morality and the construction of spiritual civilization). Unpublished manuscript.

Lin, K. Y. "The Economics of Yao Life." *Lingnan Science Journal* (Canton) 18 (1939): 409–423.

Lin Yaohua. "Zhongguo xinan diqude minzu shibie" (Ethnic identification in the region of southwest China). In *Yunnan shaoshu minzu shehui lishi diaocha ziliao huibian* (Collection of materials from historical and sociological investigations of minority nationalities in Yunnan). Kunming: Yunnan People's Publishing House, 1987.

————. "New China's Ethnology: Research and Prospects." In *Anthropology in China: Defining the Discipline*, ed. Greg Guldin, 141–161. Arnmonk, NY: M.E. Sharpe, 1990.

Litzinger, Ralph. "Returning the 'Traditional' to a Socialist-Modern Landscape." Paper presented at the American Anthropological meetings, San Francisco, 2–6 December 1992.

————. "Making Histories: Contending Conceptions of the Yao Past." In *Cultural En-*

counters on China's Ethnic Frontiers, ed. Stevan Harrell, 117–139. Seattle: University of Washington Press, 1994.

———. "Memory Work: Reconstituting the Ethnic in Post-Mao China." Cultural Anthropology 13:2 (1998): 224–255.

———. "Re-imagining the State in Post-Mao China." In Cultures of Insecurity: States, Communities and the Production of Danger, ed. Jutta Weldes, Mark Laffey, Hugh Gusterson, and Raymond Duvall, 293–318. Minneapolis: University of Minnesota Press, 1999.

Liu Baoyuan. "Lun woguo Yaozu chuantong wenhua de goucheng" (A discussion on the structure of the traditional culture of China's Yao nationality). Paper presented at Yao Studies Research Conference, Chenzhou, Hunan, 1988.

Liu Chungshee Hsien. "The Dog-ancestor Story of the Aboriginal Tribes of Southern China." Journal of the Royal Anthropological Institute of Great Britain and Ireland 62 (1932): 361–368.

Liu, Guangjing (Kuang-ching). "Worldview and Peasant Rebellion: Reflections on Post-Mao Historiography." Journal of Asian Studies 40:2 (1981): 295–326.

Liu, Lydia. "Translingual Practice: The Discourse of Individualism between China and the West." positions: east asia cultures critique 1:1 (1993): 160–193.

Liu, Yaoquan, and Hu Qiwang. "Survey of Yao Studies in China (1949–1984)." In The Yao of South China: Recent International Studies, ed. Jacques Lemoine and Chao Chien, 507–575. Paris: Pangu, Editions de l'AFEY, 1991.

Liu Yulian. "Minzuxue yu xiandaihua jiehe de yige shili dui jianshe Jinxiu Yaoshan de chubu shexiang" (Some tentative thoughts on an example of how ethnology and modernization are to be integrated for the construction of the Jinxiu Yao Mountains). Paper presented at Ethnology Research Institute of the Central Nationalities Institute, Beijing, 1983.

———. " 'Liang zhong shengchan de lilun' gei wo de qishi—luolun Chashan, Hualan, Ao Yao de shengyi wenti" (What I have learned from the "Theory of the two modes of production": A brief account of the problem of reproduction among the Chashan, Hualan, and Ao Yao). Unpublished manuscript, 1984.

———. "Shilun Daojiao wenhua yu Chashan Yao minjian wenhua zhi guangxi" (An inquiry into the relationship between Taoist culture and the folk culture of the Chashan Yao). Paper presented at Yao Studies Research Conference, Chenzhou, Hunan, 1988.

Liu, Zheng. "Population." In China's Socialist Modernization, ed. Yu Guangyuan, 527–568. Beijing: Foreign Languages Press, 1984.

Loh, Wai-fong. "From Romantic Love to Class Struggle: Reflections on the Film Liu Sanjie." In Popular Chinese Literature and the Performing Arts in the People's Republic of China, ed. Bonnie MacDouggall. 165–176. Berkeley: University of California Press, 1984.

Lu, Sheldon Hsiao-peng. "Postmodernity, Popular Culture, and the Intellectual: A Report on Post-Tiananmen China." *boundary 2* 23:2 (1996): 139–169.

Lupher, Mark. *Power Restructuring in China and Russia.* Boulder, CO: Westview Press, 1996.

MacCannell, Dean. *The Tourist: A New Theory of the Leisure Class.* New York: Schocken Books, 1976.

———. *Empty Meeting Grounds: The Tourist Papers.* London: Routledge, 1992.

MacDonald, Jeffery L. *Transnational Aspects of Iu-Mien Identity.* New York: Garland Publishing, 1997.

MacInnis, Donald E. *Religion in China Today: Policy and Practice.* Maryknoll, NY: Orbis Books, 1989.

Mackerras, Colin. *China's Minorities: Integration and Modernization in the Twentieth Century.* Hong Kong: Oxford University Press, 1994.

Madsen, Richard. Foreword to *Religion in China Today: Policy and Practice,* ed. Donald E. MacInnis. Maryknoll, NY: Orbis Books, 1989.

———. *Morality and Power in a Chinese Village.* Berkeley: University of California Press, 1984.

Malkki, Liisa. "Speechless Emissaries: Refugees, Humanitarianism, and Dehistoricization." *Cultural Anthropology* 11:3 (1996): 377–404.

———. "Things to Come: Internationalism and Global Solidarities in the Late 1990s." *Public Culture* 10:2 (1998): 431–442.

Mani, Lata. "Contentious Traditions: The Debate on Sati in Colonial India." In *The Nature and Context of Minority Discourse,* ed. Abdul R. Jan Mohammed and David Lloyd, 319–356. New York: Oxford University Press, 1990.

Mani, Lata, and Ruth Frankenberg. "The Challenge of Orientalism." *Economy and Society* 14 (1985): 174–192.

Mao Zedong. "Report on an Investigation of the Peasant Movement in Hunan, March 1927." In *Selected Readings from the Works of Mao Tse-tung.* Reprinted in Beijing: Foreign Language Publishing House, 1967.

Marcus, George. "Ethnography in/of the World System: The Emergence of Multisited Ethnography." *Annual Review of Anthropology* 24 (1995): 95–117.

———, ed. *Elites: Ethnographic Issues.* Albuquerque: School of American Research, University of New Mexico, 1983.

McCarthy, Thomas. "The Critique of Impure Reason: Foucault and the Frankfurt School." *Political Theory* 18 (1990): 437–469.

McKhann, Charles F. "The Naxi and the Nationalities Question." In *Cultural Encounters on China's Ethnic Frontiers,* ed. Stevan Harrell, 39–62. Seattle: University of Washington Press, 1994.

Miles, Douglas. "Land, Labour, and Kin Groups among Southeast Asian Shifting Cultivators." *Mankind* 8 (1972): 185–197.

———. "Yao Bride-exchange, Matrifiliation, and Adoption." *Bijdragen tot de Taal-land-en Volkenkunde* 128 (1972): 99–117.

———. "Yao Spirit Mediumship and Heredity versus Reincarnation and Descent in Pulangka." *Man* 13 (1978): 428–443.

Mitchell, Timothy. *Colonizing Egypt.* Berkeley: University of California Press, 1988.

Moore, Donald S. "Remapping Resistance: 'Ground for Struggle' and the Politics of Place." In *Geographies of Resistance*, ed. Steve Pile and Michael Keith, 87–106. London: Routledge, 1997.

Morris, Rosalind C. "Surviving Pleasure at the Periphery: Chiang Mai and the Photographies of Political Trauma in Thailand, 1976–1992." *Public Culture* 10:2 (winter 1998): 341–370.

Moseley, George. *The Party and the National Question in China.* Cambridge, MA: MIT Press, 1966.

Moser, Leo J. *The Chinese Mosaic: The Peoples and Provinces of China.* Boulder, CO: Westview Press, 1985.

Nee, Victor, and David Mozingo, eds. *State and Society in Contemporary China.* Ithaca, NY: Cornell University Press, 1983.

Nichols, Bill. *Ideology and the Image.* Bloomington: Indiana University Press, 1981.

Nora, Pierre. "Between Memory and History: Les Lieux de Memoire." *Representations* 26 (spring 1989): 7–25.

Nugent, Stephen. "The 'Peripheral Situation.'" *Annual Review of Anthropology* 17 (1988): 79–98.

Oakes, Timothy S. "Cultural Geography and Chinese Ethnic Tourism." *Journal of Cultural Geography* 12 (1992): 3–17.

Ong, Aihwa. "Anthropology, China and Modernities: The Geopolitics of Cultural Knowledge." In *The Future of Anthropological Knowledge*, ed. Henrietta L. Moore. London: Routledge, 1996.

———. "Chinese Modernities: Narratives of Nation and of Capitalism." In *Ungrounded Empires: Chinese Transnationalism as an Alternative Modernity*, ed. Aihwa Ong and Donald Nonini, 171–202. New York: Routledge, 1997.

———. *Flexible Citizenship: The Cultural Logics of Transnationality.* Durham, NC: Duke University Press, 1999.

Pandey, Gyanendra. "The Culture of History." In *In Near Ruins: Cultural Theory at the End of the Century*, ed. Nicholas Dirks, 19–38. Minneapolis: University of Minnesota Press, 1998.

Pease, Donald E. Foreword to *The Ethics of Marginality: A New Approach to Gay Studies*, by John Champagne, vii–xxii. Minneapolis: University of Minnesota Press, 1995.

Pemberton, John. *On the Subject of "Java."* Ithaca, NY: Cornell University Press, 1997.

Perry, Elizabeth. "State and Society in Contemporary China." *World Politics* 41 (1988): 579–600.

———. "Chinese Political Culture Revisited." In *Popular Protest and Political Culture in Modern China: Learning from 1989*, ed. Jeffrey N. Wasserstrom and Elizabeth J. Perry, 1–13. Boulder, CO: Westview Press, 1992.

———. "Trends in the Study of Chinese Politics: State–Society Relations." *China Quarterly* 139 (September 1994): 704–713.

Phillips, Christopher, ed. *Photography in the Modern Era: European Documents and Critical Writings, 1913–1940*. New York: Metropolitan Museum of Art/Aperture, 1989.

Pile, Steve, and Michael Keith, eds. *Geographies of Resistance*. London: Routledge, 1997.

Povinelli, Elizabeth A. "Settler Modernity and the Quest for an Indigenous Tradition." *Public Culture* 11:1 (1999): 19–48.

Prakash, Gyan. "Science Gone Native in Colonial India." *Representations* 40 (fall 1992): 153–178.

Pratt, Mary Louise. *Imperial Eyes: Travel Writing and Transculturation*. New York: Routledge, 1992.

Pu Pang. "The Seething Wave of Culture Studies." *Lilun xinxibao* (Theory information). 24 March 1986.

Qiu Pu. "Minzuxue de xin kaiduan" (A new beginning for ethnology). *Minzuxue yanjiu* 1 (1981): 1–8.

Radhakrishnan, R. "Ethnic Identity and Post-Structuralist Difference." *Cultural Critique* 6 (spring 1987): 199–220.

———. *Diasporic Mediations: Between Home and Location*. Minneapolis: University of Minnesota Press, 1996.

Rhodes, Lorna. "Panoptical Intimacies." *Public Culture* 10:2 (1998): 285–311.

Robbins, Bruce. "Introduction: The Grounding of Intellectuals." In *Intellectuals: Aesthetics, Politics, Academics*, ed. Bruce Robbins, ix–xxvii. Minneapolis: University of Minnesota Press, 1990.

Robotham, Don. "Postcolonialities: The Challenge of New Modernities." *International Social Science Journal* 49:3 (September 1997): 357–372.

Rofel, Lisa. "Rethinking Modernity: Space and Factory Discipline in China." *Cultural Anthropology* 7:1 (1992): 93–114.

Rony, Fatimah Tobing. *The Third Eye: Race, Cinema, and Ethnographic Spectacle*. Durham, NC: Duke University Press, 1996.

Rosaldo, Renato. *Culture and Truth: The Remaking of Social Analysis*. Boston: Beacon Press, 1989.

Ross, Andrew. *Universal Abandon: The Politics of Modernism*. Minneapolis: University of Minnesota Press, 1988.

Rudelson, Justin. *Oasis Identities: Uyghur Nationalism along China's Silk Road*. New York: Columbia University Press, 1977.

Russo, Alessandro. "The Probable Defeat: Preliminary Notes on the Chinese Cultural Revolution." *positions: east asia cultures critique* 6:1 (1998): 179–202.

Safran, William. "Introduction: Nation, Ethnie, Region, and Religion as Markers of Identity." In *Nationalism and Ethnoregional Identities in China*, ed. William Safran, 1–8. London: Frank Cass Publishers, 1998.

———, ed. *Nationalism and Ethnoregional Identities in China*. London: Frank Cass Publishers, 1998.

Saich, Tony. "The Search for Civil Society and Democracy in China," *Current History* (September 1994): 260–264.

Said, Edward. *Orientalism*. New York: Random House, 1978.

———. "Reflections on Exile." *Granta* 13 (1984): 158–172.

———. "The Mind of Winter: Reflections on a Life of Exile." *Harper's* (September 1984): 49–55.

———. "Representing the Colonized: Anthropology's Interlocutors." *Critical Inquiry* 15:2 (1989): 205–225.

Sakai, Naoki. "Modernity and Its Critique: The Problem of Universalism and Particularism." In *Postmodernism and Japan*, ed. Masao Miyoshi and H. D. Harootunian, 475–504. Durham, NC: Duke University Press, 1989.

Sanchez, A. R., and S. L. Wong. "On 'An Interview with Chinese Anthropologists.'" *China Quarterly* 60 (1974): 775–790.

Sangren, P. Steven. *History and Magical Power in a Chinese Community*. Stanford: Stanford University Press, 1987.

———. "'Power' against Ideology: A Critique of Foucaultian Usage." *Cultural Anthropology* 10:1 (1995): 3–40.

Saso, Michael. *Taoism and the Rite of Cosmic Renewal*. Pullman, WA: Washington State University, 1972.

Schafer, Edward H. *The Vermilion Bird: T'ang Images of the South*. Berkeley: University of California Press, 1967.

Schein, Louisa. "The Dynamic of Cultural Revival among the Miao in Guizhou." In *Ethnicity and Ethnic Groups in China*, ed. Chao Chien and Nicholas Tapp, 199–212. Hong Kong: New Asia Academic Bulletin, Chinese University of Hong Kong, 1989.

———. "The Other Goes to Market: The State, the Nation, and Unruliness in Contemporary China." *Identities* 2:3 (1996): 197–222.

———. "Gender and Internal Orientalism." *Modern China* 23:1 (1997): 69–98.

———. *Minority Rules: The Miao and the Feminine in China's Cultural Politics*. Durham, NC: Duke University Press, 1999.

Schell, Orville. "China: The End of an Era." *The Nation*, 17–24 July 1995.

Schwarcz, Vera. *The Chinese Enlightenment: Intellectuals and the Legacy of the May Fourth Movement of 1919*. Berkeley: University of California Press, 1986.

Schwartz, Benjamin. "A Marxist Controversy in China." *Far Eastern Quarterly*, 13 (1954): 143–153.

Scott, David. "The Aftermaths of Sovereignty: Postcolonial Criticism and the Claims of Political Modernity." *Social Text* 48, 14:3 (1996): 1–26.

Scott, Joan W. " 'Experience.' " In *Feminists Theorize the Political*, ed. Judith Butler and Joan W. Scott, 22–40. New York: Routledge, 1992.

Shapiro, Michael. "Moral Geographies and the Ethics of Post-sovereignty." *Public Culture* 6 (1994): 479–502.

———. *Violent Cartographies: Mapping Cultures of War*. Minneapolis: University of Minnesota Press, 1997.

She I-tse. *Zhongguo Tusi zhidu* (China's native chieftan system). Shanghai: Zhongzheng Shuju, 1947.

Shiratori, Yoshiro. *Yojin bunsho* (Yao documents). Tokyo: Kodansha, 1975.

———. *Tonan Ajin sanchi minzoku shi* (Visual ethnography: The hill tribes of Southeast Asia). Tokyo: Kodansha, 1978.

Shue, Vivian. *The Reach of the State: Sketches of the Chinese Body Politic*. Stanford: Stanford University Press, 1988.

Siu, Helen. *Agents and Victims in South China: Accomplices in Rural Revolution*. New Haven: Yale University Press, 1989.

———. "Recycling Rituals: Politics and Popular Culture in Contemporary Rural China." In *Unofficial China: Popular Culture and Thought in the People's Republic of China*, ed. Perry Link, Richard Madsen, and Paul G. Pickowicz, 121–137. Boulder, CO: Westview Press, 1989.

———. "Cultural Identity and the Politics of Difference in South China." *Daedalus* 122 (1993): 19–44.

Siu, Helen, and David Faure. Introduction to *Down to Earth: The Territorial Bond in South China*, ed. Helen Siu and David Faure, 1–20. Stanford: Stanford University Press, 1995.

Skinner, William G. "Regional Urbanization in Nineteenth-Century China." In *The City in Late Imperial China*, ed. William G. Skinner, 211–249. Stanford: Stanford University Press, 1977.

———. "Cities and the Hierarchy of Local Systems." In *The City in Late Imperial China*, ed. William G. Skinner, 275–351. Stanford: Stanford University Press, 1977.

———, ed. *The City in Late Imperial China*. Stanford: Stanford University Press, 1977.

Smith, Gary, ed. *Benjamin: Philosophy, History, Aesthetics*. Chicago: University of Chicago Press, 1989.

Soderlind, Sylvia. "The Contest of Marginalities." *Essays on Canadian Writing* 56 (1995): 96–109.

Soja, Edward W. *Postmodern Geographies: The Reassertion of Space in Critical Social Theory*. London: Verso, 1989.

Song Enzhang. "The Family System and Its Ethos among the Yunnan Yao." In *The Yao of South China: Recent International Studies*, ed. Jacques Lemoine and Chao Chien, 229–247. Paris: Pangu, Editions de l'AFEY, 1991.

Spence, Jonathan D. *The Search for Modern China*. New York: Norton, 1990.

Spivak, Gayatri Chakravorty. *In Other Worlds: Essays in Cultural Politics*. New York: Routledge, 1987.

———. *The Post-colonial Critic: Interviews, Strategies, Dialogues*, ed. Sarah Harasym. New York: Routledge, 1990.

———. "Poststructuralism, Marginality, Postcoloniality and Value." In *Literary Theory Today*, ed. Peter Collier and Helga Geyer-Ryan, 219–239. Ithaca, NY: Cornell University Press, 1990.

———. "Can the Subaltern Speak?" In *Marxism and the Interpretation of Culture*, ed. Cary Nelson and Lawrence Grossberg, 271–313. Urbana: University of Illinois Press, 1991.

Stalin, Joseph. "Marxism and the National Question." In *Collected Works*, 3: 300–384. Moscow: Progress, 1953–1955.

Stauffer, Bob. "After Socialism: Capitalism, Development, and the Search for Critical Alternatives." *Alternatives* 15 (1990): 401–430.

Stocking, George W. *Victorian Anthropology*. New York: The Free Press, 1987.

Stoler, Ann. "Making Empire Respectable: The Politics of Race and Sexual Morality in 20th Century Colonial Cultures." *American Ethnologist* 16:4 (1989): 634–660.

———. *Race and the Education of Desire: Foucault's History of Sexuality and the Colonial Order of Things*. Durham, N.C.: Duke University Press, 1995.

Strickmann, Michel. "The Tao among the Yao: Taoism and the Sinification of South China." In *Peoples and Cultures in Asiatic History*, 23–30. Tokyo: Kokasho Kankokai, 1982.

Stubel, H. "The Yao of the Province of Guangdong." *Monumenta Serica* 3 (1938): 345–384.

Su Defu. "Zai shehuizhuyi chu jiejieduan zhong fazhan yaozu diqu jingji wenhua jianshe zhi wojian" (My view of economic cultural construction in the development of Yao regions in the class stage of early socialism). Unpublished manuscript, 1988.

Su Defu and Liu Yulian. "Dayaoshan shipai zhidu xi" (An analysis of the stone tablet system in the Great Yao Mountains). In *Yaozu yenjiu lunwenji* (Collected papers on Yao research). Nanning: Guangxi Nationalities Publishing House, 1987.

———. "Dayaoshan Yaozu renmin fandui Guomindang fandong tongzhi de gaoya —Jinxiu baodong" (The Jinxiu uprising: Opposing the high-handed policies of the Guomindang reactionaries). Unpublished manuscript, 1990.

———. *Chashan Yao yanjiu wenji* (Collected essays on the tea-mountain Yao). Beijing: Central Nationalities University Publishing House, 1992.

Sun, Lung-kee. "Chinese Intellectuals' Notion of 'Epoch' (*shidai*) in the post–May Fourth Era." *Chinese Studies in History* 20:2 (1986–1987): 44–74.

Swedenburg, Ted. "The Palestinian Peasant as National Signifier." *Anthropological Quarterly* 63:1 (1990): 18–30.

———. "Occupational Hazards Revisited: Reply to Moshe Shokeid." *Cultural Anthropology* 7:4 (1992): 478–495.

Tagg, John. *The Burden of Representation: Essays on Photographies and Histories*. London: Macmillan, 1988.

Tanaka, Stefan. *Japan's Orient: Rendering Pasts into History*. Berkeley: University of California Press, 1993.

Tang Xiaobing. "Orientalism and the Question of Universality: The Language of Contemporary Chinese Literary Theory." *positions* 1:2 (1993): 389–413.

Tang Zhaomin. *Yaoshan sanji* (Miscellaneous notes on the Yao Mountains). Shanghai: Wenhua gongying she, 1948.

Thomas, Nicholas. *Colonialism's Culture: Anthropology, Travel, and Government*. Princeton, NJ: Princeton University Press, 1994.

Thongkum, Theraphan. *Guo Shan Bang: Perpetual Redaction of the Imperial Decree of Emperor Ping Huang for Protection When Traveling in the Hills*. Bangkok: Linguistics Research Unit, Faculty of Arts, Chulalongkorn University, 1991.

Tong Enzhang. "Moergen de moshi yu makesi zhuyi" (Morgan's model and Marxism). *Shehui kexue yanjiu* 12:2 (1988): 177–196.

Trachtenberg, Alan, ed. *Classic Essays on Photography*. New Haven: Leete's Island Books, 1980.

Trouillot, Michel-Rolph. *Silencing the Past: Power and the Production of History*. Boston: Beacon Press, 1995.

Tsin, Michael. "Imagining 'Society' in Early Twentieth-Century China." In *Imagining the People: Chinese Intellectuals and the Concept of Citizenship, 1890–1920*, ed. Joshua A. Fogel and Peter G. Zarrow, 212–231. Armonk, NY: M.E. Sharpe, 1997.

Tsing, Anna Lowenhaupt. *In the Realm of the Diamond Queen: Marginality in an Out-of-the Way Place*. Princeton, NJ: Princeton University Press, 1993.

Turner, Bryan. *Orientalism, Postmodernism, and Globalism*. London: Routledge, 1994.

Umemoto, Diane L. "Yao Ritual Scrolls: From Icons to Antiques." *Asia* 4:1 (1981): 30–37.

Upton, Janet. "Home on the Grasslands? Tradition, Modernity and the Negotiation of Identity by Tibetan Intellectuals in the People's Republic of China." In *Negotiating Ethnicities in China and Taiwan*, ed. Melissa Brown, 98–124. Berkeley: China Research Monograph, Institute of East Asian Studies, University of California, 1996.

Verdery, Katherine. *Nationalist Ideology under Socialism: Identity and Cultural Politics in Ceausescu's Romania*. Berkeley: University of California Press, 1995.

———. *What Was Socialism, and What Comes Next?* Princeton, NJ: Princeton University Press, 1996.

von Glahn, Richard. *The Country of Streams and Grottos: Expansion, Settlement, and the Civilizing of the Sichuan Frontier in Song Times*. Cambridge, MA: Harvard University, Council of East Asian Studies, 1987.

Walder, Andrew G. *Communist Neo-Traditionalism: Work and Authority in Chinese Industry.* Berkeley: University of California Press, 1986.

Walker, R. B. J. *Inside/Outside: International Relations in Political Theory.* New York: Cambridge University Press, 1993.

Wang, He. "Traditional Culture and Modernization: Summary and Contents on the Studies of Chinese Culture in Recent Years." *Social Sciences in China* 3 (1986), 25–36.

Wang, Jing. "*He shang* and the Paradoxes of Chinese Enlightenment." *Bulletin of Concerned Asian Scholars* 23:3 (1991): 23–32.

———. *High Culture Fever: Politics, Aesthetics, and Ideology in Deng's China.* Berkeley: University of California Press, 1996.

Wang Tonghui. *Hualan Yao shehui zuzhi* (The social organization of the Hualan Yao). Nanning: Shangwu Yinshu Guanfahang, 1936.

Wang, W. C. "Yao Religion and Education." *Lingnan Science Journal* (Canton) 18 (1939): 397–408.

Wang, Yuejin. "The Cinematic Other and the Cultural Self: De-centering the Cultural Identity of the Cinema." *Wide Angle* 11:2 (1989): 32–39.

———. "Mixing Memory and Desire: *Red Sorghum*, a Chinese Version of Masculinity and Femininity." *Public Culture* 2:1 (1989): 31–53.

Watson, Ruby S., ed. *Memory, History, and Opposition under State Socialism.* Santa Fe, NM: School of American Research Press, 1994.

Wei Yuan. "Sheng wu ji" (A record of imperial military activities, fourteenth chapter). In *Jindai Zhongguo shiliao congkan* (Collections of historical materials of contemporary China). Taibei: Taibei Cultural Publishing House, 1842.

Weller, Robert W. "Historians and Consciousness: The Modern Politics of the Taiping Heavenly Kingdom." *Social Research* 54 (1987): 731–755.

Wendt, Ronald F. "Answers to the Gaze: A Genealogical Poaching of Resistances." *Quarterly Journal of Speech* 82 (1996): 251–273.

White, Sydney D. "State Discourses, Minority Policies, and the Politics of Identity in the Lijiang Naxi People's Autonomous County." In *Nationalism and Ethnoregional Identities in China*, ed. William Safran, 9–27. London: Frank Cass Publishers, 1998.

Wiens, Harold. *China's March toward the Tropics.* Hamden, CN: Shoe String Press, 1954.

Williams, Brackette. "A Class Act: Anthropology and the Race to Nation across Ethnic Terrain." *Annual Review of Anthropology* 18 (1989): 401–444.

Wilmsen, Edwin N. "Introduction: Premises of Power in Ethnic Politics." In *The Politics of Difference: Ethnic Premises in a World of Power*, ed. Edwin N. Wilmsen and Patrick McAllister, 1–24. Chicago: University of Chicago Press, 1996.

Wong, S. L. "Phonetics and Phonology of the Yao Language." *Lingnan Science Journal* 18 (1939): 425–455.

Wu Chi-chang. "Wei ch'in liao chao pien cheng de chieh chien" (An examination of the frontier government in the Wei, Tsin, and Six dynasties). *Pien cheng kung lun* 1 (1943): 64–72.

Xu Jiewu and Deng Wentong. "Cong Yaozu zhixi wenti tanqi" (Discussion arising from the question of Yao subgroups). In *Yaozu yanjiu lunwenji* (Collected Papers on Yao Research). Nanning: Guangxi Minzu Chubanshe, 1987.

Ya Hanzhang. *Minzu wenti yu zongjiao wenti* (The nationalities problem and the problem of religion). Beijing: Zhongguo Shehui Kexue Chubanshe, 1984.

Yang, Dali L. *Beyond Beijing: Liberalization and the Regions in China*. New York: Routledge, 1997.

Yang, Mayfair Mei-hui. "The Modernity of Power in the Chinese Socialist Order." *Cultural Anthropology* 3:4 (1988): 408–427.

Yao, Shunan. "Investigating the Dayaoshan Stone Tablet System." Paper presented at a seminar on Yao Studies, Chenzhou, Hunan, 1988.

Yau, Esther. "Is China the End of Hermeneutics? Or, Political and Cultural Usages of Non-Han Women in Mainland Chinese Films." *Discourse* 11 (1989): 115–136.

Young, Robert. *White Mythologies: Writing History and the West*. New York: Routledge, 1990.

———. *Colonial Desire: Hybridity in Theory, Culture and Race*. New York: Routledge, 1995.

Zha, Jianying. *China Pop: How Soap Operas, Tabloids, and Bestsellers Are Transforming a Culture*. New York: The New Press, 1995.

Zhang Xudong. "On Some Motifs in the Chinese 'Cultural Fever' of the Late 1980s: Social Change, Ideology, and Theory." *Social Text* 39 (1994): 129–156.

———. *Chinese Modernism in the Era of the Reforms: Culture Fever, Avant-Garde Fiction, and the New Chinese Cinema*. Durham, NC: Duke University Press, 1997.

Zhang, Yingjin. "Ideology of the Body in *Red Sorghum*: National Allegory, National Roots, and Third Cinema." *East-West Film Journal* 4 (1990): 38–53.

Zhang Youjun. *Yaozu zongjiao lunji* (Collected essays on Yao religion). Nanning: Guangxi Yaozu yanjiu xuehui, 1986.

———. "A Simple Explanation of Taoism among the Yao of the One Hundred Thousand Mounts." In *The Yao of South China*, ed. Jacques Lemoine and Chiao Chien, 311–348. Paris: Pangu, Editions de l'AFEY, 1991.

Zi, Zhongyun. "The Relationship of Chinese Traditional Culture to the Modernization of China." *Asian Survey* 27 (1987): 442–458.

index

Ralph A. Litzinger is Assistant Professor in the Department of
Cultural Anthropology at Duke University.

Library of Congress Cataloging-in-Publication Data
Litzinger, Ralph A.
Other Chinas : the Yao and the politics of national belonging /
Ralph A. Litzinger.
p.   cm.
Includes bibliographical references and index.
ISBN 0-8223-2525-X (cloth : alk. paper)
— ISBN 0-8223-2549-7 (paper : alk. paper)
1. Yao (Southeast Asian people) — Ethnic identity.   2. Yao
(Southeast Asian people) — History.   3. Yao (Southeast Asian
people) — Government relations.   4. China — Ethnic relations.
5. China — Politics and government.   6. China — Social
conditions.   I. Title.
DS731.Y3 L57   2000
305.895'94—dc21   99-087369

DATE DUE